INTERMEDIATE PASCAL PROGRAMMING

McGraw-Hill Computer Science Series

Ahuja: *Design and Analysis of Computer Communication Networks*
Barbacci and Siewiorek: *The Design and Analysis of Instruction Set Processors*
Ceri and Pelagatti: *Distributed Databases: Principles and Systems*
Collins: *Intermediate Pascal Programming: A Case Study Approach*
Debry: *Communicating with Display Terminals*
Donovan: *Systems Programming*
Filman and Friedman: *Coordinated Computing: Tools and Techniques for Distributed Software*
Givone: *Introduction to Switching Circuit Theory*
Goodman and Hedetniemi: *Introduction to the Design and Analysis of Algorithms*
Katzan: *Microprogramming Primer*
Keller: *A First Course in Computer Programming Using Pascal*
Kohavi: *Switching and Finite Automata Theory*
Liu: *Elements of Discrete Mathematics*
Liu: *Introduction to Combinatorial Mathematics*
MacEwen: *Introduction to Computer Systems: Using the PDP-11 and Pascal*
Madnick and Donovan: *Operating Systems*
Manna: *Mathematical Theory of Computation*
Newman and Sproull: *Principles of Interactive Computer Graphics*
Payne: *Introduction to Simulation: Programming Techniques and Methods of Analysis*
Révész: *Introduction to Formal Languages*
Rice: *Matrix Computations and Mathematical Software*
Salton and McGill: *Introduction to Modern Information Retrieval*
Shooman: *Software Engineering: Design, Reliability, and Management*
Tremblay and Bunt: *An Introduction to Computer Science: An Algorithmic Approach*
Tremblay and Bunt: *An Introduction to Computer Science: An Algorithmic Approach, Short Edition*
Tremblay and Manohar: *Discrete Mathematical Structures with Applications to Computer Science*
Tremblay and Sorenson: *An Introduction to Data Structures with Applications*
Tremblay and Sorenson: *The Theory and Practice of Compiler Writing*
Tucker: *Programming Languages*
Wiederhold: *Database Design*
Wulf, Levin, and Harbison: *Hydra/C. mmp: An Experimental Computer System*

McGraw-Hill Series in Computer Organization and Architecture

Bell and Newell: *Computer Structures: Readings and Examples*
Cavanagh: *Digital Computer Arithmetic: Design and Implementation*
Gear: *Computer Organization and Programming: With an Emphasis on Personal Computers*
Hamacher, Vranesic, and Zaky: *Computer Organization*
Hayes: *Computer Architecture and Organization*
Hayes: *Digital System Design and Microprocessors*
Hwang and Briggs: *Computer Architecture and Parallel Processing*
Kogge: *The Architecture of Pipelined Computers*
Siewiorek, Bell, and Newell: *Computer Structures: Principles and Examples*
Stone: *Introduction to Computer Organization and Data Structures*
Stone and Siewiorek: *Introduction to Computer Organization and Data Structures: PDP-11 Edition*

INTERMEDIATE
PASCAL
PROGRAMMING
A Case Study Approach

William J. Collins

Radford University

McGraw-Hill Book Company

New York St. Louis San Francisco Auckland Bogotá Hamburg
Johannesburg London Madrid Mexico Montreal New Delhi
Panama Paris São Paulo Singapore Sydney Tokyo Toronto

This book was set in Times Roman.
The editor was Kaye Pace;
the cover was designed by Anne Canevari Green;
the production supervisor was Marietta Breitwieser.
Project supervision was done by Albert Harrison, Harley Editorial Services.
Halliday Lithograph Corporation was printer and binder.

INTERMEDIATE PASCAL PROGRAMMING
A Case Study Approach

1234567890HALHAL898765

ISBN 0-07-044652-0

Library of Congress Cataloging in Publication Data

Collins, William J. (William Joseph)
    Intermediate Pascal programming.

    (McGraw-Hill computer science series)
    Bibliography: p.
    Includes index.
    1. PASCAL (Computer program language)
I. Title.   II. Series.
QA76.73.P2C64   1986   001.64′24   85-11386
ISBN 0-07-044652-0

To Donnie and Mark
my boys of summer

CONTENTS

PREFACE

This text is intended for a second course in computer programming, and is suitable for the revised CS2 of ACM's Curriculum '78. It is assumed that the student has already completed the equivalent of a one-semester course in programming in which the Pascal language was introduced.

The primary objective of this text is to present a disciplined approach to programming. Recent advances in programming methodology are introduced early in a natural and informal way. Such principles as data abstraction, information hiding, and top-down testing are then applied in complete case studies.

Each case study starts by posing a problem in some area of computer science. We then proceed through a sequence of well-defined stages to obtain a validated program to solve that problem. Recursion is freely exploited so that this indispensable tool can become part of each student's repertoire.

SYNOPSIS

Chapter 1 provides those features of Pascal that are needed in subsequent chapters. Coverage of some of the topics, such as records and procedures, will probably constitute a review. Other topics, such as recursion and dynamic variables, will be new to many students. For the sake of the general audience, we consider Standard Pascal only.

Chapter 2 presents a systematic method for developing and validating programs. We include such important concepts as stepwise refinement, data abstraction, and design trade-offs. The programming tools analyzed here are frequently and explicitly utilized in the remaining chapters.

In Chapter 3 we introduce the abstract data type *list*. We then explore dynamic linked lists and how they can be processed recursively. The case study shows how to create and maintain a class roster. In this and other case studies, we pay special attention to data editing so that programs do not try to process incorrect data.

Chapter 4 investigates stacks and queues, first as abstract data types, then as Pascal constructs. The case study is a standard application of stacks, namely, converting an infix expression to postfix notation. Queues play an important role in computer simulation, and this leads to a discussion of random-number generators.

Another abstract data type, the directed graph, is introduced in Chapter 5. Of special interest are two kinds of directed graphs—trees and networks. In the case study, we develop a simplified version of a program that generates parse trees. Because binary trees have such wide applicability, we begin our investigation of them in this chapter and continue their study in Chapters 6 and 7. The section on networks focuses on finding critical paths.

Sorting and searching are analyzed in Chapters 6 and 7. Chapter 6 starts with criteria for evaluating a sort procedure, and then presents some simple (and inefficient) sorts. Finally, we study such powerful sorting procedures as Binary Sort Tree, Merge Sort, and Quicksort. Chapter 7 presents a parallel investigation of searching. The case-study program focuses on hashing identifiers into a symbol table. In both chapters, the analysis of algorithms is informal rather than rigorous.

Chapter 8 examines heuristic search techniques, a key topic in the fast-growing field of artificial intelligence. For the sake of simplicity, we restrict our attention to developing heuristic strategies for playing games, specifically, the eight-puzzle and tic-tac-toe.

In Chapters 3 through 8, moderately difficult programming problems are given at the end of each chapter. Because some of those problems require modifying the case-study programs, all of the case-study programs are available on diskettes. Instructors may request a free diskette for their computer system from the publisher.

ACKNOWLEDGMENTS

Robert M. Tardiff made many worthwhile suggestions for clarifying the material presented. Mary Ellen Royer was invaluable in editing the manuscript, running the programs, and general trouble-shooting. Mary Lou Malone contributed a software-engineering perspective. Ray Scanlon validated the random-number generator in Chapter 4. The assistance of the students and staff at Salisbury State College was much appreciated; special thanks to Brian Donovan, Jim Littleton, Dawn Mayonado, Mary Luke, Ray Muslimani, and Sarah Webster.

Eric Munson and Kaye Pace of McGraw-Hill provided timely encouragement, and Albert Harrison of Harley Editorial Services was cheerful and prompt during production and composition.

Finally, I am grateful to the following reviewers for their helpful advice: Lionel E. Deimel, Jr. (North Carolina State University); Brian Johnson (University of New Hampshire); Gary Marc Levin (University of Arizona); Patricia E. Murphy (University of Kentucky); Edward W. Packel (Columbia University); Richard Rink (Eastern Kentucky University); and Carol E. Wolf (Iowa State University).

William J. Collins

INTERMEDIATE PASCAL PROGRAMMING

IMPORTANT FEATURES OF PASCAL

In this chapter we consider those features of Pascal that are of critical importance in the rest of this book. In fact, mastery of them is essential for almost any advanced programming applications. You are probably already familiar with most of these topics, so this can be thought of as a review chapter. But whatever your background, do not proceed to the remaining chapters until you fully understand the material presented here.

RECORDS

A *record* is a collection of components of arbitrary types. The individual components are called "fields." For example, we can define

```
TYPE  STUDENTRECORD = RECORD
                NAME, ADDRESS        : PACKED ARRAY[1..40] OF CHAR ;
                NUMBEROFCREDITS      : 0..200 ;
                GRADEPOINTAVERAGE : REAL ;
                STUDENTID            : 0..99999
             END ;
```

This makes STUDENTRECORD a type identifier for a record type with five fields: a name field of 40 characters, an address field of 40 characters, the number of credits taken, the current grade point average and the student's five-digit identification number.

We can now declare variables of type STUDENTRECORD:

```
VAR CURRENTSTUDENT, BESTSTUDENT : STUDENTRECORD;
```

To refer to a field within a record variable, we specify the record-variable identifier followed by a period followed by the field identifier. For example,

```
IF CURRENTSTUDENT.NUMBEROFCREDITS > = 120 THEN
    WRITELN(CURRENTSTUDENT.NAME, 'IS ELIGIBLE TO GRADUATE.')
```

You can assign to a record variable the value of another record variable of the same type:

```
IF CURRENTSTUDENT.GRADEPOINTAVERAGE > BESTSTUDENT.GRADEPOINTAVERAGE THEN
    BESTSTUDENT := CURRENTSTUDENT
```

The execution of this assignment statement causes the value of each field in CURRENTSTUDENT to be stored in the corresponding field in BESTSTUDENT. Such an assignment is possible only because CURRENTSTUDENT and BESTSTUDENT have the exact same type. A detailed discussion of assignment compatibility is found on pages 18–19.

Standard Pascal requires that records be read in and written out componentwise if the input or output device is line oriented (such as a printer, card reader or cathode ray tube screen). Sometimes this requirement can be cumbersome. For example, to write out the values in CURRENTSTUDENT, one value per line, we would need

```
WRITELN(CURRENTSTUDENT.NAME) ;
WRITELN(CURRENTSTUDENT.ADDRESS) ;
WRITELN(CURRENTSTUDENT.NUMBEROFCREDITS : 3) ;
WRITELN(CURRENTSTUDENT.GRADEPOINTAVERAGE : 4 : 2) ;
WRITELN(CURRENTSTUDENT.STUDENTID : 6)
```

This can be shortened somewhat by using the WITH statement. This statement enables the fields in a record to be referenced without listing the record name (and period) each time. Thus, we can replace the five WRITELN statements with the following:

```
WITH CURRENTSTUDENT DO
    BEGIN
        WRITELN(NAME) ;
        WRITELN(ADDRESS) ;
        WRITELN(NUMBEROFCREDITS : 3) ;
        WRITELN(GRADEPOINTAVERAGE : 4 : 2) ;
        WRITELN(STUDENTID : 6)
    END
```

In defining the type STUDENTRECORD on page 1, two of the fields were (packed) arrays. We can also have an array of records:

```
TYPE   PART              = RECORD
                            PARTNUMBER      : 10000..99999 ;
                            DESCRIPTION     : PACKED ARRAY[1..30] OF CHAR ;
                            QUANTITYONHAND : 0..500
                          END ;
       CHARACTERCOUNTER = 1..30 ;

VAR INVENTORY : ARRAY[1..1000] OF PART ;
    I         : CHARACTERCOUNTER ;
```

INVENTORY is declared to be an array variable with 1000 components; each component is a record with three fields. To read in the quantity on hand for the 250th component, we would write

```
READ(INVENTORY[250].QUANTITYONHAND)
```

Similarly, to read in the description for the 400th component, we would write

```
FOR I := 1 TO 30 DO
    READ(INVENTORY[400].DESCRIPTION[I])
```

Here we have an array whose components are records, and one of the record's components is an array. In fact, the component type of a record or an array can be any type. For example,

```
TYPE   DATE = RECORD
                  YEAR          : 1960..2000 ;
                  MONTH         : 1..12 ;
                  DAYINMONTH : 1..31
              END ;

       CHECK = RECORD
                   WITHDRAWAL    : REAL ;
                   PAYEE         : PACKED ARRAY[1..30] OF CHAR ;
                   CHECKNUMBER : 1..999 ;
                   CHECKDATE     : DATE
               END ;
VAR    CHECKARRAY : ARRAY[1..500] OF CHECK ;
```

To write out the month in which the 47th check was cashed,

```
WRITE(CHECKARRAY[47].CHECKDATE.MONTH : 2)
```

It is worth noting that field identifiers, such as CHECKDATE and MONTH, may appear in an expression, but type identifiers, such as CHECK and DATE, are illegal in an expression.

Variant Records

Sometimes the number of fields and their types will depend on the value of a special field, known as the "tag" field, in a record. For example, the record for a hospital patient might vary depending on whether the patient is insured. We can write

```
TYPE   STRING   = PACKED ARRAY[1..20] OF CHAR ;

       PATIENT = RECORD
                     NAME          : STRING ;
                     ADDRESS       : STRING ;
                     CASE INSURED : BOOLEAN OF
                         FALSE : (EMPLOYER         : STRING ;
                                  YEARSEMPLOYED : 0..50) ;
                         TRUE  : (INSURER          : STRING ;
                                  DEDUCTIBLE       : 0..100000 ;
                                  PERCENTCOVERED : REAL)
                 END ;
```

```
VAR   NEWPATIENT     : PATIENT ;
      INSURANCECODE : 0..1 ;
      I              : 1..20 ;
```

Here the tag field is INSURED and its type (the "tag" type) is BOOLEAN. The variant part of the record goes from the word CASE down to (but not including) the word END. When INSURED has the value FALSE, NEWPATIENT is a record variable with only five fields: NAME, ADDRESS, INSURED, EMPLOYER and YEARSEMPLOYED. When INSURED has the value TRUE, NEWPATIENT has six fields: NAME, ADDRESS, INSURED, INSURER, DEDUCTIBLE and PERCENTCOVERED. The value of INSURED will be determined, and possibly changed, during the execution of the program. For example, part of the program might be

```
WITH NEWPATIENT DO
    BEGIN
        FOR I := 1 TO 20 DO
            READ(NAME[I]) ;

        FOR I := 1 TO 20 DO
            READ(ADDRESS[I]) ;

        READLN(INSURANCECODE) ;
        IF   INSURANCECODE = 0 THEN
            BEGIN
                INSURED := FALSE ;
                FOR I := 1 TO 20 DO
                    READ(EMPLOYER[I]) ;
                READLN(YEARSEMPLOYED)
            END

        ELSE
            BEGIN
                INSURED := TRUE ;
                FOR I := 1 TO 20 DO
                    READ(INSURER[I]) ;
                READLN(DEDUCTIBLE, PERCENTCOVERED)
            END
    END
```

If the input is

```
JOHN SMITH              22 ALBACORE ST.        0
FRED'S PIZZA PARLOR  5
```

then the value of NEWPATIENT will be as follows:

(name)	(address)	(insured)	(employer)
JOHN SMITH	22 ALBACORE ST.	FALSE	FRED'S PIZZA PARLOR
			5

(years
employed)

If, however, the input is

```
JANE DOE              16 FISHHEAD ST.        1
JOHN HANCOCK, INC.  200      0.80
```

then the value of NEWPATIENT will be

(name)	(address)	(insured)	(insurer)	
JANE DOE	16 FISHHEAD ST.	TRUE	JOHN HANCOCK, INC.	
			200	0.80
			(deductible)	(percent covered)

Notes on variant records

1. The variant fields corresponding to a particular value of the tag field must be enclosed in parentheses.
2. An empty variant field is denoted by "( )".
3. The tag field must be an ordinal type identifier.
4. There is no special END for the variant part because the variant part is terminated by the END that terminates the entire record. Thus the variant part of a record always comes at the end of the record, after the "fixed" part.
5. A record need not have a fixed part. For example, we can write

```
TYPE  SHAPE  = (LINE, POINT, TRIANGLE) ;

     OBJECT = RECORD
               CASE FIGURE : SHAPE OF
                   LINE        : (SIDE : REAL) ;
                   POINT       : ( ) ;
                   TRIANGLE : (SIDE1, ANGLE1, ANGLE2 : REAL)
              END ;
```

6. Each field identifier in a record, whether or not it has a variant part, must be distinct from any other field identifier in that record. Thus, it would be *illegal* to write

```
TYPE  SHAPE  = (LINE, POINT, TRIANGLE) ;

     OBJECT = RECORD
               CASE FIGURE : SHAPE OF
                   LINE        : (SIDE : REAL) ;
                   POINT       : ( ) ;
                   TRIANGLE : (SIDE, ANGLE1, ANGLE2 : REAL)
              END ;
```

This definition of OBJECT is illegal because SIDE occurs twice as a field identifier.

7. The tag field is optional. In the definition of PATIENT on page 3, we could have replaced the line

CASE INSURED : BOOLEAN OF

with

CASE BOOLEAN OF

If this change were made, the subsequent references to INSURED in the WITH statement would have to be omitted. The references to the variant fields within that statement would still be unambiguous by note 6.
8. The definition and manipulation of variant records require extreme care, so do not use a variant record unless it will be a clear asset to your program.

Another example of variant records is provided in Chap. 4 and in Case Study 5.1.

DYNAMIC AND POINTER VARIABLES

In several of the case studies in succeeding chapters, we will utilize one of Pascal's subtle but important features: the ability of the programmer to create and destroy variables *during* the execution of a program. The use of such variables often enables our programs to conserve space in main memory and to execute more quickly than they otherwise would. A *dynamic variable* is one that is explicitly created and destroyed *during* the execution of a program. A dynamic variable is not declared in a variable declaration part since the variable does not exist prior to execution time. In fact, a dynamic variable does not even have a name! It is always referenced indirectly, by a *pointer variable*. A pointer variable is so named because the value stored in it is the address of a dynamic variable.

The declaration of a pointer variable's type is somewhat involved since we must also specify the type of the dynamic variables to be referenced by that pointer variable. For example,

```
TYPE   ARROW          = ^STUDENTRECORD ;

       STUDENTRECORD = RECORD
                   NAME, ADDRESS       : PACKED ARRAY[1..40] OF CHAR ;
                   NUMBEROFCREDITS     : 0..200 ;
                   GRADEPOINTAVERAGE : REAL ;
                   STUDENTID           : 0..999999
                 END ;
VAR    STUDENTPOINTER : ARROW ;
```

The first type definition defines ARROW as a type identifier for a pointer type: Any variable of type ARROW will point to a dynamic variable of type STUDENTRECORD. STUDENTRECORD is then defined as a type identifier for a record type containing five fields. STUDENTPOINTER is a variable (identifier) of type ARROW. Thus STUDENTPOINTER will contain the starting address of a dynamic (record) variable with five fields.

To create a dynamic variable of type STUDENTRECORD, the predeclared procedure NEW is called. The only actual parameter is a variable which will contain the address of the dynamic variable. Thus, STUDENTPOINTER is used as the actual parameter:

NEW(STUDENTPOINTER)

The execution of this procedure statement causes space to be allocated from a special area of memory known as the "heap". Enough space is allocated to accommodate the five fields in a student record, and the starting address of this area is stored in STUDENTPOINTER. Pictorially,

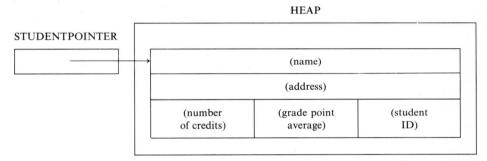

The arrow indicates that the value stored in the pointer variable STUDENT-POINTER is the address of the beginning of the area that comprises the dynamic variable. The dynamic variable is referred to by STUDENTPOINTER^. Thus, we can write

STUDENTPOINTER^.NUMBEROFCREDITS := 0 ;
READLN(STUDENTPOINTER^.GRADEPOINTAVERAGE) ;
WRITE(STUDENTPOINTER^.NAME)

To deallocate the storage given for a dynamic variable, we call the predeclared procedure DISPOSE. The only actual parameter is the pointer variable which points to the dynamic variable. Thus,

DISPOSE(STUDENTPOINTER)

will free the space that had been allocated to the dynamic variable above. This space can then be allocated to other dynamic variables. Another consequence of the call to DISPOSE is that the value of STUDENTPOINTER becomes undefined; the same fate befalls any other pointer variable which had the same value as STUDENTPOINTER just prior to the call.

The reserved word NIL denotes a value in any pointer type. This special value can be stored in a pointer variable to signify that the pointer variable does not contain the address of any dynamic variable. Thus,

STUDENTPOINTER := NIL

explicitly acknowledges that STUDENTPOINTER is not pointing to a dynamic variable. When STUDENTPOINTER has a NIL value, it would be an error to reference STUDENTPOINTER^, such as

WRITELN(STUDENTPOINTER^.GRADEPOINTAVERAGE : 4 : 2)

This is the most common error associated with pointer variables! How can such an error be made? Consider the following program segment:

```
REPEAT
   :
UNTIL (STUDENTPOINTER = NIL)
      OR (STUDENTPOINTER^.GRADEPOINTAVERAGE > 2.00)
```

Suppose STUDENTPOINTER has the value NIL at the end of the loop. Then the first operand of the operator OR will have the value TRUE. If the other operand is also evaluated,† the above-mentioned error will occur.

Virtually all applications of pointer variables and dynamic variables involve linked lists. A *linked list* is an ordered collection of records in which each record has a field that "points to" the next record in the list. The linked-list concept is developed in Chap. 3, and several additional applications are considered in Chaps, 5, 7, and 8.

FILES

Many problems in business and science require handling of vast quantities of data, more than will fit in the computer's main memory. On such occasions the information is stored outside of the main memory on a storage medium such as magnetic disk or magnetic tape. Such media are referred to as "secondary storage." In Pascal, a file type is a collection of components which reside in secondary storage. For example,

```
TYPE  PAYROLLRECORD = RECORD
                      NAME   : PACKED ARRAY[1..20] OF CHAR ;
                      SALARY : REAL
                      END ;

VAR   PAYROLLFILE : FILE OF PAYROLLRECORD ;
```

We have declared PAYROLLFILE to be a file variable; each component in the file is a record with two fields.

Disk drives and tape drives, the devices that control disks and tapes, can perform only trivial operations, so components from a file must be brought into

---

† The order of evaluation of operands is *implementation-dependent*: possibly differing between processors and not necessarily defined for any particular processor. Thus, for example, the operands may be evaluated in the given order, or in reverse order, or in parallel, or they may not both be evaluated.

main memory, one at a time. In Standard Pascal, every file must be accessed sequentially, starting with the first component in the file.† At any given time, the component most recently brought into main memory from the file is stored in a special variable, called the *buffer variable*. The buffer variable for a file is denoted by appending " ^ " to the name of the file variable. For example, the buffer variable for the file declared above is denoted by PAYROLLFILE^. The buffer variable is also used when we want to insert a component out onto the file.

In any file, the *file position* refers to the place from which the last component was brought into main memory, or the place to which the next component will be added to the file. We can detect when the file position is at the end of the file by using the predeclared function EOF whose only argument is a file variable. For example, a call to EOF(PAYROLLFILE) yields the value TRUE if the file position for PAYROLLFILE is at the end of the file; otherwise EOF(PAYROLL-FILE) is FALSE.

File Generation

Pascal provides two predeclared procedures to aid in *generating*, that is, creating a file. To illustrate the effect of these procedures, assume the following declarations:

```
VAR   SCOREFILE      : FILE OF 0..100 ;
      CURRENTSCORE : 0..100 ;
```

We use "@" to represent the end-of-file marker.

REWRITE(SCOREFILE).   REWRITE(SCOREFILE) prepares SCOREFILE for being generated: SCOREFILE becomes an empty file, the file position points to the end-of-file marker, and SCOREFILE^ is undefined. We say that SCORE-FILE is now "in the generation state."

Example If we have

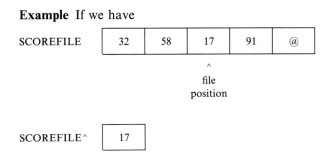

SCOREFILE

| 32 | 58 | 17 | 91 | @ |

^
file
position

SCOREFILE^

| 17 |

---

† Some versions of Pascal also permit random access to files: Any component can be brought into main memory (or stored on the file) simply by specifying the position of the component. The preceding components need not be brought in first. Random-access files are discussed in Chap. 7.

and we call REWRITE(SCOREFILE), we will have

PUT(SCOREFILE).   PUT(SCOREFILE) appends the value of SCOREFILE^ to the end of SCOREFILE. The file position points to the end-of-file marker, SCOREFILE remains in the generation state, and SCOREFILE^ becomes undefined. It is an error if SCOREFILE is not in the generation state when PUT(SCOREFILE) is called.

Example 1 If we have

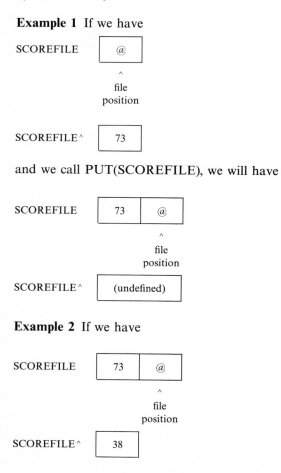

and we call PUT(SCOREFILE), we will have

SCOREFILE

| 73 | @ |

^
file
position

SCOREFILE^   (undefined)

Example 2 If we have

SCOREFILE

| 73 | @ |

^
file
position

SCOREFILE^   38

and we call PUT(SCOREFILE), we will have

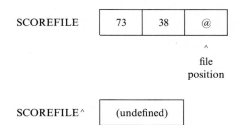

SCOREFILE

73	38	@

file
position

SCOREFILE^

(undefined)

To generate SCOREFILE from the input, we could proceed as follows:

```
REWRITE(SCOREFILE) ;

WHILE NOT EOF(INPUT) DO          (* INPUT SPECIFIED FOR CLARITY. *)
    BEGIN
        READLN(CURRENTSCORE) ;
        SCOREFILE^ := CURRENTSCORE ;
        PUT(SCOREFILE)
    END
```

For example, if the input contained

```
39
17
48
61
```

then, after the completion of the WHILE statement, we would have

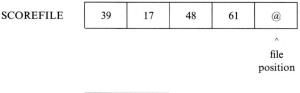

SCOREFILE

39	17	48	61	@

file
position

SCOREFILE^

(undefined)

CURRENTSCORE

61

We can abbreviate this somewhat with the help of the predeclared procedure WRITE.

```
WRITE(SCOREFILE, CURRENTSCORE)
```

is an abbreviation for

```
SCOREFILE^ := CURRENTSCORE ;
PUT(SCOREFILE)
```

Thus, to generate SCOREFILE from the input,

REWRITE(SCOREFILE) ;

```
WHILE  NOT  EOF(INPUT)  DO
    BEGIN
        READLN(CURRENTSCORE) ;
        WRITE(SCOREFILE, CURRENTSCORE)
    END
```

The above procedures perform as we have described them for any files except "text" files, described on pages 15–18.

File Inspection

Pascal also provides two predeclared procedures to aid in *inspecting* a file, that is, bringing the components of the file into main memory. To illustrate each of these procedures, we assume the following declarations:

```
VAR   SCOREFILE        : FILE OF 0..100 ;
          CURRENTSCORE,
          NEXTSCORE      : 0..100 ;
```

RESET(SCOREFILE).   RESET(SCOREFILE) prepares SCOREFILE for being inspected: the file position points to the first component in the file, and a copy of that component is stored in the buffer variable, SCOREFILE^. We say that SCOREFILE is now "in the inspection state."

Example If we have

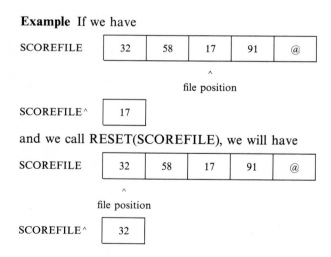

and we call RESET(SCOREFILE), we will have

Notes

1. If SCOREFILE is an empty file, a call to RESET(SCOREFILE) causes SCOREFILE^ to become undefined and EOF(SCOREFILE) to become TRUE.

2. It is an error if SCOREFILE is undefined before a call to RESET(SCORE-FILE).

GET(SCOREFILE). GET(SCOREFILE) advances the file pointer to point to the next component in the file and stores a copy of that component in SCOREFILE^. The file remains in the inspection state.

Example If we have

SCOREFILE

32	58	17	91	@

^

file position

SCOREFILE^

32

and we call GET(SCOREFILE), we will have

SCOREFILE

32	58	17	91	@

^

file position

SCOREFILE^

58

Notes

1. If there is no "next" component in the file, a call to GET(SCOREFILE) causes the file position to point to the end-of-file marker, SCOREFILE^ to become undefined, and EOF(SCOREFILE) to become TRUE.
2. It is an error if GET(SCOREFILE) is called when SCOREFILE is not in the inspection state.
3. It is an error if EOF(SCOREFILE) is already TRUE just prior to a call to GET(SCOREFILE).

To process all of SCOREFILE, we could proceed as follows:

```
RESET(SCOREFILE);     (* Brings first component into SCOREFILE^. *)
WHILE NOT EOF(SCOREFILE) DO
     BEGIN
          (* Process the component just brought in. *)
               :
          GET(SCOREFILE)
     END
```

The predeclared procedure READ is often used as an abbreviation. For example,

```
READ(SCOREFILE, CURRENTSCORE)
```

is equivalent to

CURRENTSCORE := SCOREFILE^ ;
GET(SCOREFILE)

Furthermore,

READ(SCOREFILE, CURRENTSCORE, NEXTSCORE)

is equivalent to

READ(SCOREFILE, CURRENTSCORE) ;
READ(SCOREFILE, NEXTSCORE)

File Updating

After a file has been created, we will often want to *update* the file: insert, delete, and change components in the file. This is not quite as easy as it might first appear. Suppose, for example, that RESET(SCOREFILE) has just been called and SCOREFILE is in increasing order, as follows:

SCOREFILE

32	46	48	67	81	@

^
file position

If we want to insert 53 into its correct position in the file, we would repeatedly call GET(SCOREFILE) as long as SCOREFILE^ were less than 53. When the loop is exited, SCOREFILE^ would have a value of 67. But the file is in the inspection state, so 53 cannot now be "put" into the file.

In general, updates are not performed directly on SCOREFILE. Instead, we utilize another file, such as NEWSCOREFILE. In the above example, we would call REWRITE(NEWSCOREFILE) right after calling RESET(SCOREFILE). We would still call GET(SCOREFILE) as long as SCOREFILE^ were less than 53, but in each such case, we would call WRITE(NEWSCOREFILE, SCOREFILE^) to append the current component of SCOREFILE to NEW-SCOREFILE. By the time this loop is exited, SCOREFILE^ would be 67, and NEWSCOREFILE would be

NEWSCOREFILE

32	46	48	@

^
file position

A call WRITE(NEWSCOREFILE, 53) yields

NEWSCOREFILE

32	46	48	53	@

^
file position

We would now go through another loop to append the rest of SCOREFILE to NEWSCOREFILE. This gives us

NEWSCOREFILE	32	46	48	53	67	81	@

^
file position

If we copy NEWSCOREFILE onto SCOREFILE, we will be done. But before we wipe out the original version of SCOREFILE, we should save it somewhere. Otherwise, if any of the above operations were performed incorrectly, NEWSCOREFILE might contain garbage. Copying this garbage onto SCORE-FILE would make it a worthless file. Thus, we first copy SCOREFILE onto, say OLDSCOREFILE, and then copy NEWSCOREFILE onto SCOREFILE. This copying cannot be accomplished with an assignment statement since file types are not assignment compatible (see page 19). Instead, we call COPY(SCOREFILE, OLDSCOREFILE) and COPY(NEWSCOREFILE, SCOREFILE), where the procedure COPY and related declarations in the calling program are as follows:

```
TYPE   FILETYPE = FILE OF 0..100 ;
VAR    SCOREFILE, NEWSCOREFILE, OLDSCOREFILE : FILETYPE ;

PROCEDURE COPY(VAR   SOURCEFILE, DESTINATIONFILE : FILETYPE) ;

(*   Copy SOURCEFILE onto DESTINATIONFILE.   *)

BEGIN
    RESET(SOURCEFILE) ;
    REWRITE(DESTINATIONFILE) ;

    WHILE NOT EOF(SOURCEFILE) DO
        BEGIN
            WRITE(DESTINATIONFILE, SOURCEFILE^) ;
            GET(SOURCEFILE)
        END

END ;    (* of the procedure COPY. *)
```

Text Files

There is a predefined type in Pascal:

```
TYPE   TEXT = FILE OF CHAR ;
```

A text file is subdivided into lines and each line is followed by a special, unprintable character: an end-of-line marker. For example, we can declare

```
VAR   CHARFILE                         : TEXT ;
      CURRENTCHARACTER, NEXTCHARACTER : CHAR ;
```

To generate the first line of CHARFILE,

```
REWRITE(CHARFILE) ;
WRITE(CHARFILE, 'B', 'I', 'G', ' ', 'D', 'E', 'A', 'L') ;
```

This gives us

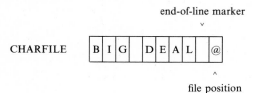

The predeclared procedure **WRITELN** appends an end-of-line marker to the end of a file. Thus,

WRITELN(CHARFILE) ;

yields the following

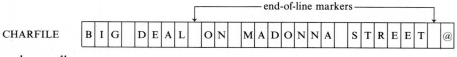

As you can see, the end-of-line marker looks like a blank character. The above WRITE and WRITELN calls could be replaced by

WRITELN(CHARFILE, 'B', 'I', 'G', ' ', 'D', 'E', 'A', 'L') :

When a textfile is in the inspection state, the predeclared procedure READLN enables us to skip over the end-of-line marker. Thus, if CHARFILE is

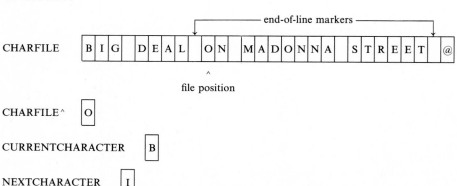

and we call

RESET(CHARFILE) ;
READLN(CHARFILE, CURRENTCHARACTER, NEXTCHARACTER)

we will have

The above call to READLN is an abbreviation for

READ(CHARFILE, CURRENTCHARACTER, NEXTCHARACTER) ;
READLN(CHARFILE)

That is why the file position is pointing to the first character (namely 'O') after the first end-of-line marker.

Detecting the end-of-line marker is accomplished by the predeclared function EOLN: a call to EOLN(CHARFILE) yields TRUE or FALSE depending on whether CHARFILE^ contains an end-of-line marker. Thus,

READLN(CHARFILE)

is an abbreviation for

WHILE NOT EOLN(CHARFILE) DO
    GET(CHARFILE) ;
GET(CHARFILE)

To provide legible input and output, the following predeclared variables are used:

VAR INPUT, OUTPUT : TEXT ;

The file INPUT contains data from your computer's standard input device, which may be a terminal or card reader, for example. The file OUTPUT contains data for your computer's standard output device, which may be a line printer or a cathode ray tube screen, for example. The procedure calls

RESET(INPUT) ;
REWRITE(OUTPUT)

have been executed prior to the start of your program's execution. Furthermore, INPUT is assumed when the file variable is omitted in a call to EOF, EOLN, READ, and READLN. Similarly, OUTPUT is assumed when the file variable is omitted in a call to WRITE, WRITELN, and PAGE.

Of special importance is that a textfile, typically INPUT, can be used for reading in INTEGER and REAL values as well as CHAR values. For example, suppose we have

VAR TEMPERATURE : −273..MAXINT ;

The execution of

READ(TEMPERATURE)

proceeds character by character as follows: First, all preceding blanks and end-of-line markers in INPUT are skipped over. Then the sign, if there is one, is saved. The succeeding collection of digit characters, up to the first nondigit character, is then read in and assembled into an integer. This integer is negated if the sign was '−', and the resulting value is stored in the variable TEMPERATURE. A REAL value is handled similarly, character by character, with appropriate care for the decimal point and 'E' (if the value is in floating point notation).

A textfile, typically OUTPUT, can be used for writing values of types INTE-GER, REAL, BOOLEAN and string, as well as CHAR.

ASSIGNMENT COMPATIBILITY

One of Pascal's most significant features is its treatment of types. A variable's type can be denoted in either of two ways: by a type identifier or by a new type. But two variables may be considered to have the same type even if those variables are denoted by different type identifiers. Thus, if we have

```
TYPE  STUDENTRECORD  = RECORD
                          NAME, ADDRESS          : PACKED ARRAY[1..40] OF CHAR ;
                          NUMBEROFCREDITS     : 0..200 ;
                          GRADEPOINTAVERAGE : REAL ;
                          STUDENTID                  : 0..99999
                       END ;

      ALUMNUSRECORD = STUDENTRECORD ;

VAR   CURRENTSTUDENT   : STUDENTRECORD ;
      ALUMNUS                   : ALUMNUSRECORD ;
```

then CURRENTSTUDENT and ALUMNUS are considered to have the same type since ALUMNUSRECORD was "equated" with STUDENTRECORD in the type definition of ALUMNUSRECORD. Thus, the assignment

```
ALUMNUS := CURRENTSTUDENT
```

is legitimate. To put it another way, the value of CURRENTSTUDENT is *assignment-compatible* with the type of ALUMNUS.

On the other hand, the Pascal standard (American National Standard Pascal, 1983, page 33) states that "Each occurrence of a new-type shall denote a type that is distinct from any other new-type." Thus, two types may be considered distinct even though their structures are identical. For example, suppose we have

```
TYPE  STUDENTRECORD  = RECORD
                          NAME, ADDRESS          :PACKED ARRAY[1..40] OF CHAR ;
                          NUMBEROFCREDITS     : 0..200 ;
                          GRADEPOINTAVERAGE : REAL ;
                          STUDENTID                  : 0..99999
                       END ;

      ALUMNUSRECORD = RECORD
                          NAME, ADDRESS          : PACKED ARRAY[1..40] OF CHAR ;
                          NUMBEROFCREDITS     : 0..200 ;
                          GRADEPOINTAVERAGE : REAL ;
                          STUDENTID                  : 0..99999
                       END ;

VAR   CURRENTSTUDENT : STUDENTRECORD ;
      ALUMNUS                 : ALUMNUSRECORD ;
```

Here, CURRENTSTUDENT and ALUMNUS do *not* have the same type, and so the assignment

ALUMNUS := CURRENTSTUDENT

would be illegal!

The issue of assignment-compatibility is important, not only in assignment statements, but also in the relationship between a value formal parameter and its corresponding actual parameter (see page 22). It will be well worth your while to study the following rules until you fully understand them.

A value of type T2 is *assignment-compatible with* (that is, can be assigned to) a variable of type T1 if and only if one of the following statements is true:

1. T1 and T2 are the same type, and that type is not a file type or a type with file components.
2. T1 is REAL and T2 is INTEGER.
3. T1 and T2 are ordinal types and the value from type T2 is one of the values in the type T1.
4. T1 and T2 are set types, whose base types are either both packed or both unpacked, and all the members of the value of type T2 are members of the base type of T1. For example, suppose we have

   VAR   FIRSTSET   : SET OF 0..100 ;
         SECONDSET : SET OF 10..20 ;

   Then [5, 10, 15, 20] is assignment-compatible with FIRSTSET, and so

   FIRSTSET := [5, 10, 15, 20]

   is legitimate. However, [5, 10, 15, 20] is *not* assignment-compatible with SECONDSET. The assignment statement

   FIRSTSET := SECONDSET ;

   is legitimate as long as SECONDSET is given a value (in the type SET OF 10..20) prior to the assignment statement. Since [13, 15, 18] is assignment-compatible with FIRSTSET, the pair of statements

   FIRSTSET   := [13, 15, 18] ;
   SECONDSET := FIRSTSET

   is legitimate.
5. T1 and T2 are string types with the same number of components. A *string* is a packed array of characters with subscripts starting at 1.

Note that for records, assignment-compatibility occurs only if both types are the same. The examples on pages 18–19 will help to clarify what *same type* means. Similarly, for arrays (except strings), assignment-compatibility occurs only if both types are the same.

Exercise 1.1 Use the following definitions and declarations to determine which assignment statements below violate the assignment-compatibility rules. In each assignment statement, assume that the expression to the right of the " := " has a value in its type.

```
TYPE   FIRSTRECORDTYPE    = RECORD
                                 FIRSTFIELD    : INTEGER ;
                                 SECONDFIELD : REAL
                             END ;

       SECONDRECORDTYPE = RECORD
                                 FIRSTFIELD    : INTEGER ;
                                 SECONDFIELD : REAL
                             END ;

       THIRDRECORDTYPE   = SECONDRECORDTYPE ;

       FIRSTARRAYTYPE    = ARRAY[1..10] OF REAL ;
       SECONDARRAYTYPE   = ARRAY[1..10] OF REAL ;

VAR    RECORD1              : FIRSTRECORDTYPE ;
       RECORD2              : SECONDRECORDTYPE ;
       RECORD3              : THIRDRECORDTYPE ;
       RECORD4, RECORD5     : RECORD
                                 FIRSTFIELD    : INTEGER ;
                                 SECONDFIELD : REAL
                             END ;

       STRING1              : PACKED ARRAY[1..10] OF CHAR ;
       STRING2              : PACKED ARRAY[1..10] OF CHAR ;

       ARRAY1               : FIRSTARRAYTYPE ;
       ARRAY2, ARRAY3       : SECONDARRAYTYPE ;

       SET1                 : SET OF 0..100 ;
       SET2                 : SET OF 50..100 ;

       FILE1, FILE2         : FILE OF REAL ;
```

(a) RECORD1.FIRSTFIELD   := 32 ;
(b) RECORD1.SECONDFIELD := 32 ;
(c) RECORD1 := RECORD2 ;
(d) RECORD2 := RECORD3 ;
(e) RECORD2 := RECORD4 ;
(f) RECORD4 := RECORD5 ;
(g) STRING1 := 'YES' ;
(h) STRING1 := STRING2 ;
(i) ARRAY2 := ARRAY1 ;
(j) ARRAY2 := ARRAY3 ;
(k) ARRAY1 := 0 ;
(l) SET1 := [20, 60] ;
(m) SET2 := [20, 60] ;
(n) SET1 := SET2 ;

(*o*) FILE1 ^ := FILE2 ;
(*p*) FILE1 ^ := 35.7 ;
(*q*) FILE2 ^ := 35 ;
(*r*) FILE1 ^ := FILE2 ^ ;
(*s*) FILE1 := FILE2 ;

PROCEDURES

A *procedure* is a named program segment that accomplishes some task. A procedure consists of a procedure heading followed by a *block*: a declarations section followed by an executable section. This is similar to the structure of a program, but a program's executable section is automatically carried out. For a procedure, the executable section is carried out only when the procedure is explicitly called in a *procedure statement*, sometimes referred to as a *procedure call*. For example,

```
PROGRAM FINDHIGHSPEED(INPUT, OUTPUT) ;

(* This program determines the higher of two velocities. *)

VAR   SPEED1, SPEED2, HIGHSPEED : REAL ;

PROCEDURE   FINDLARGER(FIRST, SECOND : REAL ; VAR   LARGER : REAL) ;

(* Determine the larger of FIRST and SECOND and store the      *)
(* larger value in LARGER. If FIRST and SECOND have the same *)
(* value, LARGER will get that value.                          *)

BEGIN
     IF FIRST > SECOND THEN
         LARGER := FIRST
     ELSE
         LARGER := SECOND
END ;   (* of the procedure FINDLARGER. *)

BEGIN
     READLN(SPEED1, SPEED2) ;

     FINDLARGER(SPEED1, SPEED2, HIGHSPEED) ;

     WRITELN('THE LARGER OF ', SPEED1 : 7 : 2, ' AND ', SPEED2 : 7 : 2, ' IS ',
             HIGHSPEED : 7 : 2)
END.
```

The first statement executed in the above program will be the READLN statement (which, in fact, is a procedure statement that calls the predeclared procedure READLN). The procedure statement

```
FINDLARGER(SPEED1, SPEED2, HIGHSPEED)
```

is executed next. The variables SPEED1, SPEED2, and HIGHSPEED in the procedure statement are called *actual parameters*: they provide values to the procedure and may have their values changed by the procedure. The procedure's name, FINDLARGER, occurs both in the procedure statement and in the procedure heading. The procedure heading also has two formal parameter sections (separated by a semicolon), with three formal parameters that correspond to the three actual parameters. Since the correspondence is strictly positional, FIRST corresponds to SPEED1, SECOND corresponds to SPEED2, and LARGER corresponds to HIGHSPEED. FIRST and SECOND are *value* formal parameters since their section does not begin with VAR. A value formal parameter gets its initial value from the corresponding actual parameter at the time the procedure is called, but the actual parameter's value is *unaffected* by the procedure. LARGER is a *variable* formal parameter since its section begins with VAR. A variable formal parameter denotes the *same variable* as the corresponding actual parameter. Thus, LARGER and HIGHSPEED are considered two names for the same variable, so any change in LARGER's value is also a change in HIGHSPEED's value.

The execution of the procedure statement is completed when the executable section of the procedure has been carried out. The executable section of the procedure assigns a value to LARGER, and thus to HIGHSPEED.

When a procedure is called, each *value* formal parameter gets its initial value from the corresponding actual parameter. Thus, the value of the actual parameter must be *assignment-compatible* with its corresponding value formal parameter. Such an actual parameter need not be a variable: it can be an arbitrary expression.

As we mentioned earlier, each *variable* formal parameter represents the same variable as the corresponding actual parameter. Thus, a variable formal parameter and its corresponding actual parameter must have the *same type*.

Pascal requires that every formal parameter have its type denoted by a type identifier. As a practical matter, the type of the corresponding actual parameter should be denoted by the *same* type identifier (unless that actual parameter is not a variable). This practice will eliminate most of the errors associated with the actual parameter-formal parameter correspondence.

Exercise 1.2 Why is it illegal for the type of a value formal parameter to be a file type?

FUNCTIONS

A function is a named program segment that calculates a *single* value. A function is similar to a procedure in that a function has formal parameters that correspond to actual parameters (often called *arguments*) when the function is called. A function differs from a procedure in the following respects:

1. A function call occurs as part of an expression, whereas a procedure call is a statement by itself.

2. A function heading includes the type of the result calculated by the function. That type must be denoted by a type identifier for a REAL, ordinal, or pointer type.
3. Each time the function is called, at least one assignment statement must be executed in which the function identifier occurs all by itself to the left of the " := ". The expression to the right of the " := " will provide the value to be returned by the function.

For example, the program on page 21 used a procedure. The following program uses a function to solve the same problem:

```
PROGRAM   FINDHIGHSPEED(INPUT, OUTPUT) ;

(* Determine the higher of two velocities. *)

VAR   SPEED1, SPEED2 : REAL ;

FUNCTION   LARGER(FIRST, SECOND : REAL) : REAL ;

(* Return the larger of FIRST and SECOND. *)

BEGIN
    IF FIRST > SECOND THEN
        LARGER := FIRST
    ELSE
        LARGER := SECOND
END ; (* of the function LARGER. *)

BEGIN
    READLN(SPEED1, SPEED2) ;
    WRITELN('THE LARGER OF ', SPEED1 : 7 : 2, ' AND ', SPEED2 : 7 : 2, ' IS ',
            LARGER(SPEED1, SPEED2) : 7 : 2)
END.
```

Pascal allows a function to have variable formal parameters as well as value formal parameters. But, since a function is used to calculate a single value, good programming practice dictates that a function have value formal parameters only. The one exception to this practice occurs when an actual parameter has a file type. The corresponding formal parameter could not be a value formal parameter because a file is not assignment-compatible with any variable, even if they are of the same type. Thus, a formal parameter corresponding to an actual parameter whose type is a file type must be a variable formal parameter.

Because procedures and functions both have structures that are similar to programs, from now on we will use the term *subprogram* to refer to a procedure or function. When a subprogram is called, the return address in the calling program (or subprogram) must be saved by the computer so it will know where to resume execution after the call is completed. Because it is possible for a subprogram to call itself (see pages 27–34), the computer needs to save quite a bit more than just the return address. For example, when a subprogram calls a subprogram, the values of the calling subprogram's local variables must be saved lest they be destroyed in the event that the subprogram is calling itself. The information saved when a subprogram calls a subprogram is referred to as the "execution state." After the call is completed, the state of execution that existed prior to the call is restored.

SCOPE

The *scope* of an identifier is that portion of the program to which the identifier's declaration (or definition) applies. To be precise, an identifier's scope consists of the remainder of the block subsequent to the point where the identifier is declared, less any enclosed headings and blocks in which it is redeclared. For example, the following program has three identifiers called RATE, each with its own scope. We indent each block for the sake of readability. (In the case studies, we will use a different indenting convention.)

```
PROGRAM SAMPLE(OUTPUT);
(* This program demonstrates the scope of identifiers. *)
  CONST RATE = 50;
  PROCEDURE PRINT1(RATE : REAL);
      VAR MILES : INTEGER;
      PROCEDURE NEST;
          CONST RATE = 10.23;
          BEGIN
              WRITELN(RATE : 5 : 2)
          END; (* of the procedure NEST. *)
      BEGIN
          WRITELN(RATE : 5 : 2);
          MILES := 0;
          NEST
      END; (* of the procedure PRINT1. *)
  PROCEDURE PRINT2;
      BEGIN
          WRITELN(RATE : 5)
      END; (* of the procedure PRINT2. *)
  BEGIN (* the executable section of the main program. *)
      WRITELN(RATE : 5);
      PRINT1(31.6);
      PRINT2
  END.
```

The definition of RATE as a constant identifier with a value of 50 applies to the entire program subsequent to that definition, except for the procedure

PRINT1. In PRINT1, the identifier RATE is declared as a REAL variable. This declaration applies to all of PRINT1's block except the procedure NEST, where RATE is defined as a constant identifier with a value of 10.23.

Thus the output from the program will be

50	(from the WRITELN statement in the main program)
31.60	(from the WRITELN statement in the procedure PRINT1)
10.23	(from the WRITELN statement in the procedure NEST)
50	(from the WRITELN statement in the procedure PRINT2)

An identifier declared in the main program block is said to be a *global* identifier. In the program SAMPLE, the global identifiers are RATE (a constant identifier with a value of 50), PRINT1, and PRINT2. Those are the only identifiers known to the main program. Thus, for example, the main program can call procedures PRINT1 and PRINT2 but cannot call the procedure NEST. An identifier declared in a procedure block is said to be a *local* identifier in that procedure. In the procedure PRINT1, the only local identifiers are NEST and MILES. In the procedure NEST, the only local identifier is the constant identifier RATE, with a value of 10.23. The identifiers NEST and MILES, as well as all the global identifiers, are *nonlocal* to the procedure NEST. The procedure PRINT2 has no local identifiers.

Since an identifier's scope does not include any prior part of the program, an identifier cannot be referred to until it is declared.† Thus, in the program SAMPLE, the procedure PRINT1 could *not* have called the procedure PRINT2, but PRINT2 could have called PRINT1 (since PRINT1's scope is the entire program subsequent to PRINT1's procedure heading). NEST could not have called PRINT2 since PRINT2 was defined after NEST. Furthermore, PRINT2 could not have called NEST since the scope of NEST is limited to the procedure PRINT1. Lastly, PRINT1 could have called (in fact, did call) NEST, and NEST could have called PRINT1 since the scope of PRINT1 is the entire program subsequent to PRINT1's procedure heading. Figure 1.1 depicts the scopes of the procedure identifiers PRINT1, NEST, and PRINT2.

A final note on scope: An identifier cannot be declared twice in the same declarations section, but a field identifier in a record is considered distinct from any other identifier in that block. For example, it would be legal to write

```
VAR   AGE   : 0..120 ;
      CHILD : RECORD
                 NAME : PACKED ARRAY[1..30] OF CHAR ;
                 AGE  : 0..17
              END ;
```

---

† There are two exceptions to this:
  1. The definition of a pointer type refers to the type (which may be subsequently defined) of the dynamic variable pointed to.
  2. A file variable may be referred to in the list of program parameters (in the program heading) before it is declared.

```
PROGRAM   SAMPLE(OUTPUT);
(* This program demonstrates the scope of identifiers. *)
   CONST RATE = 50;
   PROCEDURE PRINT1(RATE : REAL);
```

— scope of PRINT1 (including the two boxes within this one)

```
      VAR MILES : INTEGER;
      PROCEDURE NEST;

            CONST RATE = 10.23;
            BEGIN
                 WRITELN(RATE:5:2)
            END; (* of the procedure NEST.*)          ← scope of NEST
         BEGIN
            WRITELN(RATE:5:2);
            MILES := 0;
            NEST
         END; (* of the procedure PRINT1. *)

                                                      scope of PRINT2
   PROCEDURE   PRINT2;

         BEGIN
              WRITELN(RATE:5)
         END; (* of the procedure PRINT2.*)
   BEGIN   (* the executable section of the main program. *)
      WRITELN(RATE:5);
      PRINT1(31.6);
      PRINT2
   END.
```

Figure 1.1 Illustration of the scopes of the procedure identifiers PRINT1, NEST, and PRINT2.

The field identifier AGE may be referred to only in conjunction with the record variable CHILD, such as

WRITELN(CHILD.AGE)

Other references to AGE refer to the variable with values in 0..120.

Exercise 1.3 For each procedure in the following program skeleton, indicate which procedures can be called by that procedure. Also, which procedures can be called by the main program?

```
PROGRAM   LEGALCALLS(INPUT, OUTPUT);
    PROCEDURE  PROC1;
        PROCEDURE  PROC2;
            PROCEDURE  PROC3;
                BEGIN
                  ⋮
                END;  (* of procedure PROC3. *)
```

```
        BEGIN
          ⋮
        END ;   (* of procedure PROC2. *)
    PROCEDURE   PROC4;
        BEGIN
          ⋮
        END ;   (* of procedure PROC4. *)
      BEGIN
        ⋮
      END ; (* of procedure PROC1. *)
    PROCEDURE   PROC5 ;
        BEGIN
          ⋮
        END ;   (* of procedure PROC5. *)
  BEGIN   (* the executable section of the main program. *)
    ⋮
  END.
```

RECURSION

If there is any single skill that distinguishes a novice Pascal programmer from an experienced one, it is the understanding of recursion. A subprogram is *recursive* if it is defined in terms of itself. It is not difficult to insert, within a subprogram, a call to the subprogram itself. What is hard is recognizing situations for which such recursive calls are appropriate. Because recursion plays a critical role in the remainder of this text, we now present two examples to give you a feel for recognizing such situations.

Example 1 The "Towers of Hanoi" game. We have three poles: A, B, and C. We also have a number of disks of different sizes. Initially, all of the disks are on pole A, with the largest disk on the bottom, then the next largest, and so on. Figure 1.2 shows the initial configuration if we started with six disks. The object of the game is to move all of the disks from pole A to pole B; pole C is used for temporary storage. The rules of the game are:

1. Only one disk may be moved at a time.
2. No disk may ever be placed on top of a smaller disk.
3. Other than the prohibition of rule 2, any disk may be moved from any pole to any other pole.

Figure 1.2 The initial configuration for the Towers of Hanoi with six disks.

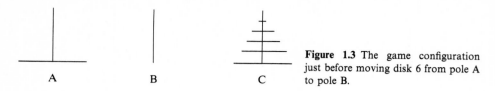

Figure 1.3 The game configuration just before moving disk 6 from pole A to pole B.

Rather than trying to decide where to move disk 1, the smallest disk, consider the situation later on when we are about to move disk 6. Since disk 6 must go at the bottom of pole B, the configuration just before we move disk 6 must be as shown in Fig. 1.3.

Thus, we must first figure out how to move five disks from pole A to pole C. Then we can move disk 6 from pole A to pole B and, finally, move the five disks from pole C to pole B. This idea has not told us where to move disk 1 initially, but we have made an important step in completing the whole game. If we can figure out how to move five disks from one pole to another, we will be done! The key feature is that we have reduced the original problem (moving six disks) to a smaller problem (moving five disks).

How can we move five disks from pole A to pole C? Easily! First we figure out how to move the top four disks from pole A to pole B, then move disk 5 to pole C, and finally move the four disks from pole B to pole C. Eventually, we will face the trivial problem of moving disk 1 from one pole to another.

We now have the strategy for moving an arbitrary number, N, of disks from pole A to pole B:

If $N = 1$, we simply move disk 1 from pole A to pole B. Otherwise,

1. Move $N - 1$ disks from pole A to pole C, using pole B as a temporary.
2. Next, move disk N from pole A to pole B.
3. Finally, move $N - 1$ disks from pole C to pole B, using A as a temporary.

This strategy naturally leads to the following recursive procedure:

```
TYPE   POSINTEGER = 1..MAXINT ;
       POLE        = 'A'..'C' ;

PROCEDURE   MOVE(N : POSINTEGER ;
                  ORIGIN, DESTINATION, TEMPORARY : POLE) ;

(* Describe the steps necessary to move N disks from an ORIGIN pole  *)
(* to a DESTINATION pole, using the other pole for TEMPORARY         *)
(* storage. The procedure does not actually effect any moves; it     *)
(* merely associates disks with poles.                               *)

BEGIN

    IF N = 1 THEN
        WRITELN('MOVE DISK 1 FROM POLE ', ORIGIN, ' TO POLE ',
                DESTINATION, '.')
```

```
    ELSE
      BEGIN
          MOVE(N − 1, ORIGIN, TEMPORARY, DESTINATION);
          WRITELN('MOVE DISK ', N : 1, ' FROM POLE ', ORIGIN,
                  ' TO POLE ', DESTINATION, '.');
          MOVE(N − 1, TEMPORARY, DESTINATION, ORIGIN)
      END

END;   (* of the procedure MOVE. *)
```

In Fig. 1.4, we present a tree, called a "recursion tree," to illustrate what would happen after an initial call of

MOVE(3, 'A', 'B', 'C')

Thus, the output would be

```
MOVE DISK 1 FROM POLE A TO POLE B.
MOVE DISK 2 FROM POLE A TO POLE C.
MOVE DISK 1 FROM POLE B TO POLE C.
MOVE DISK 3 FROM POLE A TO POLE B.
MOVE DISK 1 FROM POLE C TO POLE A.
MOVE DISK 2 FROM POLE C TO POLE B.
MOVE DISK 1 FROM POLE A TO POLE B.
```

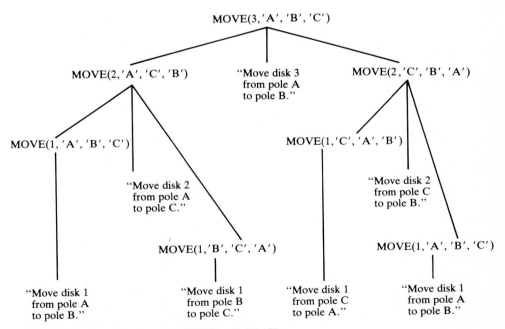

Figure 1.4 The recursion tree for MOVE(3, 'A', 'B', 'C').

Exercise 1.4 Develop a recursion tree to illustrate the execution of the procedure MOVE after an initial call of

MOVE(4, 'A', 'B', 'C')

Exercise 1.5 Let f be a function which calculates the number of moves required to move disks from one pole to another pole. From page 29, we see that $f(3) = 7$. What is $f(4)$? What is $f(5)$? Determine the general formula for $f(N)$. You may express it recursively.

Recursion is an appropriate technique if the problem has these characteristics:

1. Solving larger instances of the problem involves solving one or more smaller instances.
2. The smallest instances of the problem can be solved straightforwardly.

In the Towers of Hanoi problem, recursion was natural because moving N disks could be accomplished by moving $N - 1$ disks (twice), and moving 1 disk was trivial.

Example 2 Fibonacci Numbers The arrangement of scales on pine cones, as well as the florets of daisies and the family tree of male bees, follows the Fibonacci sequence. This sequence is named after the 13th century Italian mathematician who noticed that the breeding pattern of rabbits conformed to the sequence 1, 1, 2, 3, 5, 8, 13, 21, 34, ... In this sequence, the first two terms are both 1; after that, each term is equal to the sum of the two preceding terms (for example, $8 = 5 + 3$). This suggests that the function to calculate the Nth number in the sequence can be defined recursively:

```
TYPE   POSINTEGER = 1..MAXINT ;

FUNCTION   FIBONACCI(N : POSINTEGER) : POSINTEGER ;
(* Calculate the Nth number in the Fibonacci *)
(* sequence : 1, 1, 2, 3, 5, 8, 13, 21, 34, 55, ....   *)
BEGIN
    IF    N <= 2 THEN
          FIBONACCI := 1
    ELSE
          FIBONACCI := FIBONACCI(N - 1) + FIBONACCI(N - 2)
END ;    (* of the function FIBONACCI. *)
```

In the last assignment statement of the function, there are two recursive calls to the function FIBONACCI. The recursion tree in Fig. 1.5 shows the effect of a call to FIBONACCI(6).

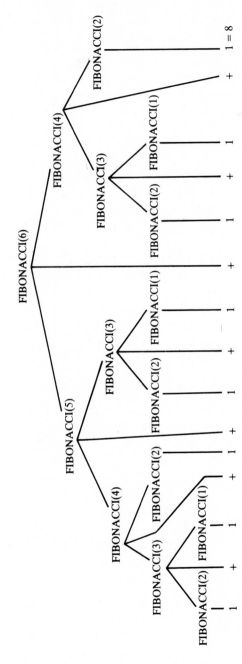

Figure 1.5 The recursion tree for the call to FIBONACCI(6).

31

Figure 1.5 shows that the above function is not efficient: For example, FIBONACCI(4) must be calculated twice. Exercise 1.6 includes a function that calculates the Nth Fibonacci number using a loop instead of recursion; such a function is called "iterative" because it has a loop. Sometimes a recursive subprogram can easily be replaced by a more efficient, iterative subprogram. Often this is not the case. During the design stage, you should neither seek nor avoid recursion. Instead, you should concentrate on solving the problem in a clear and natural way. Excessive concern for efficiency in the design stage will complicate your problem-solving efforts.

Exercise 1.6 An iterative function to calculate Fibonacci numbers is based on the following observation: Whenever we add the current and previous Fibonacci numbers to obtain the next one, we can then view the current Fibonacci number as the previous one and the next one as the current one. For example if we have

CURRENT | PREVIOUS
| 5 | | 3 |

and we add them to obtain

NEXT
| 8 |

then on the next iteration we want

CURRENT | PREVIOUS
| 8 | | 5 |

```
TYPE   POSINTEGER = 1..MAXINT ;
FUNCTION   FIBONACCI(N: POSINTEGER) : POSINTEGER ;
(* Calculate the Nth number in the Fibonacci *)
(* sequence : 1, 1, 2, 3, 5, 8, 13, 21, 34, 55, .... *)
TYPE   COUNTER = 3..MAXINT ;
VAR    PREVIOUS, CURRENT, NEXT : POSINTEGER ;
       I                       : COUNTER ;
BEGIN
    IF N <= 2 THEN
       FIBONACCI := 1
```

```
    ELSE
        BEGIN
            PREVIOUS := 1 ;
            CURRENT := 1 ;

            FOR I := 3 TO N DO
                BEGIN
                    NEXT        := CURRENT + PREVIOUS ;
                    PREVIOUS := CURRENT ;
                    CURRENT := NEXT
                END ;
            FIBONACCI := CURRENT
        END

END ; (* of the function FIBONACCI. *)
```

Trace the execution of this function after an initial call to FIBONACCI(6). How many additions were required to calculate FIBONACCI(6) in the recursive function on page 30? For both the iterative and recursive versions, determine the general formula for the number of additions required to calculate FIBONACCI(N).

Exercise 1.7 Try to develop an iterative procedure to solve the Towers of Hanoi game. *Hint:* On odd-numbered moves, the smallest disk is moved either clockwise (A → B → C) or counterclockwise (A ← B ← C) depending on whether the total number of disks is odd or even, respectively. On even-numbered moves, we make the only legal move possible to a non-smallest disk.

Indirect Recursion

We mentioned earlier (page 24) that a considerable body of information is saved every time a subprogram calls a subprogram. This information is saved to prevent its destruction in case the calling subprogram is calling itself. Can the compiler simply check to see if the subprogram is recursive and, if not, save only the return address? Such a test might be feasible if Pascal allowed direct recursion only. However, Pascal also supports indirect recursion. Thus, if subprogram A calls subprogram B and B calls A, then both A and B are recursive.†

There is a technical problem here: An identifier must be defined before it can be used. This implies that A must be defined before it can be called in B, and B must be defined before it can be called in A. Pascal avoids an impasse by means of the FORWARD directive. This informs the compiler that the rest of the

---

† Here is a formal (but recursive!) definition of "recursive." A subprogram is *active* if it is being executed or it has called an active subprogram. A subprogram is *recursive* if it can be called while it is active.

current subprogram declaration does not immediately follow but will be found farther down in the program. For example, we might have

PROCEDURE   A(X : REAL) ; FORWARD ;

PROCEDURE   B(N : INTEGER) ;

BEGIN   (∗ the executable section of procedure B. ∗)
    ⋮
    A(4.6) ;
    ⋮
END ;   (∗ of procedure B. ∗)

PROCEDURE   A ;   (∗ Note : the rest of the procedure   ∗)
                  (∗   heading must be omitted. ∗)

BEGIN   (∗ the executable section of procedure A. ∗)
    ⋮
    B(3) ;
    ⋮
END ;   (∗ of procedure A. ∗)

PROGRAMMING METHODOLOGY

In this chapter we introduce the concept of "structured programming": a systematic method for developing and validating programs. The eight-stage process we outline here will be carefully followed in the case studies presented in subsequent chapters. In addition, you will be expected to go through the same process for several moderately difficult programming assignments. The organization imposed on you by this process will help you to appreciate programming as a rigorous discipline, not a haphazard, error-prone activity.

A general outline of the process is as follows: We start by analyzing the problem (stages 1-4). Next comes the most important part of the process— designing the program (stages 5-6). We then code the program (stage 7). Finally, we validate the program (stage 8). It should be pointed out that this is an iterative process: While working on a later stage, we may find that we need to redo some or all of our work from an earlier stage.

PROBLEM ANALYSIS

The first four stages constitute an analysis of the problem. Before we can hope to develop a program to solve some problem, we must understand exactly what the problem is.

Stage 1 Statement of the Problem The problem may be stated explicitly, but often there will be some ambiguity.

Stage 2 Clarification Here we clear up any vagueness in the problem statement and give the input and output specifications. We must also provide for error handling: What action should the program take for the various errors that may occur in the input? The reason that we concern ourselves with input errors is that a program should fail gracefully when the input is incorrect. It is much more helpful to receive a program-generated message such as

"INPUT ERROR : 14 IS AN ILLEGAL FLIGHT NUMBER."

rather than a system-generated message such as

"ADDRESS EXCEPTION — REENTRANT ADDRESS 02E194."

Furthermore, we may want the program to try to process the input that follows the invalid item. Such an attempt is impossible if the program "bombed out" on the input error.

Stage 3 Sample Input Subject to the stipulations of stages 1 and 2, we choose sample input values. This list of values serves to confirm our understanding of the problem and to indicate the format of the input. Extensive test data will be provided in stage 8—Program testing and debugging.

Stage 4 Sample Output Using the Sample Input provided in stage 3, we determine what the output will be. By solving the problem in this sample case, we again confirm our understanding of the problem and also indicate the format of the output.

In addition to the "answers" to the problem, a program must produce many other details, such as headings, spacing, and description of the answers. As a general rule, the program should also print out each input value, so anyone can easily determine if the input was entered correctly and if the answers correspond to the given input. This feature is called "echo printing."

PROGRAM DESIGN

We now indicate how to design a program to solve a given problem. There are two components in the design: data types and algorithms. For the sake of clarity we will discuss them separately, but they will be developed jointly during the design of a program.

A *data type* is a collection of data values together with a set of operations. In Pascal, for example, the operations on values of the INTEGER data type include addition, subtraction and remainder (MOD). The Pascal language provides a substantial number of data types, but we need not restrict ourselves to these during program design.

One important data type that is not directly available in Pascal is the *list*, discussed extensively in Chap. 3. A list is an ordered collection of components of the same type. The list is more abstract than any Pascal data type. In fact, we might decide to implement a list in Pascal with an array or a file, depending on the size of the list and the operations to be performed on it. For example, suppose we are given the salaries of all employees at a company and we want to find out how many of those salaries are above the mean. Since the mean must be calculated before each salary can be compared to that mean, we need a data type that can hold all of the salaries. For the sake of generality, we choose the list data type. What operations will be performed on the list? We need to be able to do the following:

1. Given a salary, store the salary in the list at the first unused position.
2. Access the salary at each position (for adding and comparing).

During the design of the program, we focus on the abstract data type without regard for how it will be implemented in Pascal. This approach is referred to as "data abstraction." By utilizing data abstraction, we avoid getting bogged down in implementation details and simultaneously increase our flexibility. Of course, we must ultimately decide whether to implement the list in Pascal as an array or a file or some other Pascal type. But even this decision can later be changed without altering the design.

To implement any data type in a Pascal program, we must specify a Pascal data type and a corresponding data structure. A *data structure* is a collection of locations in memory that holds a value in a data type. For example, consider the following declarations section:

TYPE   STRING = PACKED ARRAY[1..50] OF CHAR;

VAR   LINE : STRING ;

STRING is a type identifier: It is the name of the data type PACKED ARRAY[1..50] OF CHAR. LINE is a variable identifier: It is the name of the data structure that will hold a string. The number of locations in that data structure will depend on the number of characters that can be packed into one location on the computer being used.

An *algorithm* is a list of instructions that provides the solution to a given problem. We will not specify the format of those instructions, but simply stipulate that each instruction be routinely translatable into Pascal. For all but the most trivial of problems, the initial solution statement (that is, the statement of what is to be done) must go through several levels of refinement before we achieve an algorithm. The vehicle for this refinement is the solution tree.

Stage 5 Solution Tree A *solution tree* is a visual device for illustrating the development of an algorithm by stepwise refinement. The "root" of the tree, that is, the statement from which the refinements start, is an abbreviated version of the solution statement, such as "Create a reservations system" or "Simulate a car-wash." This is successively refined until an algorithm is produced.

For a simple example, suppose we want to develop an algorithm to solve the following problem: Given the bowling scores in all the games at a recent tournament, find the highest score. We assume that there will be one score per input line and that at least one score will be given. The root of the solution tree is

Find the highest score

After some consideration, we decide to refine this statement into three statements:

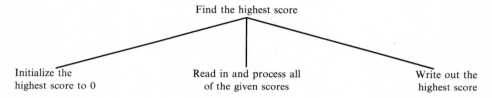

The first and last statements can easily be translated into Pascal, so they will not be refined further. In other words, they will be "leaves" in our solution tree. In analyzing the middle statement, we see that a loop is needed. Each time through the loop we will read in a score and update the highest score, if necessary. We now have the tree shown in Fig. 2.1. Notice that the "Loop until . . . ," "Read in a score," and "Update..." statements have lines coming from "Read in and process . . ." since those statements are refinements of the "Read in and process . . ." statement. It would be inappropriate to put the "Read in a score" and "Update . . ." statements under "Loop until . . ." because those two statements are *not* refinements of "Loop until . . . ."

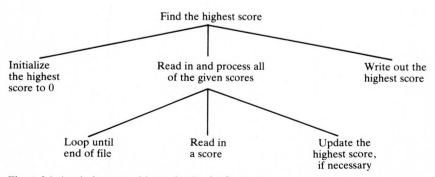

Figure 2.1 A solution tree with two levels of refinement.

Initialize the highest score to 0.	HIGHESTSCORE := 0;
Loop until end of file:	WHILE NOT EOF DO
Read in a score.	BEGIN
Update highest score, if necessary.	READLN(SCORE);
Write out the highest score.	IF SCORE > HIGHESTSCORE THEN
	HIGHESTSCORE := SCORE
	END;
	WRITELN(HIGHESTSCORE:3)

Figure 2.2 The algorithm from Fig. 2.1 and the corresponding Pascal statements.

Since each of the statements at the second level of refinement can easily be translated into Pascal, the solution tree is complete. The algorithm is obtained by listing the leaves from left to right. For the sake of readability, we indent loops and instructions under the control of "If," "Else," and "Case." Figure 2.2 shows the algorithm from Fig. 2.1. The corresponding Pascal statements are also shown.

A popular alternative to the solution tree is to develop an algorithm linearly from the solution statement. Figures 2.3 and 2.4 show the initial and final versions of the linear development of an algorithm to find the highest score.

Both Figs. 2.1 and 2.4 illustrate the development of an algorithm by stepwise refinement. The main advantage to the solution-tree approach is that refinements can be made without redrawing the tree, whereas the linear form must be recopied for each refinement beyond the first level.

For a complex problem, some of the leaves of the solution tree may correspond to Pascal procedure statements. Each such leaf will be refined in a separate tree, called a "subtree." Thus, we will have a main tree and one or more subtrees. The leaves of each subtree constitute a subalgorithm, which can routinely be translated into the executable section of a subprogram. Each subtree should accomplish a *single* task in the overall problem. When developing the main tree or a subtree, we initially concentrate on *what* is to be done, and gradually refine this into *how* it will be done. The separation of what is to be done from how it will be done is called "procedural abstraction."

Design Trade-offs

Since you have designed and written several programs on your own, you have already encountered some of the difficulties faced by professional programmers.

Find the highest score.
  Initialize the highest score to 0.
  Read in and process all of the given scores.
  Write out the highest score.

Figure 2.3 The initial version of a linearly developed algorithm for finding the highest score.

Find the highest score.
  Initialize the highest score to 0.
  Read in and process all of the given scores.
    Loop until end of file:
      Read in a score.
      Update highest score, if necessary.
  Write out the highest score.

Figure 2.4 The final version of a linearly developed algorithm for finding the highest score.

Your major problem was probably that of meeting deadlines, but you might also have contended with the following three obstacles:

1. In a multi-user environment, if your program took too long, your run may have been terminated or at least delayed until other programs were completed.
2. Similarly, if your program required too much memory, termination or delay may have resulted.
3. Each time you tried to use a new feature of Pascal, you may have spent considerable time in trying to understand its syntax and semantics—or else you simply wasted a lot of runs in a trial-and-error approach.

Often, a trade-off must be made: A method that reduces one of the three obstacles may intensify the other two. For example, suppose you had to sort a collection of up to 5000 numbers. One straightforward way to accomplish this would be to read all of the numbers into an array (which was declared to have 5000 components) and sort them with a selection sort or other simple technique. Such a procedure would be easy to design and code, but would waste space, because some of the locations in the array would normally be unused, and would run slowly (you will see why when we get to Chap. 6).

You might save space by using a linked list instead of an array, but this requires familiarity with linked lists (discussed in Chap. 3). Furthermore, the procedure would still run slowly. Alternatively, you could speed up the procedure by using an efficient sorting method such as Quicksort, discussed in Chap. 6. But what if you are not sure how Quicksort works? Is it worth learning how to use Quicksort for this one program?

There may be other factors which determine your course of action: If the procedure is part of a production program—one that is run over and over again—it may well be worth the effort to learn Quicksort. If the procedure is to be run once on a microcomputer with limited memory, learning (or relearning) how to use linked lists might be appropriate. If the procedure has to be debugged and running by midnight, you will probably be grateful that you know how to use an array and that you can implement even a trivial sorting method!

The point is that real-life programming involves hard decisions—it is not nearly enough that you can design and write programs that run. Adapting to constraints such as those mentioned above will make you a better programmer by increasing your flexibility.

None of this is to say that external constraints permit sloppy or inscrutable programs. Your primary goal should be to design and write clear programs. Other features may be needed for a particular situation, but they must be of secondary importance.

Stage 6 Structured Walkthrough Before coding your program, you should be convinced that your design is correct. It is helpful in this regard to have others examine your work, since you may already have developed an emotional attachment to what you have done. One evaluation technique that is widely used in industry is the "structured walkthrough." A structured walkthrough is performed by teams, with three or four people in each team. In a classroom context, the members of each team may be selected by the instructor or by some other means. In the structured walkthrough, each member presents her or his design; the other members of the team provide constructive criticism of that design. The individual does not advance to the next stage unless the current design is approved or there is a consensus on the changes that have to be made.

PROGRAM IMPLEMENTATION AND TESTING

The remaining two stages are concerned with the coding, testing, and debugging of the program.

Stage 7 Coding We are now ready to implement our data types and algorithm in Pascal. Each of the following features will help to make your program understandable and easily modifiable.

Hierarchy charts To outline the overall structure of our program, we provide a "hierarchy chart." A *hierarchy chart* shows the order in which the subprograms are called. This will help us to define our procedures in the proper order, since a procedure must be defined before it can be called. Figure 2.5 shows an example of a hierarchy chart. The main program, called INFIXTOPOSTFIX, calls the subprograms SETUPTRANSITIONTABLE, INITIALIZESTACK, CHECKFOR-POSITIONALERRORS, APPLYTRANSITIONTABLE, and WRITEPOST-FIXORERROR, in that order. The subprogram CHECKFORPOSITIONAL-ERRORS calls the subprogram TOKEN. Since TOKEN is also called from APPLYTRANSITIONTABLE, we say that TOKEN is a "utility" subprogram —denoted by a darkened triangle in the upper right-hand corner of its box. APPLYTRANSITIONTABLE also calls STACKEMPTY, ACCESSTOP,

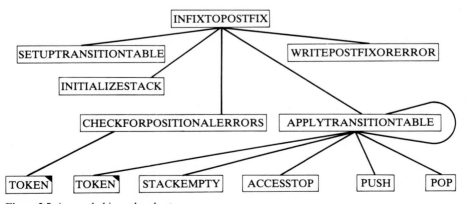

Figure 2.5 A sample hierarchy chart.

PUSH, POP, and itself. To indicate that **APPLYTRANSITIONTABLE** is recursive, we draw a line from its box that leads back to its box.

On some occasions there will be subprograms in a hierarchy chart that were not developed from subtrees. That is because those simple subprograms handle the details of input or output, or else they deal with the implementation details of some data type.

Subprogram layout Pascal allows nesting of subprograms; for example, the declaration of procedure B may occur as part of the declarations section of procedure A. See Fig. 2.6.

Figure 2.6 illustrates the problem with nested procedures: the local types and variables of procedure A are separated from A's executable section by procedure B. This separation detracts from the readability of procedure A. For this reason, subprograms will not be nested in this text. Of course, nested calls will be allowed (thus, procedure A can call procedure B). To further enhance readability, each subprogram will take up at most one page, and no subprogram will be split between two pages.

Comments At the beginning of the main program and each of the subprograms, we insert a block of comments to describe what the module does, the variables affecting and affected by the module, and any other information helpful to the reader. Comments occurring in the executable section of the program usually come from the nonleaves in the main tree for that program. Similarly, nonleaves in a subtree provide comments for the executable section of the corresponding subprogram.

```
PROCEDURE A(        );
TYPE   ──────
       ──────

VAR    ──
       ──
       ──

PROCEDURE B(        );
VAR    ──────
       ──────

BEGIN (* the executable section of procedure B. *)
  .
  .
  .
END; (* of procedure B. *)
BEGIN (* the executable section of procedure A. *)
  .
  .
  .
END; (* of procedure A. *)
```

Figure 2.6 Nesting of procedures.

Data encapsulation and information hiding As we implement our data types in Pascal, we will be careful to preserve the flexibility we gained through data abstraction. We do this by encapsulating the implementation details. For example, consider the following array implementation of a list of salaries:

```
CONST   MAXNUMBEROFSALARIES = 200 ;

TYPE    LISTSIZE  = 1..MAXNUMBEROFSALARIES ;
        LISTTYPE = RECORD
                        SALARYARRAY       : ARRAY[LISTSIZE] OF REAL ;
                        NUMBEROFSALARIES : LISTSIZE
                   END ;
VAR     SALARY : LISTTYPE ;
```

All the implementation information has been encapsulated in a record.

Now suppose we have a subprogram to count the number of above-average salaries. Such a subprogram will actually work with the elements in the list and thus will utilize the fact that an array implementation has been chosen. Other subprograms will be concerned with features of the program that do not manipulate the list, so they will not depend on the array implementation. In fact, these other subprograms would be unaffected if we decided to adopt a different implementation from the one given above. To put it another way, we have attempted to "hide" implementation information from those subprograms that do not need it. Information hiding is difficult to attain in Pascal because, as in the above example, implementation details are often specified in global type definitions. Thus, those details are accessible even to subprograms that need not utilize them.

In the case studies that follow, we strive for information hiding at the programmer level (rather than at the language level) by requiring that subprograms which do not manipulate a data type be unaffected by a change in implementation of that data type. It should be noted that two of Pascal's descendants, Ada and Modula-2, fully support information hiding.

Coding conventions There are two conventions we have adopted to standardize communication between a calling (sub)program and the subprogram called. First, the type of each variable will be given by a type identifier. This will make it easier for an actual parameter and its corresponding formal parameter to have the same type (see page 22). The second convention is that global variables are permitted in subprograms only to overcome a defect in the Pascal language. For example, Pascal has no facility for defining constant array identifiers, so an array variable whose components are constants may be used as a global variable in a subprogram (this is done in Chap. 4). The reason for this prohibition against global variables in a subprogram is that global variables bypass the normal method of communicating with a subprogram: parameters. Many a programmer has spent days trying to fix a program in which a subprogram inadvertently altered the value of a global variable.

Appendix 4 lists all the coding conventions followed in this text.

Stage 8 Program Testing and Debugging

Testing

The purpose of program testing is to determine whether any errors remain in the program. We do this by running the program with various sets of input values. We cannot test all possible input sets except for the most trivial of problems. This fact has two consequences:

1. The test data must be carefully selected to see if the program performs according to specifications. The quality of test data is more important than the quantity.
2. We cannot be certain that a program is error-free even if it passes all tests.

Top-down testing For small programs, it is convenient to code the main program and the subprograms together and to test the program as a whole. For large programs, this approach is not feasible: Finding an error in a 5000-line program is much more difficult than finding an error in a 50-line program. Thus, a systematic testing procedure should be used. In *top-down testing*, the main program is coded first and tested immediately. Once the main program has been validated, the subprograms are tested and validated, one by one, in the order in which they were designed. For example, the order of testing for the program outlined in Fig. 2.5 is as follows:

```
INFIXTOPOSTFIX
SETUPTRANSITIONTABLE
INITIALIZESTACK
CHECKFORPOSITIONALERRORS
TOKEN
APPLYTRANSITIONTABLE
STACKEMPTY
ACCESSTOP
PUSH
POP
WRITEPOSTFIXORERROR
```

To test a subprogram, the program in which the test data is run includes the main program, all previously tested (and validated) subprograms, and the subprogram now being tested. Thus, for example, Fig. 2.7 shows the environment for testing the subprogram CHECKFORPOSITIONALERRORS. Since executing the main program involves several subprogram calls, you may ask how we can test the main program or any of its subprograms before all the subprograms have been coded. The answer lies in the use of *stubs*: dummy subprograms that perform trivial or minimal tasks. For example, the stub for INITIALIZESTACK may be

```
PROCEDURE   INITIALIZESTACK(VAR   OPERATORSTACK : STACK);
BEGIN
    WRITELN('STACK  INITIALIZED')
END;   (* of the procedure INITIALIZESTACK. *)
```

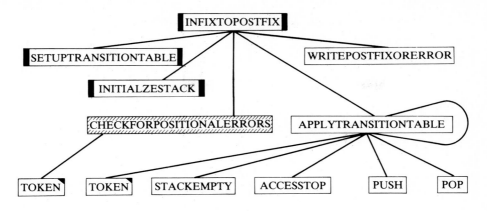

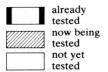
already
tested
now being
tested
not yet
tested

Figure 2.7 Testing CHECKFORPOSITIONALERRORS during top-down testing.

Similarly, the stub for STACKEMPTY may be

FUNCTION   STACKEMPTY(OPERATORSTACK : STACK) : BOOLEAN ;

BEGIN
      EMPTY := TRUE
END ;   (∗ of the procedure STACKEMPTY. ∗)

Each of these stubs will be replaced by the actual subprogram code when that subprogram is itself tested.

In addition to subdividing the testing phase, another advantage to top-down testing is that a program's most important segments, those at the higher levels, are tested early and implicitly retested with each added subprogram.

Boundary conditions Your program should produce correct answers for all valid inputs. One potential troublespot involves the handling of "boundary" conditions. For example, suppose we have designed and coded a program to read in a nonempty list of test scores, each between 0 and 100, inclusive, and write out the letter grade corresponding to the average score:

'A,' if the average score is at least 90;
'B,' if the average score is at least 80 but less than 90;
'C,' if the average score is at least 70 but less than 80;
'D,' if the average score is at least 60 but less than 70;
'F,' if the average score is less than 60.

The boundary values are 90, 80, 70, and 60. Some appropriate tests are:

TEST 1
---
90 80 100 90

TEST 2

79

TEST 3
---
60 60 60 60 59 60

The letter grades produced should be 'A,' 'C,' and 'F,' respectively.

Invalid inputs What action should your program take for invalid input? This depends on the specifications provided in the Clarification (stage 2). For example, the Clarification for the grading program just referred to might have the following:

Input values less than 0 or greater than 100 should be printed, together with the message "IS OUT OF RANGE." Such values should be ignored in calculating the average score. If no valid input is provided, the message "ERROR—NO VALID INPUT WAS PROVIDED." should be printed.

Some appropriate tests might be:

TEST 4
---
90 80 101 90

TEST 5

TEST 6

−2 85 200

TEST 7

101

For this last test, the output should be

101 IS OUT OF RANGE.
ERROR – NO VALID INPUT WAS PROVIDED.

What action should be taken for the following test?

TEST 8
---
85 9F 75

If the clarification did not specify what was to be done with a letter in the input, the program would not handle this case. Thus, a run-time error message, such as "ERROR IN READ – F IS NOT A DIGIT," would be produced. To prevent your program from aborting with nondigit, nonblank input, your input variable would have to be of type CHAR. Your program could then easily detect when the input was not in ['0' .. '9', ' '], but "constructing" an integer score out of digit characters would be nontrivial.

The point is that it is very difficult, if not virtually impossible, to require your program to fail *gracefully* for every kind of invalid input. The Clarification should prudently specify which invalid inputs are to be handled by the program, and program testing should focus on those inputs as well as selected valid inputs.

Debugging

As you begin to code and compile your program, you may discover that one or more errors have occurred. Later, as you test your program with several sets of inputs, you may encounter still more errors. The process of detecting and removing program errors is called "debugging." As with most other activities, the more you practice debugging, the better you will be at it. But your overall skill as a programmer depends on your design ability much more than on your debugging ability. An hour of design is worth a day of debugging!

We now classify the three kinds of errors which you may encounter as you debug your program.

1. *Compile-time errors.* Before your Pascal program can run on a computer, it must first be compiled into machine language. The Pascal compiler will inform you of any errors, such as missing semicolon, encountered in the attempt to compile your program. These "compile-time" errors are usually easy to fix because of (sometimes in spite of) the associated error messages.

2. *Run-time errors.* Once you have rid your program of its compile-time errors, you can execute the compiled version with input provided during Program Testing (pages 44–46). If your program attempted to divide by zero or to read after the end-of-file marker was reached, the computer would provide you with a "run-time" error message which explained what was wrong and the statement being executed when the error occurred. Run-time errors, like compile-time errors, are usually easy to fix.

3. *Hidden errors.* The true skill of debugging emerges after the compile-time and run-time errors have been eliminated. The errors that remain are "hidden" errors: No error messages are given, but the output is incorrect. Some hidden errors result from simple carelessness, such as

```
FOR I := 1 TO 10 DO ;
    BEGIN
       :
    END
```

The semicolon after DO terminates the FOR statement, so the loop consists of an empty statement. Often, a hidden error reflects a flaw in the program design. Finding such errors requires detective work. Initially, the only clue is the incorrect output. More clues can be obtained by temporarily inserting additional WRITELN statements in the program, especially at the beginning and ending of the executable section of a subprogram. These statements are removed after the errors have been detected and eliminated.

PROVING PROGRAM CORRECTNESS

Program testing cannot guarantee that a program is correct, that is, the program performs according to the specifications. An interesting alternative is to *prove* that the program is correct. The proof is developed as the program is being designed, not after the program has been coded. The fundamental concept in proving correctness is the assertion. An *assertion* consists of one or more claims about a program segment, that is, anything from a single statement up to an entire program. In particular, each procedure can be considered to contain two assertions: a *precondition* assertion that describes the assumptions at the beginning of the procedure, and a *postcondition* assertion that describes the situation when the procedure has been completed provided the precondition was true when the procedure began. For example, a binary search procedure (see Chap. 7) searches through a sorted array of components to find the position of a given element (called the *key*). We can write

```
PROCEDURE  BINARYSEARCH(A              : ARRAYTYPE ;
                        FIRST, LAST    : POSINTEGER ;
                        KEYSOUGHT      : KEYTYPE ;
                        VAR POSITION   : SUBSCRIPTTYPE ;
                        VAR MATCHFOUND : BOOLEAN) ;
(* Conduct a binary search of A[FIRST..LAST] looking for a       *)
(* record whose key field matches KEYSOUGHT.                     *)
(* Precondition : A[FIRST..LAST] in increasing order by key field. *)
(* Postcondition: If a record is found whose key field matches   *)
(*      KEYSOUGHT, POSITION gets the subscript of the matching   *)
(*      record and MATCHFOUND gets the value TRUE. Otherwise,    *)
(*      MATCHFOUND gets the value FALSE.                         *)
```

With a loop statement, we often want part of the precondition to be unchanged during each execution of the loop. This unchanging assertion is called a "loop invariant." For example, to read in and add up a list of salaries, we might have:

```
SUMOFSALARIES := 0.0 ;

(* Precondition : No salaries have yet been read in ; SUMOFSALARIES *)
(*               contains the sum of all the salaries read in so far. *)
```

```
WHILE NOT EOF DO
    (*Invariant:      SUMOFSALARIES contains the sum of all the salaries read in so far. *)
    BEGIN
        READLN(SALARY) ;
        SUMOFSALARIES := SUMOFSALARIES + SALARY
    END ;
(* Postcondition : All of the salaries have been read in and  *)
(*                 SUMOFSALARIES contains their sum. *)
```

The loop invariant is vacuously true when the loop is entered for the first time. Each execution of the loop causes a salary to be read in and added to SUMOF-SALARIES. Thus, if the invariant is true at the beginning of an execution of the loop, it will also be true after the execution of the loop. In other words, the loop *preserves* the invariant. This fact, together with the fact that the loop terminates only after all of the salaries have been read in, establishes the truth of the post-condition.

One advantage to using assertions is that it reinforces the gradual refinement of a problem statement into an algorithm. At each refinement we must verify that the relevant assertions remain true even as new assertions are established. This imposes a discipline on our design that results in clear, straightforward programs.

The main drawback to proving program correctness is that it is very difficult to achieve for complex programs, such as the ones we will be developing in subsequent chapters. This topic is generating considerable research interest at the present time, and one of the results has been new methods for formally specifying what a program is supposed to do. There are, even now, some program verification systems in operation. Roughly, such a system is provided with a formal specification and a program, and determines if the program satisfies the specification. The prospects for significant achievements in this area are reasonably good.

THREE

LIST PROCESSING

In this chapter we introduce an abstract data type, the list, that occurs in a variety of applications. After mentioning some implementations with which you are already familiar, we will devote most of the chapter to linked lists and their uses.

A *list* is an ordered collection of components of the same type. Typically, that type will be a record type. For example, a telephone directory is a list: Each component is a record consisting of a person's name, address, and telephone number; the ordering is alphabetical by the person's last name. Part of the list might look like this:

McCartney Paul	412 Abbey Rd	749–1256
McGillicuddy Lucy	95 Desilu Av	546–3261
McLaughlin Terry	261 Newbury St	535–2831

A television schedule is also a list: Each component is a record consisting of a time at which at least one program starts, together with all of the programs, with corresponding channels, that start at that time. The ordering is by day, each day is further ordered by time, and the programs for each time slot are ordered by station number. For example, we might have

Monday, October 6

    9:00 4 "The Godfather" (1971). Marlon Brando, Al Pacino. A son inherits the family business.

           5 Hogan's Heroes. Bob Crane. Klink sends Schultz to the Eastern Front.

           7 "The Maltese Falcon" (1941). Humphrey Bogart, Sidney Greenstreet. Private eye encounters low-life searching for "the stuff that dreams are made of."

Similarly, in a grocery list, each record consists of an item to be purchased. The ordering is by when the item was thought of, so the first item thought of is entered first, and so on.

What operations can be performed on a list? Figure 3.1 shows some of the operations we might want to perform on an arbitrary list.

We now consider two kinds of lists: contiguous lists and linked lists. Of special interest will be how operations such as L1–L4 in Figure 3.1 are performed with each kind of list.

CONTIGUOUS LISTS

A list is *contiguous* if, for each component in the list, the successor of that component is stored in the next physical position in the list. The most commonplace implementations of a contiguous list use an array or a file.

For an example of an array implementation, suppose we wanted to save a list of up to 200 parts, where each part consists of a part number from 0 to 99999 and a cost in dollars and cents. The ordering will be by increasing part numbers. We could write

```
TYPE   PART = RECORD
                PARTNUMBER : 0..99999 ;
                COST       : REAL
              END ;

VAR    INVENTORY    : ARRAY[1..200] OF PART ;
       NUMBEROFPARTS : 0..200 ;
```

Thus, the first component (the part with the lowest part number) will be stored in INVENTORY[1], the second component in INVENTORY[2], and so on. Each component can be referred to by specifying its subscript. If the input contains the initial list, with one part per line, we can read in the list as follows:

```
NUMBEROFPARTS := 0 ;

WHILE NOT EOF DO
    BEGIN
        NUMBEROFPARTS := NUMBEROFPARTS + 1 ;
        WITH INVENTORY[NUMBEROFPARTS] DO
            READLN(PARTNUMBER, COST)
    END
```

Since each new component is inserted in the next position in the array, this is a special case of operation L1 (see Fig. 3.1). Figure 3.2 shows what the array might contain if there were 70 parts in the input (a question mark indicates an undefined value).

L1. Insert a new component anywhere in the list.
L2. Delete a component from anywhere in the list.
L3. Change the value(s) of any component in the list.
L4. Determine the value(s) of any component in the list.

Figure 3.1 Operations that can be performed on a list.

	(Part number)	(Cost)
INVENTORY[1]	01040	216.32
INVENTORY[2]	01153	86.35
.	.	.
.	.	.
.	.	.
INVENTORY[13]	20615	120.00
INVENTORY[14]	21773	85.25
INVENTORY[15]	21805	100.25
.	.	.
.	.	.
.	.	.
INVENTORY[70]	89303	104.21
INVENTORY[71]	?	?
.	.	.
.	.	.
.	.	.
INVENTORY[200]	?	?

Figure 3.2 A list of 70 inventory parts, stored in an array with room for 200 parts.

An immediate disadvantage of an array implementation is apparent from Fig. 3.2: We had to allocate space for 200 parts even if the actual list were smaller. With an array, you must always specify, in advance, the maximum possible size and allocate the corresponding space. In some languages, such as Ada, Modula-2 and PL/I, the size of an array may shrink and grow *during* the execution of the program.

We now illustrate how to perform the operations in Fig. 3.1 on the list with 70 components shown in Fig. 3.2. In each case, we must first determine the subscript of the component. This may require a search through the list. Assume, for simplicity, that the subscript has already been determined and its value is 14.

L1. To insert a new component in INVENTORY[14], we first move IN-VENTORY[70] to INVENTORY[71], then move INVENTORY[69] to INVENTORY[70],..., and move INVENTORY[14] to INVEN-TORY[15]. Finally, we can insert the new component in INVEN-TORY[14]. On the average, each insertion will require about half of the list to be moved! This tends to make the program's run time unacceptably long, especially since each component is a multifield record.

L2. Deleting the component in INVENTORY[14] requires that all later components in the list be "bumped up" by one: INVENTORY[15] is moved to INVENTORY[14], INVENTORY[16] is moved to INVEN-TORY[15], and so on. Just as with inserting, the average deletion requires moving half of the list.

L3, L4. We can easily change or determine the value(s) of INVENTORY[14]. For example,

```
INVENTORY[14].COST := 82.25 ;
WRITELN(INVENTORY[14].COST : 7 : 2)
```

In general, an array implementation of a contiguous list is quite efficient when performing operations such as L3 and L4. For example, to change (or determine) the value of *each* component in an array, we can use a FOR statement with the loop counter as a subscript.

An array implementation of a contiguous list has the following drawbacks:

1. The maximum size of the list must be known and allocated in advance.
2. Insertions and deletions can require substantial movement of data.

For some applications, these drawbacks will be inconsequential. For example, if the maximum size is not "very" large, an array will not waste much space. If most of the insertions and deletions come at the end of the list, then the overhead of data movement is minimized.

For a large contiguous list, the only possible implementation is a file. For example, if we had up to two million parts (with seven-digit part numbers) we could write

```
TYPE   PART = RECORD
                PARTNUMBER : 0..9999999 ;
                COST         : REAL
              END ;

VAR    INVENTORY : FILE OF PART ;
```

With regard to the operations listed in Fig. 3.1, a file is similar to an array. For the special case of inserting at the end of a file, this can be accomplished straightforwardly with a WRITE or PUT as long as the file is in the generation state (see page 9). For arbitrary insertions, and for all deletions and changes, a temporary file must be created (see page 14). Determining a component's value can be accomplished in a simple loop once the file is in the inspection state (see page 12).

In summary, a file is to be preferred over an array only when the list will not fit in an array or the information is to be saved after the execution of the program.

LINKED LISTS

A *linked list* is an ordered collection of records, in which each record has a field that indicates where the next record in the list is located. Thus, the ordering is explicitly provided by this field. For example, in the linked list shown in Fig. 3.3a, each record has a height field, a weight field, and a field that points to the next record in the list. The first record in the list is referred to as the "head" of the list. For the last record in the list, we insert a bar in the third field to indicate that there is no "next" record.

As you can see, a linked list is an abstract data type (although not as abstract as the "list" data type). Before we discuss how linked lists can be implemented in

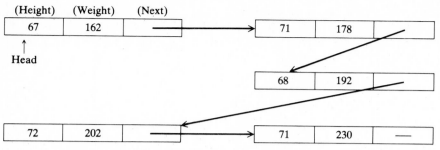

(Height) (Weight) (Next)

Figure 3.3a A linked list in which each record has three fields.

Pascal, we first illustrate how operations L1–L4 could be performed on the linked list shown in Fig. 3.3a.

L1. Suppose we want to insert

| 70 | 183 | ? |

between the second and third records of the linked list in Fig. 3.3a. Starting at the first record in the list, we follow the "next" field to get to the second record. We now give the "next" field in the record to be inserted the same value as in the "next" field of the second record. This gives us the picture shown in Fig. 3.3b.

Finally, we change the second record's "next" field to point to the record to be inserted. The resulting linked list is shown in Fig. 3.3c.

L2. To delete, say, the fourth record in the linked list of Fig. 3.3a, we proceed as follows: Starting at the first record in the list, we follow the pointer fields until we get to the third record—the one whose "next" field points to the record to be deleted. We now take the value in the "next" field of

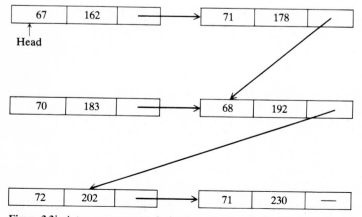

Figure 3.3b A temporary stage during insertion in a linked list.

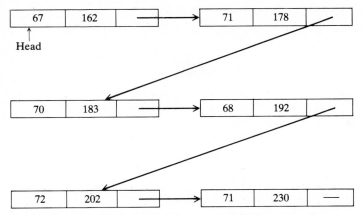

Figure 3.3c The linked list of Fig. 3.3a after an insertion was made.

the fourth record and store this value in the "next" field of the third record. As Fig. 3.3d shows, the fourth record is no longer in the linked list since there is no "next" field pointing to it.

L3, L4. These operations are handled analogously and straightforwardly: Starting at the first record in the list, we follow the pointer fields until we reach the record whose field will have its value changed (or determined). The change (or determination) is then made.

Dynamic Implementation of a Linked List

In Pascal, a linked list can be conveniently implemented with dynamic variables. For the linked list shown in Fig. 3.3a, the declarations section is

```
TYPE  LINK   = ^RATING ;
      RATING = RECORD
                  HEIGHT : 50..85 ;
                  WEIGHT : 80..300 ;
                  NEXT   : LINK
               END ;

VAR   HEAD : LINK ;
```

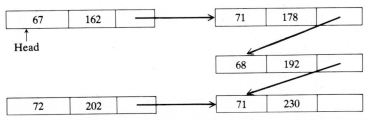

Figure 3.3d The linked list of Fig. 3.3a after deletion of the fourth record. (What had been the fourth record has been bypassed.)

LINK is a pointer-type identifier: Any variable of type LINK will point to a dynamic variable of type RATING. The pointer variable HEAD will point to the first record in the list.

As we mentioned in Chap. 1 (page 7), a dynamic variable is created by a call to the predeclared procedure NEW. For example,

NEW(HEAD)

will allocate, from the heap, enough space for a dynamic variable of type RATING. The address of the beginning of this variable is stored in HEAD. Pictorially, with question marks indicating garbage values,

We can assign values to this newly created record as follows:

```
HEAD^.HEIGHT := 67 ;
HEAD^.WEIGHT := 162 ;
HEAD^.NEXT   := NIL
```

The first line is read "Assign to the HEIGHT field of the dynamic record pointed to by HEAD the value of 67". The NEXT field of this record gets the value denoted by NIL, so we have just one record in the linked list, as shown in Fig. 3.4.

Simple Operations On a Dynamic Linked List

To help familiarize you with linked lists and their dynamic implementation, we now consider the simple operations of inserting and deleting at the head of the list. As it turns out, these two operations can easily be extended to performing insertions and deletions anywhere in a linked list. In addition to the pointer variable HEAD, assume that another pointer variable, CURRENTPOINTER, has also been declared.

Insertion at head To insert a new record at the head of the list in Fig. 3.4, we first create the new record and store values in its height and weight fields:

```
NEW(CURRENTPOINTER) ;
CURRENTPOINTER^.HEIGHT := 70 ;
CURRENTPOINTER^.WEIGHT := 158 ;
```

Figure 3.4 A linked list with just one record.

We now have

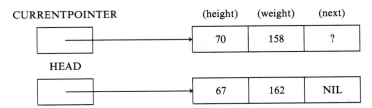

We want the record now pointed to by HEAD to come right after the record pointed to by CURRENTPOINTER, so we store HEAD's value in the NEXT field of the record pointed to by CURRENTPOINTER:

CURRENTPOINTER^.NEXT := HEAD ;

This gives us

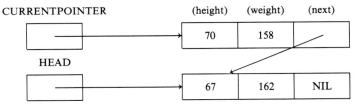

Finally, we store CURRENTPOINTER's value in HEAD so that HEAD points to the (new) head of the list:

HEAD := CURRENTPOINTER

Figure 3.5 shows the resulting, two-record list. The above analysis leads us to the following procedure (the type definitions for LINK and RATING are found on page 55):

```
PROCEDURE HEADINSERT(VAR HEAD                              : LINK ;
                         CURRENTHEIGHT, CURRENTWEIGHT : INTEGER) ;

(* Create a dynamic record, of type RATING, with CURRENTHEIGHT and      *)
(* CURRENTWEIGHT in its height and weight fields, and insert this record at the *)
(* beginning of the linked list pointed to by HEAD.                      *)

VAR   CURRENTPOINTER : LINK ;

BEGIN
     NEW(CURRENTPOINTER) ;

     WITH CURRENTPOINTER^ DO
         BEGIN
              HEIGHT := CURRENTHEIGHT ;
              WEIGHT := CURRENTWEIGHT ;
              NEXT   := HEAD
         END ;

     HEAD := CURRENTPOINTER

END ;  (* of the procedure HEADINSERT. *)
```

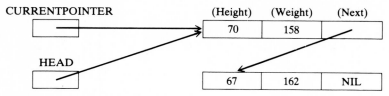

Figure 3.5 A linked list with two records.

Exercise 3.1 Show what will happen if HEAD has the value shown in Fig. 3.5 and we call

HEADINSERT(HEAD, 68, 155)

Deletion from head Deleting the first record in a linked list seems easy: We simply change HEAD to point to HEAD^.NEXT. There are two potential problems. First, if HEAD happens to be NIL, a reference to HEAD^.NEXT will be an error. To avoid this situation, we will use a boolean variable called SUCCESS. If HEAD is NIL, we set SUCCESS to FALSE to indicate that the deletion could not be made. The second potential problem is that, after a deletion, the deleted record should have its space deallocated. But, since nothing is pointing to it, DISPOSE cannot be called. This problem is avoided by saving HEAD's value (in TEMPORARYPOINTER) before changing HEAD's value to point to the next record. We can then call DISPOSE with TEMPORARYPOINTER as the actual parameter.

We have just developed the following procedure:

```
PROCEDURE  TRYTODELETEHEAD(VAR  HEAD    : LINK ;
                           VAR  SUCCESS : BOOLEAN) ;
(* Try to delete the first record from the linked list       *)
(* pointed to by HEAD. If HEAD is NIL, SUCCESS will get *)
(* the value FALSE. Otherwise, SUCCESS will get the      *)
(* value TRUE and the deletion will take place.              *)

VAR  TEMPORARYPOINTER : LINK ;
BEGIN
    IF  HEAD  =  NIL THEN
       SUCCESS := FALSE
    ELSE
       BEGIN
          SUCCESS              := TRUE ;
          TEMPORARYPOINTER := HEAD ;
          HEAD                  := HEAD^.NEXT ;
          DISPOSE(TEMPORARYPOINTER)
       END
END ;   (* of the procedure TRYTODELETEHEAD. *)
```

For example, if we have

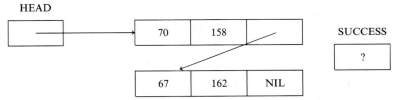

and we call TRYTODELETEHEAD(HEAD, SUCCESS), then after the call we will have

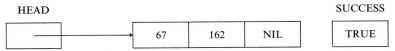

If we again call TRYTODELETEHEAD(HEAD, SUCCESS), then after the call we will have

After one more call to TRYTODELETEHEAD(HEAD, SUCCESS), we will have

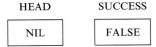

Updating a Dynamic Linked List

We now consider, for a dynamically implemented linked list, how to perform the four operations in Fig. 3.1. We will develop a procedure to insert a new component in a linked list (operation L1). The other three operations are handled analogously; they are included in the exercises and also in Case Study 3.1. We assume, for specificity, that the linked list has the underlying structure given in the declarations section on page 55. The ordering will be by increasing *weights*; the heights may be in any order. Duplicate records are not allowed; that is, no record shall be inserted if its height and weight are the same as those of a record already in the list.

We want to develop a procedure, TRYTOINSERT, with variable formal parameters HEAD and SUCCESS, and value formal parameters CURRENT-HEIGHT and CURRENTWEIGHT. The procedure will try to insert, in the linked list pointed to by HEAD, a record whose height and weight values are those of CURRENTHEIGHT and CURRENTWEIGHT, respectively. If these values match those of a record already in the list, then the insertion cannot be made, so SUCCESS will get the value FALSE. Otherwise, the insertion does take place, and SUCCESS gets the value TRUE. The insertion should preserve the

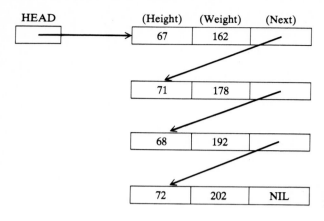

Figure 3.6 A linked list with four records.

ordering by weights. For example, suppose we started with the linked list shown in Fig. 3.6. If we call

TRYTOINSERT(HEAD, SUCCESS, 71, 195)

then after the call, the linked list would be as shown in Fig. 3.7.

To develop the procedure, TRYTOINSERT, we will focus on the head of the list. There are four cases to consider.

Case 1. If HEAD is NIL, we simply call the procedure HEADINSERT given on page 57.

Case 2. Otherwise, we can compare CURRENTWEIGHT to HEAD^. WEIGHT. If CURRENTWEIGHT < HEAD^.WEIGHT, then the new

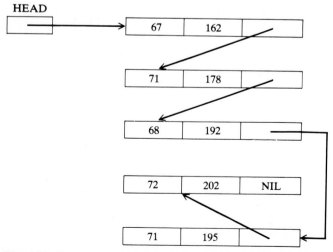

Figure 3.7 The linked list resulting from an insertion to the linked list in Fig. 3.6.

record belongs at the head of the list, so we call HEADINSERT. For example, if we started with

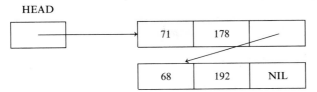

and called

TRYTOINSERT(HEAD, SUCCESS, 67, 162)

then after the call, we would have

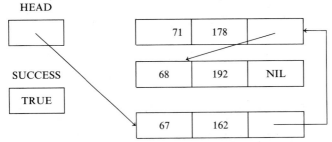

Case 3. If the new record does not belong at the head of the list, we check to make sure the new record is not a duplicate of the current head of the list. If CURRENTWEIGHT = HEAD^.WEIGHT and CURRENTHEIGHT = HEAD^.HEIGHT, then the insertion should not be made, so we set SUCCESS to FALSE.

Case 4. Otherwise, we try to insert the new record later in the list. We can rephrase this in another, significant way: To try to insert the new record later in the list, we try to insert it in the linked list pointed to by HEAD^.NEXT! We can accomplish this, within the procedure TRYTOINSERT, by calling

TRYTOINSERT(HEAD^.NEXT, SUCCESS, CURRENTHEIGHT, CURRENTWEIGHT)

Each time we make this recursive call, we are trying to insert in a *smaller* linked list. Thus, eventually, one of the earlier three cases will apply.

To illustrate the effect of this recursive call, suppose we started with the linked list shown in Fig. 3.6. If we then call

TRYTOINSERT(HEAD, SUCCESS, 71, 195)

then, at the beginning of the execution of this first call to TRYTOINSERT, we will have the picture shown in Fig. 3.8.

Since CURRENTWEIGHT is greater than HEAD^.WEIGHT, we call TRYTOINSERT a second time. The call is

TRYTOINSERT(HEAD^.NEXT, SUCCESS, CURRENTHEIGHT, CURRENTWEIGHT)

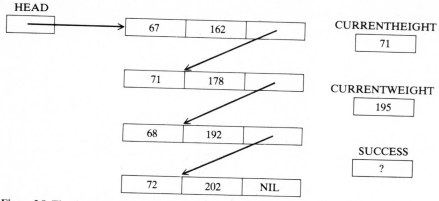

Figure 3.8 The data structures at the start of an execution of the procedure TRYTOINSERT.

During the execution of this second call, the variable formal parameter HEAD will represent the same variable as the corresponding actual parameter, namely HEAD^.NEXT. So, at the beginning of the execution of this second call, we have the picture shown in Fig. 3.9 (the original value of HEAD was automatically saved). Again we find that CURRENTWEIGHT > HEAD^.WEIGHT, so a third call to TRYTOINSERT is made:

TRYTOINSERT(HEAD^.NEXT, SUCCESS, CURRENTHEIGHT, CURRENTWEIGHT)

At the beginning of this third call, we have the picture shown in Fig. 3.10. Once again, CURRENTWEIGHT > HEAD^.WEIGHT, so TRYTOINSERT is called a fourth (and final) time:

TRYTOINSERT(HEAD^.NEXT, SUCCESS, CURRENTHEIGHT, CURRENTWEIGHT)

At the beginning of this fourth call, we have the picture shown in Fig. 3.11. Since CURRENTWEIGHT is less than HEAD^.WEIGHT, the insertion is made, via

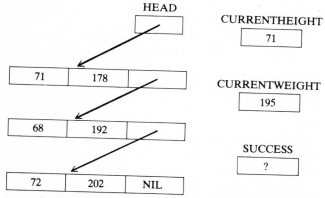

Figure 3.9 The data structures at the beginning of the second call to TRYTOINSERT.

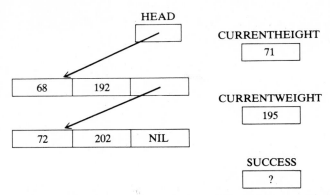

Figure 3.10 The data structures at the beginning of the third call to TRYTOINSERT.

a call to HEADINSERT. At the end of this fourth execution, the linked list looks as shown in Fig. 3.12. During the fourth execution of TRYTOINSERT, the formal parameter HEAD represented the variable HEAD^.NEXT from the third, interrupted execution of TRYTOINSERT. When that value of HEAD is restored, the linked list is as shown in Fig. 3.13. Since the third call to TRY-TOINSERT has now been completed, the value of HEAD from the second call is restored, giving us the linked list shown in Fig. 3.14. The second call to TRY-

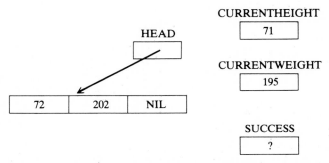

Figure 3.11 The data structures at the beginning of the fourth call to TRYTOINSERT.

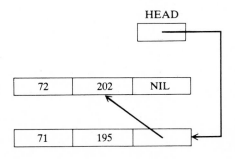

Figure 3.12 The linked list at the end of the execution of the fourth call to TRYTOINSERT.

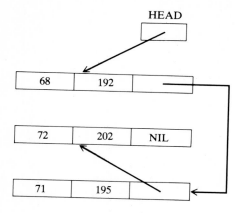

Figure 3.13 The linked list after the completion of the (earlier interrupted) third call to TRYTO-INSERT.

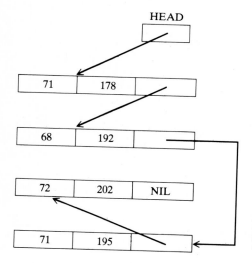

Figure 3.14 The linked list after the completion of the (earlier interrupted) second call to TRY-TOINSERT.

TOINSERT has now been completed, so the original value of HEAD is restored, giving us the linked list shown in Fig. 3.15.

We now list the procedure we have just developed:

```
PROCEDURE   TRYTOINSERT(VAR      HEAD                          : LINK ;
                        VAR      SUCCESS                       : BOOLEAN ;
                        CURRENTHEIGHT, CURRENTWEIGHT : INTEGER) ;
(* Try to insert, into the linked list pointed to by HEAD, a        *)
(* record whose height field has the value of CURRENTHEIGHT and *)
(* whose weight field has the value of CURRENTWEIGHT. The        *)
(* ordering is by increasing weights, and duplicate records          *)
(* (that is, same heights and same weights) are not permitted.    *)
(* If an attempt is made to insert a duplicate record, the           *)
(* insertion is not made and SUCCESS gets the value FALSE.       *)
(* Otherwise, the insertion is made and SUCCESS gets the value  *)
(* TRUE. The procedure HEADINSERT is listed on page 57.         *)
```

```
BEGIN

    IF HEAD = NIL THEN
        BEGIN
            HEADINSERT(HEAD, CURRENTHEIGHT, CURRENTWEIGHT) ;
            SUCCESS := TRUE
        END
    ELSE

        (* Does the new record belong at the head of the list? *)
        IF CURRENTWEIGHT < HEAD^.WEIGHT THEN
            BEGIN
                HEADINSERT(HEAD, CURRENTHEIGHT, CURRENTWEIGHT) ;
                SUCCESS := TRUE
            END
        ELSE

            (* Would the new record duplicate the record *)
            (* at the head of the list?                  *)
            IF (CURRENTHEIGHT = HEAD^.HEIGHT) AND
                   (CURRENTWEIGHT = HEAD^.WEIGHT) THEN
                SUCCESS := FALSE
            ELSE

                (* Try to insert the new record later in the list.  *)
                (* In other words, try to insert the new record in *)
                (* the linked list pointed to by HEAD^.NEXT. *)
                TRYTOINSERT(HEAD^.NEXT, SUCCESS, CURRENTHEIGHT,
                            CURRENTWEIGHT)

END ;   (* of the procedure TRYTOINSERT. *)
```

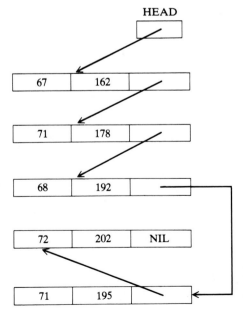

Figure 3.15 The final version of the linked list from Fig. 3.6 after a call to TRYTOINSERT (HEAD, SUCCESS, 71, 195).

Exercise 3.2 Start with the linked list in Fig. 3.6 and show what will happen after each of the following calls is made in sequence. Also, determine how many times case 4 (the recursive call) applied and which other case finally applied.

```
TRYTOINSERT(HEAD, SUCCESS, 71, 210) ;
TRYTOINSERT(HEAD, SUCCESS, 63, 162) ;
TRYTOINSERT(HEAD, SUCCESS, 71, 178)
```

Exercise 3.3 Develop a procedure, called TRYTODELETE, with variable formal parameters HEAD and SUCCESS, and value formal parameters CURRENTHEIGHT and CURRENTWEIGHT. The procedure should try to delete, from the linked list pointed to by HEAD, the record whose height field has the value of CURRENTHEIGHT and whose weight field has the value of CURRENTWEIGHT. SUCCESS will get the value of TRUE or FALSE, depending on whether the deletion can be performed. *Hint*: See the procedures TRYTOINSERT (pages 64–65) and TRYTODELETEHEAD (page 58).

Exercise 3.4 Develop a procedure, called TRYTOCHANGE, with variable formal parameters HEAD and SUCCESS, and value formal parameters CURRENTHEIGHT, CURRENTWEIGHT, and NEWHEIGHT. The procedure should try to change, in the linked list pointed to by HEAD, the height field of the record whose height field has the value of CURRENT-HEIGHT and whose weight field has the value of CURRENTWEIGHT. The new value in the height field will be that of NEWHEIGHT. SUCCESS will get the value of TRUE or FALSE, depending on whether there is a record in the list whose height field has the value of CURRENTHEIGHT and whose weight field has the value of CURRENTWEIGHT.

Exercise 3.5 It would be incorrect to try to combine the first two cases in the above procedure TRYTOINSERT, that is,

```
IF (HEAD = NIL) OR (CURRENTWEIGHT < HEAD^.WEIGHT) THEN
    BEGIN
        HEADINSERT(HEAD, CURRENTHEIGHT, CURRENTWEIGHT) ;
        SUCCESS := TRUE
    END
```

Why is this incorrect? *Hint*: See page 8.

Exercise 3.6 The last record in a list is referred to as the *tail*. For example,

```
TYPE   STRING    = PACKED ARRAY[1..30] OF CHAR ;
       POINTER   = ^EMPLOYEE ;
       EMPLOYEE = RECORD
                        NAME   : STRING ;
                        SALARY : REAL ;
                        NEXT   : POINTER
                  END ;

VAR    HEAD, TAIL : POINTER ;
```

The list is empty when both HEAD and TAIL have the NIL value. With three employees in the list we would have

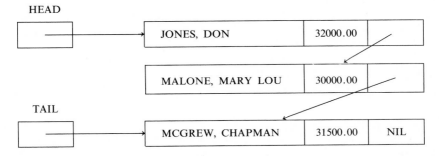

1. Develop a procedure, TAILINSERT, with variable formal parameters HEAD and TAIL, and value formal parameters CURRENTNAME and CURRENTSALARY, to insert at the tail of a list a record whose name field will have the value of CURRENTNAME and whose salary field will have the value of CURRENTSALARY.
2. Develop a procedure, TRYTODELETETAIL, with variable formal parameters HEAD, TAIL and SUCCESS, to attempt to delete from the linked list the record pointed to by TAIL.
   Hint: Consider four cases:

   Case 1. HEAD = NIL.
   Case 2. HEAD = TAIL.
   Case 3. HEAD^.NEXT = TAIL.
   Case 4. The tail comes farther down in the list, after HEAD^.NEXT.

Summary of List Implementations

In a dynamically implemented linked list, space is allocated (and deallocated) on demand: It is not necessary to preallocate space for the entire list. Of course, the pointers themselves take up some space. Also, insertions and deletions are made without moving any records: the operations are effected by adjusting pointers.

	(Height)	(Weight)	(Next)
LIST.LISTARRAY[1]	67	162	2
LIST.LISTARRAY[2]	71	178	3
LIST.LISTARRAY[3]	68	192	5
LIST.LISTARRAY[4]	72	202	0
LIST.LISTARRAY[5]	71	195	4
LIST.LISTARRAY[6]	?	?	?

LIST.HEAD

1

LIST.LISTARRAY[100]

?	?	?

Figure 3.16 A static representation of the linked list shown in Fig. 3.7.

Contrast these features with the two implementations of a contiguous list that we considered earlier in this chapter. With an array, it is necessary to preallocate space for the entire list, and each insertion or deletion requires, on the average, half of the list to be moved. One advantage to an array is that any component can be accessed once its subscript is known. For example, it is easy to access the middle component of an array by specifying the middle subscript. With a file, space is allocated on demand, but each insertion, deletion and change requires the *entire* file to be copied.†

In addition to a dynamic implementation of a linked list, an array implementation is also possible. For example, the declarations section on page 55 could be replaced by

```
CONST   MAXLISTSIZE = 100 ;

TYPE    RATING = RECORD
                     HEIGHT : 50..85 ;
                     WEIGHT : 80..300 ;
                     NEXT    : 0..MAXLISTSIZE
                 END ;


VAR     LIST : RECORD
                   LISTARRAY : ARRAY[1..MAXLISTSIZE] OF  RATING ;
                   HEAD       : 0..MAXLISTSIZE
               END ;
```

This is a *static* implementation because the maximum list size is specified and allocated in advance. In this implementation, subscripts take the place of pointers, with a subscript of 0 corresponding to a NIL pointer. For example, the linked list in Fig. 3.7 could be represented by the one in Fig. 3.16. The subscript 0 corresponds to the NIL pointer.

† Except for an insertion at the end of a file that is in the generation state.

Insertions and deletions are effected by adjusting the subscripts similarly to the pointer adjustments made in the dynamic implementation. This implementation has two major disadvantages over the dynamic implementation:

1. The maximum list size must be specified and allocated in advance.
2. When a new record is to be inserted, the programmer must determine where it should go.

Because of these disadvantages, a static implementation is used only

1. By programmers in older languages (such as BASIC, COBOL and FORTRAN) which do not support dynamic variables.†
2. By Pascal programmers who are unfamiliar with dynamic variables.

CASE STUDY 3.1: A CLASS ROSTER

Design and write a program to solve the following problem:

Problem

Create and maintain a class roster for a class that holds at most 35 students.

Clarification The information provided for each student in the input will consist of two lines. The first line contains only the word 'INSERT' or 'DELETE' columns 1–6, to indicate whether the subsequent line is to be inserted in the class roster or deleted from it. The second line contains

(a) the student's name, in columns 1 to 30, last name first, left-justfied;
(b) the student's ID, in columns 31 to 36, a six-digit positive integer;
(c) the student's class code, in columns 37–38, a two-character code to indicate whether the student is a freshman(FR), sophomore(SO), junior(JR), senior(SR), special(SP), audit(AU), or graduate(GR).

The following exceptional cases should be noted:

1. It shall be an error if no input is provided. In this case the message printed is 'NO INPUT WAS PROVIDED.'
2. If the type of update is neither 'INSERT' nor 'DELETE,' the message 'ILLEGAL UPDATE TYPE' should be printed.
3. No insertion should be made when the class is full. The corresponding error message is 'INSERTION NOT MADE—CLASS FULL.'

---

† Since these languages do not support recursion either, iteration would be needed for performing insertions and deletions.

4. If an attempt is made to insert a student already on the roster, the message 'ATTEMPT TO ADD AN ALREADY EXISTING RECORD' should be printed.
5. If an attempt is made to delete a student who is not on the roster, the message 'ATTEMPT TO DELETE A NONEXISTING RECORD' should be printed.

Each time an insertion or deletion is made (that is, except in the five cases just cited), the entire current roster should be printed in alphabetical order by students' last names.

Sample Input

```
INSERT
LEZON KAREN M.                    305229GR
INSERT
MAYHEW VALERIE M.                 202129JR
INSERT
DANE ANDREW F.                    285283JR
INSERT
HOCH KELLER P.                    185214SO
INSERT
MAYHEW VALERIE M.                 202129JR
DELETE
DANE ANDREW F.                    285283JR
INSERT
WRIGHT AMY L.                     185922JR
INSERT
RUSS DAVID F.                     252864GR
DELETE
COGDILL CATHERINE E.              421106SR
INSERT
WATSON ROBERT W.                  105221SO
DELETE
WRIGHT AMY L.                     185922SR
INSERT
RUSS DAVID F.                     252864GR
DELETE
MAYHEW VALERIE M.                 202129JR
DELETE
WRIGHT AMY L.                     185922SR
```

Sample Output

```
INSERT
LEZON KAREN M.                    305229GR
ƀ
ƀ
ƀ
CURRENT ROSTER
ƀ
```

NAME	ID	CLASS
LEZON KAREN M.	305229	GRADUATE

(*new page*)

INSERT
MAYHEW VALERIE M. 202129JR

CURRENT ROSTER

NAME	ID	CLASS
LEZON KAREN M.	305229	GRADUATE
MAYHEW VALERIE M.	202129	JUNIOR

(*new page*)

INSERT
DANE ANDREW F. 285283JR

CURRENT ROSTER

NAME	ID	CLASS
DANE ANDREW F.	285283	JUNIOR
LEZON KAREN M.	305229	GRADUATE
MAYHEW VALERIE M.	202129	JUNIOR

(*new page*)

INSERT
HOCH KELLER P. 185214SO

CURRENT ROSTER

NAME	ID	CLASS
DANE ANDREW F.	285283	JUNIOR
HOCH KELLER P.	185214	SOPHOMORE
LEZON KAREN M.	305229	GRADUATE
MAYHEW VALERIE M.	202129	JUNIOR

(*new page*)

INSERT
MAYHEW VALERIE M. 202129JR

ATTEMPT TO ADD AN ALREADY EXISTING RECORD.

(and so on).

Solution Tree Because most of the activity with the class roster involves insertions and deletions, we will use a linked list to hold the roster. To start the solution tree, we establish an empty class roster by initializing the head and the class total. After that we will test to see if any input was provided. If there was no input, an error message is produced. If there was input, then we can read and process all of it.

The initial tree is shown in Fig. 3.17.

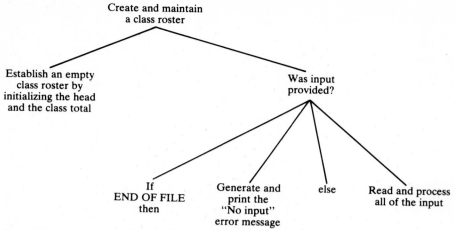

Figure 3.17 The initial version of the main tree.

To read and process the input, we need a loop that terminates when we reach the end of the file. Each time through the loop we will read in one update record, attempt to perform the update and then print out either the class roster or an error message, depending on whether the attempt was successful.

The final version of the main tree is shown in Fig. 3.18.

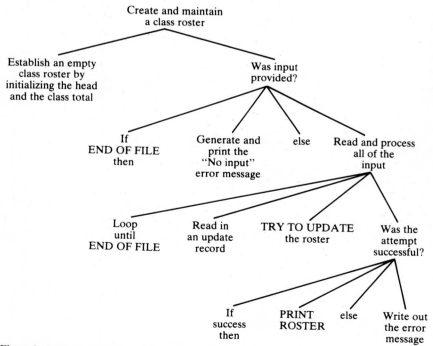

Figure 3.18 The final version of the main tree.

The subtree TRY TO UPDATE will attempt to perform the update on the class roster. This subtree will be provided with the class roster (via the head), the update record and the class total. This subtree will maintain the class roster and the class total. It will also generate any error message associated with the attempted update, and report back to the main tree that the attempted update was successful or unsuccessful.

If the type of update is an insertion, then we check to see if the class is full before trying to insert the new record in the roster. If the insertion attempt succeeds, the class total is incremented; otherwise, we have a duplicate record.

If the update type is a deletion, then we try to delete the record from the roster. If the attempt succeeds, the class total is decremented; otherwise, the record was not found.

The subtree TRY TO UPDATE is shown in Fig. 3.19.

The subtree TRY TO INSERT will attempt to insert a new record into the class roster. This subtree will be provided with the class roster (via the head) and the update record. It will maintain the class roster and report whether the attempted insertion was successful. As discussed earlier (pages 60–61), there are four cases to consider:

Case 1. The roster is empty. In this case the record is inserted at the head of the roster, successfully.

Case 2. The update record belongs before the current head of the roster. Again, the record is inserted at the head of the roster, successfully.

Case 3. If the name field of the update record matches that of the record at the head of the roster, then the attempted insertion fails.

Case 4. The update record belongs after the first record in the roster, so we try to insert it in the (shorter) roster pointed to by the "next" field in the first record.

The complete subtree is given in Fig. 3.20.

The subtree INSERT AT HEAD will insert a record at the head of a class roster. This subtree will be provided with the current head and the update record to be inserted, and will maintain the roster (via the head).

Making the insertion is straightforward. We first allocate space for a record with four fields. In the first three fields, we store the name, ID, and class codes from the update record. The "next" field will point to what is now the first record in the roster. Finally, the head of the roster is adjusted to point to this new record.

The subtree is given in Fig. 3.21.

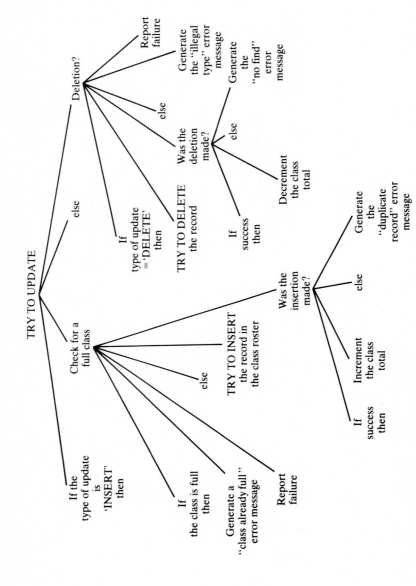

Figure 3.19 The subtree TRY TO UPDATE.

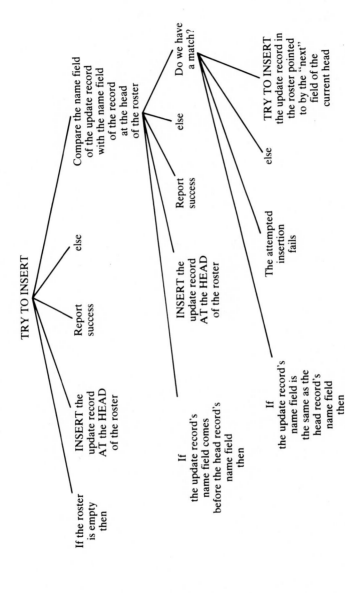

Figure 3.20 The subtree TRY TO INSERT.

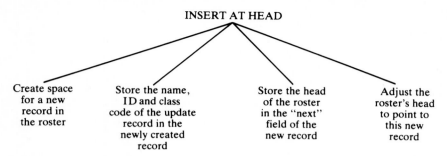

Figure 3.21 The subtree INSERT AT HEAD.

The subtree TRY TO DELETE will attempt to delete from the class roster the record whose name field matches the name in the update record. This subtree will be provided with the class roster (via the head) and the update record. It will maintain the class roster and report whether the attempted deletion was successful.

This subtree is analogous to the subtree TRY TO INSERT: the same conditions are tested, but success and failure are reversed. There are four cases to consider:

Case 1. The roster is empty. In this case, the attempted deletion fails.

Case 2. The update record's name comes before the name at the head of the roster. Again, the attempted deletion fails.

Case 3. The update name is the same as the name at the head of the roster. In this case, the deletion is made. First, we save the head's value in a temporary pointer (so we can dispose of it later). Then we adjust the head to point to the next record in the roster. After that, we can dispose of the record that used to be at the head of the roster. Finally, we report a successful deletion.

Case 4. The record to be deleted comes after the first record at the head of the roster, so we try to delete it from the (shorter) roster pointed to by the head record's "next" field.

The complete subtree is given in Fig. 3.22.

The subtree PRINT ROSTER will write out each student in the class roster. This subtree will be provided with the class roster (via the head).

We start at the head of the roster. For each record, we write out the relevant fields in that record and then advance to the next record. The subtree is shown in Fig. 3.23.

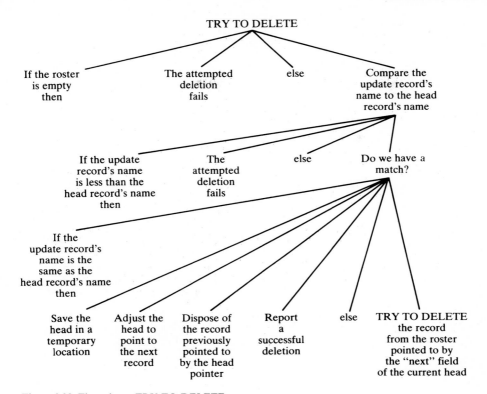

Figure 3.22 The subtree TRY TO DELETE.

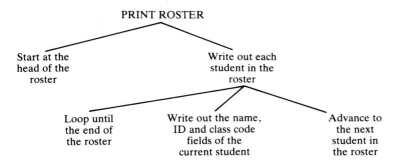

Figure 3.23 The subtree PRINT ROSTER.

Coding The discussion on pages 68–69 makes it clear that a dynamically implemented linked list is appropriate. To isolate this implementation detail, we define

```
TYPE   CLASSRANGE = 0..35 ;
       POINTER     = ^STUDENT ;
       ROSTERTYPE = POINTER :
          :
          :
VAR    ROSTERINFO : ROSTERTYPE ;
```

If we later decided to implement the linked list statically, we could define

```
TYPE   POINTER      = 0..35 ;
       ROSTERTYPE = RECORD
                       ROSTERARRAY : ARRAY[1..35] OF STUDENT ;
                       HEAD         : POINTER
                    END ;
```

The declaration of the variable ROSTERINFO would be unchanged from above.

Furthermore, we isolate the linked-list operations to a few procedures so that, for example, the linked-list implementation will be hidden from the executable section of the main program and from the procedure TRYTOUPDATE. To hide the linked-list implementation information from the executable section of the main program, we introduce a procedure called INITIALIZEROSTER, which simply sets ROSTERINFO to NIL and CLASSTOTAL to zero.

Finally, the details of reading and echo-printing each update are handled in a separate procedure, READANDECHO.

The hierarchy chart is shown in Fig. 3.24.

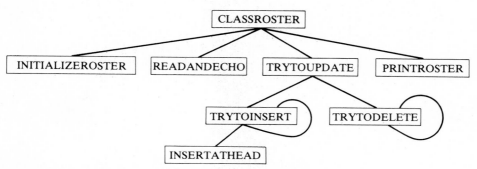

Figure 3.24 The hierarchy chart for the program CLASSROSTER.

Program

```
PROGRAM  CLASSROSTER(INPUT, OUTPUT);

(*****************************************************)
(*                                                 *)
(*    Programmer:    Bill Collins.                  *)
(*                                                 *)
(*    This program will solve the following problem: *)
(*    Create and maintain a class roster for a class *)
(*    that holds at most 35 students.  Each input record *)
(*    will take up two lines:  the type of update  *)
(*    ('INSERT' or 'DELETE') will be in columns 1 to 6 *)
(*    of the first line; the second line will contain *)
(*    the name field (columns 1 - 30, last name first), *)
(*    the id field (columns 31 - 36), and the class- *)
(*    code field (columns 37 - 38) to indicate the *)
(*    student's class.  The available class codes are *)
(*    FR (freshman), SO (sophomore), JR (junior), SR *)
(*    (senior), SP (special), AU (audit) and GR     *)
(*    (graduate).                                   *)
(*       If an insertion cannot be made (because either *)
(*    the class is full or the student is already on the *)
(*    roster) or a deletion cannot be made (because the *)
(*    student is not on the roster), an appropriate *)
(*    message should be printed.  An error message should *)
(*    also be printed if no input is provided or if the *)
(*    update type is neither 'INSERT' nor 'DELETE'.  Each *)
(*    time an insertion or deletion is made, the current *)
(*    roster should be printed in alphabetical order by *)
(*    the students' last names.                    *)
(*                                                 *)
(*****************************************************)

CONST CLASSLIMIT = 35;
      INPUTMISSINGERROR
                = 'NO INPUT PROVIDED.                        ';
      CLASSFULLERROR
                = 'INSERTION CANNOT BE MADE - CLASS FULL.    ';
      DUPLICATIONERROR
                = 'ATTEMPT TO ADD AN ALREADY EXISTING RECORD.';
      NONEXISTINGDELETIONERROR
                = 'ATTEMPT TO DELETE A NONEXISTING RECORD.   ';
      ILLEGALUPDATETYPEERROR
                = 'ILLEGAL UPDATE TYPE                       ';
      INSERTION  = 'INSERT';
      DELETION   = 'DELETE';
      NAMELENGTH = 30;
      CODELENGTH = 2;
      TYPELENGTH = 6;

TYPE  CLASSRANGE = 0..CLASSLIMIT;
      POINTER    = ^STUDENT;
      ROSTERTYPE = POINTER;
      STUDENT    = RECORD
                    NAME      : PACKED ARRAY[1..NAMELENGTH] OF CHAR;
                    ID        : 0..999999;
                    CLASSCODE : PACKED ARRAY[1..CODELENGTH] OF CHAR;
                    NEXT      : POINTER
                   END;
      UPDATE     = RECORD
                    TYPEOFUPDATE: PACKED ARRAY[1..TYPELENGTH] OF CHAR;
                    NAME        : PACKED ARRAY[1..NAMELENGTH] OF CHAR;
                    ID          : 0..999999;
                    CLASSCODE   : PACKED ARRAY[1..CODELENGTH] OF CHAR
                   END;
      MESSAGE    = PACKED ARRAY[1..42] OF CHAR;

VAR   ROSTERINFO               : ROSTERTYPE;
      CLASSTOTAL               : CLASSRANGE;
      UPDATERECORD             : UPDATE;
      ERRORMESSAGE             : MESSAGE;
      SUCCESS                  : BOOLEAN;
```

```
PROCEDURE  INITIALIZEROSTER(VAR    ROSTERINFO : ROSTERTYPE;
                           VAR    CLASSTOTAL : CLASSRANGE);

(*  Establish an empty class roster by initializing ROSTERINFO *)
(*  and CLASSTOTAL.                                            *)

BEGIN

   ROSTERINFO := NIL;
   CLASSTOTAL := 0

END;  (*  of the procedure INITIALIZEROSTER.  *)




PROCEDURE  READANDECHO(VAR    UPDATERECORD : UPDATE);

(*  Read in and echo print one UPDATERECORD.  *)

TYPE  CHARACTERCOUNTER = 1..NAMELENGTH;

VAR    I : CHARACTERCOUNTER;

BEGIN

   WITH UPDATERECORD DO
      BEGIN
         FOR I := 1 TO TYPELENGTH DO
            READ(TYPEOFUPDATE[I]);
         READLN;

         FOR I := 1 TO NAMELENGTH DO
            READ(NAME[I]);
         READ(ID);

         FOR I := 1 TO CODELENGTH DO
            READ(CLASSCODE[I]);
         READLN;

         WRITELN(TYPEOFUPDATE);
         WRITELN(NAME, ID:6, CLASSCODE);
         WRITELN;
         WRITELN;
         WRITELN
      END

END;  (*  of the procedure READANDECHO.  *)
```

```
PROCEDURE  INSERTATHEAD(UPDATERECORD      : UPDATE;
                        VAR    ROSTERINFO : ROSTERTYPE);

(*  Create a new record from fields in the UPDATERECORD and   *)
(*  insert this new record at the head of the class roster.   *)
(*  ROSTERINFO points to the head of the roster.              *)

VAR   NEWPOINTER : POINTER;

BEGIN

    NEW(NEWPOINTER);

    (*  Obtain the field values for this new record from the  *)
    (*  update record and from ROSTERINFO.                    *)
    WITH NEWPOINTER^ DO
        BEGIN
            NAME      := UPDATERECORD.NAME;
            ID        := UPDATERECORD.ID;
            CLASSCODE := UPDATERECORD.CLASSCODE;
            NEXT      := ROSTERINFO
        END;

    ROSTERINFO := NEWPOINTER

END;  (*  of the procedure INSERTATHEAD.  *)




PROCEDURE TRYTOINSERT (UPDATERECORD       : UPDATE;
                       VAR ROSTERINFO  : ROSTERTYPE;
                       VAR SUCCESS     : BOOLEAN);

(*  Attempt to insert the student from the UPDATERECORD  *)
(*  into the class roster, whose first record is pointed *)
(*  to by ROSTERINFO. The variable SUCCESS will indicate *)
(*  whether or not the insertion is made.                *)

BEGIN  (*  The executable section of TRYTOINSERT.  *)

    (*  Is the roster empty?  *)
    IF ROSTERINFO = NIL THEN
        BEGIN
            INSERTATHEAD(UPDATERECORD, ROSTERINFO);
            SUCCESS := TRUE
        END
    ELSE

        (*  Compare UPDATERECORD.NAME with ROSTERINFO^.NAME.  *)
        IF UPDATERECORD.NAME < ROSTERINFO^.NAME THEN
            BEGIN
                INSERTATHEAD(UPDATERECORD, ROSTERINFO);
                SUCCESS := TRUE
            END
        ELSE
            IF UPDATERECORD.NAME = ROSTERINFO^.NAME THEN
                SUCCESS := FALSE
            ELSE

                (*  Try to insert the new record into the  *)
                (*  roster whose first record is pointed    *)
                (*  to by ROSTERINFO^.NEXT.                 *)
                TRYTOINSERT(UPDATERECORD, ROSTERINFO^.NEXT, SUCCESS);

END;  (*  of the procedure TRYTOINSERT.  *)
```

```
PROCEDURE  TRYTODELETE (UPDATERECORD     : UPDATE;
                        VAR ROSTERINFO   : ROSTERTYPE;
                        VAR SUCCESS      : BOOLEAN);

(*  Attempt to delete, from the class roster, the record      *)
(*  whose name field matches the name in the UPDATERECORD.     *)
(*  The first record in the roster is pointed to by           *)
(*  ROSTERINFO. The variable SUCCESS will indicate whether    *)
(*  or not the deletion is achieved.                          *)

VAR   TEMPORARYPOINTER : POINTER;

BEGIN

   (*  Is the roster empty?  *)
   IF ROSTERINFO = NIL THEN
      SUCCESS := FALSE
   ELSE

      (*  Compare UPDATERECORD.NAME with ROSTERINFO^.NAME.  *)
      IF UPDATERECORD.NAME < ROSTERINFO^.NAME THEN
         SUCCESS := FALSE
      ELSE
         IF UPDATERECORD.NAME = ROSTERINFO^.NAME THEN

            (*  Delete ROSTERINFO^ from the roster.  *)
            BEGIN
               TEMPORARYPOINTER := ROSTERINFO;
               ROSTERINFO       := ROSTERINFO^.NEXT;
               DISPOSE(TEMPORARYPOINTER);
               SUCCESS := TRUE
            END
         ELSE

            (*  Try to delete the record whose name       *)
            (*  field is the same as UPDATERECORD.NAME     *)
            (*  from the roster whose first record is      *)
            (*  pointed to by ROSTERINFO^.NEXT.            *)
            TRYTODELETE(UPDATERECORD, ROSTERINFO^.NEXT, SUCCESS)

END;  (*  of the procedure TRYTODELETE.  *)
```

```
PROCEDURE  TRYTOUPDATE(UPDATERECORD          : UPDATE;
                       VAR    ROSTERINFO     : ROSTERTYPE;
                       VAR    CLASSTOTAL     : CLASSRANGE;
                       VAR    ERRORMESSAGE   : MESSAGE;
                       VAR    SUCCESS        : BOOLEAN);

(*  Attempt to perform an update to the class roster.      *)
(*  The update information is contained in UPDATERECORD.   *)
(*  The first record in the roster is pointed to by        *)
(*  ROSTERINFO. If the update can be performed, it will    *)
(*  be performed, CLASSTOTAL will be adjusted and SUCCESS  *)
(*  will get the value TRUE.  Otherwise, SUCCESS will      *)
(*  get the value FALSE and ERRORMESSAGE will indicate     *)
(*  why the attempted update failed.                       *)

BEGIN

   IF UPDATERECORD.TYPEOFUPDATE = INSERTION THEN

      (*  Check for a full class.  *)
      IF CLASSTOTAL = CLASSLIMIT THEN
         BEGIN
            ERRORMESSAGE := CLASSFULLERROR;
            SUCCESS      := FALSE
         END
      ELSE
         BEGIN

            TRYTOINSERT(UPDATERECORD, ROSTERINFO, SUCCESS);

            (*  Was the insertion attempt successful?  *)
            IF SUCCESS THEN
               CLASSTOTAL := CLASSTOTAL + 1
            ELSE
               ERRORMESSAGE := DUPLICATIONERROR

         END

   ELSE

      IF UPDATERECORD.TYPEOFUPDATE = DELETION THEN
         BEGIN

            TRYTODELETE(UPDATERECORD, ROSTERINFO, SUCCESS);

            (*  Was the deletion attempt successful?  *)
            IF SUCCESS THEN
               CLASSTOTAL := CLASSTOTAL - 1
            ELSE
               ERRORMESSAGE := NONEXISTINGDELETIONERROR

         END

      ELSE
         BEGIN
            ERRORMESSAGE := ILLEGALUPDATETYPEERROR;
            SUCCESS      := FALSE
         END

END; (*  of the procedure TRYTOUPDATE.  *)
```

```
PROCEDURE  PRINTROSTER(ROSTERINFO : ROSTERTYPE);

(*  Write out each student in the class roster whose *)
(*  first record is pointed to by ROSTERINFO.        *)

VAR   CURRENTPOINTER : PCINTER;

BEGIN

    (* Print heading. *)
    WRITELN('CURRENT ROSTER');
    WRITELN;
    WRITELN('NAME':17, 'IC':22, 'CLASS':14);
    WRITELN('-----------------------------',
            '------':11, '----------':14);

    (* Start at the beginning of the roster. *)
    CURRENTPOINTER := ROSTERINFO;

    WHILE CURRENTPOINTER <> NIL DO
        BEGIN

            (*  Write out the relevant fields for the current student.  *)
            WITH CURRENTPOINTER^ DO
                BEGIN

                    WRITE(NAME, IC:11, '       ');
                    IF CLASSCCDE = 'FR' THEN
                        WRITELN('FRESHMAN');
                    IF CLASSCCDE = 'SC' THEN
                        WRITELN('SOPHOMORE');
                    IF CLASSCCDE = 'JR' THEN
                        WRITELN('JUNIOR');
                    IF CLASSCCDE = 'SR' THEN
                        WRITELN('SENIOR');
                    IF CLASSCCDE = 'SP' THEN
                        WRITELN('SPECIAL');
                    IF CLASSCCDE = 'AU' THEN
                        WRITELN('AUDIT');
                    IF CLASSCCDE = 'GR' THEN
                        WRITELN('GRADUATE')

                END;

            (*  Advance to the next student in the roster.  *)
            CURRENTPOINTER := CURRENTPOINTER^.NEXT

        END

END;  (*  of the procedure PRINTROSTER.  *)
```

```
BEGIN   (*   the executable section of the main program.   *)

    (*   Establish an empty class roster.   *)
    INITIALIZEROSTER(ROSTERINFO, CLASSTOTAL);

    (*   Was input provided?   *)
    IF EOF THEN
        BEGIN
            ERRORMESSAGE := INPUTMISSINGERROR;
            PAGE;
            WRITELN(ERRORMESSAGE)
        END
    ELSE

        (*   Read and process all of the input.   *)
        REPEAT
            PAGE;

            (*   Read in and echo print one update record.   *)
            READANDECHO(UPDATERECORD);

            (*   Attempt to perform the update.   *)
            TRYTOUPDATE(UPDATERECORD, ROSTERINFO, CLASSTOTAL,
                        ERRORMESSAGE, SUCCESS);

            (*   Was the attempt successful?   *)
            IF SUCCESS THEN
                PRINTROSTER(ROSTERINFO)
            ELSE
                WRITELN(ERRORMESSAGE)

        UNTIL EOF;

    PAGE
END.
```

Program testing We note, at the outset, that the program will not detect all invalid inputs. For example, consider the following input:

```
INSERT
BUSHMAN JOANNE M.   320H38SO
```

Since there was no error checking for a nondigit in the ID field, the value for that field would simply be 320, and the class code would be 'H3.' Thus, no class would be printed during the printing of the roster (see the procedure PRINTROSTER).

1. In testing the main program, we used the following three stubs:

```
PROCEDURE   READANDECHO(VAR   UPDATERECORD : UPDATE) ;
BEGIN
     READLN ;
     READLN ;
     WRITELN('ONE UPDATE RECORD READ IN AND PRINTED OUT.')
END ;

PROCEDURE   TRYTOUPDATE(UPDATERECORD        : UPDATE ;
                        VAR     ROSTERINFO   : ROSTERTYPE ;
                        VAR     CLASSTOTAL   : CLASSRANGE;
                        VAR     ERRORMESSAGE : MESSAGE ;
                        VAR     SUCCESS      : BOOLEAN) ;
BEGIN
     SUCCESS := TRUE
END ;

PROCEDURE   PRINTROSTER(ROSTER : ROSTERTYPE) ;
BEGIN
     WRITELN('ROSTER PRINTED.')
END ;
```

The procedure INITIALIZEROSTER was defined completely since it was so small. For one test, no input was provided. The second test had two update records (four lines) of input; the actual values were irrelevant since READ-ANDECHO was just a stub.

2. To test READANDECHO (with the main program), the following input was used:

```
INSERT
RUSS DAVID F.                      252864GR
DELETE
LONG CRESTIN L.                    173085JR
```

3. In testing TRYTOUPDATE (with the main program and READAND-ECHO), the following new stubs were used:

```
PROCEDURE   TRYTOINSERT(UPDATERECORD   : UPDATE ;
                        VAR     ROSTERINFO : ROSTERTYPE ;
                        VAR     SUCCESS    : BOOLEAN) ;
```

```
BEGIN
    IF  UPDATERECORD.NAME = 'IMA DUPLICATE                      ' THEN
        SUCCESS := FALSE
    ELSE
        SUCCESS := TRUE
END ;

PROCEDURE   TRYTODELETE(UPDATERECORD       : UPDATE ;
                        VAR    ROSTERINFO : ROSTERTYPE ;
                        VAR    SUCCESS    : BOOLEAN) ;
BEGIN
    IF  UPDATERECORD.NAME = 'IMA PHANTOM                      ' THEN
        SUCCESS := FALSE
    ELSE
        SUCCESS := TRUE
END ;
```

The input was designed to test for valid insertions and deletions as well as the four update-related errors given in the Clarification. The following input was used:

INSERT	
SMITH JOHN A.	205163SR
INSERT	
IMA DUPLICATE	100000GR
INSRET	
IMA MISSPELLING	444444JR
DELETE	
SMITH JOHN A.	205163SR
DELETE	
IMA PHANTOM	999999AU
DELEAT	
IMA POOR SPELLER	222222FR
INSERT	
1	000001SP
INSERT	
2	000002SP
INSERT	
3	000003SP
INSERT	
4	000004SP
:	
INSERT	
35	000035SP
INSERT	
36	000036SP
DELETE	
GRAY DORIAN	221155SO
INSERT	
GETTY J. PAUL	121212SO

4. In testing TRYTOINSERT (with the main program, READANDECHO and TRYTOUPDATE), we included the complete procedure INSERTATHEAD

because of its simplicity. We also included the complete procedure PRINT-ROSTER because it would be difficult to test TRYTOINSERT without printing out the roster. The following input tested an insertion in an empty roster, insertions at the beginning, middle and end of the roster, and an attempted duplication.

```
INSERT
BUSHMAN JOANNE M.            320538SO
INSERT
GARCZYINSKI JANET L.         573079SR
INSERT
BUSHMAN JOANNE M.            320538SO
INSERT
SMITH JOHN A.               205163SR
INSERT
AARDVARK HARRY P.           784653FR
INSERT
OBRIEN KATHY M.             163062JR
```

5. The input for testing TRYTODELETE included a deletion from an empty roster, two legitimate deletions and a deletion of a record not on the roster. The following input was used:

```
DELETE
CARPENTER DAVID F.          486205AU
INSERT
SPRINGSTEEN BRUCE L.        591635SP
INSERT
WEBSTER SARAH A.            917363JR
INSERT
GUNDERSON LISA A.           819052SR
DELETE
WEBSTER SARAH A.            917363JR
DELETE
WILKERSON KATHY F.          305912GR
DELETE
SPRINGSTEEN BRUCE L.        591635SP
```

Since the program passed all of these tests, our confidence in its correctness increased. But testing can only reveal the presence of errors, not their absence.

Notes

1. The above program is essentially a sort program with some other features added on. As far as sorting itself is concerned, the program is not particularly efficient (Chap. 6 discusses what "efficient" means and also develops some efficient sort programs). The main purpose of the program is to provide a complete example of linked-list processing with recursion.
2. Most of the type definitions in the above program were required. The definitions for POINTER and STUDENT were needed to make STUDENT a

type identifier for a dynamic variable. The definitions for ROSTERTYPE, UPDATE, and MESSAGE were needed because each was used as the data type of a formal parameter. The data type of a formal parameter has to be given by a type identifier, either predefined (INTEGER, REAL, CHAR, or BOOLEAN) or defined in a type definition. The type CHARACTER-COUNTER, in the procedure READANDECHO, was defined to satisfy our convention that each variable's type be defined in a type definition.

3. The above program contains a flaw. Whether 'JOHN THOMAS E.' is less than 'JOHNSON LYNDON B.' depends on the collating sequence used, in particular, whether the blank character is less than 'S' in that sequence. In the most widely used collating sequences, ASCII and EBCDIC, the blank is less than any letter, so the program would work as expected for any input values. If you wanted a program that would work as expected for any input values and any collating sequence, then the string comparisons in the above program would have to be replaced with character-by-character comparisons. Insertions and deletions would be made in observance of the rule that the blank should be considered "smaller" than any letter.

Exercise 3.7 Modify the CLASSROSTER program so that it will work with any collating sequence.

Exercise 3.8 In the procedure PRINTROSTER above, why would the following CASE statement have been *illegal*?

```
CASE CLASSCODE OF
    'FR' : WRITELN('FRESHMAN') ;
    'SO' : WRITELN('SOPHOMORE') ;
        ⋮
END ;
```

Exercise 3.9 In the above program, we used a linked list with dynamic variables to hold the class roster. Discuss the advantages and disadvantages of each of the following alternate data structures:
(*a*) a contiguous implementation, with an array;
(*b*) a contiguous implementation, with a file;
(*c*) a static linked-list implementation, with an array; in particular, how would you replace NEW and DISPOSE?

Exercise 3.10 How would the above program have reacted if the class code 'SR' were entered as 'SE'?

Exercise 3.11 Modify the above program so that an appropriate error message would be printed if the class code were incorrect.

Exercise 3.12 Redesign each of the following as iterative procedures:

1. TRYTOINSERT.

2. TRYTODELETE.

Warning: Pay careful attention to the beginning and end of the roster.

MULTILINKED LISTS

In each linked list we have seen so far, each record had only one pointer field. We now consider several situations in which it is appropriate for each record to have more than one pointer field. The resulting list is then called a "multilinked list."

In the class roster of Case Study 3.1, suppose that we wanted the roster printed by ID numbers as well as by student names. Then we could have a pointer field to the next higher ID number as well as a pointer field to the next name. Each pointer field would need its own head, and each time an insertion or deletion was made, both the name pointers and the ID pointers would have to be adjusted. For example, suppose we had the multilinked list shown in Fig. 3.25. After an insertion of MAYHEW, VALERIE M. 202129JR, we would have the list shown in Fig. 3.26.

Such an insertion would require adjusting both pointer fields—this could be handled by designing a procedure to adjust the name pointers and another procedure to adjust the ID pointers. Could we develop a single procedure that could be called to adjust the name pointers and use the same code to adjust the ID pointers? The answer is "no" because the name and ID data types are different.

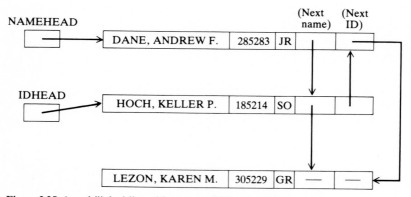

Figure 3.25 A multilinked list, with name and ID pointer fields.

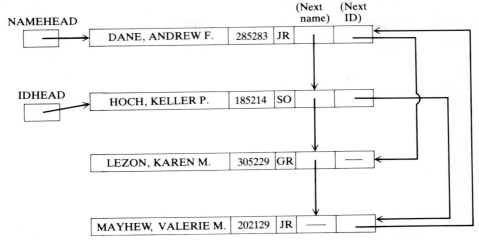

Figure 3.26 The multilinked list obtained by inserting a record into the list of Fig. 3.25.

In a condition such as

UPDATERECORD.FIELD > CURRENTPOINTER^.FIELD

the data type of FIELD could not be a name data type during one call to the procedure and be an ID data type during another call. This is just one facet of the "strong typing" facilities of Pascal.

Doubly Linked Lists

A *doubly linked list* is a multilinked list in which each record has a field which points to the previous record in the list and another field which points to the next record in the list. For example, in a text editor (that is, a program that manipulates lines of text), each line is stored in a record which also contains a pointer to the previous line and a pointer to the next line. In Fig. 3.27, some sample lines are shown.

Because of the backward and forward pointers, it is easy to traverse the list in either direction. Thus, if the next line to be processed is line 15, we would go through a loop seven times (22 − 15). Each time through the loop we would set the current line pointer's value to that of the previous line. For example, in a dynamic implementation,

CURRENTLINEPOINTER := CURRENTLINEPOINTER^.PREVIOUS

Such traversals are much more efficient than always starting at the head of the list.

Another example of forward and backward pointers is found in Case Study 8.1.

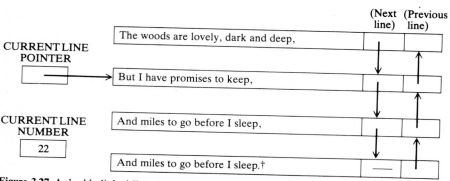

Figure 3.27 A doubly linked list.

Sparse Matrices

We now decribe another common application of multilinked lists, namely, in processing a "sparse" matrix.

Matrices are commonly used in a variety of fields, for example, in mathematics (solution of systems of linear equations), in sociology (Markov chain for studying social mobility) and in economics (input-output analysis). Some of those matrices have hundreds, even thousands, of rows and columns, but most of the entries are zero. Such matrices are called "sparse matrices" because of the sparsity of nonzero entries. As a small-scale example, consider the following matrix:

$$
\begin{bmatrix}
0 & 0 & 0 & 0 & 3 & 0 & 0 & 0 & 0 & 0 \\
5 & 0 & -1 & 0 & 0 & 0 & 9 & 0 & 0 & 0 \\
0 & 0 & 0 & 0 & 0 & 0 & 0 & 0 & 0 & 0 \\
3 & 0 & 0 & 0 & 0 & -5 & 6 & 0 & 0 & 0 \\
0 & 6 & 0 & 0 & 0 & 5 & 0 & 0 & 0 & 0 \\
0 & 0 & 0 & 0 & 0 & 0 & 0 & 0 & 0 & 0 \\
0 & 0 & 0 & 0 & 0 & 0 & 0 & 0 & 0 & 0 \\
0 & -2 & 0 & 0 & 9 & 6 & 0 & 0 & 0 & 0 \\
0 & 0 & 0 & 0 & 0 & 0 & 0 & 0 & 0 & 0 \\
3 & 18 & 0 & 0 & 0 & 0 & 0 & 0 & 0 & 0
\end{bmatrix}
$$

Here we have 10 rows and 10 columns, for a total of 100 entries, only 14 of which are nonzero. Such a matrix could be represented contiguously with a two-dimensional array. But suppose we had a sparse matrix with 1000 rows and 1000

---

† From "Stopping by Woods on a Snowy Evening," from *The Poetry of Robert Frost* edited by Edward Connery Lathem. Copyright 1923, © 1969 by Holt, Rinehart and Winston. Copyright 1951 by Robert Frost. Reprinted by permission of Holt, Rinehart and Winston, Publishers.

columns! Few Pascal compilers would allow you to declare such a large two-dimensional array, and the zero entries would occupy wasted space in any event.

An alternative implementation uses multilinked lists with one record for each nonzero entry. Each record will have five fields:

1. The row number
2. The column number
3. The nonzero value
4. A pointer to the next higher row (in the same column) that has a nonzero value
5. A pointer to the next higher column (in the same row) that has a nonzero value

For example, the above matrix would be represented as follows:

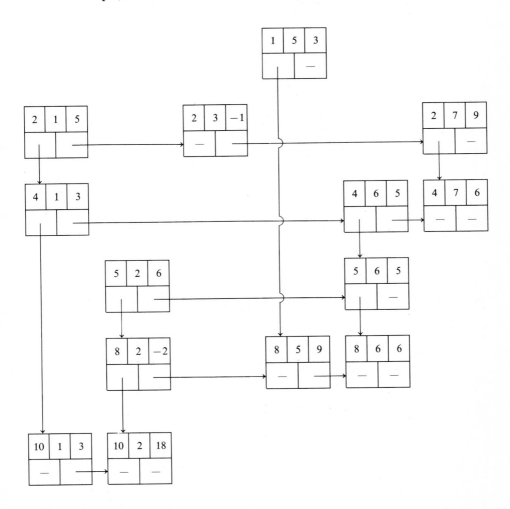

Instead of a single head, we would need an array of row heads and an array of column heads. For example, ROWHEAD[5] would contain a pointer to the first record in row 5, namely the record in the above list whose first three fields are 5, 2, and 6, respectively. Similarly, COLUMNHEAD[4] would contain a bar since the above list has no records in col. 4.

After a sparse matrix has been stored in such a multilinked list (actually, an array of multilinked lists), standard matrix operations can be performed on it. One operation is to multiply a given row by a constant value. For example, if we were to multiply each element in row 8 by 3, our multilinked list representation would then be

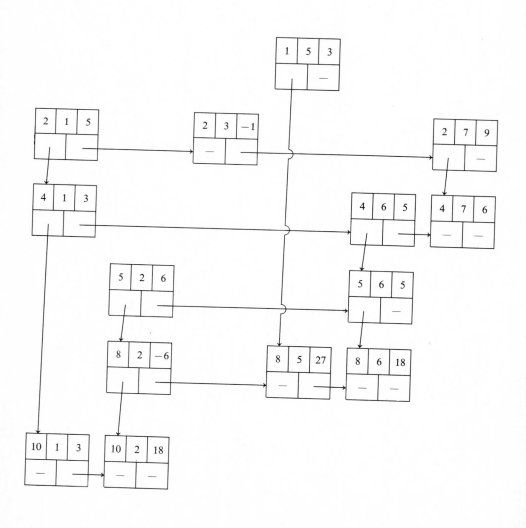

Notice that no pointers had to be changed. But what if the constant multiplier is 0? Then the effect would be to delete the given row from the list, and that requires some pointer adjustments. For example, if we multiply row 4 by 0, we would get

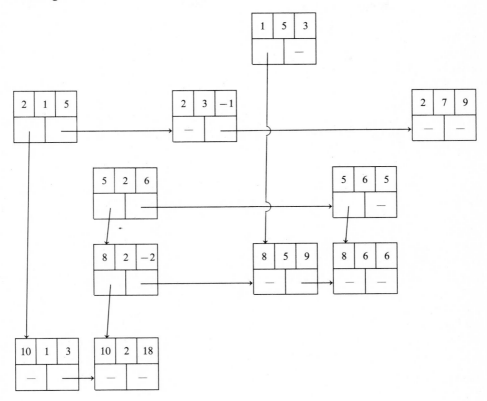

When is the multilinked list implementation preferable to the contiguous, two-dimensional-array implementation? If space is the only concern, the determination is straightforward. On most computers, a pointer variable or subscript occupies as much space as an integer variable; for simplicity let us assume that each requires one location. For a matrix with R rows, C columns and N nonzero entries, the multilinked list requires $5 * N$ locations for each nonzero entry, plus R locations for the array of row heads and C locations for the array of column heads. The total space requirements are $5 * N + R + C$ locations. The two-dimensional-array requires $R * C$ locations. Thus, the multilinked list saves space whenever $5 * N + R + C < R * C$, that is, whenever

$$N < \frac{(R-1)*(C-1)-1}{5}$$

Loosely speaking, a multilinked list saves space when less than one fifth of the entries are nonzero. However, as noted above, some matrix operations (such as multiplying a row or column by 0) take longer with a multilinked list implementation than with a two-dimensional array. Thus, a time-space trade-off may have to be made for some applications.

PROBLEMS

Problem 3.1: A Sparse Matrix

Design and write a program to solve the following problem: Multiply a given row in a sparse matrix by a given constant.

Clarification We assume that the matrix has at most 200 rows and at most 200 columns. Each entry will be an integer between -1000 and 1000. The first line of the input will contain the row (to be multiplied) and the constant multiplier, which will be an integer between -25 and 25. Each successive line will contain a row number, column number, and nonzero entry in the original matrix. The listing of nonzero entries will be in row-major order, that is, each nonzero entry in row 1 is listed first (in increasing order of column numbers), then each nonzero entry in row 2 (in increasing order of column numbers), and so on. The output will contain, in row-major order, a row number, column number and corresponding nonzero entry in the resultant matrix. The implementation of the sparse matrix *must* use multilinked lists.

Sample Input 1

8	3	
1	5	3
2	1	5
2	3	-1
2	7	9
4	1	3
4	6	-5
4	7	6
5	2	6
5	6	5
8	2	-2
8	5	9
8	6	6
10	1	3
10	2	18
185	127	5

Sample Output 1

ORIGINAL MATRIX

b̸
b̸
b̸
b̸

ROW	COLUMN	VALUE
1	5	3
2	1	5
2	3	−1
2	7	9
4	1	3
4	6	−5
4	7	6
5	2	6
5	6	5
8	2	−2
8	5	9
8	6	6
10	1	3
10	2	18
185	127	5

(*new page*)

WHEN WE MULTIPLY ROW 8 BY 3, WE GET THE FOLLOWING MATRIX:
b̸
b̸
b̸

ROW	COLUMN	VALUE
1	5	3
2	1	5
2	3	−1
2	7	9
4	1	3
4	6	−5
4	7	6
5	2	6
5	6	5
8	2	−6
8	5	27
8	6	18
10	1	3
10	2	18
185	127	5

Sample Input 2

```
  4      0
  1      5      3
  2      1      5
  2      3     -1
  2      7      9
  4      1      3
  4      6     -5
  4      7      6
  5      2      6
  5      6      5
  8      2     -2
  8      5      9
  8      6      6
 10      1      3
 10      2     18
185    127      5
```

Sample Output 2

ORIGINAL MATRIX

 b
b
b
b

ROW	COLUMN	VALUE
1	5	3
2	1	5
2	3	-1
2	7	9
4	1	3
4	6	-5
4	7	6
5	2	6
5	6	5
8	2	-2
8	5	9
8	6	6
10	1	3
10	2	18
185	127	5

(*new page*)

WHEN WE MULTIPLY ROW 4 BY 0, WE GET THE FOLLOWING MATRIX:
b̶
b̶
b̶
b̶

ROW	COLUMN	VALUE
1	5	3
2	1	5
2	3	−1
2	7	9
5	2	6
5	6	5
8	2	−2
8	5	9
8	6	6
10	1	3
10	2	18
185	127	5

Problem 3.2: A Flight Roster

Design and write a program to solve the following problem: White Knuckle Airlines schedules 12 flights daily from Salisbury, Maryland to Dover, Delaware. Create and maintain a reservations list for each flight.

Clarification Each flight carries a maximum of five passengers. Each line of input contains the request: 'ADD,' 'CANCEL,' 'FIND,' or 'LIST' in cols. 1–6, the flight number in cols. 9–10 and, unless 'LIST' is requested, the passenger's name in cols. 15–34.

The four types of requests should be handled as follows:

1. If the request is 'ADD,' then the given passenger wants to be added to the given flight; if that flight is full, then the passenger is turned away.
2. If the request is 'CANCEL,' then the given passenger should be removed from the flight list.
3. If the request is 'FIND,' then the value output should be 'YES—ON FLIGHT LIST' or 'NOT ON FLIGHT LIST.'
4. If the request is 'LIST,' then the flight list should be printed, in alphabetical order by passengers' names.

The following exceptional cases should be noted:

(a) If the request is not one of the four described above, the error message 'ERROR—ILLEGAL REQUEST' should be printed.
(b) If the flight number is not in the 1 to 12 range, then the error message 'ERROR—ILLEGAL FLIGHT NUMBER' should be printed.

(c) If the request is 'ADD' but the passenger is already on the flight list, then the error message 'ERROR – DUPLICATE NAME' should be printed.

(d) If the request is 'CANCEL' but the passenger is not on the flight list, then the error message 'ERROR—NAME NOT ON FLIGHT LIST' should be printed.

(e) If the passenger is turned away, the message 'FLIGHT ALREADY FULL —SORRY!' should be printed.

Sample Input

ADD	6	KUNDELL KENNETH
ADD	2	FAHEY PETER
ADD	2	SMITH JEFFERY
ADD	2	FAHEY KATHLEEN
ADD	3	TUFTS MARGARET
LIST	14	
ADD	2	LONG CRESTIN
FIND	2	RUSS DAVID
ADD	2	ABRESCH LINDA
FIND	2	FAHEY KATHLEEN
ADD	2	MURPHY CHARLES
CANCEL	3	FORTE FABIAN
ADD	2	HARDIN CHARLES
LIST	2	
FIND	2	MURPHY CHARLES
ADD	2	STARKEY RICHARD
CANCEL	2	FAHEY PETER
LIST	2	
ADD	2	PENNIMAN RICHARD
CANCEL	2	HARDIN CHARLES
LIST	2	
CANCEL	20	FAHEY KATHLEEN
FIND	2	MURPHY CHARLES
ADD	2	FAHEY PETER
ADD	2	PENNIMAN RICHARD
LIST	2	

Sample Output

REQUEST	FLIGHT NUMBER	NAME
ADD	6	KUNDELL KENNETH
♭		
♭		
ADD	2	FAHEY PETER
♭		
♭		
ADD	2	SMITH JEFFERY
♭		
♭		
ADD	2	FAHEY KATHLEEN

♭			
♭			
ADD	3	TUFTS MARGARET	
♭			
♭			
LIST	14		ERROR – ILLEGAL FLIGHT NUMBER
♭			
♭			
ADD	2	LONG CRESTIN	
♭			
♭			
FIND	2	RUSS DAVID	ERROR – NAME NOT ON FLIGHT LIST
♭			
♭			
ADD	2	ABRESCH LINDA	
♭			
♭			
FIND	2	FAHEY KATHLEEN	YES – ON FLIGHT LIST
♭			
♭			
ADD	2	MURPHY CHARLES	FLIGHT ALREADY FULL – SORRY!
♭			
♭			
CANCEL	3	FORTE FABIAN	ERROR – NAME NOT ON FLIGHT LIST
♭			
♭			
ADD	2	HARDIN CHARLES	FLIGHT ALREADY FULL – SORRY!
♭			
♭			
LIST	2		FLIGHT LIST

FLIGHT LIST
————————

ABRESCH LINDA
FAHEY KATHLEEN
FAHEY PETER
LONG CRESTIN
SMITH JEFFERY

♭			
♭			
FIND	2	MURPHY CHARLES	NOT ON FLIGHT LIST
♭			
♭			
ADD	2	STARKEY RICHARD	FLIGHT ALREADY FULL – SORRY!
♭			
♭			
CANCEL	2	FAHEY PETER	
♭			
♭			
LIST	2		FLIGHT LIST

FLIGHT LIST
————————

ABRESCH LINDA
FAHEY KATHLEEN
LONG CRESTIN
SMITH JEFFERY

♭
♭

ADD	2	PENNIMAN RICHARD	
♭ ♭			
CANCEL	2	HARDIN CHARLES	ERROR – NAME NOT ON FLIGHT LIST
♭ ♭			
LIST	2		FLIGHT LIST

ABRESCH LINDA
FAHEY KATHLEEN
LONG CRESTIN
PENNIMAN RICHARD
SMITH JEFFERY

♭ ♭			
CANCEL	20	FAHEY KATHLEEN	ERROR – ILLEGAL FLIGHT NUMBER
♭ ♭			
FIND	2	MURPHY CHARLES	NOT ON FLIGHT LIST
♭ ♭			
ADD	2	FAHEY PETER	FLIGHT ALREADY FULL – SORRY!
♭ ♭			
ADD	2	PENNIMAN RICHARD	ERROR – DUPLICATE NAME
♭ ♭			
LIST	2		FLIGHT LIST

ABRESCH LINDA
FAHEY KATHLEEN
LONG CRESTIN
PENNIMAN RICHARD
SMITH JEFFERY

Problem 3.3: A Small Text Editor

Develop a small text editor. (*Warning:* This is a difficult problem! It should be assigned only as a team project.)

Clarification A *text editor* is a program that manipulates text, line by line. We assume that each line is exactly 80 characters long. Each editing command begins with a dollar sign (and no other line begins with a dollar sign). There are seven editing commands:

1. $INSERT
   Each subsequent line (up to the next editing command) will be inserted in the text after the current line. For example, if the text is ("→" indicates the current line)

```
      NOW IS THE
  →  TIME FOR
      MEN TO COME TO
      THE
      AID OF THE PARTY.
```

then the sequence

```
$INSERT
ALL
GOOD
```

will cause the text to become

```
      NOW IS THE
      TIME FOR
      ALL
  →  GOOD
      MEN TO COME TO
      THE
      AID OF THE PARTY.
```

2. $DELETE   m,n

   Each line in the text between lines m and n, inclusive, will be deleted. If the current line had been in this range, the new current line will be line m − 1 (this may be line 0). For example, if the text is

```
      NOW IS THE
      TIME FOR
      ALL
  →  GOOD
      MEN TO COME TO
      THE
      AID OF THE PARTY.
```

   then the command

```
$DELETE 3,5
```

   will cause the text to become

```
      NOW IS THE
  →  TIME FOR
      THE
      AID OF THE PARTY.
```

   An appropriate error message should be printed if
   (*a*) a line number (or the comma) is omitted;
   (*b*) n is less than m;
   (*c*) m is less than 1 or n is greater than the last line number in the text.

3. $LINE   m

Line m becomes the current line. For example, if the text is

        MARESY DOATS
        AND DOESY DOATS
    → AND LITTLE LAMBSY DIVY.

then the command

$LINE   1

will make line 1 the current line:

    → MARESY DOATS
        AND DOESY DOATS
        AND LITTLE LAMBSY DIVY.

The command

$LINE   0

followed by an insert command, is used to insert lines at the beginning of the text.

   An error message should be printed if m is either less than zero or greater than the last line number in the text.

4. $CHANGE   %x%y%

In the current line, each occurrence of the string given by x will be replaced by the string given by y. For example, if the current line is

AID OF THE PARTY.

then the command

$CHANGE   %A%VO%

will cause the current line to become

VOID OF THE PVORTY.

If we then issue the command

$CHANGE   %PVO%A%

we would get

VOID OF THE ARTY.

Notes:

(a) If either x or y contains a percent sign, another delimiter should be used in the command. For example,

   $CHANGE   #0.16#16%#

(*b*) The string given by y may be the null string. For example, if the current line is

AID OF THE PARTY.

then the command

$CHANGE   %OF %%

will change the current line to

AID THE PARTY.

(*c*) An error message should be printed if the delimiter occurs fewer than three times.

5. $LAST
The *line number* of the last line in the text will be printed. For example, if the text is

   I HEARD A BIRD SING
→ IN THE DARK OF DECEMBER.
   A MAGICAL THING
   AND A JOY TO REMEMBER.

then

$LAST

will cause "4" to be printed. The text (and current line) will be unchanged.

6. $PRINT   m,n
Each line (and line number) in the text, from lines m through n, inclusive, will be printed. For example, if the text is

   WINSTON CHURCHILL ONCE SAID THAT
→ DEMOCRACY IS THE WORST
   FORM OF GOVERNMENT
   EXCEPT FOR ALL THE OTHERS.

then the command

$PRINT   1,3

will cause the following to be printed:

1 WINSTON CHURCHILL ONCE SAID THAT
2 DEMOCRACY IS THE WORST
3 FORM OF GOVERNMENT

The text (and current line) are unchanged.

An error message should be printed if

(a) a line number (or the comma) is omitted from the command;

(b) n is less than m;

(c) m is less than 1 or n is greater than the last line number in the text.

7. $DONE

This terminates the execution of the text editor.

An error message should be printed for any illegal command (such as "$END" or "?INSERT").

Sample Input (Sample Output is underlined)

```
$INSERT
YOU CAN FOOL
SOME OF THE PEOPLE
SOME OF THE TIMES,
BUT YOU CAN'T FOUL
ALL OF THE PEEPLE
ALL OF THE TIME.
$LINE 3
$PRINT 3
```

*** ERROR : MISSING COMMA.   PLEASE TRY AGAIN.

```
$PRINT 3,3
```

3   SOME OF THE TIMES,

```
$CHANGE %S%%
$PRINT 3,3
```

3   OME OF THE TIME,

```
$CHANGE %O%SO
```

*** ERROR : DELIMITER % OCCURS ONLY TWICE.   PLEASE TRY AGAIN,

```
$CHANGE %O%SO%
$PRINT 3,3
```

3   SOME SOF THE TIME.

```
CHANGE %SOF%OF%
```

*** ERROR : COMMAND MUST BEGIN WITH $. PLEASE TRY AGAIN,

```
$CHANGE   %SOF%OF%
$PRINT 3,3
```

3   SOME OF THE TIME,

```
$LINE 0
$INSERT
LINCOLN ONCE SAID THAT
YOU CAN FOOL
SOME OF THE PEOPLE
ALL THE TIME AND
ALL OF THE TIME AND
$LAST
```

<u>11</u>
$PRINT 1,11

<u>1</u>   LINCOLN ONCE SAID THAT
<u>2</u>   YOU CAN FOOL
<u>3</u>   SOME OF THE PEOPLE
<u>4</u>   ALL THE TIME AND
<u>5</u>   ALL OF THE TIME AND
<u>6</u>   YOU CAN FOOL
<u>7</u>   SOME OF THE PEOPLE
<u>8</u>   SOME OF THE TIME,
<u>9</u>   BUT YOU CAN'T FOUL
<u>10</u> ALL OF THE PEEPLE
<u>11</u> ALL OF THE TIME.
$LINE 7
$CHANGE %SOME%ALL%
$PRINT 7,7

<u>7</u>   ALL OF THE PEOPLE
$LINE 9
$CHANGE %UL%OL%
$PRINT 9,9

<u>9</u>   BUT YOU CAN'T FOOL
$LINE 10
$CHANGE %EE%EO%
$PRINT 10,10

<u>10</u> ALL OF THE PEOPLE
$DELETE 4,4
$PRINT 1,11

*** ERROR : 11 IS GREATER THAN THE LAST LINE NUMBER IN THE TEXT,
        NAMELY 10. PLEASE TRY AGAIN.
$PRINT 1,10

<u>1</u>   LINCOLN ONCE SAID THAT
<u>2</u>   YOU CAN FOOL
<u>3</u>   SOME OF THE PEOPLE
<u>4</u>   ALL OF THE TIME AND
<u>5</u>   YOU CAN FOOL
<u>6</u>   ALL OF THE PEOPLE
<u>7</u>   SOME OF THE TIME,
<u>8</u>   BUT YOU CAN'T FOOL
<u>9</u>   ALL OF THE PEOPLE
<u>10</u> ALL OF THE TIME.
$DONE

Hint: Because of the possibility of a missing line number or comma in several commands, each command line should be read in as a character string. The digit characters should then be "peeled off" and converted to a number. For example, suppose LINESTRING is a string variable (packed array of four characters) and LINENUMBER is an integer variable. If we have

LINESTRING[1]	4
LINESTRING[2]	8
LINESTRING[3]	7
LINESTRING[4]	

then we can calculate the corresponding value of LINENUMBER as follows

```
LINENUMBER := 0 ;
FOR I := 1 TO 3 DO
     LINENUMBER := 10 * LINENUMBER + (ORD(LINESTRING[I]) − ORD('0'))
```

The variable LINENUMBER would now have a value of 487.

FOUR

RESTRICTED LISTS

In this chapter we introduce two types of lists—stacks and queues—which can be updated only in a very limited way. Since our ability to manipulate them is so restricted, we are able to use convenient implementations, and this is especially fortunate since both stacks and queues have a wide variety of applications.

STACKS

A *stack* is a list in which both insertions and deletions are made at the same end, known as the "top" of the stack. For example, a tray-holder in a cafeteria forms a stack since insertions and deletions are made only from the top. To put it another way, the tray put on most recently will be the next one to be removed. This defining property of stacks is sometimes abbreviated "Last In, First Out," or LIFO. In keeping with this view, an insertion is referred to as a "push" and a deletion is referred to as a "pop."

There are exactly five operations that can be performed on a stack:

1. Initialize the stack, to make it empty.
2. Push an element onto the (top of the) stack.
3. Test the stack to see if it is empty.
4. Access the top element on the stack.
5. Pop (the top element from) the stack.

In keeping with the principle of data abstraction (page 37), we will initially focus on the abstract data type and ignore implementation details.

Figure 4.1*a* shows a stack with six elements. After the number 13 is pushed onto the stack, we get Fig. 4.1*b*. The results of two successive pops are then shown in Figs. 4.1*c* and *d*, and 4.1*e* shows what the stack looks like after the number 9 is pushed onto it.

This can be conveniently represented in a single picture if we adopt the following conventions:

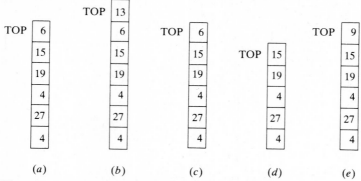

(a)   (b)   (c)   (d)   (e)

Figure 4.1 A stack through several stages of pushes and pops.

1. An element is circled to indicate it has been popped.
2. When an element is pushed, it is placed just above the previous top of the stack, unless that above location is occupied by a circled element; in that case the new element is placed at the same level as the circled element in the first empty column to the right.

Figure 4.1 could then be represented by the picture in Fig. 4.2.

Note that, at any time, the top of the stack is the highest uncircled element. For a somewhat more complicated example, consider the list of pushes and pops in Fig. 4.3. The corresponding stack picture is shown in Fig. 4.4. Let us now consider the opposite approach: to produce a stack's history from the stack picture. Suppose we start with the stack picture shown in Fig. 4.5. Since "i" appears just to the right of "p" and there is nothing under "i," we know that "i" must have been pushed just after "p" was popped. Similar analyses show that the stack's history had to be as shown in Fig. 4.6.

Figure 4.2 A single-picture stack.

1. push t
2. push a
3. push p
4. push x
5. push u
6. pop u
7. pop x
8. push v
9. push q
10. pop q
11. pop v
12. pop p
13. push i
14. push s
15. push l
16. pop l
17. push v

Figure 4.3 A list of stack operations.

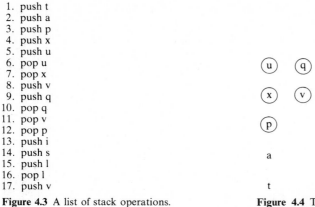

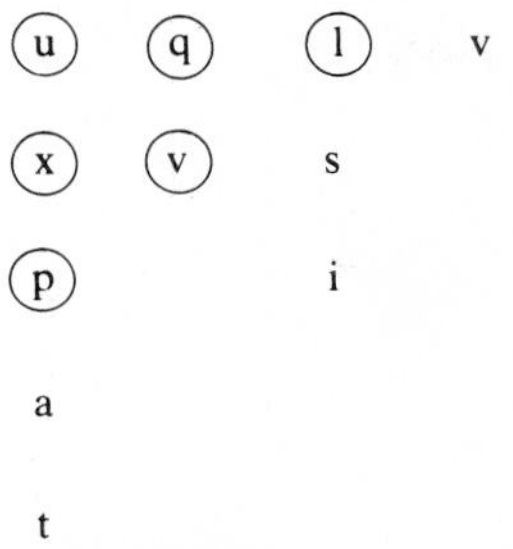

Figure 4.4 The stack picture corresponding to the operations in Fig. 4.3.

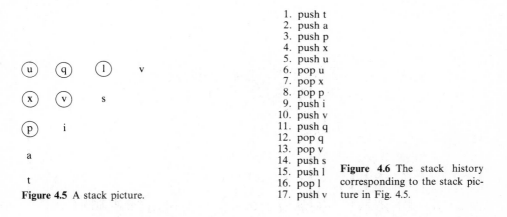

Figure 4.5 A stack picture.

1. push t
2. push a
3. push p
4. push x
5. push u
6. pop u
7. pop x
8. pop p
9. push i
10. push v
11. push q
12. pop q
13. pop v
14. push s
15. push l
16. pop l
17. push v

Figure 4.6 The stack history corresponding to the stack picture in Fig. 4.5.

Exercise 4.1 Draw a sequence of eight stack pictures (as in Fig. 4.1) for the following sequence of operations:

1. push a
2. push b
3. push c
4. pop c
5. pop b
6. push d
7. push e
8. pop e

Exercise 4.2 Draw a single-picture stack for the operations of Exercise 4.1.

Exercise 4.3 Draw a single-picture stack for the following sequence of operations:

1. push A
2. push A
3. push B
4. pop B
5. pop A
6. push X
7. push C
8. push D
9. pop D
10. pop C
11. push Y
12. pop Y
13. pop X
14. push Z
15. pop Z
16. pop A

Exercise 4.4 Trace the history of the following stack

ⓤ   v

ⓧ ⓠ ⓢ   1

ⓟ ⓥ   i

a

t

Exercise 4.5 Trace the history of the following stack

ⓧ ⓤ ⓥ ⓠ   ⓥ ⓜ

ⓟ   ⓘ ①

ⓐ   ⓢ

ⓣ

Stack Implementations

In the previous section we considered the stack as an abstract data type. To facilitate the task of writing programs to manipulate a stack, we now turn our attention to stack implementations.

There are several ways to implement a stack in Pascal. One possibility is a dynamic linked list. For example, if the type of each element is some previously defined type called ELEMENTTYPE, we can define the following:

```
TYPE  POINTER       = ^STACKRECORD ;
      STACKRECORD = RECORD
                        ELEMENT : ELEMENTTYPE ;
                        NEXT      : POINTER
                    END ;
      STACKTYPE     = RECORD
                        TOPOFSTACK : POINTER ;
                        UNDERFLOW,
                        OVERFLOW    : BOOLEAN
                    END ;
VAR   STACK         : STACKTYPE ;
```

The boolean field **UNDERFLOW** is initialized to FALSE. Its value is changed to TRUE if an attempt is made to pop an empty stack or to access the top element on an empty stack. Similarly, OVERFLOW indicates whether an attempt has been made to push onto an already full stack.

Figure 4.7 shows what a three-element stack of characters would look like, and Fig. 4.8 shows the effect of pushing 'Q' onto that stack.

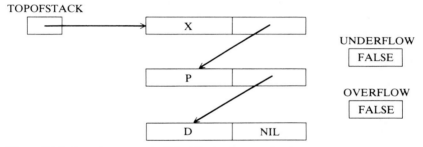

Figure 4.7 A three-element stack: linked-list implementation.

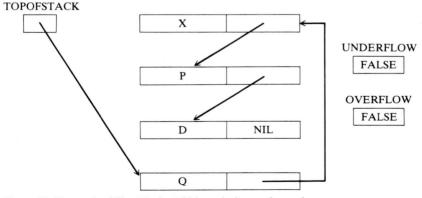

Figure 4.8 The stack of Fig. 4.7 after 'Q' is pushed onto the stack.

One advantage of a dynamic linked-list implementation is that we can have a stack of arbitrary, unspecified size, limited only by the size of the heap (see page 7). We include an OVERFLOW field in the definition of STACKTYPE because overflow may be a possibility with other implementations (for example, see page 115). Thus, a call to a "push" procedure may be followed by a test of STACK.OVERFLOW no matter what implementation is used.

Each of the five stack operations listed on page 109 can easily be handled since all of the activity takes place at the top of the stack. For the sake of completeness, we now list subprograms to accomplish those five operations.

```
PROCEDURE  INITIALIZESTACK(VAR  STACK : STACKTYPE) ;

(* Make STACK an empty stack. *)

BEGIN

    WITH STACK DO
        BEGIN
            TOPOFSTACK := NIL ;
            UNDERFLOW := FALSE ;
            OVERFLOW   := FALSE
        END

END ;   (* of the procedure INITIALIZESTACK. *)



PROCEDURE  PUSH(VAR  STACK : STACKTYPE ;
                     ELEMENT    : ELEMENTTYPE) ;

(* Push onto STACK the value of ELEMENT. *)

VAR  NEWTOP : POINTER ;

BEGIN

    WITH STACK DO
        BEGIN

            NEW(NEWTOP) ;
            NEWTOP^.ELEMENT := ELEMENT ;
            NEWTOP^.NEXT     := TOPOFSTACK ;

            (* Adjust the top of the stack. *)
            TOPOFSTACK := NEWTOP

        END

END ;   (* of the procedure PUSH. *)



FUNCTION  STACKEMPTY(STACK : STACKTYPE) : BOOLEAN ;

(* Return TRUE or FALSE, depending on whether STACK is empty. *)

BEGIN

    STACKEMPTY := STACK.TOPOFSTACK = NIL

END ;   (* of the function STACKEMPTY. *)
```

```
PROCEDURE  ACCESSTOP(VAR  STACK      : STACKTYPE ;
                         VAR   ELEMENT : ELEMENTTYPE) ;
```

(∗ If STACK is empty, STACK.UNDERFLOW gets the value TRUE. ∗)
(∗ Otherwise, ELEMENT gets a copy of the top element on STACK.   ∗)

```
BEGIN

     WITH STACK DO
         IF TOPOFSTACK = NIL THEN
             UNDERFLOW := TRUE
         ELSE
             ELEMENT := TOPOFSTACK^.ELEMENT

END ;   (∗ of the procedure ACCESSTOP. ∗)
```

```
PROCEDURE  POP(VAR  STACK      : STACKTYPE ;
                   VAR   ELEMENT : ELEMENTTYPE) ;
```

(∗ If STACK is empty, STACK.UNDERFLOW gets the value TRUE. ∗)
(∗ Otherwise, ELEMENT gets a copy of the top element on STACK   ∗)
(∗ and then that top element is deleted.   ∗)

```
VAR  NEWTOP : POINTER ;

BEGIN

     WITH STACK DO
         IF TOPOFSTACK = NIL THEN
             UNDERFLOW := TRUE
         ELSE
             BEGIN
                 ELEMENT := TOPOFSTACK^.ELEMENT ;

                 (∗ Pop the stack. ∗)
                 NEWTOP := TOPOFSTACK^.NEXT ;
                 DISPOSE(TOPOFSTACK) ;
                 TOPOFSTACK := NEWTOP
             END

END;   (∗ of the procedure POP. ∗)
```

Because insertions and deletions can be made only at the top of a stack, a contiguous, array implementation is reasonable. Of course, the maximum size of such an array must be specified in advance. Suppose, for example, we were willing to allow at most 200 elements in a stack. We could write

```
CONST  MAXSTACK  = 200 ;

TYPE     STACKTYPE = RECORD
                     STACKARRAY : ARRAY[1..MAXSTACK] OF ELEMENTTYPE ;
                     TOPOFSTACK : 0..MAXSTACK ;
                     UNDERFLOW,
                     OVERFLOW   : BOOLEAN
                 END ;

VAR      STACK      : STACKTYPE ;
```

Since TOPOFSTACK holds the subscript of the most recently pushed element, this value is the size of the stack. When TOPOFSTACK has a value of 0, the stack is empty—this is analogous to TOPOFSTACK'S being NIL in a dynamic linked-list implementation. UNDERFLOW plays the same role it did in the linked list implementation. OVERFLOW is initially FALSE, but will be changed to TRUE if an attempt is made to push when TOPOFSTACK = MAXSTACK. In Fig. 4.9 we show what a three-element stack might look like.

The five stack operations on page 109 can be handled as easily with an array implementation as with a linked list implementation. For example, we now present the PUSH and POP procedures.

```
PROCEDURE  PUSH(VAR  STACK : STACKTYPE ;
                     ELEMENT    : ELEMENTTYPE) ;
(* If STACK is full, STACK.OVERFLOW gets the value TRUE. *)
(* Otherwise, push onto the stack the value of ELEMENT.        *)
BEGIN

    WITH STACK DO
        IF TOPOFSTACK = MAXSTACK THEN
            OVERFLOW := TRUE
        ELSE
            BEGIN
                TOPOFSTACK                       := TOPOFSTACK + 1 ;
                STACKARRAY[TOPOFSTACK] := ELEMENT
            END

END ;   (* of the procedure PUSH. *)
```

```
PROCEDURE  POP(VAR  STACK     : STACKTYPE ;
                    VAR   ELEMENT : ELEMENTTYPE) ;
(* If STACK is empty, STACK.UNDERFLOW gets the value *)
(* TRUE. Otherwise, ELEMENT gets a copy of the top      *)
(* element on STACK.                                                *)
BEGIN

    WITH STACK DO
        IF TOPOFSTACK = 0 THEN
            UNDERFLOW := TRUE
        ELSE
            BEGIN
                ELEMENT      := STACKARRAY[TOPOFSTACK] ;
                TOPOFSTACK := TOPOFSTACK - 1
            END

END ;   (* of the procedure POP. *)
```

TOPOFSTACK   1   D

    3

                    2   P

UNDERFLOW

   FALSE   3   X

OVERFLOW

   FALSE   200   **Figure 4.9** An array implementation of a stack.

In the procedure POP, there is no need to delete the popped element from the stack since any array component with subscript greater than TOPOFSTACK will be ignored.

How does the dynamic linked-list implementation compare with the contiguous, array implementation with respect to time and space requirements? The linked-list implementation is substantially slower since its pushes and pops must call the predeclared procedures NEW and DISPOSE. Neither implementation is space-efficient: In a linked list, the pointer fields take up extra space; with an array, the maximum stack size must be specified and allocated in advance.

With each implementation, we hid the information about that implementation inside the five subprograms that actually manipulate the stack. Thus, if we wrote a program using one implementation and later decided to switch to the other implementation, the change could be made easily.

Exercise 4.6 If we use the above array implementation of a stack, why would it be incorrect to process pops as follows?

```
WITH STACK DO
    BEGIN
        ELEMENT     := STACKARRAY[TOPOFSTACK];
        TOPOFSTACK := TOPOFSTACK − 1 ;
        IF TOPOFSTACK < 0 THEN
            UNDERFLOW := TRUE
    END
```

Postfix Notation

We now consider an important application of stacks: translating an arithmetic expression from infix notation to postfix notation. In infix notation, the kind you are familiar with, an operator is placed between its operands. For example, if we temporarily restrict ourselves to single-letter identifiers, parentheses and the binary operators $+$, $-$, $*$, and $/$, then Fig. 4.10 shows several valid expressions in infix notation.

A + B
B – C * D
(B – C) * D
A – C – H / B * C
A – (C – H) / (B * C)   **Figure 4.10** Several expressions in infix notation.

The order in which operations are to be performed is determined by the usual rules for arithmetic:

1. Multiplication and division have higher precedence than addition and subtraction. For example, if we have

$$A - B * C$$

then the multiplication will be performed before the subtraction.
2. Within each precedence level, operations are performed from left to right. For example, if we have

$$A - B + C$$

then the subtraction will be performed before the addition.
3. Parentheses can be used to alter the order in which operations are performed. For example, if we have

$$A - (B + C)$$

then the addition will be performed before the subtraction.

In Fig. 4.11 we indicate how the expressions in Fig. 4.10 would be evaluated. In the expression B – C * D, the two operands for " – " are B and the product of C and D. In (B – C) * D the first operand for " * " is the difference between B and C; the second operand is D.

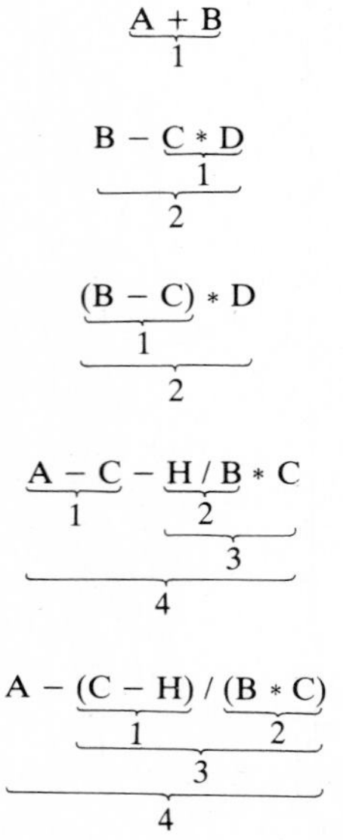

$$\frac{A + B}{1}$$

B – $\frac{C * D}{1}$

$$\underbrace{\qquad\qquad}_{2}$$

(B – C) * D
$$\underbrace{\quad 1 \quad}$$
$$\underbrace{\qquad\qquad}_{2}$$

A – C – H / B * C
  1   2
        3
  4

A – (C – H) / (B * C)
       1   2
           3
       4

Figure 4.11 The order in which each expression in Fig. 4.10 would be evaluated.

The translation of arithmetic (infix) expressions into machine language is one of the most noteworthy parts of a compiler. In fact, the most famous of the early compilers, FORTRAN (from FORmula TRANslator), was named for its ability to translate arithmetic formulas into machine language. Rather than directly translating infix expressions into machine language, modern compilers utilize an intermediate form known as *postfix notation* (invented by Jan Lukasiewicz, a Polish logician). In postfix notation, an operator is placed immediately after its operands, so parentheses are unnecessary and therefore not used. Figure 4.12 shows the postfix form for each of the expressions in Fig. 4.10.

In converting an infix expression such as

$$A + B - C * D$$

to postfix notation, the order of the operands is unchanged, so each operand can be moved to the postfix string as soon as it is encountered. Operators, on the other hand, must be placed after their operands, so when an operator is encountered in the infix expression, it must be temporarily saved. In fact, the position of an operator in the resulting postfix string cannot be determined until we know its precedence relative to the next operator in the original infix expression. Thus, when " + " is encountered above, we cannot move it (from its temporary storage place) to the postfix string until we see " − ". We then realize that " + " should be performed first and so we move it to postfix, which would then be "A B +". The " − " itself is now temporarily saved. When "*" is encountered, we know that " − " has a lower precedence than "*", so " − " should not be moved to postfix until after "*" has been moved there. Of course, "*" must be temporarily saved until its operands have been moved to the postfix string.

The temporary storage facility referred to in the previous paragraph is handled most conveniently by a stack. The rules governing the use of the operator stack are:

1. Initially, the stack is empty.
2. If an operator is encountered and the stack is empty, the operator is pushed onto the stack.
3. If the current operator has higher precedence than the operator on the top of the stack, the current operator is pushed onto the stack. Otherwise the operator on the top of the stack is popped to the postfix string; the current operator is then compared to the top of the stack (and either rule 2 or rule 3 will be applied.)

Infix	Postfix
A + B	AB+
A + B − C * D	AB+CD*−
(B − C) * D	BC−D*
A − C − H / B * C	AC−HB/C*−
A − (C − H) / (B * C)	ACH−BC*/−

Figure 4.12 Several expressions, both in infix and postfix form.

4. When the end of the infix expression has been reached the stack is popped to the postfix string until the stack is empty.

For example, the conversion of

$$A + B - C * D$$

to postfix is traced in Fig. 4.13.

How are parentheses handled? When a left parenthesis is encountered in the infix expression, it is immediately pushed onto the operator stack, but its precedence will be lower than any of the binary operators. When a right parenthesis is encountered, the stack is repeatedly popped to postfix until the corresponding left parenthesis is on the top of the stack. Then the left parenthesis is popped, both left and right parentheses are discarded and the scan of the infix expression is resumed. For example, Fig. 4.14 traces the steps in the conversion of

$$X - (Y - (A + B * Z) + D / H) * X$$

Current character	Operator stack	Postfix string
A	empty	A
+	+	A
B	+	AB
−	(+) −	AB+
C	(+) −	AB+C
*	* (+) −	AB+C
D	* (+) −	AB+CD
	(*) (+) −	AB+CD*
	(*) (+) (−)	AB+CD*−

Figure 4.13 The use of a stack in converting A + B − C * D to postfix notation.

Current character	Operator stack	Postfix string
X	empty	X
−	−	X
(	(−	X
Y	(−	XY
−	− (−	XY
(	(− (−	XY
A	(− (−	XYA
+	+ (− (−	XYA
B	+ (− (−	XYAB
*	* + (− (−	XYAB

Figure 4.14a Converting

$$X - (Y - (A + B * Z) + D/H) * X.$$

The process is continued in Figs. 4.13b and c.

	Operator stack	Postfix string
Z	* + (− (−	XYABZ
)	(*) (+) (() − (	XYABZ*+
+	(*) (+) (() (−) + (−	XYABZ*+−
D	(*) (+) (() (−) + (−	XYABZ*+−D
/	(*) (+) (() / (−) + (−	XYABZ*+−D
H	(*) (+) (() / (−) + (−	XYABZ*+−DH

Figure 4.14b Continuation of the conversion into postfix notation of

$$X - (Y - (A + B * Z) + D/H) * X.$$

)   ⊛ + (− (XYABZ*+−DH/+
      ⊘ +

*   ⊛ + (− (XYABZ*+−DH/+
      ⊘ +
       *

X   ⊛ + (− (−   XYABZ*+−DH/+X*−
      ⊘ +
       *

Figure 4.14*c* The final steps in the conversion into postfix notation of

$$X - (Y - (A + B * Z) + D/H) * X.$$

to postfix notation. A summary of the conversion process is shown in the table in Fig. 4.15.

Such a table is called a "transition table" because it directs the transition from infix notation to postfix notation. Paradoxically, it is easier to translate from infix to postfix to machine language than it is to translate directly from infix to machine language. That is because a direct infix-to-machine-language translation must continually scan back and forth over the infix expression to make sure

TOP CHARACTER ON STACK

		(	+,− .	*,/	Empty
	Identifier	MOVE TO POSTFIX	MOVE TO POSTFIX	MOVE TO POSTFIX	MOVE TO POSTFIX
	End of expression	ERROR	POP TO POSTFIX	POP TO POSTFIX	DONE
CURRENT CHARACTER	)	POP;PITCH '(' & ')'	POP TO POSTFIX	POP TO POSTFIX	ERROR
	(	PUSH	PUSH	PUSH	PUSH
	+,−	PUSH	POP TO POSTFIX	POP TO POSTFIX	PUSH
	*,/	PUSH	PUSH	POP TO POSTFIX	PUSH

Figure 4.15 The transition table for the infix-to-postfix conversion.

that the code is generated in the proper order according to the rules for arithmetic on page 118.

In the next case study we develop a program to convert simple infix expressions into postfix notation. We then show how easily the program can be modified to accommodate such features as the assignment operator and exponentiation.

Exercise 4.7 Translate each of the following infix expressions into postfix notation. Use a single-picture stack for temporary storage of operators.

a. A * B − H

b. A − B − H

c. A + B / H

d. A * B / H

e. X − (Y + A * Z)

f. X − (Y + A) * Z

g. X − (Y − (A + B * Z) + D / H) * X

h. (X − Y − (A + B)) * (Z − D) / H * X

CASE STUDY 4.1: CONVERTING FROM INFIX TO POSTFIX

Design and write a program to solve the following problem:

Problem

Given a list of arithmetic expressions in infix notation, convert each one to postfix notation.

Clarification Each line of input will contain an infix expression of at most 40 characters, left justified. For convenience in recognizing and handling the end of an expression, a semicolon will be inserted at the end of each infix expression. Other than that, the infix expression may not have any symbols except single-letter identifiers, parentheses, and the binary operators +, −, *, and /. The following errors should be detected:

1. It is an error if a left parenthesis does not have a subsequent matching right parenthesis. It is also an error if a right parenthesis does not have a preceding matching left parenthesis.

2. No identifier may be immediately preceded by either a right parenthesis or another identifier.

3. No operator may be immediately preceded by either a left parenthesis or another operator.
4. No left parenthesis may be immediately preceded by either an identifier or a right parenthesis.
5. No right parenthesis may be immediately preceded by either an operator or a left parenthesis.

If an expression violates any one of the above rules, an appropriate error message should be printed. Only the first such error in an infix expression need be detected.

Sample Input

```
X − Y + Z ;
X − (Y + Z) ;
X − Y(+ Z) ;
X − (Y − (A + B ∗ Z) + D / H) ∗ X ;
X − (Y − (A + B ∗ Z) + D / H ∗ X ;
A ∗ B + C / D − H ∗ I ;
```

Sample Output

```
INFIX EXPRESSION : X − Y + Z ;
POSTFIX EXPRESSION: XY − Z +
♭
♭
INFIX EXPRESSION : X − (Y + Z) ;
POSTFIX EXPRESSION: XYZ + −
♭
♭
INFIX EXPRESSION : X − Y(+ Z) ;
ERROR: LEFT PARENTHESIS PRECEDED BY IDENTIFIER OR RIGHT PARENTHESIS.
♭
♭
INFIX EXPRESSION : X − (Y − (A + B ∗ Z) + D / H) ∗ X ;
POSTFIX EXPRESSION: XYABZ ∗ + − DH / + X ∗ −
♭
♭
INFIX EXPRESSION : X − (Y − (A + B ∗ Z) + D / H ∗ X ;
ERROR : UNMATCHED PARENTHESIS.
♭
♭
INFIX EXPRESSION : A ∗ B + C / D − H ∗ I ;
POSTFIX EXPRESSION: AB ∗ CD / + HI ∗ −
```

Solution Tree The conversion process will be driven by the transition table in Fig. 4.15, so we must set up that table before we can perform any conversions.

After the transition table has been set up, we can read in the infix expressions and write out the postfix strings and error messages. This will be done in a loop, so our main tree starts out as shown in Fig. 4.16.

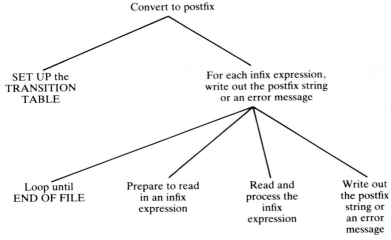

Figure 4.16 The initial version of the main tree.

What preparations must be made before we can read and process an infix expression and write out the postfix string or error message? The output decision rests on whether an error has been found in the infix expression, so we initially establish that no errors have been found so far. Furthermore, both the stack and the postfix string should initially be empty.

To read and process one infix expression, we loop until either a semicolon is reached or an error has been found. For each character read in, we apply the transition table to that character provided no errors have been found. But the transition table allows us to detect only the first kind of error (unmatched parenthesis), so the four positional errors must be checked *before* a given character has been processed via the transition table. Each positional error checks the previous character, so these checks should not be made the first time through the loop. At the end of one pass through the loop, the current character will be the previous character for the next pass through the loop.

The complete main tree is shown in Fig. 4.17.

The subtree SET UP TRANSITION TABLE will create the transition table shown in Fig. 4.15. The row and column subscripts are not the individual characters themselves because there are too many of them. Instead, the characters will be grouped together into different classes, called "tokens." A *token* is the smallest meaningful unit in a program. Thus, for this problem, we can think of the tokens as the following ordered list of values: IDENTIFIER, END OF EXPRESSION, RIGHT PARENTHESIS, LEFT PARENTHESIS, ADDING OPERATOR (for addition and subtraction), MULTIPLYING OPERATOR (for multiplication and division), and EMPTY.

The row and column subscripts will be the infix tokens and stack tokens, respectively. In the ordering of tokens just given, only the first six can represent the current character, and only the last four can represent the top character on the stack, so we need define only 24 table entries.

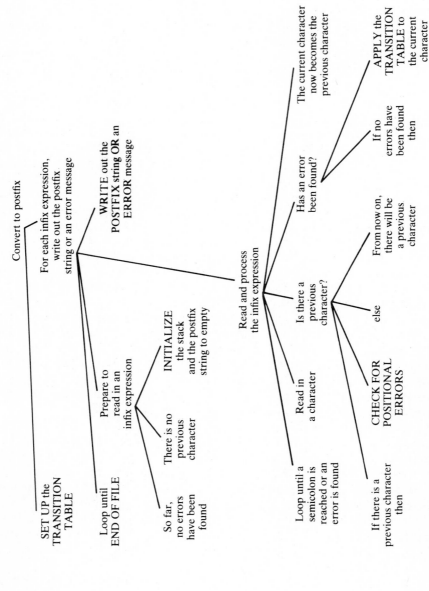

Figure 4.17 The main tree for converting from infix to postfix.

The component type for the table entries will also be enumerated, with values denoted by MOVE TO POSTFIX, PUSH ON STACK, POP TO POSTFIX, ERROR, POP AND PITCH, and DONE. We use PUSH ON STACK to distinguish this constant identifier from the procedure identifier PUSH.

The straightforward subtree is partly shown in Fig. 4.18.

We now develop the subtree CHECK FOR POSITIONAL ERRORS. From the current character's token and the previous character's token, we see if there is an incompatibility according to the four positional errors described in the Clarification. A separate function subtree, TOKEN, will determine, for a given character, the token class containing that character.

The CHECK FOR POSITIONAL ERRORS subtree is outlined in Fig. 4.19.

The APPLY TRANSITION TABLE subtree determines the infix token and processes that token in a loop. In the loop the stack token is determined and the action then taken depends on the corresponding table entry. Notice that the loop is executed more than once only if the table entry is POP TO POSTFIX; the loop is executed again so that the current character can be compared to the new character on the top of the stack. The ERROR entry applies only if we have an unmatched parenthesis. There is no action to be taken if the table entry is DONE.

According to the transition table in Fig. 4.14, a pop will take place only when there is something on the stack. Furthermore, we try to access the top element on the stack only if the stack is not empty. Thus, underflow is impossible, so we need not test for it in this subtree. We do not test for overflow here because the Clarification (pages 123–124) did not specify what action should be taken if the infix string, and thus the operator stack, gets too large. Of course, the PUSH procedure *will* still determine if overflow occurs in case the Clarification is later modified to require special action in the event of overflow.

The APPLY TRANSITION TABLE subtree is shown in Fig. 4.20.

The function subtree TOKEN returns the token class containing the given character. The token EMPTY is not included here because it is associated, not with a character, but with the condition of an empty stack.

The subtree is outlined in Fig. 4.21.

The action taken by the subtree WRITE POSTFIX OR ERROR depends on whether an error has been found in the infix expression. If no errors have been found, the postfix string is written out. Otherwise, the appropriate error message is written out.

The subtree is shown in Fig. 4.22.

Coding We choose the array implementation of a stack for the sake of increased speed (see page 117). The five associated subprograms were not included in the design because they were dependent on the implementation chosen.

The hierarchy chart for the program is given in Fig. 4.23. In the subsequent program, the five stack-related subprograms are all listed together for the sake of modularity. Thus the ordering of subprograms is slightly different from that indicated in the hierarchy chart.

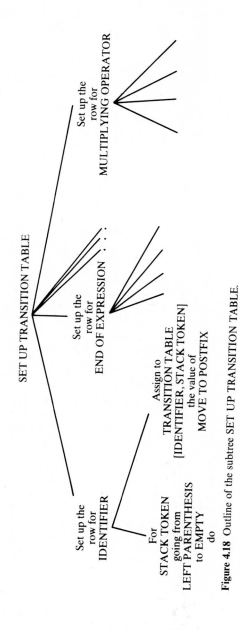

Figure 4.18 Outline of the subtree SET UP TRANSITION TABLE.

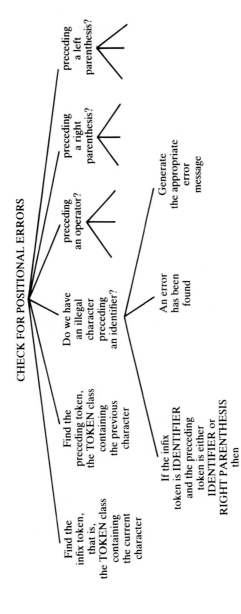

CHECK FOR POSITIONAL ERRORS

Find the
infix token,
that is,
the TOKEN class
containing
the current
character

Find the
preceding token,
the TOKEN class
containing
the previous
character

Do we have
an illegal
character
preceding
an identifier?

preceding
an operator?

preceding
a right
parenthesis?

preceding
a left
parenthesis?

If the infix
token is IDENTIFIER
and the preceding
token is either
IDENTIFIER or
RIGHT PARENTHESIS
then

An error
has been
found

Generate
the appropriate
error
message

Figure 4.19 Outline of the subtree CHECK FOR POSITIONAL ERRORS.

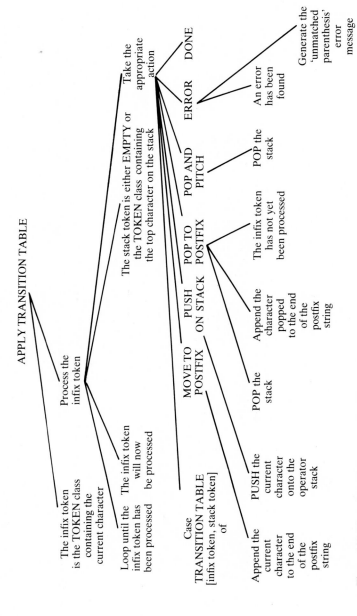

Figure 4.20 The subtree APPLY TRANSITION TABLE.

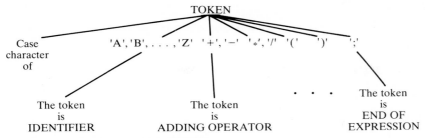

Figure 4.21 Outline of the subtree TOKEN.

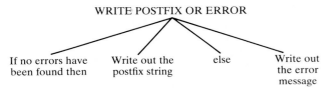

Figure 4.22 The subtree WRITE POSTFIX OR ERROR.

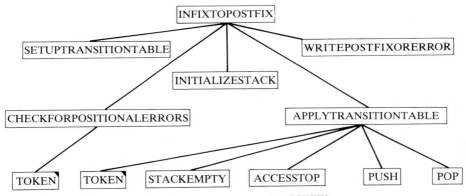

Figure 4.23 The hierarchy chart for the program INFIXTOPOSTFIX.

In the program, the stack and postfix string are arrays of single characters. We used the type identifier ELEMENTTYPE for the component type. Since ELEMENTTYPE is equated with CHAR in a type definition, we might just as well have used CHAR as the component type for this version of the program. But there are substantial advantages to using ELEMENTTYPE for a type identifier. If we later decide to alter the component type—for example, to use tokens or strings instead of characters—we need change only those parts of the program that manipulate the characters. This increased flexibility is clearly visible in the five stack subprograms: They may be viewed as a "package" that can be inserted into any program that manipulates stacks, regardless of the component type. We can even store them in a subprogram library and call them as needed in a stack related program.

```
PROGRAM  INFIXTOPOSTFIX(INPUT, OUTPUT);

(********************************************************************)
(*                                                                  *)
(*   PROGRAMMER : BILL COLLINS.                                     *)
(*                                                                  *)
(*     This program will solve the following problem: Given a list of *)
(*  arithmetic expressions in infix notation, convert each one to post- *)
(*  fix notation. Each line of input will contain an infix expression of *)
(*  of at most 40 characters, left-justified. A semicolon occurs at the *)
(*  end of each expression to aid in recognizing and handling the end of *)
(*  an expression.  Other than that, the infix expressions may not have *)
(*  any characters except single-letter identifiers, parentheses and the *)
(*  binary operators  +, -, *, and /.  Each of the following errors *)
(*  should generate an appropriate error message:                  *)
(*     1.  A left parenthesis without a subsequent matching right paren- *)
(*         thesis; a right parenthesis without a preceding matching left *)
(*         parenthesis.                                             *)
(*     2.  An identifier immediately preceded by either an identifier or *)
(*         a right parenthesis.                                    *)
(*     3.  An operator immediately preceded by either an operator or a *)
(*         left parenthesis.                                       *)
(*     4.  A left parenthesis immediately preceded by either an identi- *)
(*         fier or a right parenthesis.                            *)
(*     5.  A right parenthesis immediately preceded by either an opera- *)
(*         tor or a left parenthesis.                              *)
(*  Only the first such error in an infix expression need  be detected. *)
(*                                                                  *)
(********************************************************************)

CONST STRINGLENGTH        = 40;
      MAXSTACK            = STRINGLENGTH;
      EXPRESSIONTERMINATOR = ';';
      UNMATCHEDPARENTHESISERROR =
   'ERROR: UNMATCHED PARENTHESIS.                                   ';
      BEFOREIDENTIFIERERROR =
   'ERROR: IDENTIFIER PRECEDED BY IDENTIFIER OR RIGHT PARENTHESIS.  ';
      BEFOREOPERATORERROR =
   'ERROR: OPERATOR PRECEDED BY OPERATOR OR LEFT PARENTHESIS.       ';
      BEFORELEFTPARENTHESISERROR =
   'ERROR: LEFT PARENTHESIS PRECEDED BY IDENTIFIER OR RIGHT PARENTHESIS.';
      BEFORERIGHTPARENTHESISERROR =
   'ERROR: RIGHT PARENTHESIS PRECEDED BY OPERATOR OR LEFT PARENTHESIS. ';

TYPE  ELEMENTTYPE = CHAR;
      ERRORSTRING = PACKED ARRAY[1..68] OF CHAR;
      TOKENTYPE   = (IDENTIFIER, ENDOFEXPRESSION, RIGHTPARENTHESIS,
                     LEFTPARENTHESIS, ADDINGOPERATOR,
                     MULTIPLYINGOPERATOR, EMPTY);
      ACTION      = (MOVETOPOSTFIX, PUSHONSTACK, POPTOPOSTFIX,
                     POPANDPITCH, ERROR, DONE);
      INFIXRANGE  = IDENTIFIER..MULTIPLYINGOPERATOR;
      STACKRANGE  = LEFTPARENTHESIS..EMPTY;
      TABLE       = ARRAY[INFIXRANGE, STACKRANGE] OF ACTION;
      POSTFIXTYPE = RECORD
                       STRING : PACKED ARRAY[1..STRINGLENGTH] OF ELEMENTTYPE;
                       LENGTH : 0..STRINGLENGTH
                    END;
      STACKTYPE   = RECORD
                       STACKARRAY : ARRAY[1..MAXSTACK] OF ELEMENTTYPE;
                       TOPOFSTACK : 0..MAXSTACK;
                       UNDERFLOW,
                       OVERFLOW   : BOOLEAN
                    END;

VAR   CURRENTELEMENT, PREVIOUSELEMENT                   : ELEMENTTYPE;
      THEREISAPREVIOUSELEMENT, NOERRORSHAVEBEENFOUND : BOOLEAN;
      ERRORMESSAGE                                     : ERRORSTRING;
      TRANSITIONTABLE                                  : TABLE;
      POSTFIX                                          : POSTFIXTYPE;
      OPERATORSTACK                                    : STACKTYPE;
```

```
PROCEDURE  INITIALIZESTACK(VAR    STACK : STACKTYPE);

(*  Make STACK an empty stack.  *)

BEGIN

    WITH STACK DO
       BEGIN
          TOPOFSTACK := 0;
          UNDERFLOW  := FALSE;
          OVERFLOW   := FALSE
       END

END;  (*  of the procedure INITIALIZESTACK.  *)




PROCEDURE  PUSH(VAR    STACK : STACKTYPE;
               ELEMENT      : ELEMENTTYPE);

(*  If STACK is full, STACK.OVERFLOW gets the value TRUE.  *)
(*  Otherwise, push onto STACK the value of ELEMENT.       *)

BEGIN

    WITH STACK DO
       IF TOPOFSTACK = MAXSTACK THEN
          OVERFLOW := TRUE
       ELSE
          BEGIN
             TOPOFSTACK                := TOPOFSTACK + 1;
             STACKARRAY[TOPOFSTACK] := ELEMENT
          END

END;  (*  of the procedure PUSH.  *)




FUNCTION  STACKEMPTY(STACK : STACKTYPE) : BOOLEAN;

(*  Return TRUE or FALSE, depending on whether STACK is empty.  *)

BEGIN

    STACKEMPTY := STACK.TOPOFSTACK = 0

END;  (*  of the function STACKEMPTY.  *)




PROCEDURE  ACCESSTOP(VAR    STACK   : STACKTYPE;
                     VAR    ELEMENT : ELEMENTTYPE);

(*  If STACK is empty, STACK.UNDERFLOW gets the value TRUE.     *)
(*  Otherwise, ELEMENT gets a copy of the top element on STACK. *)

BEGIN

    WITH STACK DO
       IF TOPOFSTACK = 0 THEN
          UNDERFLOW := TRUE
       ELSE
          ELEMENT := STACKARRAY[TOPOFSTACK]

END;  (*  of the procedure ACCESSTOP.  *)
```

```
PROCEDURE  POP(VAR    STACK   : STACKTYPE;
               VAR    ELEMENT : ELEMENTTYPE);

(*  If STACK is empty, STACK.UNDERFLOW gets the value TRUE.     *)
(*  Otherwise, ELEMENT gets a copy of the top element on STACK  *)
(*  and then that top element is deleted.                       *)

BEGIN

    WITH STACK DO
        IF TOPOFSTACK = 0 THEN
            UNDERFLOW := TRUE
        ELSE
           BEGIN
              ELEMENT := STACKARRAY[TOPOFSTACK];
              TOPOFSTACK := TOPOFSTACK - 1
           END

END;  (*  of the procedure POP.  *)




FUNCTION  TOKEN(ELEMENT : ELEMENTTYPE) : TOKENTYPE;

(*  Return the token corresponding to the given    *)
(*  element.  The token "empty" is not included    *)
(*  here since it is associated, not with any      *)
(*  element, but with the condition of an empty    *)
(*  stack.                                         *)

BEGIN
    CASE ELEMENT OF
        'A','B','C','D','E','F',
        'G','H','I','J','K','L',
        'M','N','O','P','Q','R',
        'S','T','U','V','W','X',
                      'Y','Z' : TOKEN := IDENTIFIER;
                      '+','-' : TOKEN := ADDINGOPERATOR;
                      '*','/' : TOKEN := MULTIPLYINGOPERATOR;
                          '(' : TOKEN := LEFTPARENTHESIS;
                          ')' : TOKEN := RIGHTPARENTHESIS;
                          ';' : TOKEN := ENDOFEXPRESSION
    END

END;  (*  of the function TOKEN.  *)
```

```
PROCEDURE  SETUPTRANSITIONTABLE;

(*  Assign values to locations in the transition table. The       *)
(*  stack token "empty" means that the operator stack is empty.    *)
(*  This procedure has no parameters, but the variable             *)
(*  TRANSITIONTABLE is treated as a global constant.               *)

VAR    INFIXTOKEN : INFIXRANGE;
       STACKTOKEN : STACKRANGE;

BEGIN

    (*  Set up identifier row.  *)
    FOR STACKTOKEN := LEFTPARENTHESIS TO EMPTY DO
        TRANSITIONTABLE[IDENTIFIER, STACKTOKEN] := MOVETOPOSTFIX;

    (*  Set up endofexpression row.  *)
    TRANSITIONTABLE[ENDOFEXPRESSION, LEFTPARENTHESIS]       := ERROR;
    TRANSITIONTABLE[ENDOFEXPRESSION, ADDINGOPERATOR]        :=POPTOPOSTFIX;
    TRANSITIONTABLE[ENDOFEXPRESSION, MULTIPLYINGOPERATOR]   :=POPTOPOSTFIX;
    TRANSITIONTABLE[ENDOFEXPRESSION, EMPTY]                 := DONE;

    (*  Set up right parenthesis row.  *)
    TRANSITIONTABLE[RIGHTPARENTHESIS, LEFTPARENTHESIS]      :=POPANDPITCH;
    TRANSITIONTABLE[RIGHTPARENTHESIS, ADDINGOPERATOR]       :=POPTOPOSTFIX;
    TRANSITIONTABLE[RIGHTPARENTHESIS,MULTIPLYINGOPERATOR]   :=POPTOPOSTFIX;
    TRANSITIONTABLE[RIGHTPARENTHESIS, EMPTY]                := ERROR;

    (*  Set up leftparenthesis row.  *)
    FOR STACKTOKEN := LEFTPARENTHESIS TO EMPTY DO
        TRANSITIONTABLE[ LEFTPARENTHESIS, STACKTOKEN] := PUSHONSTACK;

    (*  Set up addingoperator row.  *)
    TRANSITIONTABLE[ADDINGOPERATOR, LEFTPARENTHESIS]        := PUSHONSTACK;
    TRANSITIONTABLE[ADDINGOPERATOR, ADDINGOPERATOR]         := POPTOPOSTFIX;
    TRANSITIONTABLE[ADDINGOPERATOR, MULTIPLYINGOPERATOR]    := POPTOPOSTFIX;
    TRANSITIONTABLE[ADDINGOPERATOR, EMPTY]                  := PUSHONSTACK;

    (*  Set up multiplyingoperator row.  *)
    TRANSITIONTABLE[MULTIPLYINGOPERATOR, LEFTPARENTHESIS]:= PUSHONSTACK;
    TRANSITIONTABLE[MULTIPLYINGOPERATOR, ADDINGOPERATOR] := PUSHONSTACK;
    TRANSITIONTABLE[MULTIPLYINGOPERATOR, MULTIPLYINGOPERATOR] :=
                                                  POPTOPOSTFIX;
    TRANSITIONTABLE[MULTIPLYINGOPERATOR, EMPTY]          := PUSHONSTACK

END;  (*  of the procedure SETUPTRANSITIONTABLE.  *)
```

```
PROCEDURE  CHECKFORPOSITICNALERRORS(CURRENTELEMENT,
                                    PREVIOUSELEMENT     : ELEMENTTYPE;
                                    VAR NOERRORSHAVEBEENFOUND: BOOLEAN;
                                    VAR ERRORMESSAGE    : ERRORSTRING);

(*  Check the CURRENTELEMENT in conjunction with the        *)
(*  PREVIOUSELEMENT to see if there is an incompatibility    *)
(*  according to the four positional errors described in the *)
(*  comments at the beginning of     this program. If an     *)
(*  error is discovered, the variable NOERRORSHAVEBEENFOUND is *)
(*  set to FALSE and ERRORMESSAGE gets the type of the error. *)

VAR   INFIXTOKEN, PRECEDINGTCKEN : INFIXRANGE;

BEGIN
    INFIXTOKEN     := TOKEN(CURRENTELEMENT);
    PRECEDINGTCKEN := TOKEN(PREVIOUSELEMENT);

    (*  Check for an error before an identifier.  *)
    IF (INFIXTOKEN = IDENTIFIER) AND (PRECEDINGTOKEN
         IN [IDENTIFIER, RIGHTPARENTHESIS]) THEN
        BEGIN
           NOERRORSHAVEBEENFOUND := FALSE;
           ERRORMESSAGE          := BEFOREIDENTIFIERERROR
        END;

    (*  Check for an error before an operator.  *)
    IF (INFIXTOKEN IN [ADDINGOPERATOR, MULTIPLYINGOPERATOR])
           AND (PRECEDINGTOKEN IN [LEFTPARENTHESIS,
           ADDINGOPERATOR, MULTIPLYINGOPERATOR]) THEN
        BEGIN
           NOERRORSHAVEBEENFOUND := FALSE;
           ERRORMESSAGE          := BEFOREOPERATORERROR
        END;

    (*  Check for an error before a right parenthesis.  *)
    IF (INFIXTOKEN = RIGHTPARENTHESIS) AND (PRECEDINGTOKEN
           IN [LEFTPARENTHESIS, ADDINGOPERATOR,
           MULTIPLYINGOPERATOR]) THEN
        BEGIN
           NOERRORSHAVEBEENFOUND := FALSE;
           ERRORMESSAGE          := BEFORERIGHTPARENTHESISERROR
        END;

    (*  Check for an error before a left parenthesis.  *)
    IF (INFIXTOKEN = LEFTPARENTHESIS) AND (PRECEDINGTCKEN
           IN [IDENTIFIER, RIGHTPARENTHESIS]) THEN
        BEGIN
           NOERRORSHAVEBEENFOUND := FALSE;
           ERRORMESSAGE          := BEFORELEFTPARENTHESISERROR
        END

END;  (*  of the procedure CHECKFORPOSITIONALERRORS.  *)
```

```
PROCEDURE  APPLYTRANSITIONTABLE(CURRENTELEMENT             : ELEMENTTYPE;
                               VAR POSTFIX                 : POSTFIXTYPE;
                               VAR OPERATORSTACK           : STACKTYPE;
                               VAR NOERRORSHAVEBEENFOUND: BOOLEAN;
                               VAR ERRORMESSAGE            : ERRORSTRING);

(*  Process the infix token( that is, the token corresponding to the   *)
(*  CURRENTELEMENT) by applying the transition table to that token     *)
(*  and the token for the top operator on the OPERATORSTACK. This      *)
(*  procedure is provided with the current element, the postfix        *)
(*  string and its current length, the operator stack, and a TRUE      *)
(*  value for the variable NOERRORSHAVEBEENFOUND. The procedure may     *)
(*  update any of these except the current element. In addition, if    *)
(*  an error is detected, it must be the unmatched parenthesis error,   *)
(*  so ERRORMESSAGE will get the appropriate value.                    *)

VAR    INFIXTOKEN        : INFIXRANGE;
       STACKTOKEN        : STACKRANGE;
       TOKENPROCESSED : BOOLEAN;
       TOPELEMENT        : ELEMENTTYPE;

BEGIN

   INFIXTOKEN := TOKEN(CURRENTELEMENT);

   (*  Process the infix token.  *)
   REPEAT
      TOKENPROCESSED := TRUE;

      (*  Determine the stack token.  *)
      IF STACKEMPTY(OPERATORSTACK) THEN
         STACKTOKEN := EMPTY
      ELSE
         BEGIN
            ACCESSTOP(OPERATORSTACK, TOPELEMENT);
            STACKTOKEN := TOKEN(TOPELEMENT)
         END;

      (*  Take action based on transition table entry.  *)
      CASE  TRANSITIONTABLE[INFIXTOKEN, STACKTOKEN] OF

         MOVETOPOSTFIX : WITH POSTFIX DO
                           BEGIN
                              LENGTH             := LENGTH + 1;
                              STRING[LENGTH] := CURRENTELEMENT
                           END;

         PUSHONSTACK   : PUSH(OPERATORSTACK, CURRENTELEMENT);

         POPTOPOSTFIX  : BEGIN
                           POP(OPERATORSTACK, TOPELEMENT);
                           WITH POSTFIX DO
                              BEGIN
                                 LENGTH             := LENGTH + 1;
                                 STRING[LENGTH] := TOPELEMENT
                              END;

                           (*  The loop must be executed again.  *)
                           TOKENPROCESSED := FALSE

                         END;
```

```
        POPANDPITCH      : POP(OPERATORSTACK, TOPELEMENT);

        ERROR            : BEGIN
                              NOERRORSHAVEBEENFOUND := FALSE;
                              ERRORMESSAGE      := UNMATCHEDPARENTHESISERROR
                           END;

        DONE             : (* Take no action. *)

     END (* of the CASE statement. *)

   UNTIL TOKENPROCESSED

END; (* of the procedure APPLYTRANSITIONTABLE. *)




PROCEDURE WRITEPOSTFIXORERROR( NOERRORSHAVEBEENFOUND : BOOLEAN;
                              POSTFIX               : POSTFIXTYPE;
                              ERRORMESSAGE          : ERRORSTRING);

(*  If NOERRORSHAVEBEENFOUND has the value TRUE, write out the *)
(*  POSTFIX string. Otherwise, read and echo print the rest of *)
(*  the infix string and then write out the ERRORMESSAGE.      *)

TYPE  COUNTER = 1..STRINGLENGTH;

VAR   I               : COUNTER;
      CURRENTELEMENT : ELEMENTTYPE;

BEGIN

        IF NOERRORSHAVEBEENFOUND THEN
           BEGIN

              (* Write out the postfix expression. *)
              WRITELN;
              WRITE('POSTFIX EXPRESSION: ');
              WITH POSTFIX DO
                 FOR I := 1 TO LENGTH DO
                    WRITE(STRING[I])
           END
        ELSE
           BEGIN

              (* Read and echo print the rest of the infix string. *)
              WHILE NOT EOLN DO
                 BEGIN
                    READ(CURRENTELEMENT);
                    WRITE(CURRENTELEMENT)
                 END;

              WRITELN;
              WRITE(ERRORMESSAGE)

           END;

        WRITELN;
        WRITELN;
        WRITELN

END; (* of the procedure WRITEPOSTFIXORERROR. *)
```

```
BEGIN  (*  The executable section of the main program.  *)

   PAGE;

   SETUPTRANSITIONTABLE;

   (*  Read and process all of the infix expressions     *)
   (*  and output the postfix strings and error messages.  *)
   WHILE NOT (EOF) DO
      BEGIN

         WRITE('INFIX EXPRESSION :  ');

         (*  Initialize some variables.  *)
         NOERRORSHAVEBEENFOUND   := TRUE;
         THEREISAPREVIOUSELEMENT := FALSE;
         POSTFIX.LENGTH          := 0;
         INITIALIZESTACK(OPERATORSTACK);

         (*  Read and process one infix expression.  *)
         REPEAT

            READ(CURRENTELEMENT);
            WRITE(CURRENTELEMENT);

            (*  Is there a previous element?  *)
            IF THEREISAPREVIOUSELEMENT THEN
               CHECKFORPOSITIONALERRORS(CURRENTELEMENT, PREVIOUSELEMENT,
                                        NOERRORSHAVEBEENFOUND, ERRORMESSAGE)
            ELSE
               THEREISAPREVIOUSELEMENT := TRUE;

            IF NOERRORSHAVEBEENFOUND THEN
               APPLYTRANSITIONTABLE (CURRENTELEMENT, POSTFIX, OPERATORSTACK,
                                     NOERRORSHAVEBEENFOUND, ERRORMESSAGE);

            PREVIOUSELEMENT := CURRENTELEMENT

         UNTIL (CURRENTELEMENT = EXPRESSIONTERMINATOR) OR
               (NOERRORSHAVEBEENFOUND = FALSE);

         (*  Write out the postfix string or an error message.  *)
         WRITEPOSTFIXORERROR(NOERRORSHAVEBEENFOUND, POSTFIX, ERRORMESSAGE);

         (*  Prepare to read in the next infix string.  *)
         READLN

      END;

   PAGE
END.
```

Program Testing

1. Testing the main program:

   Test 1a
   ————

   (no input)

   Test 1b
   ————

   A + B ;
   A ;

2. Testing CHECKFORPOSITIONALERRORS (and TOKEN): Each of the four positional errors was tested, along with several valid inputs.

   Test 2a
   ————

   A * B − C + D ;
   A * BC + D ;
   A + (B − (C * D − E / F + (G − H) − (I + J * (K − L))) * M − N) ;
   A + (B − C)D ;
   A + (B − C) * D ;
   X − * Y ;
   A * B + (* C) ;
   X + Y(* Z) ;
   X * (Y + Z)(+ A) ;
   A * (B −) ;
   A + ( ) ;

3. Testing APPLYTRANSITIONTABLE (and SETUPTRANSITIONTABLE and the five stack subprograms): Each of the 24 entries in the transition table was tested.

   Test 3a
   ————

   X − (A + B * (C + D) − E / F ;
   A + B * C + D) ;
   A + (B − C)) * D ;
   A − (B ;
   A * B − C + D ;
   A + (B − (C * D − E / F + (G − H) − (I + J * (K − L))) * M − N) ;
   (A) ;
   A ;
   ((((A)))) ;
   A * (B / C) ;
   A * B + C − X * Y * Z − G ;

Notes on Case Study 4.1

1. Several programming languages have a mechanism by which constant arrays can be defined prior to execution time—FORTRAN's DATA statement, COBOL's VALUE clause and PL/I's INITIAL attribute are examples. Since

Standard Pascal has no such facility, we had to declare TRANSITION-TABLE to be an array variable and explicitly assign values to its components. The use of that array as a global variable was justified because it was treated as if it were a constant array. Under normal circumstances, any variable used in a procedure should be either local to the procedure or one of the procedure's formal parameters. Global variables in a procedure usually reflect poor communication between a procedure and its calling program.

2. The array TRANSITIONTABLE had only six rows and four columns because the 26 letters were grouped together into the token IDENTIFIER. How many locations would have been needed if we had used the characters themselves instead of tokens? Since Pascal has no standard collating sequence, the only data type that would necessarily include letters,'+,' '−,' '∗,' '/,' and ';' is CHAR itself! The declaration

VAR   TRANSITIONTABLE : ARRAY[CHAR,CHAR] OF ACTION ;

could then require as many as $256 ∗ 256$ locations, depending on the collating sequence used. Such an array, even when packed, could exceed the memory available for variables on some versions of Pascal.

Exercise 4.8 Modify the above program to accommodate the following additional requirements:

1. Each error should be explicitly noted; for example,

X − Y(+ Z) ;

should generate the message

ERROR: LEFT PARENTHESIS PRECEDED BY IDENTIFIER

Similarly, 'UNMATCHED PARENTHESIS' should be replaced by 'UNMATCHED LEFT PARENTHESIS' or 'UNMATCHED RIGHT PARENTHESIS,' whichever is appropriate.
2. Include error detection for the following:
   (*a*) The first character should not be an operator.
   (*b*) The last character before the semicolon should not be an operator.
   (*c*) The infix expression should not be more than 40 characters long.
   (*d*) The infix expression should not contain illegal symbols.
3. Allow the infix expression to contain blank characters. They should, of course, be passed over in the processing of the infix expression.

Exercise 4.9 An expression in postfix notation can be evaluated with the help of an additional stack, called a "run stack" since the evaluation takes place at run time. Each operand's value is pushed onto the run stack when it is encountered in the postfix string. When a binary operator is encountered, the top two values are popped from the run stack, the binary operator is applied to them, and the result is pushed onto the stack.

For example, suppose the original infix expression is

A + B * C − D

In postfix notation, we would have

ABC * + D −

If A, B, C, and D have run-time values of 3, 4, 5, and 6, respectively, the evaluation would proceed as follows:

1. The values of A, B, and C would be pushed:

    5
    4
    3

2. When "*" is encountered, 4 and 5 are popped from the stack and multiplied; the product is then pushed onto the stack:

    20
     3

3. When "+" is encountered, 20 and 3 are popped from the stack and added; the sum is pushed onto the stack:

    23

4. The value of D is pushed onto the stack:

     6
    23

5. When "−" is encountered, 6 and 23 are popped and 6 is subtracted from 23; the difference is pushed:

    17

Thus, 17 is the value of the expression (both in infix and in postfix notations). Evaluate each of the following expressions. Assume that the values of A, B, C, and D are 3, 4, 5, and 6, respectively.

a. AB + C * D −

b. ABCD + * −

c. AB + CD * −

HANDLING TOKENS

In the above program the postfix expression contained characters instead of tokens. This was appropriate since the output was to contain the characters arranged in postfix notation. In an actual Pascal compiler, the characters in the input string would be ignored after they were grouped into tokens. The token classes are:

1. identifier
2. unsigned number
3. directive
4. label
5. character string
6. special symbol

where the class "special symbol" includes reserved words (also called *word symbols*), parentheses, operators, brackets, and delimiters (semicolon, comma, colon, period, and double period).

The structure of tokens varies widely among compilers. Typically, each token has a generic part to indicate its class and a specific part that contains an address where more information may be found. For example, the specific part of an identifier's token could contain an address into a table, called a *symbol table*. At that address would be stored the identifier, its type, initial value, and other information helpful to the compiler. For example, we could define

```
TYPE   TOKENCLASS  = (IDENTIFIER, UNSIGNEDNUMBER, DIRECTIVE, LABELCLASS,
                      CHARACTERSTRING, RESERVEDWORD, OTHERSPECIALSYMBOL) ;
       SMALLSTRING = PACKED ARRAY[1..2] OF CHAR ;

       TOKEN       = RECORD
                       CASE CLASS: TOKENCLASS OF
                         IDENTIFIER          : (IDPOINTER :
                                                  SYMBOLTABLEADDRESS) ;
                         UNSIGNEDNUMBER      : (NUMBERPOINTER :
                                                  CONSTANTTABLEADDRESS) ;
                         DIRECTIVE           : (POINTERTODIRECTIVE :
                                                  SYMBOLTABLEADDRESS) ;
                         LABELCLASS          : (LABELVALUE :
                                                  0..9999) ;
                         CHARACTERSTRING     : (STRINGPOINTER :
                                                  STRINGSPACEADDRESS) ;
                         RESERVEDWORD        : (WORDPOINTER :
                                                  SYMBOLTABLEADDRESS) ;
                         OTHERSPECIALSYMBOL : (SYMBOLRECORD :
                                                  RECORD
                                                    SYMBOL : SMALLSTRING ;
                                                    PRIORITY : 0...10
                                                  END)
                     END ;
```

Notice that we split the class "special symbol" into reserved words (with a pointer to the symbol table) and "other" special symbols. For elements of this latter group, we include the symbol itself (two characters, left justified) and its priority.

These uniform-length tokens would then be used instead of the characters themselves. A "push," for example, would cause a token to be pushed onto the operator stack. The postfix string would then consist of tokens only. We will use this approach in subsequent discussions, without specifying the form of the tokens.

EXTENSIONS TO THE POSTFIX CONVERSION ALGORITHM

Let us now extend the above conversion process. We adopt the approach just indicated, namely that infix characters are immediately converted into tokens and all subsequent processing is done to the tokens, not to the characters themselves.

We first consider the assignment operator, represented in Pascal and Ada by ":=", in BASIC, COBOL, and FORTRAN by "=" and in APL by "←." Since the processing involves tokens only, the particular representation is irrelevant for our purposes, except that ":=" is interesting to consider because it suggests the possibility of writing a Pascal compiler in Pascal!† When the token for the assignment operator is encountered, it is pushed onto the stack. Since this should be the last operation performed in an assignment statement, it is given a lower precedence than other operators. The new version of the Transition Table is shown in Fig. 4.24.

Exponentiation is not available in most versions of Pascal, but it is a commonplace arithmetic operation and is available in most programming languages,

---

† It would be silly to write a Pascal program to compile any Pascal program into machine language because the compiler itself would first have to be compiled into machine language. However, it is possible and even commonplace to write a "bootstrap" compiler—a compiler for a mini version of a language which is then used in developing a compiler for the full language. We would start with a subset of Pascal from which we could define every feature not in the subset. For example, the subset would include the REPEAT and IF statements but not the FOR, WHILE or CASE statements, since these can be defined in terms of REPEAT and IF. We would need a compiler to translate any "mini-Pascal" program into machine language. This compiler could be written in assembly language, for example (or, as Wirth himself did, in FORTRAN). Naturally, a compiler for mini-Pascal would be much simpler to write than a compiler for all of Pascal. We could then write a compiler for Pascal in mini-Pascal and our task would be complete, as the following picture shows:

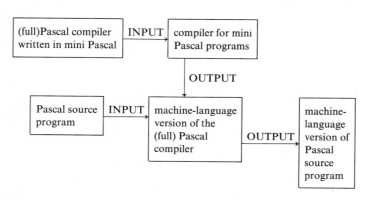

INFIX TOKEN	STACK TOKEN				
	Left parenthesis	Adding operator	Multiplying operator	Assignment operator	Empty
Identifier	MOVE TO POSTFIX	MOVE TO POSTFIX	MOVE TO POSTFIX	MOVE TO POSTFIX	MOVE TO POSTFIX
End of expression	ERROR	POP TO POSTFIX	POP TO POSTFIX	POP TO POSTFIX	DONE
Right parenthesis	POP AND PITCH	POP TO POSTFIX	POP TO POSTFIX	ERROR	ERROR
Left parenthesis	PUSH	PUSH	PUSH	PUSH	PUSH
Adding operator	PUSH	POP TO POSTFIX	POP TO POSTFIX	PUSH	PUSH
Multiplying operator	PUSH	PUSH	POP TO POSTFIX	PUSH	PUSH
Assignment operator	ERROR	ERROR	ERROR	ERROR	PUSH

Figure 4.24 Transition Table, including assignment operator.

so we will now consider it. Again, the programmatic representation (usually " ↑ " or "∗∗") is irrelevant since the tokens are processed. One issue to be decided is the order in which exponentiations are performed. In arithmetic, exponentiations are performed from right to left, so

$$2^{2^4} = 2^{16} = 65536$$

whereas $(2^2)^4 = 256$. FORTRAN, PL/I, APL, and COBOL perform exponentiations from right to left, but ALGOL and BASIC perform exponentiations from left to right. The significance of the distinction is this: If the infix token is exponentiation and the stack token is exponentiation, a right-to-left evaluation prescribes a PUSH (so the latter exponentiation will be performed before the earlier one), whereas a left-to-right scheme mandates a POP TO POSTFIX.

> **Exercise 4.10** Determine the exponentiation row and the exponentiation column in a transition table extended from Fig. 4.24. Exponentiations should be evaluated from right to left and should have a higher priority than multiplications and divisions.

QUEUES

A *queue* is a list in which insertions are made at one end, called the "tail," and deletions are made at the other end, called the "head." For example, the planes waiting to take off from an airport form a queue, with planes getting in line at the tail and taking off from the head of the list. The customers at a checkout counter also form a queue, as does the list of programs waiting for an available tape drive. In a queue the first to enter will be the first to leave, so we say that a queue is a "First In, First Out" list—FIFO for short.

There are exactly five operations that can be performed on a queue, and they are almost identical to the five stack operations. The queue operations are:

1. Initialize the queue, to make it empty.
2. Insert an element at the tail of the queue.
3. Test the queue to see if it is empty.
4. Access the element at the head of the queue.
5. Delete the element at the head of the queue.

Figure 4.25 shows a queue through several stages of insertions and deletions.

Exercise 4.11 Make the following changes to the queue shown in Fig. 4.25*d*:
(*a*) Delete Suzy
(*b*) Insert Dawn.

Queue Implementations

Just as with a stack, a queue may be implemented with a linked list or a contiguous list. For a dynamic linked-list implementation of a queue of elements, we could have

Brian	Jane	Suzy	Bob	Tom	Elly	Karen

HEAD   TAIL

(*a*) A queue with seven elements.

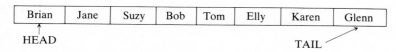

(*b*) After Glenn is inserted.

(*c*) After Brian is deleted.

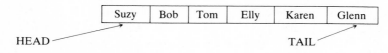

(*d*) After Jane is deleted.

Figure 4.25 A queue through several stages of insertions and deletions.

```
TYPE   POINTER        = ^QUEUERECORD ;
       QUEUERECORD =   RECORD
                           ELEMENT : ELEMENTTYPE ;
                           NEXT     : POINTER
                       END ;

       QUEUETYPE      = RECORD
                           HEAD, TAIL              : POINTER ;
                           UNDERFLOW, OVERFLOW  : BOOLEAN
                       END ;

VAR    QUEUE : QUEUETYPE ;
```

We define an empty queue to be one in which both HEAD and TAIL are NIL. The five queue operations can be straightforwardly implemented. For example, here is a procedure to implement insertion in a queue. Note that we do not test for overflow since we do not know the size of the heap.

```
PROCEDURE   QUEUEINSERTION(VAR   QUEUE : QUEUETYPE ;
                          ELEMENT     : ELEMENTTYPE) ;

(* Insert at the tail of QUEUE the value of ELEMENT. *)

BEGIN
    WITH  QUEUE  DO
        BEGIN

            (* Is the queue empty? *)
            IF  (HEAD = NIL)  AND  (TAIL = NIL)  THEN
                BEGIN
                    NEW(TAIL) ;
                    HEAD := TAIL
                END
            ELSE
                BEGIN
                    NEW(TAIL^.NEXT) ;
                    TAIL := TAIL^.NEXT
                END ;

            (* Fill in values in the tail's fields. *)
            TAIL^.ELEMENT := ELEMENT ;
            TAIL^.NEXT     := NIL
        END
END ;   (* of the procedure QUEUEINSERTION. *)
```

For example, suppose that the queue were empty and ELEMENTTYPE was a record type with a name and cost fields. If ELEMENT contained

TED WILLIAMS	48.13

and we called QUEUEINSERTION(QUEUE, ELEMENT), the result would be the queue shown in Fig. 4.26. If ELEMENT later contained

KAYE HOLLOWAY	61.25

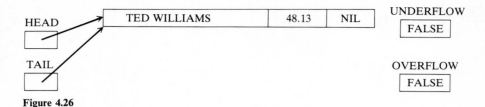

Figure 4.26

and we called QUEUEINSERTION(QUEUE, ELEMENT), we would get the queue shown in Fig. 4.27.

Since deletions take place at the head of the queue, the procedure QUEUE-DELETION is similar to the procedure POP developed earlier (page 115). The only new feature is that a deletion from a single-element queue requires that TAIL, as well as HEAD, be set to NIL.

```
PROCEDURE  QUEUEDELETION(VAR  QUEUE    : QUEUETYPE ;
                        VAR  ELEMENT : ELEMENTTYPE) ;

(* If QUEUE is empty, QUEUE.UNDERFLOW gets the value TRUE. *)
(* Otherwise, ELEMENT gets a copy of the element at the head      *)
(* of QUEUE and that element is then deleted.                     *)

VAR  NEWHEAD : POINTER ;

BEGIN

    WITH QUEUE DO
        IF (HEAD = NIL) AND (TAIL = NIL) THEN
            UNDERFLOW := TRUE
        ELSE

            (* The deletion can be made. *)
            BEGIN
                ELEMENT := HEAD^.ELEMENT ;

                (* Is this a single-element queue? *)
                IF  HEAD = TAIL  THEN
                    BEGIN
                        DISPOSE(HEAD) ;
                        HEAD := NIL ;
                        TAIL := NIL
                    END
                ELSE
                    BEGIN
                        NEWHEAD := HEAD^.NEXT ;
                        DISPOSE(HEAD) ;
                        HEAD := NEWHEAD
                    END
            END

END ;   (* of the procedure QUEUEDELETION. *)
```

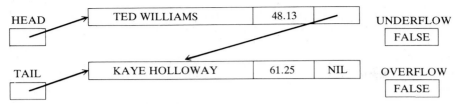

Figure 4.27 A dynamic implementation of a two-element queue.

If, for example, we start with the queue shown in Fig. 4.27, and call QUEUE-DELETION(QUEUE, ELEMENT), the result would be the queue shown in Fig. 4.28. If the procedure were called again, we would get an empty queue: Both HEAD and TAIL would have the value NIL. If the procedure were called another time, UNDERFLOW would get the value TRUE, indicating that no deletion took place.

Exercise 4.12 Why would it be incorrect to use the following statements to delete the only record in a single-element queue?

```
NEWHEAD := HEAD ;
HEAD     := HEAD^.NEXT;
DISPOSE   (NEWHEAD)
```

A dynamic implementation, such as the one above, permits a queue of arbitrary size, bounded only by the size of the heap. If we choose instead to implement a queue contiguously, by an array, the maximum queue size must be specified in advance, such as:

```
CONST   MAXQUEUE = 200 ;

TYPE    QUEUETYPE = RECORD
                    QUEUEARRAY : ARRAY[1..MAXQUEUE] OF ELEMENTTYPE ;
                    HEAD, TAIL    : 0..MAXQUEUE ;
                    UNDERFLOW,
                    OVERFLOW     : BOOLEAN
                END ;

VAR     QUEUE : QUEUETYPE ;
```

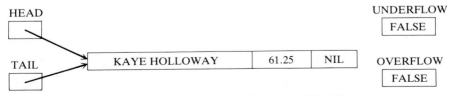

Figure 4.28 The queue resulting from a deletion to the queue in Fig. 4.27.

Here, an empty queue means that both HEAD and TAIL have a value of 0. Just as with the linked-list representation, an insertion is in an empty queue and a deletion from a single-element queue are special cases since both HEAD and TAIL must be adjusted.

Typically, an insertion causes TAIL to increase by one and a deletion causes HEAD to increase by one. For example, suppose that we had the five-element queue shown in Fig. 4.29.

If three insertions and four deletions were now made, we would get the queue shown in Fig. 4.30.

Notice that the list tends to slide down the array. This is because HEAD and TAIL are incremented but never decremented. Eventually, we could get something such as the six-customer queue shown in Figure 4.31.

How should the next insertion be handled? Since there is plenty of space left in the array, setting OVERFLOW to TRUE would be inappropriate. Instead, we

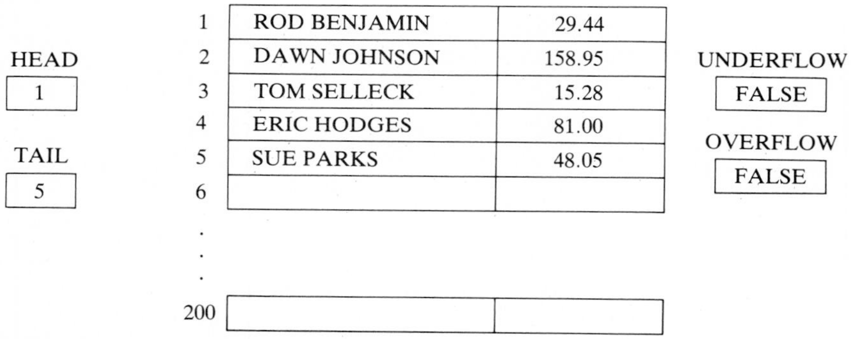

1	ROD BENJAMIN	29.44	
HEAD	2	DAWN JOHNSON	158.95
1	3	TOM SELLECK	15.28
	4	ERIC HODGES	81.00
TAIL	5	SUE PARKS	48.05
5	6		

HEAD

1

TAIL

5

UNDERFLOW

FALSE

OVERFLOW

FALSE

Figure 4.29 An array implementation of a five-element queue.

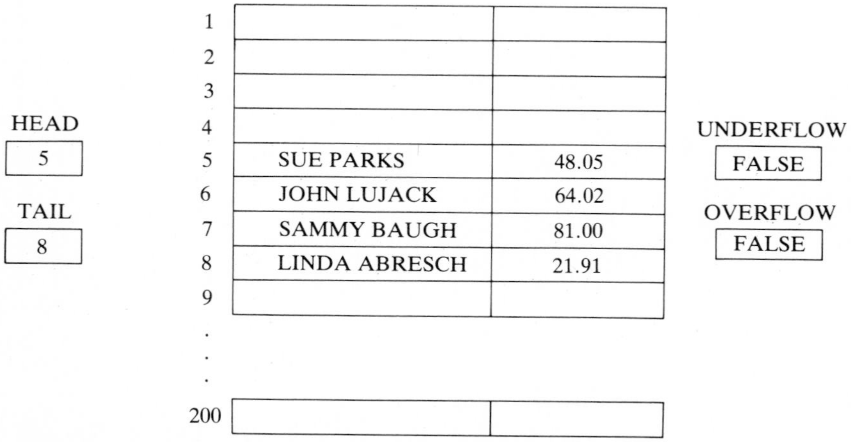

HEAD

5

TAIL

8

1		
2		
3		
4		
5	SUE PARKS	48.05
6	JOHN LUJACK	64.02
7	SAMMY BAUGH	81.00
8	LINDA ABRESCH	21.91
9		

UNDERFLOW

FALSE

OVERFLOW

FALSE

Figure 4.30 An array implementation of a four-element queue.

	1		

HEAD

195

TAIL

200

	194		
	195	BARBARA MALCHOW	47.18
	196	MARY LUKE	54.05
	197	LISA STAMP	7.55
	198	BRIAN DONOVAN	50.75
	199	NED GARVER	161.14
	200	JILL PETERS	91.07

UNDERFLOW

FALSE

OVERFLOW

FALSE

Figure 4.31 An array implementation of a six-element queue.

1	NORINE COLE	28.77
2		

HEAD

195

TAIL

1

194		
195	BARBARA MALCHOW	47.18
196	MARY LUKE	54.05
197	LISA STAMP	7.55
198	BRIAN DONOVAN	50.75
199	NED GARVER	161.14
200	JILL PETERS	91.07

Figure 4.32 A seven-element queue: Norine Cole comes after Jill Peters.

simply set TAIL equal to 1 and make the insertion at the very beginning of the array, as shown in Fig. 4.32.

What we have now is a *circular* queue since position 1 is, in effect, the successor of position 200.

Queue overflow will occur if an insertion is attempted when the head occupies the position where the tail's successor should go. For example, if HEAD is 195 and TAIL is 194, then the next insertion belongs in position 195, but this is already occupied (by the head), so we have an overflow condition. In general, overflow would occur if, just prior to an insertion, either TAIL + 1 = HEAD or TAIL = MAXQUEUE and HEAD = 1, in other words, if (TAIL MOD MAXQUEUE) + 1 = HEAD.

We now develop a procedure to insert an element in a circular queue. We have discussed the possibility that the attempt might fail because of overflow.

Otherwise, the attempt will succeed and the insertion procedure is analogous to the linked-list version on page 147.

```
PROCEDURE  QUEUEINSERTION(VAR  QUEUE : QUEUETYPE ;
                            ELEMENT   : ELEMENTTYPE) ;
(* If QUEUE is already full, then QUEUE.OVERFLOW gets the *)
(* value TRUE. Otherwise, the element is inserted at the    *)
(* tail of QUEUE.                                           *)
BEGIN

    WITH QUEUE DO

        (* Is the queue already full? *)
        IF (TAIL MOD MAXQUEUE) + 1 = HEAD THEN
            OVERFLOW := TRUE
        ELSE
            BEGIN   (* The insertion will be made. *)

                (* Is the queue now empty? *)
                IF (HEAD = 0) AND (TAIL = 0) THEN
                    BEGIN
                        HEAD := 1 ;
                        TAIL  := 1
                    END
                ELSE
                    TAIL := (TAIL MOD MAXQUEUE) + 1 ;

                QUEUEARRAY[TAIL] := ELEMENT

            END

END ;   (* of the procedure QUEUEINSERTION. *)
```

In spite of its overflow-checking and modular arithmetic, the above procedure executes faster than the linked-list version on page 147. That is because insertion in a linked list requires a call to the procedure NEW.

Exercise 4.13 Develop a procedure to delete an element from a circular queue.

COMPUTER SIMULATION

A *system* is a collection of interacting parts. We are often interested in studying the behavior of a system, for example, an economic system, a political system, an ecological system or even a computer system. Because systems are usually complicated, we may utilize a model to make our task manageable. A *model*, that is, a simplification of a system, is designed so that we may study the behavior of the system.

A physical model is similar to the system it represents, except in scale or intensity. For example, we might create a physical model of tidal movements in the Chesapeake Bay or of a proposed shopping center. War games and scrimmages are also examples of physical models. Unfortunately, some systems cannot be modelled physically with currently available technology—there is, as yet, no physical substance that could be expected to behave like the weather. Often, as with pilot training, a physical model may be too expensive, too dangerous, or simply inconvenient.

Sometimes we may be able to represent the system with a mathematical model: a set of assumptions and equations. A mathematical model is certainly more tractable than a physical model. In many cases, such as DISTANCE = RATE * TIME and the pythagorean theorem, the mathematical model can be solved analytically in a reasonable amount of time. Many mathematical models, however, do not have such a handy solution. For example, most differential equations cannot be solved analytically, and an economic model with thousands of equations cannot be solved by hand in a reasonable period of time.

In such cases the mathematical model is usually solved on a computer. Computer models are essential in complex systems such as weather forecasting, space flight, and urban planning. The use of computer models is called "computer simulation." Some advantages of computer models over physical models are

1. *Safety.* Flight simulators can assail pilot trainees with a welter of dangerous situations such as hurricanes and hijackings, but no one gets hurt.†
2. *Economy.* Simulation games such as the *Business Management Laboratory* (Jenson, 1977) enable students to run a hypothetical company in competition with other students. If the company goes "belly up," the only recrimination is a lower grade for the students.
3. *Speed.* The computer makes predictions soon enough for you to act on them. This feature is essential in almost every simulation, from the stock market to national defense.
4. *Flexibility.* If the results you get do not conform to the system you are studying, all you have to do is change your model. This feedback‡ feature is shown in Fig. 4.33.

† Except once, when a trainee panicked because one of his engines failed during a blizzard. He "bailed out" of his simulated cockpit and broke his ankle when he hit the floor.

‡ *Feedback* is a process in which the factors that produce a result are themselves affected by that result.

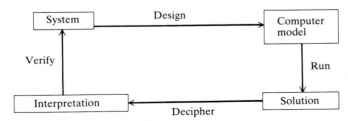

Figure 4.33 Feedback in computer simulation.

The above benefits are so compelling that computer simulation has become the accepted method for studying complex systems. This is not to say that computer simulation is a panacea for all systems problems. The simplification required to model a system automatically introduces a disparity between the model and the system. And, of course, prediction is always a risky business. For these reasons, a disclaimer such as the following usually precedes the results of a computer simulation : "If the relationships among the variables are as described and if the initial conditions are as described, then the consequences will probably be as follows...."

Many simulations involve queues: traffic at toll booths, checkout lines at supermarkets, airplanes in a holding pattern, and so on. The first problem in the Problems section deals with simulating a queue of cars at a car wash.

PROBLEMS

Problem 4.1 A Simulated Car Wash

Design and write a program to solve the following problem: Simulate traffic flow at Speedo's Car Wash. The input consists of the number of minutes during which cars may arrive and a list of arrival times.† There is one station in the car wash, and each car takes exactly ten minutes getting washed. At any time there can be at most five cars waiting to be washed—if another car arrives then, it is turned away and considered an "overflow"; the technical term for this situation is "balking." The output should consist of the arrivals and departures as they occur as well as the following summary statistics: the average queue length, the average waiting time per customer, and the number of overflows.

Clarification The arrival and departure times will be listed in whole minutes from the beginning of the simulation. For each arrival and departure, there should be one line of output, with the time of the event, either the word "ARRIVAL" all by itself, the words "ARRIVAL—OVERFLOW" (if the car just arriving is turned away), or the word "DEPARTURE" followed by the time elapsed since that car's arrival (that is, the time spent waiting in the queue plus the ten minutes getting washed). If a car arrives when the queue is empty and no cars are being washed, the car starts getting washed—it is not put on the queue. If an arrival and departure occur during the same minute, the departure is processed first.

The average queue length is found by adding up the queue lengths at the end of each minute of the simulation and dividing by the total number of minutes (until the last departure). Alternatively, the average queue length can be calculated by adding up the number of minutes each customer was on the queue and dividing by the total number of minutes. The average waiting time is determined by adding up the waiting times for each customer and dividing by the number of

---

† A method for generating these arrival times is considered on pages 157–159.

customers served. *Note*: A customer leaves the queue (and stops waiting) once the car starts through the ten-minute wash cycle. The average queue length and average waiting time should be rounded to one fractional digit.

Sample Input

300	(total number of minutes during which arrivals may occur)
28	
40	
70	
70	
95	
100	
114	
116	
121	
125	
125	
151	
153	
154	
154	
159	
162	
166	
170	
198	
199	
202	
212	
237	
242	
255	
291	
295	

Sample Output

THE SIMULATED CAR WASH WILL ACCEPT CUSTOMERS FOR 300 MINUTES.

♭

♭

TIME	EVENT		ELAPSED TIME
28	ARRIVAL		
38		DEPARTURE	10
40	ARRIVAL		
50		DEPARTURE	10
70	ARRIVAL		
70	ARRIVAL		
80		DEPARTURE	10
90		DEPARTURE	20

95	ARRIVAL		
100	ARRIVAL		
105		DEPARTURE	10
114	ARRIVAL		
115		DEPARTURE	15
116	ARRIVAL		
121	ARRIVAL		
125		DEPARTURE	11
125	ARRIVAL		
125	ARRIVAL		
135		DEPARTURE	19
145		DEPARTURE	24
151	ARRIVAL		
153	ARRIVAL		
154	ARRIVAL		
154	ARRIVAL		
155		DEPARTURE	30
159	ARRIVAL		
162	ARRIVAL – OVERFLOW		
165		DEPARTURE	40
166	ARRIVAL		
170	ARRIVAL – OVERFLOW		
175		DEPARTURE	24
185		DEPARTURE	32
195		DEPARTURE	41
198	ARRIVAL		
199	ARRIVAL		
202	ARRIVAL		
205		DEPARTURE	51
212	ARRIVAL		
215		DEPARTURE	56
225		DEPARTURE	59
235		DEPARTURE	37
237	ARRIVAL		
242	ARRIVAL		
245		DEPARTURE	46
255		DEPARTURE	53
255	ARRIVAL		
265		DEPARTURE	53
275		DEPARTURE	38
285		DEPARTURE	43
291	ARRIVAL		
295		DEPARTURE	40
295	ARRIVAL		
305		DEPARTURE	14
315		DEPARTURE	20

♭
♭
THE AVERAGE QUEUE LENGTH WAS 1.7 CARS.
♭
THE AVERAGE WAITING TIME PER CUSTOMER WAS 21.0 MINUTES.
♭
THE NUMBER OF OVERFLOWS WAS 2.

Randomizing the Arrival Times

It is not necessary that the arrival times be read in. They can be generated by your program provided it is given the *mean arrival time*, that is, the average time between arrivals. We now outline how this could be done. First we must introduce the concept of a random number. Given a collection of numbers, a number is selected *randomly* from the collection if each number has an equal chance of being selected. A number so chosen is called a *random number*.† The following function produces a random integer between 1 and 131071. Each time the function is called, the new random integer is generated from the previous one. Strictly speaking, the sequence so generated is not random since it is explicitly determined by the function; but it *appears* to be random if you do not have access to the function that generates it.

```
CONST    UPPERLIMIT = 131071 ;
         VELOCITY   = 9806 ;

TYPE     RANGE      = 1..UPPERLIMIT ;

FUNCTION   RANDOM(PREVIOUSRANDOMINTEGER : RANGE) : RANGE ;

(* This function produces a random integer in the given range. *)
BEGIN
       RANDOM := ((VELOCITY * PREVIOUSRANDOMINTEGER) MOD UPPERLIMIT) + 1
END ;   (* of the function RANDOM. *)
```

Warning: In a production environment, larger values for UPPERLIMIT and VELOCITY should be used. This may necessitate rewriting the above function as a machine-language routine (to avoid an overflow error during the multiplication). Consult Knuth, 1981, chap. 3, for details.

Suppose that the *seed*, that is, the initial argument, is arbitrarily chosen as 5000. Then the first random integer generated will be (9806 * 5000 MOD 131071) + 1, namely, 9447. We can then use 9447 as an argument to RANDOM, and thus obtain a second random integer, (9806 * 9447 MOD 131071) + 1, namely, 101157. Continuing this process, we get a list of random integers.

What if we wanted (as we will below) to generate a list of random real numbers between 0 and 1 instead of random integers between 1 and 131071? If RANDOMINTEGER contains the result of calling the function RANDOM, then

RANDOMREAL := RANDOMINTEGER/UPPERLIMIT

---

† If we generate a long list of numbers, eventually the same number will occur twice. But then the sequence generated from that point on will duplicate an earlier sequence, since if two numbers are the same, their successors will be the same, and their successors' successors will be the same, etc. For this reason, the numbers generated are called "pseudorandom numbers."

will produce a random real number which is greater than 0 and less than or equal to 1. For example, for the two random integers generated above, the corresponding values of RANDOMREAL would be

0.0721   (that is, 9447/131071) and

0.7718   (that is, 101157/131071).

We now define a function that calculates the distribution of times between arrivals. The mathematical justification for the following discussion is beyond the scope of this book—the interested reader may consult Hogg, 1983, pages 162 ff. Let X be any time between arrivals. Then $F(X)$, the probability that the time until the next arrival will be at least X minutes from now, is given by

F(X) = EXP(− X / MEANARRIVALTIME)

For example, $F(0) = EXP(0) = 1$; that is, it is certain that the next arrival will take at least 0 minutes from now. Similarly, F(MEANARRIVALTIME) = EXP(−1) ≈ 0.4; F(10000 ∗ MEANARRIVALTIME) is approximately 0. The graph of the function F is shown in Fig. 4.34.

To generate the arrival times randomly, we introduce an integer variable called TIMETILLNEXTARRIVAL, which will contain the number of minutes from the current time until the next arrival. We determine the value for TIME-TILLNEXTARRIVAL as follows. According to the distribution function F given above, the probability that the next arrival will take at least TIMETILL-NEXTARRIVAL minutes is given by

EXP(− TIMETILLNEXTARRIVAL / MEANARRIVALTIME)

This expression represents a probability, that is, a real number between 0 and 1. To randomize this probability, we associate the expression with RANDOM-REAL:

RANDOMREAL = EXP(− TIMETILLNEXTARRIVAL / MEANARRIVALTIME)

The appropriate value for TIMETILLNEXTARRIVAL is found by solving this equation for TIMETILLNEXTARRIVAL:

TIMETILLNEXTARRIVAL := ROUND(− MEANARRIVALTIME ∗ LN(RANDOMREAL))

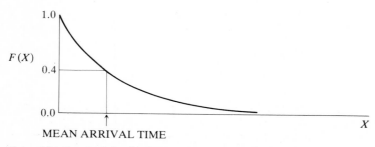

Figure 4.34 Graph of the distribution of interarrival times.

For example, if the mean arrival time is 12 minutes and the list of random real numbers starts with 0.0721 and 0.7718, then the first two values of TIMETILL-NEXTARRIVAL will be

32   (that is, ROUND(−12 ∗ LN(0.0721))) and

3   (that is, ROUND(−12 ∗ LN(0.7718))).

Thus the first customer will arrive 32 minutes after the car wash opens and the second customer will arrive 3 minutes after that.

Problem 4.2 Car Wash, Revisited

Modify your design and program for Prob. 4.1 so that the input merely consists of the mean arrival time in minutes and the number of minutes during which cars may arrive: the actual arrival times must be generated by your program. Use 12 and 300 for the Sample Input. The Sample Output should be similar to that shown for Prob. 4.1 but the exact values depend on the random number generator used, the seed and even the physical representation of REAL values on your computer.

Problem 4.3 A Flight Roster, Revisited

Design and write a program (or modify your design and program for Prob. 3.2) to solve the following problem: White Knuckle Airlines schedules 12 flights daily from Salisbury, Maryland to Dover, Delaware. Create and maintain a flight list and a *waiting list* for each flight.

Clarification Each flight carries a maximum of five passengers. Each line of Sample Input contains the request: 'ADD,' 'CANCEL,' 'FIND,' or 'LIST' in cols. 1–6, the flight number in cols. 9 and 10 and, unless 'LIST' is requested, the passenger's name in cols. 15–34.

The four types of requests should be handled as follows:

1. If the request is 'ADD,' then the given passenger wants to be added to the given flight. If that flight is full, then the passenger is put at the tail of the waiting list for that flight.
2. If the request is 'CANCEL,' then the given passenger should be removed from the flight list (or from the waiting list). If the passenger was removed from the flight list, then the head of the waiting list should be added to the flight list (unless the waiting list is already empty).
3. If the request is 'FIND,' then the value output should be 'YES—ON FLIGHT LIST,' 'YES—ON WAITING LIST' or 'NOT ON EITHER LIST.'
4. If the request is 'LIST,' then the flight list should be printed, in alphabetical order by passengers' names. The waiting list for that flight should also be printed, by order in which names were added to it; thus the first passenger put on the waiting list is printed first, and so on.

The following exceptional cases should be noted:

(a) If the request is not one of the four described above, the error message 'ERROR—ILLEGAL REQUEST' should be printed.
(b) If the flight number is not in the 1 to 12 range, then the error message 'ERROR—ILLEGAL FLIGHT NUMBER' should be printed.
(c) If the request is 'ADD' but the passenger is already on the flight list or the waiting list, then the error message 'ERROR—DUPLICATE NAME' should be printed.
(d) If the request is 'CANCEL' but the passenger is not on the flight list or the waiting list, then the error message 'ERROR—NAME NOT ON EITHER LIST' should be printed.

Sample Input

ADD	6	KUNDELL KENNETH
ADD	2	FAHEY PETER
ADD	2	SMITH JEFFERY
ADD	2	FAHEY KATHLEEN
ADD	3	TUFTS MARGARET
LIST	14	
ADD	2	LONG CRESTIN
FIND	2	RUSS DAVID
ADD	2	ABRESCH LINDA
FIND	2	FAHEY KATHLEEN
ADD	2	MURPHY CHARLES
CANCEL	3	FORTE FABIAN
ADD	2	HARDIN CHARLES
LIST	2	
FIND	2	MURPHY CHARLES
ADD	2	STARKEY RICHARD
CANCEL	2	FAHEY PETER
LIST	2	
ADD	2	PENNIMAN RICHARD
CANCEL	2	HARDIN CHARLES
LIST	2	
CANCEL	20	FAHEY KATHLEEN
FIND	2	MURPHY CHARLES
ADD	2	FAHEY PETER
ADD	2	PENNIMAN RICHARD
LIST	2	

Sample Output

REQUEST	FLIGHT NUMBER	NAME
ADD	6	KUNDELL KENNETH
b		
b		
ADD	2	FAHEY PETER

♭
♭
ADD   2   SMITH JEFFERY
♭
♭
ADD   2   FAHEY KATHLEEN
♭
♭
ADD   3   TUFTS MARGARET
♭
♭
LIST   14   ERROR — ILLEGAL FLIGHT NUMBER
♭
♭
ADD   2   LONG CRESTIN
♭
♭
FIND   2   RUSS DAVID   ERROR — NAME NOT ON EITHER LIST
♭
♭
ADD   2   ABRESCH LINDA
♭
♭
FIND   2   FAHEY KATHLEEN   YES — ON FLIGHT LIST
♭
♭
ADD   2   MURPHY CHARLES
♭
♭
CANCEL   3   FORTE FABIAN   ERROR — NAME NOT ON EITHER LIST
♭
♭
ADD   2   HARDIN CHARLES
♭
♭
LIST   2   FLIGHT LIST
                                                          ─────────

                                                          ABRESCH LINDA
                                                          FAHEY KATHLEEN
                                                          FAHEY PETER
                                                          LONG CRESTIN
                                                          SMITH JEFFERY
                                                          ♭
                                                          ♭
                                                          ♭
                                                          WAITING LIST
                                                          ─────────

                                                          MURPHY CHARLES
                                                          HARDIN CHARLES
♭
♭
FIND   2   MURPHY CHARLES   YES — ON WAITING LIST
♭
♭

```
ADD            2      STARKEY RICHARD
♭
♭
CANCEL         2      FAHEY PETER
♭
♭
LIST           2                              FLIGHT LIST
                                              _____

                                              ABRESCH LINDA
                                              FAHEY KATHLEEN
                                              LONG CRESTIN
                                              MURPHY CHARLES
                                              SMITH JEFFERY
                                              ♭
                                              ♭
                                              ♭
                                              WAITING LIST
                                              _____

                                              HARDIN CHARLES
                                              STARKEY RICHARD
♭
♭
ADD            2      PENNIMAN RICHARD
♭
♭
CANCEL         2      HARDIN CHARLES
♭
♭
LIST           2                              FLIGHT LIST
                                              _____

                                              ABRESCH LINDA
                                              FAHEY KATHLEEN
                                              LONG CRESTIN
                                              MURPHY CHARLES
                                              SMITH JEFFERY
                                              ♭
                                              ♭
                                              ♭
                                              WAITING LIST
                                              _____

                                              STARKEY RICHARD
                                              PENNIMAN RICHARD
♭
♭
CANCEL        20      FAHEY KATHLEEN      ERROR — ILLEGAL FLIGHT NUMBER
♭
♭
FIND           2      MURPHY CHARLES      YES — ON FLIGHT LIST
♭
♭
ADD            2      FAHEY PETER
♭
♭
ADD            2      PENNIMAN RICHARD    ERROR — DUPLICATE NAME
```

♮
♮
LIST   2

FLIGHT LIST
_____

ABRESCH LINDA
FAHEY KATHLEEN
LONG CRESTIN
MURPHY CHARLES
SMITH JEFFERY
♮
♮
♮
WAITING LIST
_____

STARKEY RICHARD
PENNIMAN RICHARD
FAHEY PETER

Problem 4.4 CONVERTTOPOSTFIX, Revisited

Modify the program CONVERTTOPOSTFIX to accommodate the assignment operator ":=" and the exponentiation operator "∗∗". Exponentiations should be evaluated from *right to left*.

Clarification The characters in the original infix expression should be converted to tokens. The first field in each token will be its class. The only two token classes will be IDENTIFIER and OPERATOR. For an identifier, the second field will contain the symbol table address in which the identifier is stored. For example, the identifier A will be tokenized as

     class   address

IDENTIFIER	100

100	A

The first identifier should be stored at location 100, the second at location 101, and so on.

    For an operator token, the second field will contain the operator and the third field will contain the operator's priority. Thus, assuming "+" has a priority of 2, its token is

     class   symbol priority

OPERATOR	+	2

    The postfix output should consist of addresses (for the identifiers) and operators.

Sample Input

A + B * C ;
A := − B ;
X := X + (−Y ** Z ** (A / B)) ;
A := − B + C * A ** X / Y − B ;

Sample Output

ADDRESSES ARE ASSIGNED AS FOLLOWS: THE FIRST IDENTIFIER IN THE INFIX STRING IS STORED AT LOCATION 100, THE SECOND AT LOCATION 101, AND SO ON.

INFIX   : A + B * C ;
POSTFIX : 100 101 102 * +
♭
♭
INFIX   : A := − B ;
POSTFIX : 100 101 − :=
♭
♭
INFIX   : X := X + (−Y ** Z ** (A / B)) ;
POSTFIX : 100 100 101 102 103 104 / ** ** − + :=
♭
♭
INFIX   : A := − B + C * A ** X / Y − B ;
POSTFIX : 100 101 − 102 100 103 ** * 104 / + 101 − :=

FIVE

DIRECTED GRAPHS

Since a list is an ordered collection of components, the components can be organized in a linear fashion. We now turn our attention to directed graphs, which provide a nonlinear organization of components. Of special interest are two types of directed graphs, namely trees and networks.

DEFINITIONS

A *directed graph* consists of a collection of components called *nodes* and a collection of arrows, each of which starts at a node and ends at a node. Figure 5.1 shows several directed graphs.

We begin our study of directed graphs by defining some terms as they apply to directed graphs.

A *path* is a consecutive sequence of two or more nodes joined by appropriately oriented arrows. Thus, in Fig. 5.1a,

$$BDEF$$

is a path from B to F. Similarly

$$ABDEFDEDEFH$$

is a path from A to H. A simpler path from A to H is

$$ABDEFH$$

There is no path from D to B, nor from H to any node.

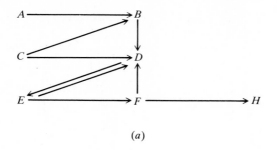

(a)

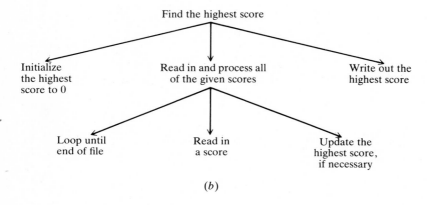

(b)

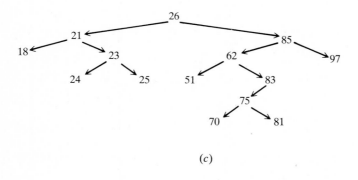

(c)

(d)

Figure 5.1 Several directed graphs.

The *successor set* of a given node is the set of all nodes to which there is a path from the given node. Thus, in Fig. 5.1*d*, the successor set of 385 is {483, 480, finish}. In Fig. 5.1*c*, the successor set of 26 consists of all the other nodes in the graph.

A *cycle* is a path in which the first and last nodes are the same and there are no other repeats. In Fig. 5.1*a*,

$$DEFD$$

is a cycle. So is

$$EDE$$

The graphs in Figs. 5.1*b*, *c*, and *d* are *acyclic*, that is, they have no cycles.

For any node X in a graph, the *indegree* of X, written

$$in(X)$$

is the number of arrows coming into X. Similary, the *outdegree* of X, written

$$out(X)$$

is the number of arrows going out of X. In Fig. 5.1*a*, $in(A) = 0$, $in(B) = 2$, $in(D) = 4$, $out(A) = 1$, $out(C) = 2$, $out(E) = 2$, $out(H) = 0$.

A node whose indegree is 0 is called a *source*; a node whose outdegree is 0 is called a *sink*. In Fig. 5.1*a*, nodes A and C are sources; node H is a sink. Figure 5.1*d* has a single source, namely "start," and a single sink, namely "finish."

A directed graph is *connected* if, for any pair of nodes X and Y, there is a positive integer N and a consecutive sequence of nodes $X_1, X_2, \ldots, X_N$ such that $X = X_1$, $Y = X_N$ and for each i between 1 and $N - 1$, there is an arrow from X_i to X_{i+1} or an arrow from X_{i+1} to X_i. Informally, a graph is connected if it is all one piece. All the graphs in Fig. 5.1 are connected. Figure 5.2 shows a directed graph that is not connected. Henceforth we assume connectedness when we use the term "directed graph."

Exercise 5.1 Use the directed graph in Fig. 5.1*a* for each of the following:

(*a*) Find a path from A to H.
(*b*) Find two paths from C to D which include F.
(*c*) How many paths are there from C to B?
(*d*) For each of the seven nodes, find the node's successor set.
(*e*) How many cycles does the graph have?
(*f*) Find $in(C)$, $in(F)$, $in(H)$, $out(B)$, $out(D)$, $out(F)$.

Figure 5.2 A directed graph (with five nodes) that is not connected.

Exercise 5.2 Find the indegree of each node in Fig. 5.1*b*. How many sources are there? How many sinks?

TREES

We now restrict our attention to a special kind of directed graph, the tree. A *tree* is a (connected) directed graph in which one node is a source and every other node has an indegree of 1. The source in a tree is called the *root*. Figures 5.1*b* and 5.1*c* are both trees. It follows from the above definition that, in every tree, the root's successor set consists of all other nodes. Furthermore, a tree cannot contain any cycles; in fact, between any two nodes there is at most one path. In a tree we use the term *branch* instead of "arrow" and *leaf* instead of "sink".

If there is a branch from node *X* to node *Y*, then *X* is called the *parent* of *Y* and *Y* is called the *child* of *X*. Nodes with the same parent are called *siblings*. In the tree in Fig. 5.1*c*, 51 and 83 are siblings since they have 62 as their parent.

A tree is *ordered* if each group of siblings is ordered, from left to right. Figure 5.3 shows two *different*, ordered trees. Henceforth we consider only trees that are ordered.

We adopt the widely accepted but unnatural convention that the root will be placed at the top of the tree and that all the arrows (that is, branches) will point downward. We can thus omit the head of each arrow and simply use a straight line.

Exercise 5.3 Use your general understanding of the following terms to define them with respect to trees:

(*a*) ancestor;
(*b*) descendant;
(*c*) cousin;
(*d*) forest.

In Chap. 4 we converted simple arithmetic expressions from infix notation to postfix notation and, in passing, detected certain errors in the infix expression. We now develop a powerful tool for examining entire programs as well as simple expressions. A special kind of tree, the *parse tree*, plays a role in this development.

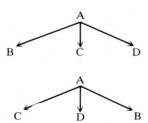

Figure 5.3 Two different, ordered trees.

FORMAL GRAMMARS

One of the most important concepts in computer science is that of a formal grammar. This notion is crucial in the explicit definition of a programming language such as Pascal. A formal grammar for a language prescribes which strings of symbols are allowed in the language. A formal grammar for a language has four components:

1. A set of terminal symbols—the symbols actually used in the language. For example, Pascal allows letters and digits, as well as "(", ";", ":", and so on.
2. A set of nonterminal symbols—these are used to describe parts of the language. To make the nonterminals easily distinguishable from the terminals, we use lowercase letters for the nonterminals and bracket them with metalinguistic† symbols "⟨" and "⟩". Some nonterminals used in Pascal are ⟨identifier⟩, ⟨compound statement⟩, and ⟨procedure heading⟩.
3. A set of rules that define each nonterminal as a string of symbols, each of which must be either a terminal or a nonterminal. (As a special case we include the empty string, represented by the metalinguistic symbol "#".) To describe these rules, we use the following metalinguistic symbols besides "⟨", "⟨", and "#":
   ::= means *is defined to be*
   | means *or*; this is used to indicate alternate definitions of a nonterminal.

   The defined nonterminal occurs to the left of the "::="; the defining terminals and nonterminals occur on the right-hand side. For example, in a grammar for Pascal, we could define the nonterminal ⟨variant selector⟩ as

   ⟨variant selector⟩::=⟨tag type⟩|⟨tag field⟩:⟨tag type⟩

4. A start symbol, that is, a special nonterminal whose definition is applied first whenever we want to generate an acceptable string in the language. In a grammar for Pascal, for example, the start symbol would be ⟨program⟩.

How can we generate, from the rules, a string of terminal symbols? We begin with the start symbol and choose a rule to apply. If the resulting string contains nonterminals, we choose rules to apply to each of those nonterminals. Each time we apply a rule to a nonterminal, we replace that nonterminal in the current string by the right-hand side of the rule applied. We continue making replacements according to the rules until, finally, the current string contains no nonterminals. Since the current string then consists of terminal symbols only, we are done.

The language generated by a grammar is the set of all strings of terminal symbols that can be obtained by the process discussed in the previous paragraph.

---

† That is, these symbols are used, neither as terminals nor as nonterminals, but to help define the grammar itself.

Example 1 Figure 5.4 defines a grammar for a very simple language. It is sufficient to list the rules of the grammar since we will always define the start symbol in the first rule and the nonterminals are always bracketed.

Let us determine the language defined by this grammar. Any string in the language can be obtained by applying the given rules. For example, we can replace ⟨s⟩ by A, so

$$A$$

all by itself is a legitimate string (of terminal symbols) in the language. Suppose, instead, we first apply the rule

$$⟨s⟩ ::= ⟨s⟩ \text{ BB}$$

Then we have two choices for the rule to be applied next:

$$⟨s⟩ ::= A$$

or

$$⟨s⟩ ::= ⟨s⟩ \text{ BB}$$

If we chose the rule ⟨s⟩ ::= A, we would derive

$$ABB$$

as a string in the language. This derivation can be depicted in a tree (called a "derivation tree") in which the start symbol is the root and, for any parent, its children are obtained from the right-hand-side of the rule applied to the parent. Thus we would have

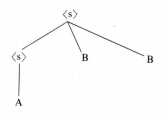

The leaves in each derivation tree constitute one terminal string in the language.

<s> ::= A | <s> BB   **Figure 5.4** A grammar for a simple language.

Another derivation tree is obtained by applying the rule $\langle s \rangle ::= \langle s \rangle$ BB twice followed by $\langle s \rangle ::= A$:

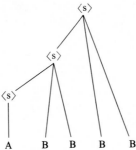

Since the rule $\langle s \rangle ::= \langle s \rangle$ BB may be applied over and over again, the size of each string in the language is determined by the number of times that rule is applied. The entire language is {A, ABB, ABBBB, ABBBBBB, ...}. Each string in the language consists of the letter A followed by an even number (possibly zero) of B's.

Example 2 Figure 5.5 defines a grammar for very simple arithmetic expressions. This grammar has three nonterminals and six terminals. The size of a terminal string in the language is determined by the number of times the rules

$$\langle expression \rangle ::= \langle expression \rangle + \langle term \rangle$$

and

$$\langle term \rangle ::= \langle term \rangle * \langle factor \rangle$$

are applied. For example, we can develop the derivation trees shown in Fig. 5.6.

One important feature of the grammar in Fig. 5.5 is that it preserves the normal order for carrying out arithmetic operations. This may seem strange since the rule for "+" appears before the rule for "*" in the grammar, but consider the following tree:

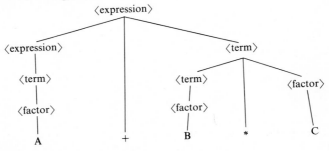

```
<expression>  ::= <term> | <expression> + <term>
<term>        ::= <factor> | <term> * <factor>
<factor>      ::= A | B | C | D
```

Figure 5.5 A grammar for very simple arithmetic expressions.

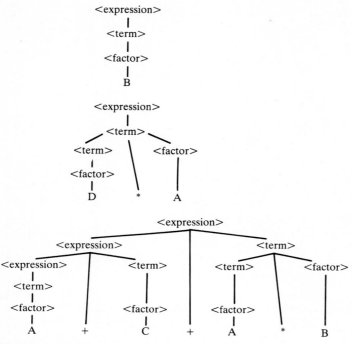

Figure 5.6 Some derivation trees from the grammar in Fig. 5.5.

In the evaluation of A + B ∗ C, the operator "+" cannot be applied until the values of its two operands are known. The value of its right operand requires that "∗" be applied, so multiplications will be performed before additions, as usual.

Could we simply generate a different tree in which "+" would have to be performed before "∗"? Suppose we had the following:

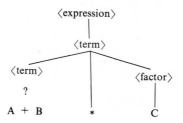

We would now be at an impasse: There is no sequence of rules that could transform ⟨term⟩ into A + B. The only tree with A + B ∗ C as its terminal string must start with the rule ⟨expression⟩ ::= ⟨expression⟩ + ⟨term⟩, and so, as required, the multiplication will be performed before the addition.

Furthermore, additions are performed from left to right and multiplications are performed from left to right. For example, consider the following tree:

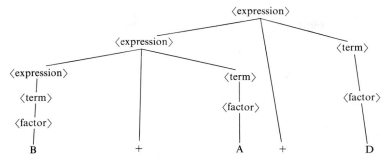

The second "+" cannot be applied until both of its operands' values are known, and obtaining the value of its left operand requires that the first "+" be applied. Notice that, if the first rule in the grammar of Fig. 5.5 had been

⟨expression⟩ ::= ⟨term⟩ | ⟨term⟩ + ⟨expression⟩

then additions would be performed from right to left.

In general, the further an operator's rule is from the root, the sooner the operator will be applied in the evaluation of the expression.

Exercise 5.4 Let us modify the grammar in Fig. 5.5 so that parentheses will be included in the resulting language. Since parenthesized subexpressions should be evaluated first, the nonterminal defined using parentheses should itself be used in defining multiplication:

⟨expression⟩ ::= ⟨term⟩ | ⟨expression⟩ + ⟨term⟩
⟨term⟩   ::= ⟨factor⟩ | ⟨term⟩ ∗ ⟨factor⟩
⟨factor⟩   ::= A | B | C | D | (⟨expression⟩)

Use this grammar to develop derivation trees that generate

(*a*) A ∗ (B + C)
(*b*) A ∗ (B + C ∗ (D + B) + A)

Exercise 5.5 Modify the grammar in Fig. 5.5 so that multiple-letter identifiers and multiple-digit numbers are included in the resulting language.

Hint: Fill in the missing rules:

⟨expression⟩ ::= ⟨term⟩ | ⟨expression⟩ + ⟨term⟩
⟨term⟩   ::= ⟨factor⟩ | ⟨term⟩ ∗ ⟨factor⟩
⟨factor⟩   ::= ⟨identifier⟩ | ⟨number⟩
⟨identifier⟩ ::= ⟨letter⟩ | ⟨identifier⟩⟨letter⟩
⟨letter⟩   ::= A | B | C | D
⟨number⟩   ::=
⟨digit⟩   ::=

Exercise 5.6 Consider the following modification of the grammar in Fig. 5.5 (" ↑ " represents the exponentiation operator):

⟨expression⟩ ::= ⟨term⟩ | ⟨expression⟩ + ⟨term⟩
⟨term⟩   ::= ⟨factor⟩ | ⟨term⟩ * ⟨factor⟩
⟨factor⟩   ::= ⟨primary⟩ | ⟨primary⟩ ↑ ⟨factor⟩
⟨primary⟩   ::= A | B | C | D

Develop derivation trees that generate

(*a*) A ↑ B + C
(*b*) A * B ↑ C
(*c*) A * B ↑ C ↑ D * B

Because of the way the grammar was written, the evaluation of expressions will proceed as follows: exponentiations will be performed first, from *right to left*, followed by multiplications, from left to right, followed by additions, from left to right. Modify the grammar so that exponentiations will be performed from left to right.

Exercise 5.7 Determine the language generated by the following grammar:

⟨s⟩ ::= A ⟨s⟩ C | B

Exercise 5.8 Determine the language generated by the following grammar.

⟨s⟩ ::= A ⟨s⟩ | B ⟨t⟩ | B
⟨t⟩ ::= ⟨t⟩ C | C

Compare that language with the language generated by

⟨x⟩ ::= B ⟨y⟩ | A ⟨x⟩
⟨y⟩ ::= # | ⟨y⟩ C

Hint: " # " is a metalinguistic symbol, not a terminal symbol. Thus, it does not appear in any terminal string. For example, if we apply the first rule for ⟨x⟩ and then apply the first rule for ⟨y⟩, the terminal string generated is simply

B

PARSING

In the previous section we derived terminal strings from the start symbol by applying the grammar's rules. We now investigate a much more practical problem: Given a grammar and a string of terminals, determine whether the string is in the language defined by the grammar. In particular, suppose that the grammar defines a programming language such as Pascal or COBOL. Given a string of terminal symbols, we determine whether the string constitutes a program in the language. In so doing we can discover the syntactic (that is, grammatical) structure of the program. This syntactic analyzing, also called "parsing," is one of the main tasks of a compiler.

To illustrate how this works, consider the grammar in Fig. 5.7—it defines the syntax of a very simple, Pascal-like language.

Figure 5.8 shows a program in the language defined by the grammar in Fig. 5.7 (spaces are inserted for clarity).

We can "prove" that the above program is syntactically correct by means of the tree in Fig. 5.9. Such a tree is called a *parse tree* rather than a derivation tree because its development begins with, rather than ends with, the terminal string.

Exercise 5.9 Use the grammar shown in Fig. 5.7 to develop a parse tree for the following program:

```
BEGIN
    A1 := 105 ;
    B  := 2 − A1 − 5 * 10
END.
```

Exercise 5.10 Use the grammar shown in Fig. 5.7 to attempt to develop a parse tree for the following incorrect program:

```
BEGIN
    A := 5
    B := 10
END.
```

`<program>`	::= BEGIN `<statement list>` END.
`<statement list>`	::= `<assignment statement>` |
	`<assignment statement>` ; `<statement list>`
`<assignment statement>`	::= `<identifier>` := `<expression>`
`<identifier>`	::= `<letter>` | `<identifier>` `<digit>` | `<identifier>` `<letter>`
`<letter>`	::= A | B | C | D
`<digit>`	::= 0 | 1 | 2 | 3 | 4 | 5 | 6 | 7 | 8 | 9
`<expression>`	::= `<term>` | `<expression>` `<adding operator>` `<term>`
`<term>`	::= `<factor>` | `<term>` `<multiplying operator>` `<factor>`
`<factor>`	::= `<identifier>` | `<number>` | (`<expression>`)
`<adding operator>`	::= + | −
`<multiplying operator>`	::= * | /
`<number>`	::= `<digit>` | `<digit>` `<number>`

Figure 5.7 A grammar for a very simple language.

```
BEGIN
    B := 5;
    CA := 7 * B
END.
```
Figure 5.8 A program in the language defined by the grammar in Fig. 5.7.

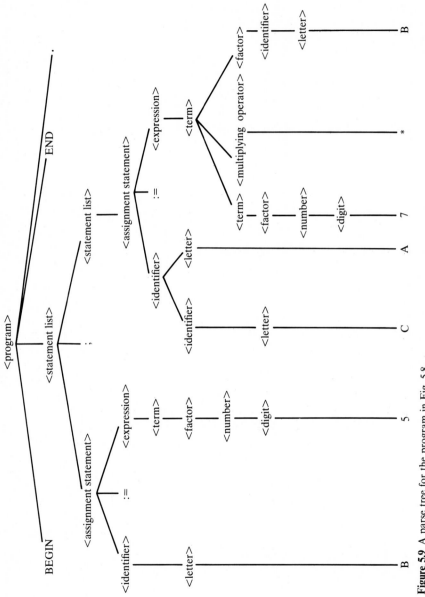

Figure 5.9 A parse tree for the program in Fig. 5.8.

Recursive Descent Parsing (optional)

What strategy should we use for developing an algorithm to parse a given (purported) program? Several possibilities are available. One is to expand the postfix conversion algorithm (pages 117–123) so that the transition table includes all the tokens in the language; the parser is then called an "operator precedence parser." Another approach uses a grammar such as the one in Fig. 5.7. Starting with ⟨program⟩, we guess which rule to try whenever we have a choice. For example, ⟨expression⟩ can be defined either as ⟨term⟩ or as ⟨expression⟩ ⟨adding operator⟩ ⟨term⟩. If we later discover that our guess is inconsistent with the input string, we must *backtrack*; that is, we retrace our steps (and undo the actions taken) until we get back to the point in the parse where the bad guess was made. We then make another guess. Since the grammar in Fig. 5.7 has many choices, a considerable amount of computer time would be devoted to backtracking. Such inefficiency makes backtracking unsuitable for a realistic parser.

Fortunately, there is a way that the grammar in Fig. 5.7 can be rewritten so that the same language is defined but the parsing algorithm has no need for backtracking. The algorithm is called a *recursive descent parser*. The word "recursive" is used because a nonterminal can be defined in terms of itself. "Descent" indicates that we start at the root of the parse tree and work our way down to the leaves. At each stage in the partially completed parse tree, the parser applies a rule to the *leftmost* nonterminal which is currently a leaf.

We need to rewrite the grammar in two parts. In the first part of the revised grammar, we define the tokens from the terminal symbols. In the second part of the grammar we define the nonterminals from the tokens. The reason a recursive descent parser can avoid backtracking is that the rules for nonterminals are defined in such a way that the parser can always determine, *from the next token*, which rule to apply (to the leftmost nonterminal in the partially completed parse tree). In other words, given the nonterminal to be matched and the token that begins the match, the rule is uniquely determined.

We will define the tokens first because it is easier and also because it will help motivate the subsequent definition of nonterminals. Since tokens constitute an intermediate form between the nonterminals and the terminals, we treat them as nonterminals when defining those tokens from terminals, but treat them as terminals when defining the nonterminals from the tokens. Figure 5.10 defines the eleven tokens of our language.† We use the nontokens ⟨letter⟩ and ⟨digit⟩ for convenience in defining the tokens.

Using the grammar in Fig. 5.10, we can always determine the next token in the input string. We would now like to use these tokens as terminal symbols in a grammar. The nonterminals will be the same as those from the grammar of Fig. 5.7, less any that were defined in Fig. 5.10. Thus, the nonterminals we need to

---

† This ad hoc approach to tokens has the advantage of simplifying the description of how the parser works. In Case Study 5.1, we will revert to the more practical method of having a small number of token classes (see page 191).

```
<begin>                  ::= BEGIN
<end>                    ::= END
<period>                 ::= .
<semicolon>              ::= ;
<identifier>             ::= <letter> | <identifier> <letter> | <identifier> <digit>
<letter>                 ::= A | B | C | D
<digit>                  ::= 0 | 1 | 2 | 3 | 4 | 5 | 6 | 7 | 8 | 9
<colon equals>           ::= :=
<adding operator>        ::= + | −
<multiplying operator>   ::= * | /
<number>                 ::= <digit> | <digit> <number>
<left parenthesis>       ::= (
<right parenthesis>      ::= )
```

Figure 5.10 Definition of tokens for a simple, Pascal-like language.

define are ⟨program⟩, ⟨statement list⟩, ⟨assignment statement⟩, ⟨expression⟩, ⟨term⟩ and ⟨factor⟩. We now define each of these six nonterminals in such a way that, whenever the parser needs to apply a rule to one of these nonterminals, it will know which rule to apply. It will know because either there will be only one rule for that nonterminal, or there will be a choice of rules, each beginning with a different token. In this latter case, the parser will know which rule to apply because it will know what is the next token obtained from the input string.

1. The first rule is straightforward:

   ⟨program⟩ ::= BEGIN ⟨statement list⟩ END PERIOD

2. Since the definition of ⟨statement list⟩ must always start with ⟨assignment statement⟩ followed by zero or more instances of SEMICOLON ⟨assignment statement⟩, we can rewrite the ⟨statement list⟩ rule as

   ⟨statement list⟩   ::= ⟨assignment statement⟩⟨rest of statement list⟩

   ⟨rest of statement list⟩ ::= # | SEMICOLON ⟨assignment statement⟩ ⟨rest of statement list⟩

   This implies that the choice of rules for ⟨rest of statement list⟩ will not be made until the rule for ⟨assignment statement⟩ has been followed all the way down to the tokens. After we have encountered all the tokens related to ⟨assignment statement⟩, the next token (namely, SEMICOLON or END) tells us whether the rule for ⟨rest of statement list⟩ must be # or SEMICOLON ⟨assignment statement⟩ ⟨rest of statement list⟩.

3. The rule for ⟨assignment statement⟩ is straightforward:

   ⟨assignment statement⟩ ::= IDENTIFIER COLONEQUALS ⟨expression⟩

4. The rule for ⟨expression⟩ must be rewritten from its form in Fig. 5.7 since the right-hand side permits a starting choice between the nonterminals ⟨term⟩ and ⟨expression⟩.

   We can eliminate the choice by noting that an expression must always begin with a term; that term will always be followed by a token (either

ADDINGOPERATOR, END, SEMICOLON, MULTIPLYINGOPERA-
TOR, or RIGHTPARENTHESIS). In particular, the definition of ⟨expres-
sion⟩ must allow that ⟨term⟩ may be followed by zero or more instances of
ADDINGOPERATOR ⟨term⟩. Thus, we can define ⟨expression⟩ as

⟨expression⟩   ::= ⟨term⟩⟨rest of expression⟩

⟨rest of expression⟩ ::= # | ADDINGOPERATOR ⟨term⟩ ⟨rest of expression⟩

5. The definition of ⟨term⟩ is handled similarly:

⟨term⟩   ::= ⟨factor⟩ ⟨rest of term⟩

⟨rest of term⟩ ::= # | MULTIPLYINGOPERATOR ⟨factor⟩ ⟨rest of term⟩

6. Finally, the rule for ⟨factor⟩ is straightforward:

⟨factor⟩ ::= IDENTIFIER | NUMBER |

    LEFTPARENTHESIS ⟨expression⟩ RIGHTPARENTHESIS

This last rule permits a choice, but the choice is among tokens, not
among nonterminals, and in any event, the choice is forced since the parser
will know at that time whether the next token is IDENTIFIER, NUMBER
or LEFTPARENTHESIS.

Figure 5.11 summarizes the two parts of the revised grammar for our simple
language.

In Case Study 5.1 we will use the grammar in Fig. 5.11 to develop a recursive
descent parser for a given purported program in our simple language.

To illustrate how a recursive descent parser could utilize such a grammar,
consider the following program:

```
BEGIN
    A := 5 ;
    B := 6
END.
```

```
<begin>                  ::= BEGIN
<end>                    ::= END
<period>                 ::= .
<semicolon>              ::= ;
<identifier>             ::= <letter> | <identifier> <letter> | <identifier> <digit>
<letter>                 ::= A | B | C | D
<digit>                  ::= 0 | 1 | 2 | 3 | 4 | 5 | 6 | 7 | 8 | 9
<colon equals>           ::= :=
<adding operator>        ::= + | −
<multiplying operator>   ::= * | /
<number>                 ::= <digit> | <digit> <number>
<left parenthesis>       ::= (
<right parenthesis>      ::= )
```

Figure 5.11a Definition of tokens from terminals. Note that ⟨letter⟩ and ⟨digit⟩ are nontokens; they
simply facilitate the definition of the tokens ⟨identifier⟩ and ⟨number⟩.

```
<program>             ::= BEGIN <statement list> END PERIOD
<statement list>      ::= <assignment statement> <rest of statement list>
<rest of statement list> ::= SEMICOLON <assignment statement> <rest of statement list> | #
<assignment statement> ::= IDENTIFIER COLONEQUALS <expression>
<expression>          ::= <term> <rest of expression>
<rest of expression>  ::= ADDINGOPERATOR <term> <rest of expression> | #
<term>                ::= <factor> <rest of term>
<rest of term>        ::= MULTIPLYINGOPERATOR <factor> <rest of term> | #
<factor>              ::= IDENTIFIER | NUMBER |
                          LEFTPARENTHESIS <expression> RIGHTPARENTHESIS
```

Figure 5.11*b* Definition of nonterminals from tokens.

Before the parser can operate on such a program, the terminals must be grouped together into tokens. This task falls on a part of the compiler known as the "scanner" or "lexical analyzer." In the case study to follow, the parser will repeatedly call the scanner to obtain the next token.

In token form, the above program would be

```
BEGIN
IDENTIFIER
COLONEQUALS
NUMBER
SEMICOLON
IDENTIFIER
COLONEQUALS
NUMBER
END
PERIOD
```

Initially, the next token would be **BEGIN**. The parse begins with an application of the rule defining ⟨program⟩:

1. ⟨program⟩ ::= BEGIN ⟨statement list⟩ END PERIOD
   The parser must now apply the rule for ⟨statement list⟩. (The next token is now IDENTIFIER).
2. ⟨statement list⟩ ::= ⟨assignment statement⟩ ⟨rest of statement list⟩
   The partially completed parse tree is now as shown in Figure 5.12.

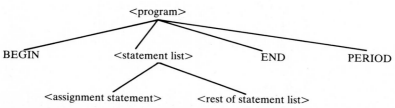

Figure 5.12 A partially completed parse tree.

The leftmost nonterminal leaf is ⟨assignment statement⟩, so the rule for that nonterminal is applied next. (We need not decide which rule to apply to ⟨rest of statement list⟩ until that becomes the leftmost nonterminal leaf in the partially completed parse tree.)

3. ⟨assignment statement⟩ ::= IDENTIFIER COLONEQUALS ⟨expression⟩

Since this rule has a nonterminal, namely ⟨expression⟩, on the right-hand side, we must apply the rule for ⟨expression⟩ next. (The next token is now NUMBER).

4. ⟨expression⟩ ::= ⟨term⟩ ⟨rest of expression⟩
5. ⟨term⟩ ::= ⟨factor⟩ ⟨rest of term⟩
6. ⟨factor⟩ ::= NUMBER

At this point the next token is SEMICOLON, so we know that the rule for ⟨rest of term⟩ must be

7. ⟨rest of term⟩ ::= #

Similarly, we know that the rule for ⟨rest of expression⟩ must be

8. ⟨rest of expression⟩ ::= #

Since the next token is still SEMICOLON, the rule for ⟨rest of statement list⟩ is

9. ⟨rest of statement list⟩ ::= SEMICOLON ⟨assignment statement⟩
⟨rest of statement list⟩

The partially completed parse tree is now as shown in Fig. 5.13. The next rule applied will be the one for ⟨assignment statement⟩. Completion of the parse tree is left as an exercise.

Exercise 5.11 Complete the parse tree in Fig. 5.13 for the program on page 182.

Exercise 5.12 Show that the eleven tokens in Fig. 5.10 could have been defined without using ⟨digit⟩ or ⟨letter⟩.

Hint: The rule for ⟨number⟩ would have 20 choices.

Exercise 5.13 Use the grammar in Fig. 5.11*a* to determine, in order, the tokens of the following program:

```
BEGIN
    A5 := B + (27 − A * B)
END.
```

Exercise 5.14 Use the grammar in Fig. 5.11*b* to develop a parse tree for the following program:

```
BEGIN
    C := 10 ;
    B := C * (C + 1 / 10) − C
END.
```

At each stage in the parse, determine the next token (from the grammar in Fig. 5.11*a*).

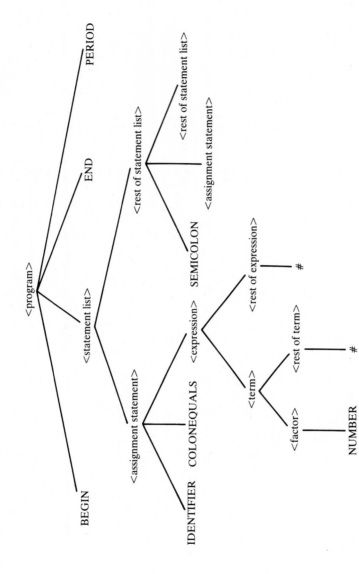

Figure 5.13 A nearly completed parse tree.

CASE STUDY 5.1: A RECURSIVE DESCENT PARSER (OPTIONAL)

Design and write a program to solve the following problem:

Problem

Develop a recursive descent parser for the language defined by the grammar in Fig. 5.11b.

Clarification The input will consist of a purported program in the language. The program may include blanks and end-of-line markers, such as the example given in Fig. 5.8. Of course, neither blanks nor end-of-line markers are allowed within the components of any token. The output will be a linear version of the parse tree. The terminal symbols that comprise the next token will be printed on a new line as soon as they are scanned. Each rule will be printed on a new line as soon as that rule has been determined. If an error is encountered during the attempted parse, the word "ERROR" and the expected next token should be printed on a new line. The parse should then be resumed from that point. The input may contain any number of syntactic errors, that is, those that violate the rules in Fig. 5.11b, but we assume that there are no lexical errors, that is, those that violate the rules in Fig. 5.11a. To avoid continual checking for end-of-file, we assume that each program will contain either an END or a period (or both), and if there is a period, it will immediately follow the END.

Sample Input

```
BEGIN
    B  := 5 ;
    CB := B + 2 * 10
END.
```

Sample Output

TERMINAL(S)	RULE OR ERROR MESSAGE
BEGIN	
	⟨program⟩ ::= BEGIN ⟨statement list⟩ END PERIOD
B	
	⟨statement list⟩ ::= ⟨assignment statement⟩ ⟨rest of statement list⟩
	⟨assignment statement⟩ ::= IDENTIFIER COLONEQUALS ⟨expression⟩
:=	
5	
	⟨expression⟩ ::= ⟨term⟩ ⟨rest of expression⟩
	⟨term⟩ ::= ⟨factor⟩ ⟨rest of term⟩
	⟨factor⟩ ::= NUMBER
;	
	⟨rest of term⟩ ::= #
	⟨rest of expression⟩ ::= #
	⟨rest of statement list⟩ ::= SEMICOLON ⟨assignment statement⟩ ⟨rest of statement list⟩

TERMINAL(S)	RULE OR ERROR MESSAGE
CB	
	⟨assignment statement⟩ ::= IDENTIFIER COLONEQUALS ⟨expression⟩
:=	
B	
	⟨expression⟩ ::= ⟨term⟩ ⟨rest of expression⟩
	⟨term⟩ ::= ⟨factor⟩ ⟨rest of term⟩
	⟨factor⟩ ::= IDENTIFIER
+	
	⟨rest of term⟩ ::= #
	⟨rest of expression⟩ ::= ADDINGOPERATOR ⟨term⟩
	⟨rest of expression⟩
2	
	⟨term⟩ ::= ⟨factor⟩ ⟨rest of term⟩
	⟨factor⟩ ::= NUMBER
*	
	⟨rest of term⟩ ::= MULTIPLYINGOPERATOR ⟨factor⟩ ⟨rest of term⟩
10	
	⟨factor⟩ ::= NUMBER
END	
	⟨rest of term⟩ ::= #
	⟨rest of expression⟩ ::= #
	⟨rest of statement list⟩ ::= #

PARSE COMPLETE

For convenience, we also show the tree form, in Fig. 5.14, with the terminals for each identifier and number at the end of a dotted line.

Solution Tree The main tree is fairly simple: We get the first token and then start the parse. To get a token, we call the subtree SCANNER, which provides the next token from the input characters.

Since the essential job of the parser is to apply rules for the nonterminals, we have a separate subtree for each nonterminal. In general, the subtree for a given nonterminal recognizes the longest string of input that matches the given nonterminal. The subtree has access to the next token and, at the conclusion of the subtree, the next token is the first one following the matched string. Thus, the main tree calls the PROGRAM subtree to start the parse.

The complete main tree is given in Fig. 5.15.

The SCANNER subtree assembles the next token from the input string. We start by skipping over all blanks and end-of-line markers. We then read in the first character in the terminal string that comprises the next token. Once the first character has been classified, it is an easy matter to determine what the next token is.

Notes

1. We leave for the coding stage the details of echo printing the terminals, since they would merely clutter up the subtree.

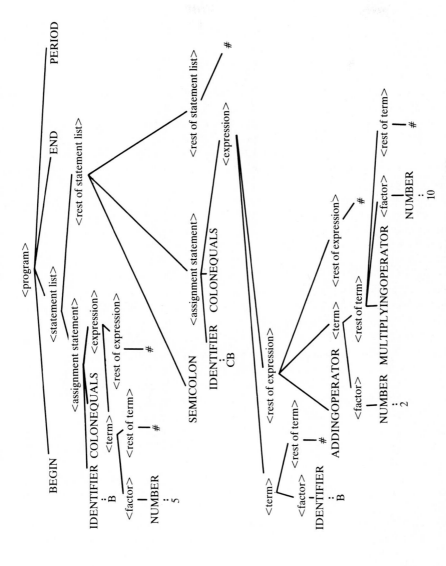

Figure 5.14 The parse tree for the program given in the Sample Input on page 183.

185

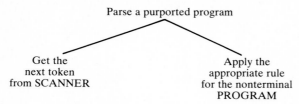

Figure 5.15 The main tree for the recursive descent parser.

2. We adopt the approach outlined on pages 142–144: There will be a small number of token classes, and the token class will determine the number and types of the other fields in a token. For the sake of simplicity, we ignore the problem of posting and accessing identifiers and reserved words in the symbol table. Since BEGIN and END are the only reserved words we have to deal with, we arbitrarily assign them symbol-table addresses of 100 and 101, respectively.

In Chap. 7, we introduce a method for efficiently posting and accessing names in a symbol table. Problem 7.1 extends the current case study to creating and maintaining the symbol table. This extension would be essential in developing a compiler.

3. A realistic scanner would devote considerable effort to detecting lexical errors, such as having a letter within a number (for example 32X7).

The subtree SCANNER is given in Fig. 5.16.

The subtree PROGRAM determines the rule to apply when the nonterminal is 〈program〉. Since the grammar in Fig. 5.11*b* has only one rule with 〈program〉 on the left-hand side, that must be the rule. So we write out this rule, check for the expected tokens, and call the STATEMENTLIST subtree.

When we return from the STATEMENTLIST subtree, the next token must represent either END or a period. If it is the former, we must check to see if there is a subsequent token and whether that next token represents a period.

The complete subtree for PROGRAM is given in Fig. 5.17.

In the subtree STATEMENTLIST, we write out the rule defining 〈statement list〉 and then call the ASSIGNMENTSTATEMENT and RESTOFSTATE-MENTLIST subtrees. See Fig. 5.18.

In the ASSIGNMENTSTATEMENT subtree, we write out the rule for 〈assignment statement〉, check for the appropriate tokens and call the EXPRES-SION subtree.

The ASSIGNMENT STATEMENT subtree is given in Fig. 5.19.

The EXPRESSION subtree writes out its rule and then calls the TERM and RESTOFEXPRESSION subtrees. See Fig. 5.20.

The TERM subtree, shown in Fig. 5.21, is similar to the one for EXPRES-SION.

At the start of the subtree FACTOR, the next token must represent either an identifier, a number or a left parenthesis (in this last case, a call to the EXPRES-SION subtree is made). After seeing one of these, SCANNER is called so that the

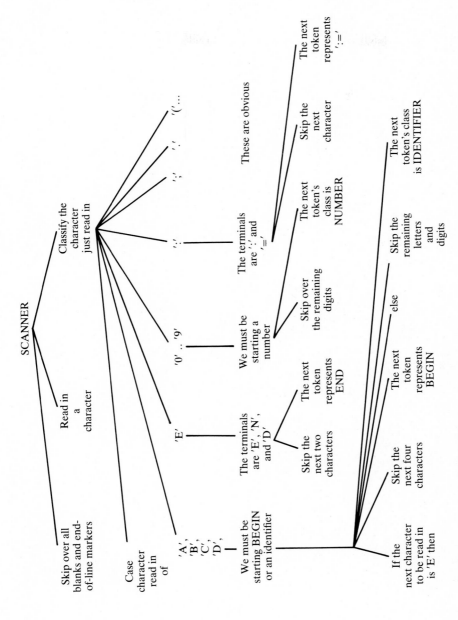

Figure 5.16 The subtree SCANNER.

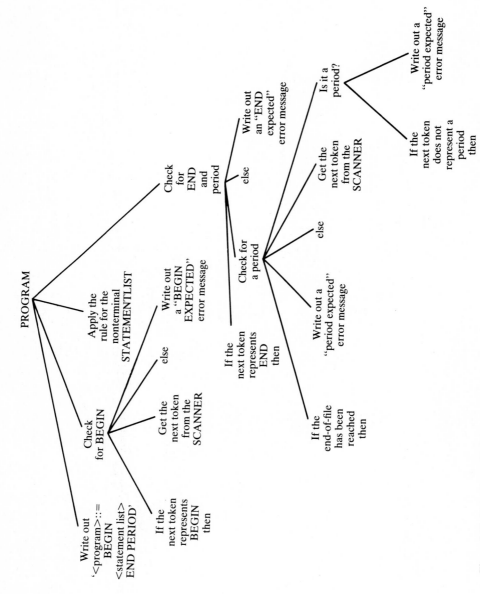

Figure 5.17 The subtree PROGRAM.

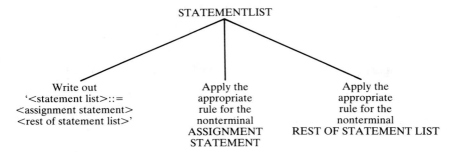

Figure 5.18 The subtree STATEMENTLIST.

RESTOFTERM, RESTOFEXPRESSION and RESTOFSTATEMENTLIST subtrees can choose the appropriate rule to apply. The subtree is given in Fig. 5.22.

The RESTOFTERM subtree decides which rule for ⟨rest of term⟩ is to be applied by examining the next token. If that token represents a multiplying operator, then the rule "⟨rest of term⟩ ::= MULTIPLYINGOPERATOR ⟨factor⟩ ⟨rest of term⟩" is appropriate. Otherwise the rule is "⟨rest of term⟩ ::= # ". See Fig. 5.23.

The RESTOFEXPRESSION subtree, shown in Fig. 5.24, is similar to that for RESTOFTERM.

The RESTOFSTATEMENTLIST subtree is straightforward if the next token represents a semicolon. Otherwise, if the next token's class is IDENTI-FIER, we assume that the semicolon is missing and this is the beginning of an assignment statement. Otherwise, if the next token represents either an END or a period, we simply apply the "empty rest of statement list" rule. If, however, the next token represents neither a semicolon, an identifier, an END or a period, then we should try to recover by skipping over the next token. For example, suppose the program were as follows:

```
BEGIN
    A := 3 := 5 ;
    C := 10
END.
```

We should skip over the second ":=" and then try to apply one of the above rules. Since none of them apply, we skip over the "5" and get to the semicolon. One of the above rules can now be applied.

The subtree is given in Fig. 5.25.

Coding The hierarchy chart is shown in Fig. 5.26. In the program, the procedures are listed in the reverse of the order of the calling sequence because a procedure must be defined before it can be called. Since EXPRESSION calls TERM and TERM calls FACTOR and FACTOR calls EXPRESSION, the program uses the FORWARD directive (see page 33) for the procedure EXPRESSION to tell the

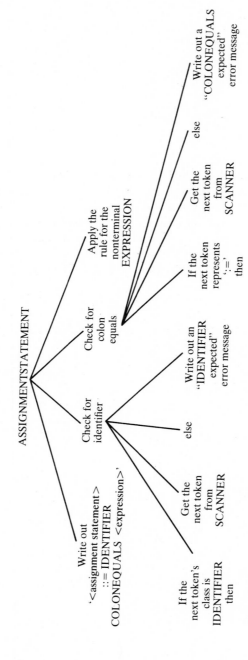

Figure 5.19 The subtree ASSIGNMENTSTATEMENT.

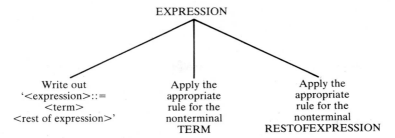

Figure 5.20 The subtree EXPRESSION.

compiler that the definition of this procedure is found farther down. To avoid conflict with the standard identifier PROGRAM, the subtree named PROGRAM corresponds to the procedure MAINPROGRAM.

We will use a variant record for the type of a token. The first field will contain the token's class : IDENTIFIER, UNSIGNEDNUMBER, RESERVED-WORD or OTHERSPECIALSYMBOL. The type of the second field will depend on the value of the class field. For example, if the class is OTHERSPECIAL-SYMBOL, the second field will contain the symbol itself as a two-character string.

Working with variant records requires special care. For example, in the ASSIGNMENTSTATEMENT subtree, one of the leaves is "If the next token represents a ' := ' then." When we translate this into Pascal, we cannot simply write

> IF (NEXTTOKEN.CLASS = OTHERSPECIALSYMBOL) AND
> (NEXTTOKEN.SYMBOL = ' := ') THEN

The reason this compound condition is incorrect is that if the next token's class is not OTHERSPECIALSYMBOL, then it is an error to refer to the SYMBOL field (recall, from page 8, that the operands for AND may be evaluated in any order). We avoid this pitfall by writing

> IF NEXTTOKEN.CLASS = OTHERSPECIALSYMBOL THEN
> IF NEXTTOKEN.SYMBOL = ' := ' THEN

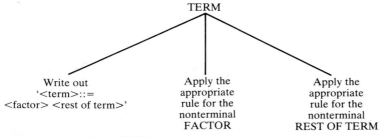

Figure 5.21 The subtree TERM.

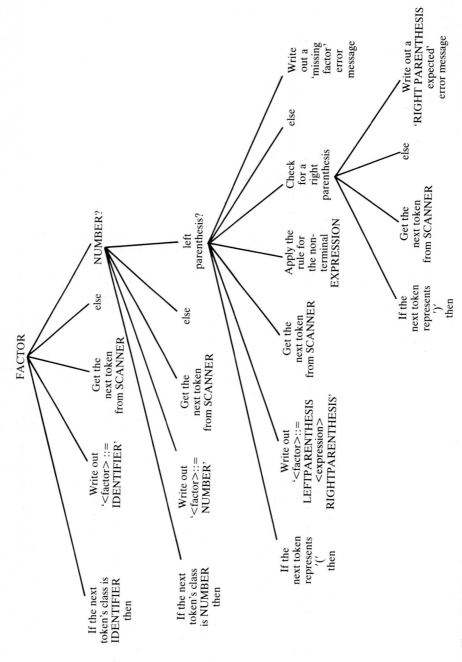

Figure 5.22 The subtree FACTOR.

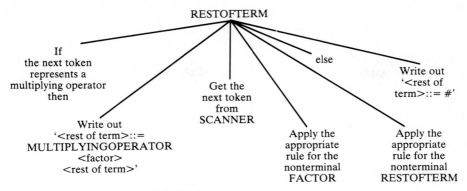

Figure 5.23 The subtree RESTOFTERM.

In coding some of the subtrees, we may have several legal alternatives for the next token. For example, in the RESTOFSTATEMENTLIST subtree, the next token may be a semicolon, an identifier, an END, or a period. In such situations, we avoid the above-mentioned pitfall by using a CASE statement. In fact, as its form suggests, a variant record is often processed with a CASE statement.

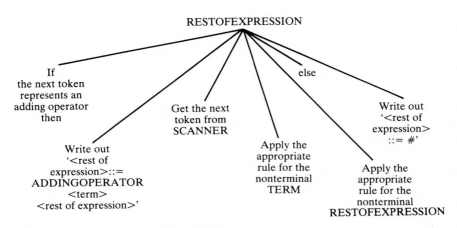

Figure 5.24 The subtree RESTOFEXPRESSION.

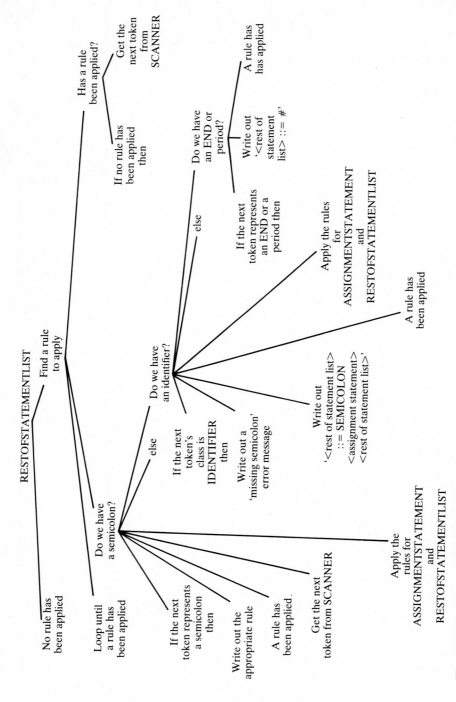

Figure 5.25 The subtree RESTOFSTATEMENTLIST.

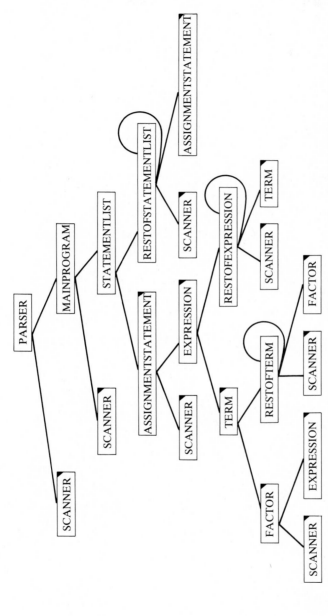

Figure 5.26 The hierarchy chart for PARSER. The calls from a utility procedure, such as ASSIGNMENTSTATEMENT are shown only once.

```
PROGRAM   PARSER(INPUT, OUTPUT);

(*************************************************************)
(*                                                         *)
(*   PROGRAMMER: BILL COLLINS.                             *)
(*                                                         *)
(*   Develop a recursive descent parser for the language  *)
(*   defined by the grammar in Figure 5.11b. The Sample   *)
(*   Input will consist of a purported program in the     *)
(*   language. The program may include blanks and         *)
(*   end-of-line markers, but not within the components of *)
(*   any token. The output will consist of an input       *)
(*   echo and a linear version of the parse tree, down to *)
(*   the tokens. At each stage in the corresponding parse *)
(*   tree, the rule defining the leftmost nonterminal will *)
(*   be applied next.                                     *)
(*       If an error is encountered during the attempted  *)
(*   parse, an appropriate error message is printed. The  *)
(*   program detects syntactic errors only, that is,      *)
(*   violations of the rules given in Figure 5.11(b), not *)
(*   lexical errors - violations of the rules in          *)
(*   Figure 5.11(a). We assume that each program will     *)
(*   contain an END or a period, and if there is a period,*)
(*   it will immediately follow the word END.             *)
(*                                                         *)
(*************************************************************)

CONST BEGINSADDRESS              = 100; (*an arbitrarily chosen location *)
                                        (*where 'BEGIN' could be stored  *)
                                        (*in the symbol table.           *)
      ENDSADDRESS                = 101;
      MISSINGBEGIN               = 'ERROR - "BEGIN" EXPECTED.';
      MISSINGSEMICOLON           = 'ERROR - SEMICOLON EXPECTED.';
      MISSINGEND                 = 'ERROR - "END" EXPECTED.';
      MISSINGPERIOD              = 'ERROR - PERIOD EXPECTED.';
      MISSINGIDENTIFIER          = 'ERROR - IDENTIFIER EXPECTED.';
      MISSINGCOLONEQUALS         = 'ERROR - COLON EQUALS EXPECTED.';
      MISSINGFACTOR              =
        'ERROR - IDENTIFIER, NUMBER, OR LEFT PARENTHESIS EXPECTED.';
      MISSINGRIGHTPARENTHESIS =
        'ERROR - RIGHT PARENTHESIS EXPECTED.';


TYPE  TOKENCLASS                = (IDENTIFIER, UNSIGNEDNUMBER, RESERVEDWORD,
                                   OTHERSPECIALSYMBOL);
      SYMBOLTABLEADDRESS   = 0..500;
      CONSTANTTABLEADDRESS = 0..500;
      SMALLSTRING          = PACKED ARRAY[1..2] OF CHAR;
      TOKENTYPE   = RECORD
                       CASE CLASS : TOKENCLASS OF
                          IDENTIFIER         : (IDPOINTER :
                                                  SYMBOLTABLEADDRESS);
                          UNSIGNEDNUMBER     : (NUMBERPOINTER :
                                                  CONSTANTTABLEADDRESS);
                          RESERVEDWORD       : (WORDPOINTER :
                                                  SYMBOLTABLEADDRESS);
                          OTHERSPECIALSYMBOL : (SYMBOL :
                                                  SMALLSTRING)
                    END;

VAR   NEXTTOKEN : TOKENTYPE;
```

```
PROCEDURE  SCANNER(VAR NEXTTOKEN : TOKENTYPE);

(*  Derive the NEXTTOKEN from the input string. In scanning the input  *)
(*  string to obtain the next token, the buffer variable INPUT^ serves  *)
(*  as a one-character lookahead.  The terminals that comprise the      *)
(*  next token are echo printed.                                        *)

CONST BLANK = ' ';

VAR   CURRENTCHARACTER : CHAR;
      I                : INTEGER;

BEGIN

    (*  Skip over end-of-line markers and blanks.  *)
    WHILE EOLN OR (INPUT^= BLANK) DO
       IF EOLN THEN  (*  Skip over the end-of-line marker.  *)
          BEGIN
              READLN;
              WRITELN
          END
       ELSE  (*  Skip over the blank.  *)
          READ(CURRENTCHARACTER);

    (*  Read in and classify the next terminal.  *)
    READ(CURRENTCHARACTER);
    WRITE(CURRENTCHARACTER);
    IF CURRENTCHARACTER IN [';','.','(',')','+','-','*','/',':'] THEN
       NEXTTOKEN.CLASS := OTHERSPECIALSYMBOL;

    WITH NEXTTOKEN DO
       CASE CURRENTCHARACTER OF

       ';'              : SYMBOL := '; ';

       '.'              : SYMBOL := '. ';

       '('              : SYMBOL := '( ';

       ')'              : SYMBOL := ') ';

       '+'              : SYMBOL := '+ ';

       '-'              : SYMBOL := '- ';

       '*'              : SYMBOL := '* ';

       '/'              : SYMBOL := '/ ';

       ':'              : BEGIN (*The next terminal is '='.*)
                              READ (CURRENTCHARACTER);
                              WRITE (CURRENTCHARACTER);
                              SYMBOL := ':='
                          END;

       'E'              : BEGIN  (* The next two terminals are 'N', 'D'. *)
                              FOR I := 1 TO 2 DO
                                  BEGIN
                                      READ(CURRENTCHARACTER);
                                      WRITE(CURRENTCHARACTER)
                                  END;
                              CLASS        := RESERVEDWORD;
                              WORDPOINTER := ENDSADDRESS
                          END;

       '0', '1', '2',
       '3', '4', '5',
       '6', '7', '8',
       '9'              : BEGIN  (*  We have a number.  *)
                              WHILE INPUT^ IN ['0'..'9'] DO
```

```
                            BEGIN
                                READ(CURRENTCHARACTER);
                                WRITE(CURRENTCHARACTER)
                            END;
                        CLASS := UNSIGNEDNUMBER
                    END;

    'A','B','C','D': IF INPUT^ = 'E' THEN   (*  The terminal string  *)
                                            (*  is 'BEGIN'.          *)
                        BEGIN
                            FOR I := 1 TO 4 DO
                                BEGIN
                                    READ(CURRENTCHARACTER);
                                    WRITE(CURRENTCHARACTER)
                                END;
                            CLASS       := RESERVEDWCRD;
                            WORDPOINTER := BEGINSADDRESS
                        END
                    ELSE  (*  We have an identifier.  *)
                        BEGIN
                            WHILE INPUT^ IN
                                ['A','B','C','D','0'..'9'] DO
                                BEGIN
                                    READ(CURRENTCHARACTER);
                                    WRITE(CURRENTCHARACTER)
                                END;
                            CLASS := IDENTIFIER
                        END


    END;  (*  of the CASE statement.  *)
    WRITELN
END;  (*  of the procedure SCANNER.  *)



PROCEDURE  EXPRESSION(VAR NEXTTOKEN : TOKENTYPE); FORWARD;
```

```
PROCEDURE   FACTOR(VAR NEXTTOKEN : TOKENTYPE);

(*   Process the nonterminal <factor>.   This procedure is   *)
(*   provided with the current value of NEXTTOKEN and        *)
(*   obtains the new value for NEXTTOKEN.                     *)

CONST FACTORIDENTIFIERRULE  = '<factor>::=IDENTIFIER';
      FACTORNUMBERRULE      = '<factor>::=NUMBER';
      FACTORPARENTHESISRLLE =
       '<factor>::=LEFTPARENTHESIS <expression> RIGHTPARENTHESIS';

BEGIN

    (*  Determine which rule applies.  *)
    WITH NEXTTOKEN DO
      CASE CLASS OF

        IDENTIFIER          : BEGIN
                                WRITELN(' ':10,FACTORIDENTIFIERRULE);
                                SCANNER(NEXTTOKEN)
                              END;

        UNSIGNEDNUMBER      : BEGIN
                                WRITELN(' ':10,FACTORNUMBERRULE);
                                SCANNER(NEXTTOKEN)
                              END;
        OTHERSPECIALSYMBOL  : IF SYMBOL = '( ' THEN
                                BEGIN
                                  WRITELN (' ':10,FACTORPARENTHESISRULE);
                                  SCANNER(NEXTTOKEN);
                                  EXPRESSION(NEXTTOKEN);
                                  IF NEXTTOKEN.CLASS = OTHERSPECIALSYMBOL
                                        THEN
                                        IF NEXTTOKEN.SYMBOL = ') ' THEN
                                            SCANNER(NEXTTOKEN)
                                        ELSE
                                            WRITELN(' ':10,
                                                    MISSINGRIGHTPARENTHESIS)
                                    ELSE
                                        WRITELN (' ':10,
                                                 MISSINGRIGHTPARENTHESIS)
                                END
                              ELSE
                                  WRITELN(' ':10, MISSINGFACTOR);

        RESERVEDWORD        : WRITELN(' ':10, MISSINGFACTOR)

      END
END; (*  of the procedure FACTOR.  *)
```

```
PROCEDURE  RESTOFTERM(VAR NEXTTOKEN : TOKENTYPE);

(*  Process the nonterminal <rest of term>. This procedure    *)
(*  is provided with the current value  of NEXTTOKEN and       *)
(*  obtains the new value of NEXTTOKEN.                        *)

CONST FULLRESTOFTERMRULE  =
      '<rest of term>::=MULTIPLYINGOPERATOR <factor> <rest of term>';
      EMPTYRESTOFTERMRULE = '<rest of term>::=  ';

BEGIN
    IF NEXTTOKEN.CLASS = OTHERSPECIALSYMBOL THEN
       IF (NEXTTOKEN.SYMBOL = '* ') OR (NEXTTOKEN.SYMBOL = '/ ') THEN
          BEGIN
             WRITELN(' ':10, FULLRESTOFTERMRULE);
             SCANNER(NEXTTOKEN);
             FACTOR(NEXTTOKEN);
             RESTOFTERM(NEXTTOKEN)
          END
       ELSE
          WRITELN(' ':10, EMPTYRESTOFTERMRULE)
    ELSE
       WRITELN(' ':10, EMPTYRESTOFTERMRULE)
END;  (*  of the procedure RESTOFTERM.  *)




PROCEDURE  TERM(VAR NEXTTOKEN : TOKENTYPE);

(*  Process the nonterminal <term>.  This procedure  *)
(*  is provided with the current value of NEXTTOKEN  *)
(*  and indirectly changes that value through        *)
(*  procedure calls.                                 *)

CONST RULEFORTERM = '<term>::=<factor> <rest of term>';

BEGIN
    WRITELN(' ':10, RULEFORTERM);
    FACTOR(NEXTTOKEN);
    RESTOFTERM(NEXTTOKEN)
END;  (*  of the procedure TERM.  *)




PROCEDURE  RESTOFEXPRESSION(VAR NEXTTOKEN : TOKENTYPE);

(*  Process the nonterminal <rest of expression>.  This procedure  *)
(*  is provided with the current value of NEXTTOKEN and obtains the *)
(*  new value of NEXTTOKEN.                                        *)

CONST FULLRESTOFEXPRESSIONRULE  =
'<rest of expression>::=ADDINGOPERATOR <term> <rest of expression>';
      EMPTYRESTOFEXPRESSIONRULE = '<rest of expression>::=  ';

BEGIN
    IF NEXTTOKEN.CLASS = OTHERSPECIALSYMBOL THEN
       IF (NEXTTOKEN.SYMBOL = '+ ') OR
          (NEXTTOKEN.SYMBOL = '- ') THEN
          BEGIN
             WRITELN(' ':10, FULLRESTOFEXPRESSIONRULE);
             SCANNER(NEXTTOKEN);
             TERM(NEXTTOKEN);
             RESTOFEXPRESSION(NEXTTOKEN)
          END
       ELSE
          WRITELN(' ':10, EMPTYRESTOFEXPRESSIONRULE)
    ELSE
       WRITELN(' ':10, EMPTYRESTOFEXPRESSIONRULE)
END;  (*  of the procedure RESTOFEXPRESSION.  *)
```

```
PROCEDURE EXPRESSION;

(*  Process the nonterminal <expression>.  This procedure   *)
(*  is provided with the current value of NEXTTOKEN and      *)
(*  indirectly changes that value through procedure calls.   *)

CONST RULEFOREXPRESSION =
         '<expression>::=<term> <rest of expression>'; -

BEGIN
   WRITELN(' ':10, RULEFOREXPRESSION);
   TERM(NEXTTOKEN);
   RESTOFEXPRESSION(NEXTTOKEN)
END;  (*  of the procedure EXPRESSION.  *)




PROCEDURE  ASSIGNMENTSTATEMENT(VAR NEXTTOKEN : TOKENTYPE);

(*  Process the nonterminal <assignment statement>.  This procedure   *)
(*  is provided with the current value of NEXTTOKEN and obtains the   *)
(*  new value of NEXTTOKEN.                                           *)

CONST RULEFORASSIGNMENT =
   '<assignment statement>::=IDENTIFIER COLONEQUALS <expression>';

BEGIN

   WRITELN(' ':10, RULEFORASSIGNMENT);

   (*  Check for identifier.  *)
   IF NEXTTOKEN.CLASS = IDENTIFIER THEN
      SCANNER(NEXTTOKEN)
   ELSE
      WRITELN(' ':10, MISSINGIDENTIFIER);

   (*  Check for colonequals.  *)
   IF NEXTTOKEN.CLASS = OTHERSPECIALSYMBOL THEN
      IF NEXTTOKEN.SYMBOL = ':=' THEN
         SCANNER(NEXTTOKEN)
      ELSE
         WRITELN(' ':10, MISSINGCOLONEQUALS)
   ELSE
      WRITELN(' ':10,MISSINGCOLONEQUALS);

   EXPRESSION(NEXTTOKEN)
END;  (*  of the procedure ASSIGNMENTSTATEMENT.  *)
```

```
PROCEDURE  RESTOFSTATEMENTLIST(VAR NEXTTOKEN : TOKENTYPE);

(*  Process the nonterminal <rest of statement list>.  This procedure   *)
(*  is provided with the current value of NEXTTOKEN and obtains the new  *)
(*  value of NEXTTOKEN.                                                  *)

CONST EMPTYRESTOFSTATEMENTLISTRULE = '<rest of statement list>::=   ';
(*    We do not define a constant identifier for the "full"     *)
(*    rest-of-statement-list rule because that rule will not     *)
(*    fit on one line.                                           *)

VAR   RULEAPPLIED : BOOLEAN;

BEGIN

    RULEAPPLIED  :=  FALSE;

    (* Find a rule to apply. *)
    REPEAT

        WITH NEXTTOKEN DO
            CASE CLASS OF

                OTHERSPECIALSYMBOL : IF SYMBOL = '; ' THEN
                                         BEGIN
                                             WRITELN(' ':10,
                                             '<rest of statement list>::=',
                                             'SEMICOLON <assignment statement>',
                                             ' <rest of statement list>');
                                             RULEAPPLIED := TRUE;
                                             SCANNER(NEXTTOKEN);
                                             ASSIGNMENTSTATEMENT(NEXTTOKEN);
                                             RESTOFSTATEMENTLIST(NEXTTOKEN)
                                         END
                                     ELSE
                                         IF SYMBOL = '. ' THEN
                                             BEGIN
                                                 WRITELN(' ':10,
                                                     EMPTYRESTOFSTATEMENTLISTRULE);
                                                 RULEAPPLIED := TRUE
                                             END;

                IDENTIFIER         : BEGIN
                                         WRITELN(' ':10, MISSINGSEMICOLON);
                                         WRITELN(' ':10,
                                         '<rest of statement list>::=',
                                         'SEMICOLON <assignment statement>',
                                         '<rest of statement list>');
                                         RULEAPPLIED := TRUE;
                                         ASSIGNMENTSTATEMENT(NEXTTOKEN);
                                         RESTOFSTATEMENTLIST(NEXTTOKEN)
                                     END;

                RESERVEDWORD       : IF WORDPOINTER = ENDSADDRESS THEN
                                         BEGIN
                                             WRITELN(' ':10,
                                                 EMPTYRESTOFSTATEMENTLISTRULE);
                                             RULEAPPLIED := TRUE
                                         END;

                UNSIGNEDNUMBER      : (* Do nothing.*)

            END; (* of the CASE statement. *)

            (* Has a rule been applied yet? *)
            IF NOT(RULEAPPLIED) THEN (* skip to next token. *)
                SCANNER(NEXTTOKEN)

        UNTIL RULEAPPLIED  (* same as "UNTIL RULEAPPLIED = TRUE" *)

    END; (* of the procedure RESTOFSTATEMENTLIST. *)
```

```
PROCEDURE  STATEMENTLIST(VAR NEXTTOKEN : TOKENTYPE);

(*   Process the nonterminal <statement list>.  This procedure   *)
(*   is provided with the current value of NEXTTOKEN and          *)
(*   indirectly changes that value through procedure calls.       *)

CONST RULEFORSTATEMENTLIST =
   '<statement list>::=<assignment statement> <rest of statement list>';

BEGIN
   WRITELN(' ':10, RULEFORSTATEMENTLIST);
   ASSIGNMENTSTATEMENT(NEXTTOKEN);
   RESTOFSTATEMENTLIST(NEXTTOKEN)
END;  (*  of the procedure STATEMENTLIST.  *)
```

```
PROCEDURE  MAINPROGRAM(VAR NEXTTOKEN : TOKENTYPE);

(*  Process the nonterminal <program>; The name "MAINPROGRAM" *)
(*  was chosen to avoid conflict with the standard Pascal      *)
(*  identifier "PROGRAM."  This procedure is provided with     *)
(*  the initial value of NEXTTOKEN and obtains, ultimately,    *)
(*  the final value of NEXTTOKEN.                              *)

CONST RULEFORPROGRAM =
      '<program>::=BEGIN <statement list> END PERIOD';

BEGIN
    WRITELN(' ':10, RULEFORPROGRAM);

    (*  Check for BEGIN.  *)
    IF NEXTTOKEN.CLASS = RESERVEDWORD THEN
        IF NEXTTOKEN.WORDPOINTER = BEGINSADDRESS THEN
            SCANNER(NEXTTOKEN)
        ELSE
            WRITELN(' ':10,MISSINGBEGIN)
    ELSE
        WRITELN(' ':10,MISSINGBEGIN);

    (* Apply the rule for <statement list>. *)
    STATEMENTLIST(NEXTTOKEN);

    (* Check for END. *)
    IF NEXTTOKEN.CLASS = RESERVEDWORD THEN
        IF NEXTTOKEN.WORDPOINTER = ENDSADDRESS THEN

            (* Check for a period after the END. *)
            IF EOLN THEN
                WRITELN(' ':10,MISSINGPERIOD)
            ELSE
                BEGIN
                    SCANNER(NEXTTOKEN);
                    IF NEXTTOKEN.CLASS = OTHERSPECIALSYMBOL THEN
                        BEGIN
                            IF NEXTTOKEN.SYMBOL <> '. ' THEN
                                WRITELN(' ':10,MISSINGPERIOD)
                        END
                    ELSE
                        WRITELN(' ':10,MISSINGPERIOD)
                END
        ELSE
            WRITELN(' ':10,MISSINGEND)
    ELSE
        WRITELN(' ':10,MISSINGEND)
END;  (*  of the procedure MAINPROGRAM.  *)




BEGIN  (*  the executable section of the main program.  *)

    (*  Print headings.  *)
    PAGE;
    WRITELN('TERMINAL(S)    RULE OR ERROR MESSAGE');
    WRITELN('----------    ---------------------');

    (*  Get the first token.  *)
    SCANNER(NEXTTOKEN);

    (*  Apply the <PROGRAM> rule.  *)
    MAINPROGRAM(NEXTTOKEN);

    WRITELN(' ':10, 'PARSE COMPLETE');
    PAGE
END.
```

Program Testing

1. Testing the main program and the procedure SCANNER:

   Test 1a

   ```
   BEGIN
       A57C := 52873 + B9 ;
       C7   := A40A * 0
   END.
   ```

2. Testing the procedure MAINPROGRAM (the STATEMENTLIST stub simply keeps scanning until the next token is an END or a period):

   Test 2a   (A correct program)

   ```
   BEGIN
       CAB7 := 426 ;
       A5C  := 2 ;
       B    := 1 * (B + B)
   END.
   ```

   Test 2b   (Missing BEGIN)

   ```
       A60 := 5 ;
       D   := A60 + 1
   END.
   ```

   Test 2c   (Missing END)

   ```
   BEGIN
       A := 5 ;
       B := 10
   ```

   Test 2d   (Missing period)

   ```
   BEGIN
       A := B + C * D
   END
   ```

   Test 2e   (Missing period)

   ```
   BEGIN
       A := B + C * D
   END ;
   ```

3. Testing the procedures STATEMENTLIST and RESTOFSTATEMENT-LIST (the ASSIGNMENTSTATEMENT stub simply keeps scanning until the next token is a semicolon, identifier, END or period):

   Test 3a   (A correct program)

   ```
   BEGIN
       BAD := 53 ;
       CAD := 54
   END.
   ```

Test 3b   (Missing semicolon)

```
BEGIN
    BAD := 53
    CAD := 54
END.
```

4. Testing the ASSIGNMENTSTATEMENT procedure:

Test 4a   (A correct program)

```
BEGIN
    B  := 7 ;
    C  := 5 + D ;
    BC := BC + 1
END.
```

Test 4b   (Missing identifier)

```
BEGIN
    A := 5 ;
    7 := B
END.
```

Test 4c   (Missing ":="; actually, it is misplaced)

```
BEGIN
    A := 7 ;
    A + 5 := 0
END.
```

5. Testing the rest of the procedures:

Test 5a   (A simple, correct program)

```
BEGIN
    A := 0
END.
```

Test 5b   (A more complex, correct program)

```
BEGIN
    A := 15 + 7 * C / (BAD − CAD) ;
    C := (((A + (7 + B) − 1) − 2) * 3) / 4 ;
    A := A + (5 * B / D / B / A / C * BA + 14 − 0 ;
    ABABCA := 1523719
END.
```

Test 5c   (Missing factors)

```
BEGIN
    A := := 5 ;
    B := ;
    C := * 7
END.
```

Test 5d   (Missing right parenthesis)

```
BEGIN
    A := 5 + (C + 10 * (D − 5);
    B := 0
END.
```

Note on Case Study 5.1 In a compiler, the parser does not output the parse tree, even in linear form. Instead, when the parser determines which rule to apply, it calls the next essential procedure in a compiler—the semantic analyzer—which associates meaning with the program's components. For example, '+' indicates that an addition is to be performed.

Exercise 5.15 In testing the above program, we did not check for a missing adding operator or multiplying operator. Why not?

Exercise 5.16 Modify the above program to include the possibility the input might contain neither an "END" nor a period.

Exercise 5.17 Use the syntax of Pascal in Appendix 1 to show that

CURRENTCHARACTER IN [';' , '.' , '(']

is a valid expression.
    Hint: Build a parse tree with ⟨expression⟩ at the root.

BINARY TREES

In this section we consider a restricted type of tree which has a convenient implementation and a variety of interesting applications. A *binary tree* is a tree which either is empty or consists of a root and two binary trees, called the "left" and "right" subtrees of the root. Thus, in a binary tree, the outdegree of each node is less than or equal to two. Fig. 5.27 shows five binary trees. Because we distinguish between left and right subtrees, the binary tree in Fig. 5.27d is different from the binary tree in Fig. 5.27e, although they are the same when viewed simply as trees.

A binary tree can be implemented as a multilinked list in which each record has a "left pointer" field and a "right pointer" field. For example, the binary tree in Fig. 5.27b can be implemented by the dynamic multilinked list shown in Fig. 5.28.

There will always be some wasted space (that is, NIL pointers) in such a representation of a binary tree, but the wastage is much less than that in a multilinked structure for an arbitrary tree. For example, in the parse tree on page 182, one of the nodes (namely the root) has four branches. Thus each node in the corresponding linked list would need four pointer fields. Over 75 percent of those pointers would have a NIL value!

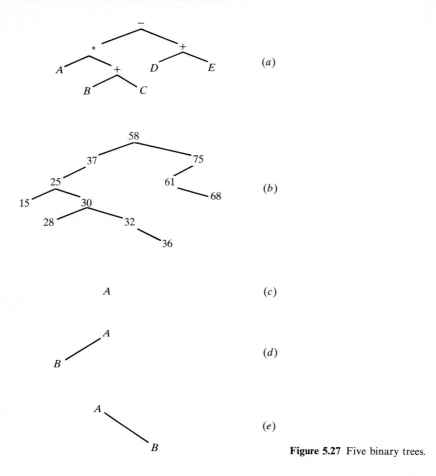

(a)

(b)

(c)

(d)

(e)

Figure 5.27 Five binary trees.

Fortunately, there is an algorithm to convert an arbitrary tree into a binary tree without loss of information. The binary tree can then be efficiently represented by a multilinked list as above. To convert an arbitrary tree into an equivalent binary tree, the strategy is as follows:

Each node in the original tree will be a node in the binary tree. Let X be any node in the original tree. The children of X in the binary tree are determined as follows:

1. In the binary tree, X's left child will be the leftmost child of X in the original tree. If X had no children in the original tree, X will have no left child in the binary tree.
2. In the binary tree, X's right child will be the sibling *of* X (in the original tree) that is just to the right of X. If X had no siblings to its right in the original tree, X will have no right child in the binary tree.

For a simple example, if the original tree is

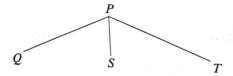

then the binary-tree representation would be

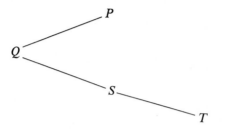

Figure 5.29 shows a more complex tree and its binary-tree equivalent. The original tree would require 10 non-NIL pointers and 34 NIL pointers, whereas the binary representation would have 10 non-NIL pointers and only 12 NIL pointers. The trade-off for this space advantage is that it takes longer to access the nodes. For example, in the original tree, node *H* can be accessed from the root with just two pointer references (*A*'s pointer to *C* and *C*'s pointer to *H*). In the binary tree, accessing *H* from the root requires five pointer references.

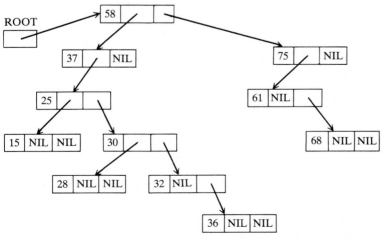

Figure 5.28 A multilinked list implementation of the binary tree in Fig. 5.27*b*.

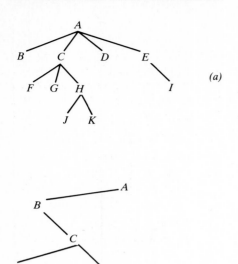

(a)

(b)

Figure 5.29 A tree and its binary equivalent.

Exercise 5.18 Generate a binary-tree representation for the following tree.

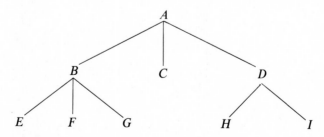

Exercise 5.19 How many NIL pointers are there in the multilinked list representation of any binary tree with 10 nodes? With 1000 nodes?

Exercise 5.20 Develop a strategy to "recover" the original structure of a tree from its binary representation. Apply that strategy to obtain the original tree in Exercise 5.18 from its binary representation.

Traversing a Binary Tree

A *traversal* of a binary tree is an algorithm that accesses each node in the tree exactly once. The accessed node may simply be printed as it is encountered or may be subjected to some kind of processing. Each traversal imposes an ordering on the nodes in the tree, namely, the order in which they are accessed. Three kinds of traversals are of special interest. Each of the three algorithms is naturally recursive since binary trees themselves are defined recursively.

1. *Left branch, Right branch, Node traversal*, abbreviated LRN. Starting at the root, we first access each node's left branch, then the node's right branch, and finally the node itself. This is a recursive algorithm since each left and right branch can be thought of as a subtree on its own. For example, if we apply an LRN traversal to the tree in Fig. 5.27a, we start by accessing the root's left branch. But the left branch is itself a subtree, so we must apply an LRN traversal to that subtree:

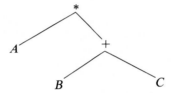

This subtree's left branch is simply A, so A is the first node accessed. The subtree's right branch is another subtree, namely

For this subtree, the LRN rule gives the ordering $BC+$. The previous subtree's root (namely "$*$") can now be accessed, so the ordering so far is

$$ABC + *$$

We now traverse the right branch of the original tree and finally, the root. The complete ordering is

$$ABC + * DE + -$$

If we think of the nonleaf nodes as operators and the branches as operands, then an LRN traversal produces postfix notation! For this reason, an LRN traversal is also called a "postorder" traversal.

2. *Left branch, Node, Right branch traversal* (LNR). Starting at the root, we first access each node's left branch, then the node itself, and finally the node's right branch. For example, an LNR traversal of the binary tree of test scores in Fig. 5.27*b* produces the ordering

15, 25, 28, 30, 32, 36, 37, 58, 61, 68, 75

The fact that the scores are listed in increasing order is no coincidence—a binary tree for which LNR produces a sorted list is called a "binary sort tree."

Thus, a binary sort tree is a binary tree which is empty or in which all the values in the left subtree are less than or equal to the root's value and all the values in the right subtree are greater than the root's value. This property applies, recursively, to each node in a binary sort tree since each node is itself the root of a binary subtree.

How can we create a binary sort tree from an unsorted list of test scores? Essentially, we need a procedure for inserting a test score in a binary sort tree. The strategy follows from the above property: If the tree is empty, insert the score at the root. For a nonempty tree, if the score is less than or equal to the root's score, insert the score in the root's left branch; otherwise, insert the score in the root's right branch.

This leads to the following procedure:

```
TYPE   SCORETYPE = 0..100 ;
       POINTER   = ^NODE ;
       NODE      = RECORD
                       SCORE        : SCORETYPE ;
                       LEFT, RIGHT : POINTER
                   END ;
PROCEDURE   INSERT(TESTSCORE :SCORETYPE ; VAR   ROOT :POINTER) ;
(* Insert TESTSCORE into the binary sort tree pointed to by ROOT. *)
BEGIN
    (* Is the tree empty so far? *)
    IF  ROOT = NIL  THEN
        BEGIN
            NEW(ROOT) ;
            ROOT^.SCORE := TESTSCORE ;
            ROOT^.LEFT  := NIL ;
            ROOT^.RIGHT := NIL
        END
    ELSE

        IF  TESTSCORE <= ROOT^.SCORE  THEN

            (* Follow the left branch. *)
            INSERT(TESTSCORE, ROOT^.LEFT)
```

ELSE

    (∗ Follow the right branch. ∗)
    INSERT(TESTSCORE, ROOT^.RIGHT)

END ; (∗ of the procedure INSERT. ∗)

For example, suppose we started with the following unsorted list of test scores:

42 51 19 37 42 86 71 10 75 22 31 42

The corresponding binary sort tree would be

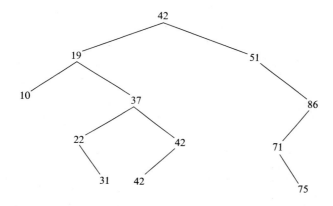

An LNR traversal is sometimes referred to as an "inorder" traversal because it produces infix notation when applied to an expression tree such as the one in Fig. 5.27a:

$$A * (B + C) - (D + E)$$

Parentheses were inserted when the child operator's priority was less than or equal to the priority of its parent operator.

3. *Node, Left branch, Right branch traversal*, abbreviated NLR. Starting at the root, we first access the node itself, then the node's left branch, and finally the node's right branch. For example, an NLR traversal of the tree in Fig. 5.27a yields

$$- * A + BC + DE$$

Since each operator immediately precedes its operands, an NLR traversal is sometimes referred to as a "preorder" traversal. We will see this traversal again in Chap. 8, where it has still another name: "depth-first" traversal.

Binary trees are further analyzed in Chaps. 6 and 7.

Exercise 5.21 Produce an LRN traversal from the following binary tree:

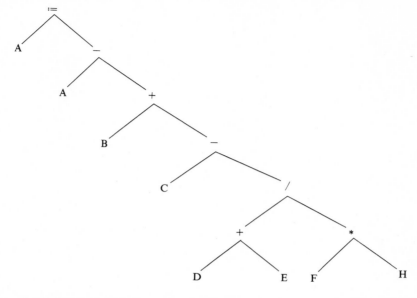

Exercise 5.22 Produce LNR and NLR traversals for the tree in Exercise 5.21.

Exercise 5.23 Develop a binary sort tree from the following list:

32   17   10   86   75   82   10   75   21

How many calls to INSERT (page 212) would be needed if we started with an empty tree?

Exercise 5.24 Find a different, unsorted arrangement of the numbers in Exercise 5.23 for which the binary sort tree would be the same as in that exercise.

Exercise 5.25 Find a different, unsorted arrangement of the numbers in Exercise 5.23 for which the binary sort tree would be different from the tree in that exercise but the LNR ordering would be the same.

NETWORKS

A *network* is an acyclic directed graph with one source and one sink, where each node in the graph has a "weight" field containing a nonnegative integer.† Figure 5.30 shows a network with seven nodes; the weight of each node is encircled.

---

† An alternative representation of a network associates the weights with the arrows rather than the nodes. For a comparison of this representation with the one we use, see Wiest, 1977.

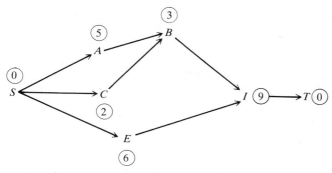

Figure 5.30 A network, with weights encircled.

By convention, the source and sink are labeled S and T (for START and TERMINUS), respectively. If we view the whole network as a project and the nodes as activities, the weight of a node may be thought of as the cost of the activity or as the length of time to complete the activity. For convenience, we henceforth interpret the weight of a node as the length of time in days to complete the corresponding activity. Thus, for example, activity A will be completed 5 days after it starts. Activity B requires 3 days, but B cannot be begun until both A and C have been completed since A and C are immediate predecessors of B.

How long will the entire project take? Since the network is small, we can calculate the project's length by hand. We first determine the start and finish times of each activity in the project. Since job S has no immediate predecessors, we can start job S at day 0. Since S's duration is 0 days, we will finish job S on day 0. Thus jobs A, C, and E can'be started at day 0 and will be finished on days 5, 2, and 6, respectively. What about job B? Since both A and C must be completed before B can be started, the start time for job B is day 5 and, since B takes three days, its finish time is day 8. Since we now know when I's immediate predecessors will finish (B on day 8, E on day 6), we conclude that I will start on the day that its latest predecessor ends, namely, on day 8. Since I takes nine days, I can finish and T can start (and finish) on the 17th day. Thus the entire project will be completed in 17 days.

From the start and finish times, shown in Fig. 5.31, we can glean additional information about the project.

Associated with the length of the project is the path (or paths) from S to T whose weights add up to the project's length. Such a path is called a *critical path*. A critical path is calculated, in reverse, starting with T. We then follow the immediate predecessors until we arrive back at S. If a given node has more than one immediate predecessor, choose from among the immediate predecessors the one whose finish time is latest. Thus, the critical path in Figure 5.30 is

SABIT

If, in calculating a critical path, two of the immediate predecessors have the same (latest) finish time, then we will have two critical paths. For example, the network in Fig. 5.32 has two critical paths: *SABDGT* and *SACEIT*.

Activity	Start time	Finish time
S	0	0
A	0	5
C	0	2
E	0	6
B	5	8
I	8	17
T	17	17

Figure 5.31 The start and finish times of each activity in the network in Fig. 5.30.

Notice that if we wanted to speed up the project, we must shorten the length of an activity on each critical path. Similarly, activities F and H can be started later or stretched out (up to a point) without affecting the length of the project. This may allow valuable resources to be reallocated to activities on the critical path, thus speeding them up.

Exercise 5.26 Draw the network defined by the following table:

Activity	Duration	Immediate predecessors
S	0	
A	5	S
B	4	S
C	5	A
D	4	A, B
E	2	C, D
F	3	D, E
G	9	B
H	6	C, F, G
I	8	H
J	12	G
T	0	I, J

Exercise 5.27 Find the critical path through the network in Exercise 5.26. How long will the project take?

Exercise 5.28 Construct a network with three critical paths.

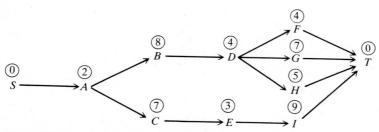

Figure 5.32 A network with two critical paths.

With a little relabelling we can obtain a convenient implementation of a network. For example, consider the network defined in Exercise 5.26. Each activity is assigned a job number according to its position in the table. Thus, S is job number 1, E is job number 6, and so on. Immediate predecessors are specified by numbers, so E's predecessor list would be 4, 5. The resulting table is shown in Fig. 5.33. We use zero for S's immediate predecessor to indicate that S has no immediate predecessor.

We can now handle an arbitrary number of activities, each of which can be specified by a string of characters, not just a single character. For example, if we wanted the network to allow up to 100 activities and each activity to be a string of 10 characters, we could use the following implementation, in which the immediate predecessors are stored in a linked list:

```
CONST   STRINGLENGTH            = 10 ;
        MAXNUMBEROFACTIVITIES = 100 ;
        JOBRANGE                = 1..MAXNUMBEROFACTIVITIES ;

TYPE    POINTER = ^PREDECESSOR ;
        NODE    = RECORD
                    ACTIVITY      :PACKED ARRAY[1..STRINGLENGTH] OF CHAR ;
                    BACKPOINTER : POINTER ;
                    DURATION,
                    STARTTIME,
                    FINISHTIME    : 0..MAXINT ;
                 END ;
        PREDECESSOR = RECORD
                        JOBNUMBER                 : JOBRANGE ;
                        OTHERPREDECESSORPOINTER : POINTER
                      END ;

ARRAYTYPE = ARRAY[JOBRANGE] OF NODE ;

VAR     NETWORK : ARRAYTYPE ;
```

Figure 5.34 shows what this array would contain if we started with the network in Fig. 5.33 and calculated the appropriate start and finish times:

Job number	Activity	Duration	Immediate predecessors
1	S	0	0
2	A	5	1
3	B	4	1
4	C	5	2
5	D	4	2, 3
6	E	2	4, 5
7	F	3	5, 6
8	G	9	3
9	H	6	4, 7, 8
10	I	8	9
11	J	12	8
12	T	0	10, 11

Figure 5.33 An alternate description of the network of Exercise 5.26.

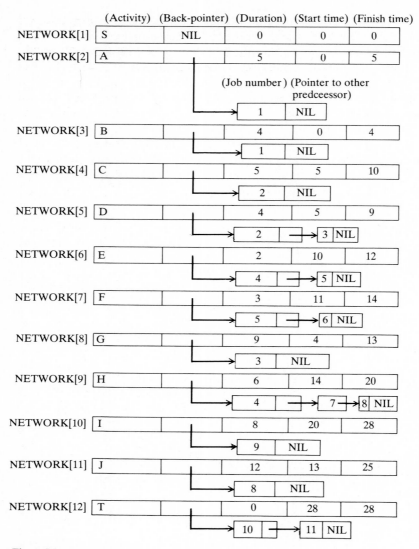

Figure 5.34 An array implementation of the network in Fig. 5.33.

PROBLEMS

Problem 5.1 A Family Tree

Given a list of parent-child relationships, determine the relationships between each pair in another list.

Clarification The first part of the input will contain a list of pairs of names. Each name will consist of up to ten letters, left justified. The first name in the pair represents the parent of the person whose name is given second. Each parent will have, at most, two children. For each parent-child pair except the first, the parent in the pair will be the child of some parent listed earlier. Thus the list of parent-child pairs constitutes a binary tree whose root is the parent given in the first pair. The list of parent-child pairs concludes with a dummy pair, "END   END". This will be followed by a list of pairs of names for which the relationships must be determined. For example, if two of the parent-child pairs were

JOHN   KAREN

KAREN   BOB

then the relationship for the pair

JOHN   BOB

would be "grandparent" because John is the grandparent of Bob. Only the following relationships need be determined:

parent

child

grandparent

grandchild

sibling

aunt/uncle

nephew/niece

cousin

We consider first-cousins only, so two people are cousins if they are not siblings but have the same grandparent.

An error message should be printed if

1. A parent attempts to have more than two children.
2. A relationship is sought for a person not in the tree.

Sample Input

JOHN	KAREN
KAREN	BOB
BOB	JANE
KAREN	PAUL
PAUL	TERRY
PAUL	JOAN
JOHN	RACHEL
RACHEL	TOM
END	END
BOB	PAUL
BOB	JANE
BOB	TOM
KAREN	TOM
KAREN	JOAN
RACHEL	TERRY
JOAN	KAREN

Sample Output

PARENT	CHILD
JOHN	KAREN
KAREN	BOB
BOB	JANE
KAREN	PAUL
PAUL	TERRY
PAUL	JOAN
JOHN	RACHEL
RACHEL	TOM

RELATIONSHIPS

BOB IS THE SIBLING OF PAUL.
BOB IS THE PARENT OF JANE.
BOB IS A COUSIN OF TOM.
KAREN IS AN AUNT/UNCLE OF TOM.
KAREN IS A GRANDPARENT OF JOAN.
RACHEL AND TERRY ARE NOT RELATED.
JOAN IS A GRANDCHILD OF KAREN.

(Each name's trailing blanks are omitted in the printing of a relationship, so there is only one space between "BOB" and "IS" in the first sentence under "RELATIONSHIPS")

Problem 5.2 A House-Construction Project

Design and write a program to solve the following problem: Given the schedule of activities for a house construction project, determine the length of the project and find all critical paths.

Clarification Each line of input will contain the following information about an activity:

1. The job number, in cols. 1–3;
2. The activity, in cols. 5–40 ;
3. The duration of this activity (in days), in cols. 42–43;
4. The immediately preceding job numbers for this activity, in cols. 45–70; each such job number will be smaller than the current job number and each except the last will be followed by a comma.

The output will consist of the length of the project in days and the job numbers (in increasing order) for each critical path.

Sample Input

(job number)	(activity)	(duration)	(immediate predecessors)
1	START	0	0
2	CLEAR AND EXCAVATE	3	1
3	POUR FOOTERS	1	2
4	POUR FOUNDATION	5	3
5	INSTALL ROUGH PLUMBING	3	4
6	ERECT FRAME AND ROOF	7	4
7	LAY BRICKWORK	4	4
8	INSTALL CHIMNEY AND ROOF SHINGLES	2	6
9	INSTALL ROUGH WIRING	2	6
10	INSTALL INSULATION	5	6,7
11	INSTALL DRY WALL	5	4,9,10
12	INSTALL HARDWOOD FLOOR	4	5
13	INSTALL KITCHEN EQUIPMENT	3	12
14	DO INTERIOR TRIM	3	12
15	COMPLETE PLUMBING	2	12
16	PAINT EXTERIOR	6	6
17	PAINT INTERIOR	5	13,14
18	INSTALL CARPETING	3	17
19	COMPLETE ELECTRICAL WORK	2	13
20	COMPLETE MECHANICAL WORK	3	15,17
21	HOOKUP UTILITIES	1	19,20
22	POUR CONCRETE DRIVEWAY	2	11
23	LANDSCAPE	4	21,22
24	CLEAN UP	2	8,16,18,23
25	TERMINUS	0	24

Sample Output

JOB NUMBER	ACTIVITY	DURATION (IN DAYS)	IMMEDIATE PREDECESSORS
1	START	0	
2	CLEAR AND EXCAVATE	3	1
3	POUR FOOTERS	1	2
4	POUR FOUNDATION	5	3
⋮			
24	CLEAN UP	2	8,16,18,23
25	TERMINUS	0	24

THE ENTIRE PROJECT WILL TAKE 34 DAYS.

EACH OF THE FOLLOWING IS A CRITICAL PATH:

1, 2, 3, 4, 5, 12, 13, 17, 20, 21, 23, 24, 25
1, 2, 3, 4, 5, 12, 14, 17, 20, 21, 23, 24, 25
1, 2, 3, 4, 6, 10, 11, 22, 23, 24, 25

Exercise 5.29 An activity's *late finish time* is the latest time that the activity can be completed without delaying the completion of the entire project. The *late start time* of an activity is the latest time it can be started without delaying the completion of the entire project. The calculation of late finish times and late start times is done in an alternating fashion, working backward from T. For T, its late finish time and late start time are both equal to its normal finish time. For any other activity, its late finish time is the minimum of the late start times of its immediate successors. An activity's late start time is its late finish time minus its duration.

For example, in Fig 5.32, T's late finish time and late start time are both equal to 21. Therefore, F's late finish time is 21 (T's late start time). F's late start time is 17: F's late finish time (21) minus its duration (4). Similarly, G's late finish time is 21 and its late start time is 14; H's late finish time is 21 and its late start time is 16. Since D has F, G, and H as immediate successors, D's late finish time is the minimum of the late start times of F, G, and H, namely 14. D's late start time is 10: D's late finish time (14) minus its duration (4). Calculate the late start and late finish times for all of the activities in the network in Prob. 5.2.

Exercise 5.30 An activity's *slack time* is the difference between its late start time and its normal start time. For example, for job number 18 in Prob. 5.2, its late start time is 29 days and its normal start time is 24 days, so its slack time is five days. Thus it can be delayed by five days without delaying the completion of the entire project. Calculate the slack time for each job in the network in Prob. 5.2. What is the slack time of each job on a critical path?

SIX

SORTING

One of the most common computer operations is *sorting*, that is, putting a list in order. From simple, one-time sorts for small lists to highly efficient sorts for frequently used mailing lists and dictionaries, the ability to design a sort procedure is an essential skill in every programmer's repertoire. Because sorting is so widely used and so many different sorting techniques are available, we should start with some criteria by which various sorts can be evaluated. Our treatment, for the most part, will be informal. A rigorous analysis of sorting (and searching) can be found in Knuth's encyclopedic work *Fundamental Algorithms, Volume 3: Sorting and Searching*, Addison Wesley, 1973.

MEASURES OF EFFICIENCY

As with any other programming problem, sorting involves time, space, and familiarity trade-offs as discussed in Chap. 2. In particular, if the list to be sorted is small, or if the sort is to be used only once or twice, familiarity with a particular sorting routine may be the paramount consideration. Even so, the ubiquitousness of sorting applications should compel you to become familiar with a variety of sorting algorithms. Furthermore, sorts designed for small lists are often applied to large lists, and sorts intended to be used once have a way of staying around for years, so unfamiliarity is often merely an excuse for laziness.

Space is seldom a determining factor in selecting a sort procedure because most of the major sort procedures have approximately the same space requirements. Thus the most important criteria for measuring a sort's efficiency is the time to run the procedure. Because a procedure's run time depends on the computer (as well as the compiler) used, we prefer a machine-independent criterion that correlates with a sort's run time. The standard measure of sort efficiency is the *sort effort*: the average number of comparisons between items to sort the data. This average is calculated over all possible initial arrangements of the items to be sorted. The sort effort is a function of the size of the list to be sorted; the identifier N is customarily used to represent the list size. For example, if one algorithm has a sort effort of $(N^2 - N)/2$ comparisons and another has a sort effort of $\text{trunc}(2N \ln N)$ comparisons, then Fig. 6.1 shows how these sort efforts compare for various values of N.

For small values of N, the differences are negligible, while for larger values the second sort effort is more efficient than the first. In fact, for large N, the first sort effort is dominated by the N^2 term, which gets increasingly larger than the dominant term in the second sort effort, $N \ln N$. To facilitate classifying sort efforts, we generally concentrate on dominant terms. The formalization of this is *O notation*: to say that a sort effort is "of order N^2," abbreviated $O(N^2)$, means that the N^2 term is "dominant" for large values of N.† The sorts we will consider in this chapter fall neatly into one of two classes: those that are $O(N \ln N)$ and those that are $O(N^2)$. It can be shown (see Kruse, 1984, pages 152–155) that, for comparison-based‡ sorts, the best sort effort possible is $O(N \ln N)$. Thus, we can view the two classes of sort efforts as "bad" [that is, $O(N^2)$] and "good" [that is, $O(N \ln N)$].

† Formally, a function $f(N)$ is $O[g(N)]$ if for some positive integer K, whenever $N >= K$,

$$\frac{1}{K} < \frac{f(N)}{g(N)} < K$$

The idea is that the ratio $f(N) / g(N)$ does not get very large or very small, so $g(N)$ may be used to approximate $f(N)$. For example, the sort effort $(N^2 - N)/2$ is $O(N^2)$ since

$$\frac{(N^2 - N)/2}{N^2} = \frac{1}{2} - \frac{1}{2N}$$

and, for any $N >= 4$

$$\frac{1}{4} < \frac{1}{2} - \frac{1}{2N} < 4$$

So, for $N >= 4$

$$\frac{1}{4} < \frac{(N^2 - N)/2}{N} < 4$$

In the notation of calculus, a function $f(N)$ is $O[g(N)]$ if

$$0 < \lim_{N \to \infty} \frac{f(N)}{g(N)} < \infty$$

‡ Most sorting requires comparisons between items. In a few situations, this is not necessary. For example, if you wanted to sort 100 different integers, each with a value between 1 and 100, you could set up an integer array with subscripts from 1 to 100, and store the item with value i at location i.

N	$(N^2 - N)/2$	trunc($2N$ ln N)
5	10	16
10	45	46
20	190	119
100	4,950	921
1000	499,500	13,815

Figure 6.1 Comparison of two sort efforts for several values of N.

In addition to the sort effort (that is, the average case), we are also interested in the worst case for a sort algorithm, that is, the initial arrangement of the N items requiring the most comparisons in the sorting. Sometimes the best case for an algorithm may also be worth noting.

Some other criteria for measuring a sort's performance are the number of swaps and the average distance moved during each swap. Sort procedures that move items over large distances during an average swap are, in general, more efficient than those that require several swaps to move an item to its final resting place.

SIMPLE SORT TECHNIQUES

To illustrate each of the sorts in this section, we use the following list of 10 integers:

59 46 32 81 46 55 87 43 70 80

We now present three methods for sorting a list of N elements $a_1, a_2, \ldots, a_N$ into increasing order. Of course a sort into decreasing order would be handled similarly. Also, these methods work equally well for strings or numbers.

Selection Sort Find the position of the smallest of $a_1, a_2, \ldots, a_N$ and swap the number in that position with the number in position 1; a_1 now contains the smallest number. Then find the position of the smallest of $a_2, a_3, \ldots, a_N$ and swap the number in that position with the number in position 2. Continue until, finally, the smallest of a_{N-1} and a_N is swapped into position $N - 1$.

The following procedure performs a selection sort on a list implemented as an array. For the sake of information hiding, we encapsulate the array information in a record type, called LISTTYPE. Thus a calling program need not be aware of the fact that the list is implemented as an array.

```
(* COMPONENTTYPE can be any type for which "<" is defined, namely, *)
(* any string type or scalar type.                                 *)
TYPE   LISTSIZERANGE = 1..MAXLISTSIZE;
       LISTTYPE      = RECORD
                           A : ARRAY[LISTSIZERANGE] OF COMPONENTTYPE ;
                           N : LISTSIZERANGE
                       END ;
```

```
PROCEDURE   SELECTIONSORT(VAR   LIST : LISTTYPE) ;

(* Perform a Selection Sort on LIST, implemented as A[1..N]. *)
VAR   I, J, POSITION : LISTSIZERANGE ;
      TEMPORARY : COMPONENTTYPE ;

BEGIN
    WITH LIST DO
        FOR I := 1 TO N − 1 DO
            BEGIN

                (* Find the position of the Ith-smallest component in A. *)
                POSITION := I ;
                FOR J := I + 1 TO N DO
                    IF A[J] < A[POSITION] THEN
                        POSITION := J ;

                IF I <> POSITION THEN
                    BEGIN (* Swap A[I] with A[POSITION] *)
                        TEMPORARY := A[I] ;
                        A[I]          := A[POSITION];
                        A[POSITION] := TEMPORARY
                    END
            END
END ;   (* of the procedure SELECTIONSORT. *)
```

Figure 6.2 shows how this method applies to the sample list of numbers on page 225. Each pass† is represented by one line, in which the position to the right of the bracket will get the smallest remaining number and the caret ("^") points to that smallest number.

What is the sort effort for the Selection Sort? To get the smallest element into position 1 requires $N − 1$ comparisons. Since position 1 is ignored from that point on, the number of comparisons needed to get the second smallest element into position 2 is only $N − 2$. The total number of comparisons to sort the whole list is

$$(N − 1) + (N − 2) + (N − 3) + \cdots + 2 + 1$$

To determine the value of this sum in terms of N, we write down the series twice: once in decreasing order and once in increasing order.

$$(N − 1) + (N − 2) + (N − 3) + \cdots + 2 + 1$$
$$1 + 2 + \cdots + (N − 3) + (N − 2) + (N − 1)$$

Notice that $(N − 1) + 1 = N$, $(N − 2) + 2 = N$, $(N − 3) + 3 = N$, $\cdots$. By adding up the two copies of the original series, we get $N − 1$ sums, each of which has a value of N. Thus,

$$2 * [(N − 1) + (N − 2) + (N − 3) + \cdots + 2 + 1] = (N − 1) * N$$

---

† A pass is a loop that accesses some segment of a list.

[59	46	32	81	46	55	87	43	70	80
32	[46	59	81	46	55	87	43	70	80
32	43	[59	81	46	55	87	46	70	80
32	43	46	[81	59	55	87	46	70	80
32	43	46	46	[59	55	87	81	70	80
32	43	46	46	55	[59	87	81	70	80
32	43	46	46	55	59	[87	81	70	80
32	43	46	46	55	59	70	[81	87	80
32	43	46	46	55	59	70	80	[87	81
32	43	46	46	55	59	70	80	81	87

Figure 6.2 A Selection Sort.

From this equation, we get

$$(N - 1) + (N - 2) + (N - 3) + \cdots + 2 + 1 = (N^2 - N)/2$$

You can also verify this equation if you are familiar with mathematical induction. The sort effort, $(N^2 - N)/2$, is $O(N^2)$. Since the number of comparisons is independent of the particular arrangement of the data, the best case and worst case both require $(N^2 - N)/2$ comparisons.

The space requirements for the Selection Sort are modest: N list items plus one temporary. The number of swaps is at most $N - 1$, which is the minimum number of swaps required to sort an arbitrary list of N values. The average distance moved in a swap during the first pass is $(N - 1)/2$ positions; during the last pass the average swap distance is $1/2$ positions. The average swap distance over all passes is $N/4$ positions. This would be an impressive statistic except that, sometimes, a component can be moved far from its final resting place. For example, in pass 2 of Fig. 6.2, 46 is moved from position 2 to position 8, but 46 belongs in position 3.

Exercise 6.1 Develop a procedure for a selection sort on a list implemented as a dynamic linked list. Assume the following type definitions:

```
TYPE  POINTER       = ^ELEMENT ;
      ELEMENT       = RECORD
                          VALUE : COMPONENTTYPE ;
                          NEXT  : POINTER
                      END ;
      LISTSIZERANGE = 1..MAXLISTSIZE ;
      LISTTYPE      = RECORD
                          HEAD : POINTER ;
                          N    : LISTSIZERANGE
                      END ;
      COMPONENTTYPE can be any type for which "<" is defined.
```

Bubble Sort For I going from 1 to $N - 1$, compare a_I with a_{I+1}, swapping if $a_I > a_{I+1}$. This will cause the largest number to be stored in (bubble up to ?) position N. Then reset I to 1 and make another pass through the list. Continue making passes until the list is sorted. To prevent needless comparisons on successive passes, each pass goes only as far as the last interchange from the previous pass. For example, if the last pair swapped on the previous pass consisted of a_7 and a_8, then a_8, a_9, $a_{10} \cdots$ must be in their final correct positions. Therefore, in the next pass I would go from 1 to 6, so we would compare only up to a_6 and a_7.

The following procedure performs a Bubble Sort on a list. For the sake of variety, we assume that the list is implemented as a dynamic linked list. The code for bubble sorting an array is slightly simpler (see Exercise 6.2).

```
(* COMPONENTTYPE can be any type for which " < " is defined, *)
(* namely, any string or scalar type.                        *)
TYPE      POINTER       = ^ELEMENT ;
          ELEMENT       = RECORD
                              VALUE : COMPONENTTYPE ;
                              NEXT  : POINTER
                          END ;
          LISTSIZERANGE = 1..MAXLISTSIZE ;
          LISTTYPE      = RECORD
                              HEAD : POINTER ;
                              N    : LISTSIZERANGE
                          END ;
```

59	46	32	81	46	55	87	43	70	80
^	^	(swap)							
46	59	32	81	46	55	87	43	70	80
	^	^	(swap)						
46	32	59	81	46	55	87	43	70	80
		^	^	(no swap)					
46	32	59	81	46	55	87	43	70	80
			^	^	(swap)				
46	32	59	46	81	55	87	43	70	80
				^	^	(swap)			
46	32	59	46	55	81	87	43	70	80
					^	^	(no swap)		
46	32	59	46	55	81	87	43	70	80
						^	^	(swap)	
46	32	59	46	55	81	43	87	70	80
							^	^	(swap)
46	32	59	46	55	81	43	70	87	80
								^	^ (swap)
46	32	59	46	55	81	43	70	80	87

Figure 6.3 The first pass in a Bubble Sort: the largest number bubbles up to the last position.

PROCEDURE BUBBLESORT(VAR LIST : LISTTYPE) ;

```
     (* Perform a Bubble Sort on the linked LIST. *)
VAR     I, FINALVALUE,
        SWAPPOSITION      : LISTSIZERANGE ;
        TEMPORARY         : COMPONENTTYPE ;
        NOSWAPSMADE       : BOOLEAN ;
        CURRENTPOINTER : POINTER ;
BEGIN
   WITH LIST DO
      BEGIN
         FINALVALUE := N ;

         (* Keep making passes through the list until no more *)
         (* swaps can be made.                                *)
         REPEAT
            NOSWAPSMADE := TRUE ;

            (* Make a pass throught the list. *)
            CURRENTPOINTER := HEAD ;
            FOR I := 1 TO FINALVALUE  −1 DO
               BEGIN
                  IF CURRENTPOINTER^.VALUE > CURRENTPOINTER^.NEXT^.VALUE
                            THEN
                     BEGIN
                        (* Swap values *)
                        TEMPORARY                    := CURRENTPOINTER^ VALUE ;
                        CURRENTPOINTER^.VALUE := CURRENTPOINTER^.NEXT^.VALUE ;
                        CURRENTPOINTER^.NEXT^.VALUE := TEMPORARY ;

                        (* Update SWAPPOSITION and NOSWAPSMADE. *)
                        SWAPPOSITION := I ;
                        NOSWAPSMADE := FALSE
                     END ;
                  CURRENTPOINTER := CURRENTPOINTER^.NEXT
               END ;
            IF NOSWAPSMADE = FALSE THEN
               FINALVALUE := SWAPPOSITION
         UNTIL NOSWAPSMADE
      END
END ;  (* of the procedure BUBBLESORT. *)
```

Figure 6.3 shows the comparisons and swaps during the *first* pass through the sample list. Carets point to the two numbers now being compared.

Since the last swap in the first pass was between a_9 and a_{10}, in the second pass I will go from 1 to 8. After the second pass we get

32 46 46 55 59 43 70 80 81 87

Since the last swap in the second pass was between a_8 and a_9, in the third pass I will go from 1 to 7. After the third pass we have

32 46 46 55 43 59 70 80 81 87

The third largest number, 80, is now in its proper position (position 8). Also, since there were no swaps from positions 6 through 8, the numbers in positions 6 and 7 (namely, 59 and 70) are already in their correct positions, so in the fourth pass I will go from 1 to 4. The remaining four passes yield

```
32  46  46  43  55  59  70  80  81  87
32  46  43  46  55  59  70  80  81  87
32  43  46  46  55  59  70  80  81  87
32  43  46  46  55  59  70  80  81  87
```

The final pass, which required no interchanges, had to be made since 32 and 43 had not been compared before.

The worst case of a Bubble Sort, when the original list is in decreasing order, requires $(N^2 - N)/2$ comparisons. The best case occurs when the original list happens to be in increasing order, in which case only $N - 1$ comparisons need be made. The calculation of the sort effort (and even the formula itself!) is quite complex. See Knuth, 1973, pages 106–111, for details. The essential feature is that it is $O(N^2)$.

How does the Bubble Sort compare with the Selection Sort? Their sort efforts are of the same order, namely, $O(N^2)$. For both sorts, the worst case requires $(N^2 - N)/2$ comparisons. In the best case for the Bubble Sort, when the list is already in increasing order, the number of comparisons is only $N - 1$, whereas the Selection Sort always requires $(N^2 - N)/2$ comparisons. Thus, the Bubble Sort is better than the Selection Sort when the list is increasing order, or nearly so. The space requirements for the two sorts are the same: N locations for the list plus one temporary location (plus N pointers, in a linked-list implementation). A significant disadvantage of the Bubble Sort is that it requires a large number of swaps. The average number of swaps for the Bubble Sort is $(N^2 - N)/4$, compared to only $N - 1$ for the Selection Sort. The reason that the Bubble Sort uses so many swaps is that the distance moved during each swap is always just one position. A further disadvantage of the Bubble Sort is that it is somewhat harder to program than the Selection Sort.

As Knuth (Knuth, 1973, page 111) says, "In short, the bubble sort seems to have nothing to recommend it, except a catchy name and the fact that it leads to some interesting theoretical problems."

Exercise 6.2 Develop a procedure to perform a Bubble Sort on a list implemented as an array. Use the type definitions for LISTSIZERANGE and LISTTYPE shown on page 225.

Insertion Sort In an Insertion Sort, we sort the successive sublists $\{a_1\}$, $\{a_1, a_2\}$, $\{a_1, a_2, a_3\}$, ..., and finally, $\{a_1, ..., a_N\}$. At each stage after the first, we have a sorted sublist in which we want to insert one item. Thus, for I going from 2 to N, we start with $\{a_1, ..., a_{I-1}\}$ already sorted. We then "sift" a_I down to its proper position in $\{a_1, ···, a_{I-1}\}$, and we have $\{a_1, ..., a_I\}$ sorted. For example, if we start with the list of 10 numbers on page 225, Fig. 6.4 shows what the list would look like *after* each of the nine stages (a caret shows the position of I during each stage, and items to the right of the caret are in their original positions).

The sifting down is accomplished in a *right-to-left* scan starting at position *I*. We let *J* hold the position of the item being sifted. In the loop we compare a_J with its predecessor: If a_J is less than its predecessor, we swap them and decrement *J*. The loop continues until a_J's final position has been found, that is, until either no swap takes place in the loop or *J*, when decremented, gets the value of 1.

The following procedure performs an Insertion Sort on a list implemented as an array.

```
(* COMPONENTTYPE can be any type for which "<" is defined, *)
(* namely, any string type or scalar type.                 *)

TYPE   LISTSIZERANGE = 1..MAXLISTSIZE ;
       LISTTYPE      = RECORD
                          A : ARRAY[LISTSIZERANGE] OF COMPONENTTYPE ;
                          N : LISTSIZERANGE
                       END ;

PROCEDURE   INSERTIONSORT(VAR   LIST : LISTTYPE) ;

(* Perform an insertion sort on LIST, implemented as A[1..N]. *)

VAR   I, J             : LISTSIZERANGE ;
      TEMPORARY        : COMPONENTTYPE ;
      POSITIONFOUND : BOOLEAN ;
BEGIN
    WITH LIST DO
       FOR I := 2 TO N DO

          (* INVARIANT : A[1..I − 1] is already sorted. *)
          BEGIN
              J                     := I ;
              POSITIONFOUND := FALSE ;

              (* Sift A[J] down to its proper position. *)

              REPEAT
                 IF  A[J] < A[J − 1] THEN
                    BEGIN
                        (* Swap. *)
                        TEMPORARY := A[J] ;
                        A[J]            := A[J − 1] ;
                        A[J − 1]        := TEMPORARY ;

                        (* Decrement and check J. *)
                        J := J − 1 ;
                        IF  J = 1 THEN
                              POSITIONFOUND := TRUE
                    END
                 ELSE
                       POSITIONFOUND := TRUE
              UNTIL  POSITIONFOUND


          END  (* of the FOR  statement. *)
END ;  (* of the procedure INSERTIONSORT. *)
```

Notice that, in the REPEAT loop, the variable TEMPORARY is always assigned the same value, namely, the value originally in A[I]. Thus, we can take these assignments to and from TEMPORARY outside of the REPEAT statement. This yields the following improved version of the Insertion Sort procedure:

```
(* COMPONENTTYPE can be any type for which "<" is defined, *)
(* namely, any string type or scalar type.                 *)
TYPE   LISTSIZERANGE = 1..MAXLISTSIZE ;
       LISTTYPE      = RECORD
                           A : ARRAY[LISTSIZERANGE] OF COMPONENTTYPE ;
                           N : LISTSIZERANGE
                       END ;

PROCEDURE   INSERTIONSORT(VAR   LIST : LISTTYPE) ;

(* Perform an insertion sort on LIST, implemented as A[1..N]. *)

VAR   I, J               : LISTSIZERANGE ;
      TEMPORARY          : COMPONENTTYPE ;
      POSITIONFOUND : BOOLEAN ;
BEGIN
      WITH LIST DO
          FOR I := 2 TO N DO
              (* INVARIANT : A[1..I − 1] is already sorted. *)
              BEGIN
                  J               := I ;
                  TEMPORARY       := A[J] ;
                  POSITIONFOUND := FALSE ;

                  (* Sift A[J] down to its proper position. *)
                  REPEAT
                      IF TEMPORARY < A[J − 1] THEN
                          BEGIN
                              A[J] := A[J − 1] ;
                              J    := J − 1 ;
                              IF J = 1 THEN
                                  POSITIONFOUND := TRUE
                          END
                      ELSE
                          POSITIONFOUND := TRUE
                  UNTIL POSITIONFOUND ;

                  A[J] := TEMPORARY

              END   (* of the FOR statement. *)
END ;   (* of the procedure INSERTIONSORT. *)
```

To illustrate the workings of this version of INSERTIONSORT, let us trace the execution of the FOR loop when I = 8 and the array A contains:

32 46 46 55 59 81 87 43 70 80

(Initially)	59	46	32	81	46	55	87	43	70	80
	46	59	32	81	46	55	87	43	70	80
		^								
	32	46	59	81	46	55	87	43	70	80
			^							
	32	46	59	81	46	55	87	43	70	80
				^						
	32	46	46	59	81	55	87	43	70	80
					^					
	32	46	46	55	59	81	87	43	70	80
						^				
	32	46	46	55	59	81	87	43	70	80
							^			
	32	43	46	46	55	59	81	87	70	80
								^		
	32	43	46	46	55	59	70	81	87	80
									^	
	32	43	46	46	55	59	70	80	81	87
										^

Figure 6.4 Successive stages in an Insertion Sort.

A[1..7] is already sorted. We set TEMPORARY equal to 43, and initialize J to 8 and POSITIONFOUND to FALSE. During the first execution of the REPEAT loop, 43 is less than the value stored in A[7], namely 87, so A[8] is set to 87 and J is decremented to 7. During the second execution of the REPEAT loop, 43 is less than the value stored in A[6], namely 81, so A[7] is set to 81 and J is decremented to 6. After four more executions of the REPEAT loop, we get

32 46 46 46 55 59 81 87 70 80

with J = 2, TEMPORARY = 43 and POSITIONFOUND still FALSE.

During the next execution of the loop, 43 is not less than A[1], namely 32, so POSITIONFOUND is set to TRUE and we fall through the loop. After leaving the loop, A[2] gets TEMPORARY's value of 43, so we have

32 43 46 46 55 59 81 87 70 80

The difference between the two versions of INSERTIONSORT may not appear to be significant, but a slight optimization in an innermost loop can cause a drastic improvement in run time. Jon Bentley reported (Bentley, 1984) that the above change reduced the execution time of his Insertion Sort by two thirds.

We now analyze the revised procedure INSERTIONSORT. If the list is initially in increasing order, the number of comparisons required is only $N - 1$. If the list is initially in decreasing order, the number of comparisons required is $1 + 2 + \cdots + N - 1$, which is $(N^2 - N)/2$. For the sort effort, each execution of the FOR statement requires, on the average, that $A[I]$ be compared with half of the preceding items. Thus the sort effort is, approximately, $1/2 + 2/2 + 3/2 + \cdots + (N - 1)/2 = (1 + 2 + \cdots + N - 1)/2 = (N^2 - N)/4$, which is $O(N^2)$. The exact value of the sort effort is derived in Exercise 6.5. There are only $N - 1$ swaps performed (but approximately $(N^2 - N)/4$ "moves"). Thus, for a list that is in order, or nearly so, the revised Insertion Sort is more efficient than the Bubble Sort or the Selection Sort. We will utilize this fact later in the chapter.

We mentioned earlier (page 224) that a sort algorithm is inferior if its sort effort is $O(N^2)$; the previous three sorts fall into that class. Later in this chapter we will encounter three "good" sorts; that is, their sort efforts are $O(N \ln N)$.

Exercise 6.3 In what respect is a dynamic linked list implementation of the list more efficient than a contiguous array implementation for an insertion sort? In what respect is a dynamic linked list implementation less efficient?

Exercise 6.4 Why would it be incorrect to replace the above REPEAT statement with

```
WHILE (TEMPORARY < A[J − 1]) AND (J > 1) DO
    BEGIN
        A[J] := A[J − 1] ;
        J    := J − 1
    END ;
```

Hint: The error occurs when J has a value of 1.

Exercise 6.5 Show that the sort effort for Insertion Sort is given by

$$\frac{N^2 + N}{4} + \frac{N}{2} - \sum_{K=1}^{N} \frac{1}{K}$$

where $\sum_{K=1}^{N} 1/K$, read as "the sum, as K goes from 1 to N, of $1/K$," is an abbreviation for

$$\frac{1}{1} + \frac{1}{2} + \frac{1}{3} + \cdots + \frac{1}{N}$$

Hint: First show that the average number of comparisons to insert the Kth item is

$$\sum_{I=1}^{K-2} \frac{I}{K} + \frac{2(K-1)}{K}$$

which is $(K + 2)(K - 1)/2K$. For example, to insert a new item into a sorted four-item list will require:

exactly one comparison one fifth of the time;
exactly two comparisons one fifth of the time;
exactly three comparisons one fifth of the time;
exactly four comparisons two fifths of the time.

(The last case is doubly likely since it includes the possibility that the new item belongs between the first and second items as well as the possibility that the new item belongs in front of the first item.) Thus the sort effort is

$$\sum_{K=1}^{N} \frac{(K+2)(K-1)}{2K} = \sum_{K=1}^{N} \frac{K^2}{2K} + \sum_{K=1}^{N} \frac{1}{2} - \sum_{K=1}^{N} \frac{1}{K}$$

Incidentally, for $N > 10$, ln N is a good approximation to

$$\sum_{K=1}^{N} \frac{1}{K}$$

(see Kruse, 1984, page 414), so the sort effort is still dominated by the N^2 term.

MULTILEVEL AND INDEX SORTING

In the previous section we developed several sorting procedures and applied them to a list in which each component had but one field. These methods may also be applied to sorting multifield records, but complications can arise. For example, consider the list in Fig. 6.5.

Suppose we wanted to sort this list as follows: Sort by division; within each division, sort by salary. In this case the division field is called the "primary key" field and the salary field is the "secondary key" field, used in comparisons only when two records have the same values in their primary key fields. Thus, for example, in a Bubble Sort, if a record's division were greater than the division of the next record, the two records would be swapped. If, however, both records had the same division, then the salary fields would be compared. After all the required swaps were made, we would get the list shown in Fig. 6.6. Of course the same principle applies to sorting by three or more fields.

One problem associated with sorting multifield records, even if there is no secondary field, is that swaps can involve moving large quantities of data. This can be avoided by means of an *index sort*, in which a separate array, called an "index array," holds the position of each element in the list. The positions may be in the form of subscripts (if the list itself is stored as an array) or pointers (if the list is stored as a linked list.) For example, if the list in Fig. 6.5 were stored as an array, then the index array would originally contain the values shown in Fig. 6.7a. After being sorted with division and salary as primary and secondary keys, respectively, the list itself would be unchanged, but the index array would be as

(Name)	(Division)	(Salary)
BUCCHIANERI, KRISTA	3	22000
CALABRIA, PETER	4	18750
CRONIN, JOSEPH	4	17000
DIMOND, JOHN	2	25000
ELDRIDGE, SHENISE	2	21000
HOGAN, LAWRENCE	3	21000
JOHNSON, KIM	1	24500
MARTIN, GEORGE	2	22000
SMITH, JOHN	4	18000
TALBOT, BARBARA	4	15000
VERNON, JANE	3	21500
YEAGER, JAMES	1	25000
YOUNG, PAUL	1	23000

Figure 6.5 A list with three fields per record.

(Name)	(Division)	(Salary)
YOUNG, PAUL	1	23000
JOHNSON, KIM	1	24500
YEAGER, JAMES	1	25000
ELDRIDGE, SHENISE	2	21000
MARTIN, GEORGE	2	22000
DIMOND, JOHN	2	25000
HOGAN, LAWRENCE	3	21000
VERNON, JANE	3	21500
BUCCHIANERI, KRISTA	3	22000
TALBOT, BARBARA	4	15000
CRONIN, JOSEPH	4	17000
SMITH, JOHN	4	18000
CALABRIA, PETER	4	18750

Figure 6.6 The list of Fig. 6.5 sorted by salary within divisions.

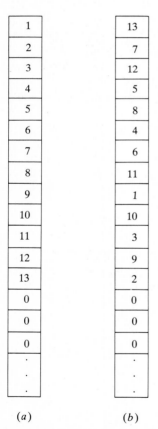

(a)   (b)

Figure 6.7(a) An index array for the list of Fig. 6.5. (b) The same index array after sorting with division and salary as primary and secondary keys, respectively.

shown in Fig. 6.7*b*. A zero entry in the index array implies that the corresponding list position contains garbage. Thus, for example, the first element of the index array contains 13, the subscript of the "smallest" record:

YOUNG, PAUL   1   23000

The second element of the index array contains 7, the subscript of the second "smallest" record:

JOHNSON, KIM   1   24500

Notice that the original list is unchanged. The comparisons are performed on its elements, but *the interchanges are made in the index array.* Since only subscripts are moved, large-scale data transfers are avoided. This advantage becomes even more compelling when the records contain a large number of fields, a common occurrence in commercial applications.

Furthermore, by maintaining several index arrays, we can save the results of sorting the list in several different ways. For example, consider Fig. 6.7 as showing two index arrays instead of one index array whose values have been changed. We then have the list sorted alphabetically (Fig. 6.7*a*) and by salary within divisions (Fig. 6.7*b*). A list with more than one index array is called an "inverted list."

Exercise 6.6 Sort the list in Fig. 6.6; use the salary field as the primary key and the name field as the secondary key.

Exercise 6.7 Show what the index array would contain if the list in Fig. 6.5 were sorted by salary.

SUPERIOR SORTS

We now present three sort procedures with sort effort of $O(N \ln N)$, which, as mentioned earlier, is optimal for comparison based sorts. Each of these sorts is based on the principle of "divide and conquer": The strategy for sorting the entire list is (recursively) applied to the sublists.

Binary Sort Tree

We mentioned earlier that the sort effort for the Insertion Sort was $O(N^2)$, indicating an inefficient sort. A version of the Insertion Sort, in which the list is implemented as a binary tree rather than an array, fares much better. The resulting sort method, known as a "Binary Sort Tree," was described in Chap. 5 (pages 212–213). If we apply it to the list given on page 225, we get the binary tree shown in Fig. 6.8.

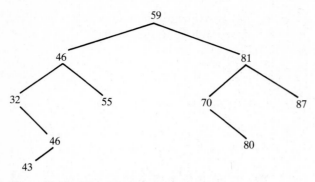

Figure 6.8 The Binary Sort Tree for the list on page 225.

The worst case for the Binary Sort Tree occurs when the original list is in reverse order. For example, if the original list had been

87 81 80 70 59 55 46 46 43 32

then the resulting Binary Sort Tree would be as shown in Figure 6.9.

In general, sorting a reverse-ordered list of N elements requires $1 + 2 + \cdots + N - 1 = (N^2 - N)/2$ comparisons if a Binary Sort Tree is used. (Of course the algorithm does not know that the list is in reverse order!) Thus the worst case requires $O(N^2)$ comparisons. The situation is not much better if the original list is in increasing order: The number of comparisons is reduced (slightly) only if there are ties. For example, if the original list had been

32 43 46 46 55 59 70 80 81 87

then the resulting Binary Sort Tree would be as shown in Fig. 6.10.

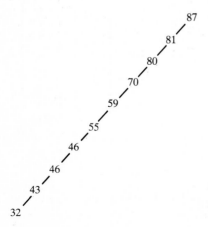

Figure 6.9 The Binary Sort Tree for a list in decreasing order.

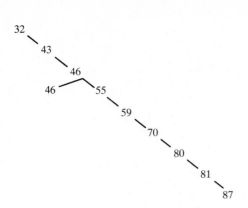

Figure 6.10 The Binary Sort Tree for a list in increasing order with one tie.

The best case occurs when the resulting tree is *perfectly balanced*, that is, each leaf is the same distance from the root and each nonleaf has two branches. For example, if the original list were

59 81 46 70 55 32 30 80 87 90 83 46 58 62 49

then the resulting Binary Sort Tree would be as shown in Fig. 6.11.

In general, sorting a perfectly balanced tree with N nodes requires

$$(N + 1)[\log_2 (N + 1) - 2] + 2$$

comparisons—see Exercise 6.9. Since

$$\log_2 N = (\ln N)/(\ln 2)$$

the number of comparisons required in the best case is $O(N \ln N)$.

The sort effort is, approximately, $2 N \ln N - 2.7 N$, but the proof is beyond the scope of this text (see Knuth, 1973, pages 427–428). Since this sort effort is $O(N \ln N)$, we have finally seen an "efficient" sort. The only drawback occurs when the list is in order or reverse order, or nearly so. Another nice feature is that there are no swaps and only N moves (one for each insertion). The speed of the binary sort tree is somewhat slowed by the N calls to the procedure NEW and the recursive calls (on the average, $O(N \ln N)$ of them) within the procedure INSERT on page 212. Also, $2N$ extra locations (for pointers) are required.

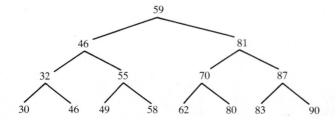

Figure 6.11 A perfectly balanced Binary Sort Tree.

Exercise 6.8 How many leaves are there in a perfectly balanced binary tree with N nodes?

Exercise 6.9 (This exercise requires familiarity with the principle of mathematical induction.) Show that a perfectly balanced tree with N nodes can be sorted with

$$(N + 1)[\log_2 (N + 1) - 2] + 2$$

comparisons.

    Hint 1: First show that the number of comparisons required is

$$1 * 0 + 2 * 1 + 4 * 2 + 8 * 3 + \cdots + (N + 1)/2 * \log_2 \frac{N + 1}{2},$$

where each term in the sum is the product of the number of nodes at a given level in the tree and the number of comparisons needed to place each of those nodes. Thus the first level is occupied by the root alone, with no comparisons required. The second level contains the root's two children, each of which can be placed with just one comparison. The third level contains the root's four grandchildren, each of which can be placed with just two comparisons.

    Hint 2: Use mathematical induction to show that

$$\sum_{i=1}^{M} (2^i * i) = (M - 1)2^{M+1} + 2$$

Now let $M = \log_2 [(N + 1)/2]$.

Exercise 6.10 Use a Binary Sort Tree to sort the following list:

41 82 39 40 41 40 56 68 70 75 71 50

Merge Sort

Another efficient sorting technique is merge sorting. We first consider a simple merge procedure; later, we will show how these simple merges can be combined to accomplish a merge sort. Suppose we have two lists $a_1, \ldots, a_M$ and $b_1, \ldots, b_N$, both of which are in increasing order. We want to merge them into a list $c_1, \ldots, c_{M+N}$ which will also be in increasing order. Starting with a_1 and b_1, we repeatedly compare one element from list a and one element from list b: The smaller is stored in list c and the next comparison is between the larger of the two elements and the next element in the list which had the smaller element. When one of the original lists has been exhausted, we move the rest of the other list to list c.

    For example, suppose we wanted to merge the following two lists:

a: 26, 38, 55, 57, 61, 64, 67

b: 46, 47, 53, 78, 80, 84

Then the following pairs would be compared:

26,46   38,46   55,46   55,47   55,53   55,78   57,78   61,78   64,78   67,78

After each comparison, the smaller element is moved to list c. Since the last comparison forced the last element in list a to be moved to c, the remaining elements of list b (namely 78, 80, and 84) are then moved to c.

How many comparisons are made during a merge? After each comparison, one element (from list a or list b) is moved to list c. After all the comparisons have been made, the remainder of list a or list b is moved to list c. The size of this remnant may be anywhere from 1 to the larger of list a or list b. If the remnant is a single element, then the number of previous moves—and hence comparisons—was $N + M - 1$. If the remnant was the larger of one of the original lists, then the number of previous moves—and hence comparisons—was the smaller of N and M. Hence, during a merge, the number of comparisons ranges from the smaller of N and M (best case) to $N + M - 1$ (worst case).

To sort a list $a_1, \ldots, a_N$ by this technique, we would first sort pairs of elements

$$a_1 \text{ and } a_2; a_3 \text{ and } a_4; a_5 \text{ and } a_6; \text{ and so on}$$

Successive pairs are then merged into quadrules; this can easily be done with the help of a temporary list. The quadrules are then merged into octuples stored back in the original list. This "Ping-Pong" merging of the original and temporary lists is continued until the entire list is sorted. Figure 6.12 illustrates this process in sorting a 14-element list.

From our earlier analysis of a simple merge, we know that each pass in a Merge Sort requires anywhere from N DIV 2 comparisons (best case) to $N - 1$ comparisons (worst case). The number of passes is equal to the number of times N can be divided by 2. To express this as an integer, we use

$$\text{TRUNC } (\log_2 (N - 1)) + 1.$$

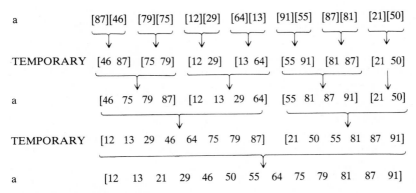

Figure 6.12 A Merge Sort example.

Thus, since the number of comparisons per pass is always $O(N)$, the sort effort is $O(N \ln N)$. A more careful analysis (see Kruse, 1984, pages 164–166) reveals that the actual sort effort is, approximately, $1.4 N \ln N - N$, which is quite close to the theoretical minimum for comparison based sorts, namely, $\log_2(N!)$. A further advantage of Merge Sort is that it requires only $O(N \ln N)$ comparisons even in the worst case.

Note that the temporary list doubles the storage requirements if the original and temporary lists are stored in arrays. If the original list is stored as a dynamic linked list, the merging is accomplished by adjusting pointers, so no temporary list is required.

Later in this chapter, we show how a file can be sorted by combining a Merge Sort with Quicksort, discussed in the next section.

Exercise 6.11 Develop a procedure, MERGE, to merge two arrays of N elements each into a third array with $2N$ elements.

Quicksort

One of the most efficient and, therefore, widely used sorting techniques is *Quicksort*, developed by C. A. R. Hoare (Hoare, 1962). We now outline the Quicksort procedure; a detailed development is postponed until Case Study 6.1.

Essentially, the Quicksort procedure is a simple application of the principle of "divide and conquer." To "Quicksort" an array A, we first partition the array into a left subarray and a right subarray such that each element in the left subarray is less than or equal to each element in the right subarray. We then Quicksort the left and right subarrays and we are done. Since this last sentence is easily implemented with two (recursive) calls to a Quicksort procedure, we will concentrate on the partitioning phase.

The partitioning begins by selecting an element of the array; the chosen element is referred to as the "pivot." For purposes of discussion, let us choose the middle element as the pivot. For example, suppose we started with the following array A:

19   56   28   101   47   16   39   54   27   18   92   45   61   72

Then 39 would be the pivot since it is in the middle position, namely, position $(1 + 14)$ DIV 2. We now want to move to the left-hand side of the array all the elements that are less than or equal to 39 and move to the right-hand side of the array all the elements that are greater than or equal to 39. Elements with a value of 39 may end up in either subarray, and the two subarrays need not have the same size. To accomplish this partitioning, we introduce two counters: one of them starts at position 1 and works upward, and the other starts at position 14 and works downward. The upcounter is looking for elements greater than or equal to 39 and the downcounter is looking for elements less than or equal to 39.

In the above example, the upcounter is incremented once before it stops (at 56); then the downcounter is decremented four times before it stops (at 18). We have

19 56 28 101 47 16 39 54 27 18 92 45 61 72
    ^   ^

   upcounter   downcounter

We now swap these two elements. This gives us

19 18 28 101 47 16 39 54 27 56 92 45 61 72
    ^   ^

upcounter   downcounter

Upcounter is now incremented twice and stops (at 101). Downcounter is decremented once and stops (at 27). After swapping, we get

19 18 28 27 47 16 39 54 101 56 92 45 61 72
        ^   ^

    upcounter   downcounter

Upcounter is incremented once and stops (at 47). Downcounter is decremented twice and stops (at 39). After swapping, we get

19 18 28 27 39 16 47 54 101 56 92 45 61 72
             ^   ^

    upcounter   downcounter

Upcounter is incremented twice and stops (at 47). Downcounter is decremented once and stops (at 16). Upcounter is now greater than or equal to downcounter and, since each element has been examined, no more swaps need to be made. We now have

19 18 28 27 39 16 47 54 101 56 92 45 61 72
           ^   ^

    downcounter upcounter

The left subarray goes from position 1 to 6 (= downcounter); the right subarray goes from postion 7 (= upcounter) to 14. Each element in the left subarray is less than or equal to each element in the right subarray. We now apply the above procedure to each subarray.

In partitioning $A[1..6]$, the pivot is 28. Upcounter starts at position 1 and is incremented twice until it stops (at 28). Downcounter starts at position 6 and stops right away (at 16). After swapping, we get

19 18 16 27 39 28
    ^   ^

  upcounter downcounter

Upcounter is incremented twice and stops (at 39). Downcounter is decremented twice and stops (at 27). Since upcounter is now greater than or equal to downcounter, no more swaps can be made.

19 18 16 27 39 28
           ^ ^

  downcounter upcounter

The two subarrays just created are $A[1..4]$ and $A[5..6]$. To Quicksort $A[1..4]$, we begin partitioning with 18 as the pivot. Upcounter starts at position 1 and stops right away (at 19). Downcounter starts at position 4 and is decremented once until it stops (at 16). After swapping, we get

```
16   18   19   27
^         ^
upcounter  downcounter
```

Upcounter is incremented once and stops (at 18) and downcounter is decremented once and stops (at 18). Since upcounter is now greater than or equal to downcounter, no more swaps can be made. The left subarray consists of $A[1..1]$ and the right subarray consists of $A[3..4]$. Since $A[2]$ is already in its correct final position, we leave it where it is. In general, whenever upcounter and downcounter stop at the same position, we omit that element (which has the same value as the pivot) from either subarray. The left subarray, $A[1..1]$ is already (trivially) sorted. Quicksorting the right subarray, $A[3..4]$ is left as an exercise, as is the Quicksorting of the previous right subarrays: $A[5..6]$ and $A[7..14]$.

The following notes may clarify some of the details of Quicksorting.

1. We use an array implementation rather than a linked list because we can directly calculate the middle element of an array.
2. In partitioning a subarray, each element, including the pivot itself, is compared to the pivot. Therefore, all possible swaps will be carried out.
3. No attempt is made to sort an empty subarray or a subarray consisting of a single element. Thus, to sort an array of size N, we must call the Quicksort procedure approximately N times. Later in this chapter we will show how the number of calls to Quicksort can be drastically reduced.
4. When we partition a subarray into two parts, the number of comparisons required is, approximately, equal to the size of the subarray (since each element is compared to the pivot). By note 3, approximately N partitions are required to sort an array of size N. Thus, Quicksort is most efficient when a partition splits a subarray into two parts that have the same size. For example, Fig. 6.13 shows repeated partitions of an array with 16 elements (subarray sizes are encircled).

Since each partition split its (sub)array into two equal parts, the number of partitioning levels in the above tree is $\log_2(16)$, namely 4. The total number of comparisons is, approximately, 64 (that is, $N \log_2 N$, where $N = 16$). For an array size of N, if we get equal size subarrays for each partition, the total number of comparisons is, approximately, $N \log_2 N$.

Contrast the above tree with the tree shown in Fig. 6.14. For an array of size N, the number of comparisons in this worst case is $(N + 2) + (N + 1) + \cdots + 5 + 4 = (N - 1)(N + 6)/2 = N^2 + 5N - 6/2$

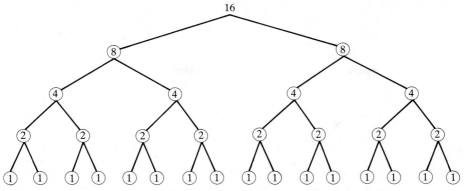

Figure 6.13 Repeated partitions, into equal sized subarrays, of an array with 16 elements.

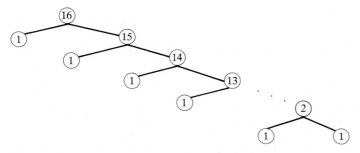

Figure 6.14 Worst case partitioning: each partition produces a subarray of size 1.

5. The rationale for choosing the middle element as the pivot is this: If the array is already sorted, or roughly so, the middle element is the best choice. Otherwise, the middle element is as good a (blind) choice as any other.

Exercise 6.12 Complete the Quicksort partitioning of the subarray in positions 7 to 14 on page 243; the elements are

47   54   101   56   92   45   61   72

We now develop a program to implement the Quicksort method described above.

CASE STUDY 6.1: SORTING ZIP CODES BY QUICKSORT

Design and write a program to solve the following problem:

Problem

Use the Quicksort method to sort a list of zip codes into increasing order.

Clarification Each line of input will contain a zip code between 00001 and 99999, inclusive. The list will contain at most 1000 zip codes.

Sample Input

```
02119
01784
21801
55121
33351
42106
21801
20210
34788
10537
01905
```

Sample Output

THE ZIP CODES AS GIVEN:

```
02119
01784
21801
55121
33351
42106
21801
20210
34788
10537
01905
```
(*new page*)

THE ZIP CODES IN INCREASING ORDER:

```
01784
01905
02119
10537
20210
21801
21801
33351
34788
42106
55121
```

Solution Tree The main tree is fairly simple. We start by establishing that no zip codes have yet been read in. We then read all of the zip codes into an array. As we read in the zip codes, we will keep track of how many there are. After the zipcodes have been read in, we Quicksort all the elements in the zip code array from position 1 to the number of zip codes. Finally, we write out the sorted zip codes.

The main tree is shown in Fig. 6.15.

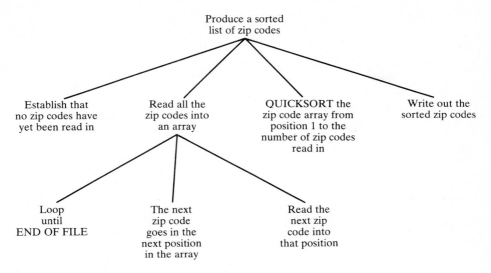

Figure 6.15 The main tree for sorting a list of zipcodes.

We now develop the QUICKSORT subtree. Rather than refer explicitly to an array of zip codes, we will suggest the generality of this subtree by working with an array called A. We want to Quicksort that part of the array from a given first position to a given last position.

We start by checking that the subarray contains at least two elements. If so, we partition the subarray into two parts, a left subarray and a right subarray. We then apply QUICKSORT to each of these subarrays.

The subtree is given in Fig. 6.16.

Finally, we develop the PARTITION subtree. We want to partition the array A, going from some first to some last position, into a left subarray (with a first and last position) and a right subarray (with a first and last position).

We start by establishing the initial conditions that must be set before all the swaps can be carried out: We must initialize the pivot, the upcounter and the downcounter. We then go through a loop which continues until the upcounter is

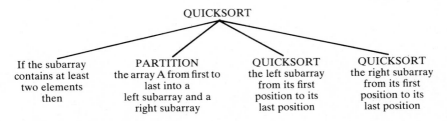

Figure 6.16 The subtree QUICKSORT.

greater than or equal to the downcounter. Each time through the loop, we try to find a pair to swap. If we succeed, we swap them. After the swapping is completed, we determine the left and right subarrays.

The subtree so far is as shown in Fig. 6.17.

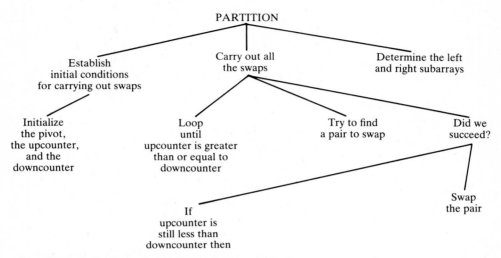

Figure 6.17 The initial version of the subtree PARTITION.

In trying to find a pair to swap, we keep incrementing upcounter as long as A[upcounter] is less than the pivot. We then keep decrementing downcounter as long as A[downcounter] is greater than the pivot.

Determining the left and right subarrays is straightforward. Recall that when upcounter and downcounter end up with the same value, the corresponding element goes in neither subarray.

The complete PARTITION subtree is shown in Fig. 6.18.

Coding We use nondescript entities such as ARRAYTYPE and COMPONENT-TYPE so that the QUICKSORT procedure, as is, can be called for sorting an arbitrary array. Each zipcode is stored in a packed array of five characters so that leading zeroes can easily be printed. If we had stored each zipcode in an integer variable, a zipcode such as 02119 would have been printed as 2119.

The inner loops within the PARTITION procedure cannot be implemented with WHILE statements. For example, suppose we wrote

```
WHILE A[UPCOUNTER] < PIVOT DO
    UPCOUNTER := UPCOUNTER + 1 ;

WHILE A[DOWNCOUNTER] > PIVOT DO
    DOWNCOUNTER := DOWNCOUNTER - 1 ;
```

Then the assignment statement in each loop would never be executed if A[FIRST] and A[LAST] happened to have the same value as PIVOT. Thus, the outer loop would be an infinite loop!

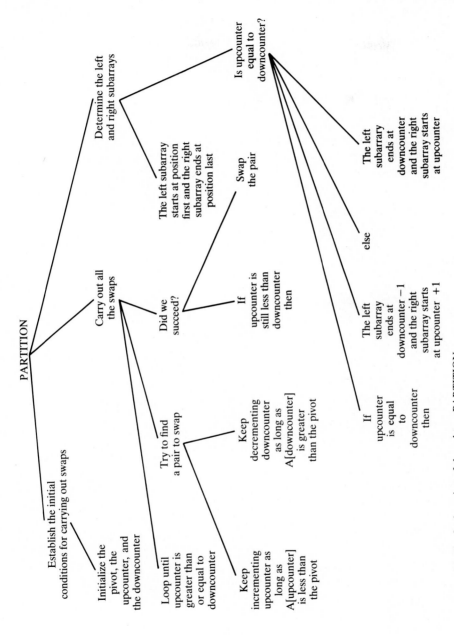

Figure 6.18 The final version of the subtree PARTITION.

The appropriate method for implementing the inner loops is the REPEAT statement:

```
REPEAT
    UPCOUNTER := UPCOUNTER + 1
UNTIL A[UPCOUNTER] > = PIVOT ;

REPEAT
    DOWNCOUNTER := DOWNCOUNTER - 1
UNTIL A[DOWNCOUNTER] < = PIVOT ;
```

To ensure that A[FIRST] will be compared to the pivot, we initialize UP-COUNTER to FIRST − 1 before entering the outer loop. Similarly, DOWN-COUNTER is initialized to LAST + 1.

Figure 6.19 contains the hierarchy chart for this program.

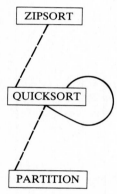

Figure 6.19 The hierarchy chart for the program ZIPSORT.

```
PROGRAM  ZIPSORT(INPUT,OUTPUT);


(******************************************************************)
(*                                                                *)
(*    PROGRAMMER: BILL COLLINS.                                   *)
(*                                                                *)
(*    Solve the following problem: given a list of up to          *)
(*    1000 zip codes, sort it into increasing order.              *)
(*    Each line of input will contain a zip code                  *)
(*    between 1 and 99999, inclusive.                             *)
(*                                                                *)
(******************************************************************)


CONST  MAXNUMBEROFZIPCODES = 1000;


TYPE   CHARCOUNTER   = 1..5;
       SUBSCRIPTTYPE = 1..MAXNUMBEROFZIPCODES;
       COMPONENTTYPE = PACKED ARRAY[CHARCOUNTER] OF CHAR;
       ARRAYTYPE     = ARRAY[SUBSCRIPTTYPE] OF COMPONENTTYPE;
       LISTSIZERANGE = 0..MAXNUMBEROFZIPCODES;

VAR    ZIPCODE            : ARRAYTYPE;
       I                  : CHARCOUNTER;
       N                  : LISTSIZERANGE;
       J                  : SUBSCRIPTTYPE;
```

```
PROCEDURE   PARTITION(VAR   A                    : ARRAYTYPE;
                      FIRST, LAST                : INTEGER;
                      VAR   LEFTFIRST, LEFTLAST,
                            RIGHTFIRST, RIGHTLAST : INTEGER);

(*  Partition A[FIRST..LAST] into two subarrays,        *)
(*  A[LEFTFIRST, LEFTLAST] and A[RIGHTFIRST, RIGHTLAST],  *)
(*  such that each element in the left subarray is less  *)
(*  than or equal to each element in the right subarray.  *)

VAR   PIVOT, TEMPORARY         : COMPONENTTYPE;
      UPCOUNTER, DOWNCOUNTER : INTEGER;

BEGIN

    (*  Establish the initial conditions for carrying out swaps.  *)
    PIVOT                := A[(FIRST + LAST) DIV 2];
    UPCOUNTER            := FIRST - 1; (* will be incremented *)
                                       (* before being used.  *)
    DOWNCOUNTER          := LAST + 1;

    (*  Carry out all possible swaps.  *)
    REPEAT

        (*  Try to find a pair to swap.  *)
        REPEAT
            UPCOUNTER := UPCOUNTER + 1
        UNTIL A[UPCOUNTER] >= PIVOT;
        REPEAT
            DOWNCOUNTER := DOWNCOUNTER - 1
        UNTIL A[DOWNCOUNTER] <= PIVOT;

        (*  Did we find a pair to swap?  *)
        IF UPCOUNTER < DOWNCOUNTER THEN
            BEGIN  (*  Swap the pair *)
                TEMPORARY       := A[UPCOUNTER];
                A[UPCOUNTER]    := A[DOWNCOUNTER];
                A[DOWNCOUNTER] := TEMPORARY
            END

    UNTIL UPCOUNTER >= DOWNCOUNTER;

    (*  Determine the left and right subarrays. Note, at  *)
    (*   this time, UPCOUNTER >= DOWNCOUNTER.              *)
    LEFTFIRST := FIRST;
    RIGHTLAST := LAST;
    IF UPCOUNTER = DOWNCOUNTER THEN
        BEGIN
            LEFTLAST   := DOWNCOUNTER - 1;
            RIGHTFIRST := UPCOUNTER + 1
        END
    ELSE
        BEGIN
            LEFTLAST   := DOWNCOUNTER;
            RIGHTFIRST := UPCOUNTER
        END


END; (*  of the procedure PARTITION.  *)
```

```
PROCEDURE  QUICKSORT(VAR    A      : ARRAYTYPE;
                     FIRST, LAST : INTEGER);

(*  Apply QUICKSORT to A[FIRST..LAST].  *)

VAR   LEFTFIRST, LEFTLAST, RIGHTFIRST, RIGHTLAST : INTEGER;

BEGIN

   (*  Sort, provided the subarray A[FIRST..LAST] contains  *)
   (*  at least two elements.                               *)
   IF LAST - FIRST >= 1 THEN
      BEGIN

         (*  Partition A[FIRST..LAST] into a left subarray  *)
         (*  and a right subarray.                          *)
         PARTITION(A, FIRST, LAST, LEFTFIRST, LEFTLAST, RIGHTFIRST,
                   RIGHTLAST);

         (*  Apply QUICKSORT to the left and right subarrays.  *)
         QUICKSORT(A, LEFTFIRST, LEFTLAST);
         QUICKSORT(A, RIGHTFIRST, RIGHTLAST)

      END

END;  (*  of the procedure QUICKSORT.  *)




BEGIN  (*  The executable section of the main program.  *)

   (*  Print heading.  *)
   PAGE;
   WRITELN ('THE ZIP CODES AS GIVEN :');
   WRITELN;

   N := 0;

   (*  Read the input into the array ZIPCODE.  *)
   WHILE NOT EOF DO
      BEGIN
         N := N + 1;

         (*  Read in one zip code.  *)
         FOR I := 1 TO 5 DO
            READ(ZIPCODE[N][I]);
         READLN;

         WRITELN (ZIPCODE[N] : 5)
      END;

   (*  Sort the array ZIPCODE.  *)
   IF N > 0 THEN
      QUICKSORT(ZIPCODE, 1, N);

   (*  Print out the sorted array.  *)
   PAGE;
   WRITELN('THE ZIP CODES IN INCREASING ORDER:');
   WRITELN;
   FOR J := 1 TO N DO
      WRITELN(ZIPCODE[J] : 5);
   PAGE
END.
```

Program Testing

1. Testing the main program:

   <u>Test 1a</u>

   (no input)

   <u>Test 1b</u>

   02119
   01784
   21801
   55121
   33351

2. Testing QUICKSORT:

   <u>Test 2a</u>

   13210

   <u>Test 2b</u>

   74170
   08540
   19689

3. Testing PARTITION:

   <u>Test 3a</u>   (All equal values)

   21801
   21801
   21801
   21801

   <u>Test 3b</u>   After all swaps made, UPCOUNTER > DOWNCOUNTER)

   21801
   12016
   55207

   <u>Test 3c</u>   (After all swaps made, UPCOUNTER = DOWNCOUNTER = 1)

   12105
   31210

   <u>Test 3d</u>   (After all swaps made, UPCOUNTER = DOWNCOUNTER > 1)

   08532
   12016
   20801

   <u>Test 3e</u>   (The Sample Input on page 373)

   02119
   01784
   21801

```
55121
33351
42106
21801
20210
34788
10537
01905
```

Exercise 6.13 In the procedure PARTITION, each REPEAT statement will terminate if an element is found whose value is *equal to* that of the pivot. This can result in needless swaps. Could we eliminate this situation by changing ">=" to ">" in the condition controlling the first REPEAT statement and changing "<=" to "<" in the second? Hint: Suppose the list were

21205   28640   25428

QUICKENING QUICKSORT

Sorting is such a commonplace operation that it will be well worth our while to revise QUICKSORT to make it as efficient as possible. A detailed analysis of Quicksort and how to improve it is given in Sedgewick, 1975. We focus on three areas of improvement.

I1. Choosing the pivot. We mentioned earlier (Note 4, page 244) that QUICKSORT works best when each partition splits its subarray into two, roughly equal parts. Choosing the pivot is a critically important operation since, the closer the pivot is to the median† of the subarray, the closer the partition will come to splitting the subarray into two equal parts. Singleton (see Singleton, 1969) suggests a simple but effective method for choosing the pivot: Let the pivot be the median of the first, middle, and last elements in the (unsorted) subarray. For example, if the subarray is

19   18   39   27   28   16

the pivot is the median of {19, 39, 16}, namely 19. Notice that the middle element in the subarray, 39, would be a terrible choice for a pivot.

---

† The median of a list is the middle value when the list is sorted. Thus, for example, the median of

38   12   96   45   49

is 45. If a list, when sorted, has two "middle" values, the median is the average of those two values. For example, the median of

38   12   96   45   90   49

is 47 [= (45 + 49)/2].

I2. Sorting small subarrays. One of the drawbacks to QUICKSORT is that the extensive partitioning machinery is employed even for small subarrays. For example, to sort a two-element subarray, the PARTITION procedure lumbers along and eventually produces two, single-element subarrays. The same sorting could be accomplished directly:

```
IF A[FIRST] > A[LAST] THEN
    BEGIN  (* Swap them. *)
        TEMPORARY := A[FIRST] ;
        A[FIRST]    := A[LAST] ;
        A[LAST]     := TEMPORARY
    END
```

Thus, to optimize the program's speed, small subarrays should not be Quicksorted. The cutoff value for the subarray size usually ranges from 6 to 30, depending on the machine used. Rather than directly sorting the small subarrays as they are encountered, we ignore them during QUICKSORT. To do this, we replace

```
IF LAST − FIRST >= 1 THEN
```

by

```
IF LAST − FIRST >= CUTOFFVALUE THEN
```

When QUICKSORT is finished, the array will not be sorted, but it will be "almost" sorted. It will consist of small clumps such that all the elements in a clump are less than or equal to those in any clump to its right. Since the array is almost sorted, INSERTIONSORT (pages 232–233) can finish up the entire array. The original call

```
QUICKSORT(ZIPCODE, 1, NUMBEROFZIPCODES);
```

is replaced by

```
QUICKSORT(ZIPCODE, 1, NUMBEROFZIPCODES) ;
INSERTIONSORT(ZIPCODE, NUMBEROFZIPCODES) ;
```

I3. Translating into machine language. A computer can execute a program only if the program is coded in the machine language for that computer (see Appendix 5, Computers and Computer Languages). Because a Pascal compiler is a general-purpose translator for Pascal programs, its code will often be less efficient than the code you could get by hand-translating the Pascal program into assembly language and then assembling the resulting program. Sedgewick found that the code produced for his Quicksort by standard compilers was at least *three* times as slow as his own assembly-language implementation (see Sedgewick, 1975). Assembly-language coding is beyond the scope of this text, but one related issue, *recursion*, merits our attention here.

Recursion is not straightforwardly handled by a computer. We mentioned in Chap. 1 (page 24) that whenever a subprogram calls a subprogram, the state of the calling subprogram must be saved to prevent its destruction in the event that the call might be a recursive one. The state of the calling subprogram includes the return address, local variables, calling parameters and the result (if the calling subprogram is a function). The information in the state is pushed onto a stack. This allows nested calls, and the calling subprogram's state is restored (by a pop) after the completion of the call.

In translating QUICKSORT into assembly language by hand, we must create and maintain our own stack. One advantage to this is that we can decide what has to be saved on the stack—a compiler would have to save the subprogram's entire state. All we need to stack are the first and last subscripts of any subarray to be partitioned later. In keeping with improvement I2, we will consider a subarray for partitioning only if its size is greater than some cutoff value.

To minimize our stack needs, after each partitioning we will stack the first and last subscripts of the larger subarray, because the smaller subarray can be subdivided fewer times than the larger one. With this improvement, the maximum stack size will occur when each partition splits the subarray into two equal parts. $\text{Log}_2 N$ is the number of times that N can be divided by 2 until we reach 1, so we will stack, at most, $\log_2 N$ subscript pairs. Thus, for example, even with a cutoff value of 1, a 50-element stack could accommodate all the necessary subscript pairs for an array of 30 million elements! The tradeoff for this decrease in space is the increased time needed to determine which subarray is larger.

Essentially, the recursion-free version of QUICKSORT works as follows: We start with an empty stack and then keep partitioning until the stack is once again empty. After each partition, we push the subscripts of the larger subarray (if it is bigger than the cutoff value) onto the stack and prepare to partition the smaller subarray, if it is big enough; if not, we pop the stack, if possible.

Here is the recursion-free version of the program to Quicksort zip codes. It can straightforwardly be translated into assembly language. We have also incorporated improvements I1 and I2.

For the sake of efficiency, we omit the UNDERFLOW and OVERFLOW fields when manipulating the stack of subscript pairs. Furthermore, to avoid any extraneous WITH statements, we make no attempt at information hiding.

```
PROGRAM  ZIPSORT(INPUT,OUTPUT);


(*******************************************************************)
(*                                                                 *)
(*   PROGRAMMER: BILL COLLINS.                                     *)
(*                                                                 *)
(*   Solve the following problem: Given a list of up to            *)
(*   1000 zip codes, sort it into increasing order.                *)
(*   Each line of input will contain a zip code                    *)
(*   between 1 and 99999, inclusive.                               *)
(*                                                                 *)
(*******************************************************************)


CONST  MAXNUMBEROFZIPCODES = 1000;
       MAXSTACK            = 50;

(*  The identifiers SUBSCRIPTTYPE, COMPONENTTYPE and ARRAYTYPE   *)
(*  are nondescript so that the procedure QUICKSORT can be       *)
(*  general.                                                     *)
TYPE  CHARCOUNTER    = 1..5;
      SUBSCRIPTTYPE  = 1..MAXNUMBEROFZIPCODES;
      COMPONENTTYPE  = PACKED ARRAY[1..5] OF CHAR;
      ARRAYTYPE      = ARRAY[SUBSCRIPTTYPE] OF COMPONENTTYPE;
      LISTSIZERANGE  = 0..MAXNUMBEROFZIPCODES;
      STACKRANGE     = 0..MAXSTACK;
      STACKARRAY     = ARRAY[1..MAXSTACK] OF SUBSCRIPTTYPE;

VAR   ZIPCODE            : ARRAYTYPE;
      I                  : CHARCOUNTER;
      N                  : LISTSIZERANGE;
      J                  : SUBSCRIPTTYPE;




PROCEDURE  FINDMEDIANOFTHREE(X, Y, Z     : COMPONENTTYPE;
                            VAR   MEDIAN : COMPONENTTYPE);

(*  Find the median of X, Y and Z.   *)

BEGIN

    IF X >= Y THEN
       IF Y >= Z THEN
          MEDIAN := Y
       ELSE
          IF X >= Z THEN
             MEDIAN := Z
          ELSE
             MEDIAN := X
    ELSE
       IF X >= Z THEN
          MEDIAN := X
       ELSE
          IF Y >= Z THEN
             MEDIAN := Z
          ELSE
             MEDIAN := Y

END;  (*  of the procedure FINDMEDIANOFTHREE.  *)
```

```
PROCEDURE  PARTITION(VAR    A                        : ARRAYTYPE;
                     FIRST, LAST                     : INTEGER;
                     VAR   LEFTFIRST, LEFTLAST,
                           RIGHTFIRST, RIGHTLAST : INTEGER);

(*  Partition A[FIRST..LAST] into two subarrays,          *)
(*  A[LEFTFIRST, LEFTLAST] and A[RIGHTFIRST, RIGHTLAST],   *)
(*  such that each element in the left subarray is less    *)
(*  than or equal to each element in the right subarray.   *)

VAR   PIVOT, TEMPORARY       : COMPONENTTYPE;
      UPCOUNTER, DOWNCOUNTER : INTEGER;

BEGIN

    (*  Establish the initial conditions for carrying out swaps.  *)
    FINDMEDIANOFTHREE(A[FIRST], A[(FIRST + LAST) DIV 2], A[LAST], PIVOT);
    UPCOUNTER           := FIRST - 1; (* will be incremented *)
                                      (* before being used.  *)
    DOWNCOUNTER         := LAST + 1;

    (*  Carry out all possible swaps.  *)
    REPEAT

        (*  Try to find a pair to swap.  *)
        REPEAT
           UPCOUNTER := UPCOUNTER + 1
        UNTIL A[UPCOUNTER] >= PIVOT;
        REPEAT
           DOWNCOUNTER := DOWNCOUNTER - 1
        UNTIL A[DOWNCOUNTER] <= PIVOT;

        (*  Did we find a pair to swap?  *)
        IF UPCOUNTER < DOWNCOUNTER THEN
           BEGIN  (*  Swap the pair. *)
              TEMPORARY        := A[UPCOUNTER];
              A[UPCOUNTER]     := A[DOWNCOUNTER];
              A[DOWNCOUNTER]   := TEMPORARY
           END
    UNTIL UPCOUNTER >= DOWNCOUNTER;

    (*  Determine the left and right subarrays. Note, at  *)
    (*   this time, UPCOUNTER >= DOWNCOUNTER.              *)
    LEFTFIRST := FIRST;
    RIGHTLAST := LAST;
    IF UPCOUNTER = DOWNCOUNTER THEN
       BEGIN
          LEFTLAST   := DOWNCOUNTER - 1;
          RIGHTFIRST := UPCOUNTER + 1
       END
    ELSE
       BEGIN
          LEFTLAST   := DOWNCOUNTER;
          RIGHTFIRST := UPCOUNTER
       END

END;  (*  of the procedure PARTITION.  *)
```

```
PROCEDURE  PUSHPAIR(FIRST, LAST      : SUBSCRIPTTYPE;
                     VAR    STACK      : STACKARRAY;
                     VAR    TOPOFSTACK : STACKRANGE);

(*  Push the pair of subscripts FIRST and LAST onto the  *)
(*  stack.  Adjust TOPOFSTACK prior to each push.         *)

BEGIN

    TOPOFSTACK            := TOPOFSTACK + 1;
    STACK[TOPOFSTACK] := FIRST;
    TOPOFSTACK            := TOPOFSTACK + 1;
    STACK[TOPOFSTACK] := LAST

END;  (*  of the procedure PUSHPAIR.  *)




PROCEDURE  POPPAIR(VAR    FIRST, LAST : SUBSCRIPTTYPE;
                     STACK            : STACKARRAY;
                     VAR    TOPOFSTACK : STACKRANGE);

(*  Pop the pair of values FIRST and LAST from the stack.  *)
(*  Adjust TOPOFSTACK after each pop.                       *)

BEGIN

    (*  LAST is popped first because it was  *)
    (*    most recently pushed.                *)
    LAST       := STACK[TOPOFSTACK];
    TOPOFSTACK := TOPOFSTACK - 1;
    FIRST      := STACK[TOPOFSTACK];
    TOPOFSTACK := TOPOFSTACK - 1

END;  (*  of the procedure POPPAIR.  *)
```

```
PROCEDURE  QUICKSORT(VAR    A      : ARRAYTYPE;
                     FIRST, LAST : SUBSCRIPTTYPE);

(*  Apply QUICKSORT to A[FIRST..LAST].  *)

CONST CUTOFFVALUE = 10;  (*  A subarray will be partitioned only if    *)
                         (*  its size is greater than the cutoff value *)

VAR    STACK                      : STACKARRAY;
       TOPOFSTACK                 : STACKRANGE;
       LEFTFIRST, LEFTLAST,
       RIGHTFIRST, RIGHTLAST      : INTEGER;
       ALLPARTITIONSHAVEBEENMADE : BOOLEAN;

BEGIN  (*  the executable section of QUICKSORT.  *)

   IF LAST - FIRST >= CUTOFFVALUE THEN
      BEGIN

         TOPOFSTACK := 0;
         ALLPARTITIONSHAVEBEENMADE := FALSE;

         (*  Keep partitioning until all partitions have been made *)
         REPEAT
            PARTITION(A, FIRST, LAST, LEFTFIRST, LEFTLAST,
                      RIGHTFIRST, RIGHTLAST);

            (*  Push (the first and last subscripts of) the larger  *)
            (*  subarray onto the stack.  Prepare to partition the  *)
            (*  smaller subarray.                                   *)
            IF LEFTLAST - LEFTFIRST > RIGHTLAST - RIGHTFIRST THEN
               BEGIN

                  (*  Push the left subarray, if it is big enough.  *)
                  IF LEFTLAST - LEFTFIRST >= CUTOFFVALUE THEN
                     PUSHPAIR(LEFTFIRST, LEFTLAST, STACK, TOPOFSTACK);

                  (*  Prepare to partition the right subarray,  *)
                  (*  if it is big enough.                      *)
                  IF RIGHTLAST - RIGHTFIRST >= CUTOFFVALUE THEN
                     BEGIN
                        FIRST := RIGHTFIRST;
                        LAST  := RIGHTLAST
                     END
                  ELSE  (*  Prepare to partition the subarray  *)
                        (*  on the top of the stack.           *)
                     IF TOPOFSTACK > 0 THEN
                        POPPAIR(FIRST, LAST, STACK, TOPOFSTACK)
                     ELSE
                        ALLPARTITIONSHAVEBEENMADE := TRUE

               END
            ELSE
               BEGIN

                  (*  Push the right subarray, if it is big enough.  *)
                  IF RIGHTLAST - RIGHTFIRST >= CUTOFFVALUE THEN
                     PUSHPAIR(RIGHTFIRST, RIGHTLAST, STACK, TOPOFSTACK);

                  (*  Prepare to partition the left subarray,  *)
                  (*  if it is big enough.                     *)
                  IF LEFTLAST - LEFTFIRST >= CUTOFFVALUE THEN
                     BEGIN
```

```
                        FIRST := LEFTFIRST;
                        LAST  := LEFTLAST
                 END
              ELSE  (*  Prepare to partition the subarray  *)
                    (*  on the top of the stack.           *)
                 IF TOPOFSTACK > 0 THEN
                    POPPAIR(FIRST, LAST, STACK, TOPOFSTACK)
                 ELSE
                    ALLPARTITIONSHAVEBEENMADE := TRUE
         END

      UNTIL ALLPARTITIONSHAVEBEENMADE

   END

END;  (*  of the procedure QUICKSORT.  *)




PROCEDURE  INSERTIONSORT(VAR    A : ARRAYTYPE; N : SUBSCRIPTTYPE);

(*  Perform an insertion sort on A[1..N].  *)

VAR    I, J            : SUBSCRIPTTYPE;
       TEMPORARY       : COMPONENTTYPE;
       POSITIONFOUND : BOOLEAN;

BEGIN

   FOR I := 2 TO N DO

      (*  INVARIANT : A[1..I - 1] is already sorted.  *)
      BEGIN
         J             := I;
         TEMPORARY     := A[J];
         POSITIONFOUND := FALSE;

         (*  Sift A[J] down to its proper position.  *)
         REPEAT
            IF TEMPORARY < A[J - 1] THEN
               BEGIN
                  A[J] := A[J - 1];
                  J    := J - 1;
                  IF J = 1 THEN
                     POSITIONFOUND := TRUE
               END
            ELSE
               POSITIONFOUND := TRUE
         UNTIL POSITIONFOUND;

         A[J] := TEMPORARY

      END  (*  of the FOR statement.  *)

END;  (*  of the procedure INSERTIONSORT.  *)
```

```
BEGIN   (*  The executable section of the main program.  *)

    (*  Print heading.  *)
    PAGE;
    WRITELN ('THE ZIP CODES AS GIVEN :');
    WRITELN;

    N := 0;

    (*  Read the input into the array ZIPCODE.  *)
    WHILE NOT EOF DO
        BEGIN
            N := N + 1;

            (*  Read in one zip code.  *)
            FOR I := 1 TO 5 DO
                READ(ZIPCODE[N][I]);
            READLN;

            WRITELN(ZIPCODE[N] : 5)
        END;

    (*  Sort the array ZIPCODE.  *)
    IF N > 0 THEN
        BEGIN
            QUICKSORT(ZIPCODE, 1, N);
            INSERTIONSORT(ZIPCODE, N)
        END;

    (*  Print out the sorted array.  *)
    PAGE;
    WRITELN('THE ZIP CODES IN INCREASING ORDER:');
    WRITELN;
    FOR J := 1 TO N DO
        WRITELN(ZIPCODE[J]);
    PAGE
END.
```

Program Testing

1. Testing the main program:

   <u>Test 1a</u>
   (no input)

   <u>Test 1b</u>
   02119
   01784
   21801
   55121
   33351
   02119

2. Testing **QUICKSORT**, **PUSHPAIR**, and **POPPAIR** (the stub for **PARTITION** simply splits the array in two):

   <u>Test 2a</u>   (array size less than cutoff value)
   02119
   01784
   21801
   55121
   33351
   02119

   <u>Test 2b</u>   (one call to **PARTITION**)
   21801
   55835
   90704
   71620
   78558
   80599
   10625
   80559
   21802
   30505

   <u>Test 2c</u>   (seven calls to **PARTITION**)
   (There were 50 zipcodes in this test.)

3. Testing **INSERTIONSORT**:

   <u>Test 3a</u>   (same as Test 2a)
   <u>Test 3b</u>   (same as Test 2b)
   <u>Test 3c</u>   (same as Test 2c)

4. Testing **PARTITION** and **FINDMEDIAN**:

   <u>Test 4a</u>   (one call to **PARTITION**)
   (Same as Test 3b)
   <u>Test 4b</u>   (several calls to **PARTITION**)
   (Same as Test 3c)

ANALYSIS OF QUICKSORT

We now informally analyze the performance of the above Quicksorting method, with a cutoff value of 10. Full details are available in Sedgewick, 1977. First, let us determine the sort effort. Since each partition produces two subarrays, the Quicksorting may be represented by a binary tree. For example, if we started with $A[1..5000]$, the tree might be as shown in Fig. 6.20.

The first partition requires either $N + 1$ or $N + 2$ comparisons, depending on whether DOWNCOUNTER is either equal to or less than UPCOUNTER when the partition is complete. Similarly, in partitioning the two subarrays at level 1, the total number of comparisons required is $N + 2$, $N + 3$, or $N + 4$. In general, with a cutoff value of 10, the number of comparisons at any level is, at most, $12N/10$. The sort effort is equal to the average number of comparisons per level times the average number of levels. The average number of levels is, approximately, the number of times that N can be divided by 2 until we reach 10, that is, $\log_2 (N/10)$. Thus, the sort effort during QUICKSORT is $O(N) * O(\log_2 N)$, which is $O(N \ln N)$. Since the resulting array is nearly sorted. INSERTIONSORT performs close to its best case: $N - 1$ comparisons. Since $O(N \ln N) + O(N) = O(N \ln N)$, the overall sort effort is $O(N \ln N)$. The actual value of the sort effort is, approximately, $1.7\, N \ln N$ comparisons. By eliminating redundant comparisons between the pivot and itself, we can reduce the sort effort to (approximately) $1.7N \ln N - 3.7N$ comparisons, at a cost of slightly complicating the code. Other sort procedures, for example, Binary Sort Tree and Merge Sort, also have sort efforts that are $O(N \ln N)$, but empirical tests have shown Quicksort to be, on the average, the fastest of all known sorts. Without doubt, one of the factors in Quicksort's impressive performance is that its inner loops (the REPEAT loops in the PARTITION procedure) can be implemented very efficiently in machine code: an increment, a comparison, and a conditional branch.

In the best case, an already sorted list, QUICKSORT requires $\log_2 (N/10)$ levels of partitioning, with, approximately, $11N/10$ comparisons per level. INSERTIONSORT requires $N - 1$ comparisons at the end, so the total number of comparisons is, approximately, $N \log_2 N$.

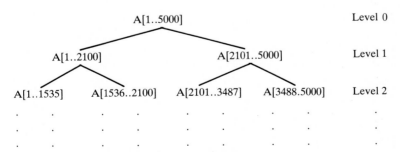

Figure 6.20 A possible partitioning of $A[1..5000]$.

The worst case occurs when we have $O(N)$ levels of partitioning rather than $O(\log_2 N)$ levels. This will happen when each partition creates a very large subarray and a very small subarray, that is, when the pivot is not a "middle" value but close to or equal to an extreme value. For example, suppose we start with the following (assume a cutoff value of 1 for simplicity):

100   0   0   90   0   0   0   100

The pivot is 100, and after the first partitioning, we get

[100   0   0   90   0   0   0]   [100]

The right subarray is ignored. For the left subarray, the pivot is 90. After partitioning, we get

[0   0   0   0   0]   [90   100]

In the worst case, which happens very infrequently, the number of comparisons is $O(N^2)$. Recall that for Merge Sort, the number of comparisons is always $O(N \ln N)$. Thus, Quicksort does not always provide the best sorting technique. For a comparison of Quicksort and Merge Sort on random lists, see Prob. 6.1. As a general rule, Quicksort will execute faster even when Merge Sort requires fewer comparisons.

The number of swaps is always less than or equal to the number of comparisons, so we will have $O(N \ln N)$ swaps, on the average. Since UPCOUNTER and DOWNCOUNTER start at opposite ends of the subarray, the average distance covered during each swap is relatively large (unlike Bubble Sort).

The space requirements are modest: N locations for the array, a stack that holds at most $\log_2 N$ subscript pairs, and a few additional locations for counters, temporaries and boolean variables.

Figure 6.21 summarizes the six sort procedures we have discussed in this chapter. Merge Sort is the best procedure if we want to consider sort effort only: The number of comparisons is kept low because almost every merge is between equal-sized sublists. But keeping track of those sublists makes Merge Sort execute more slowly than, say, Quicksort.

The role of the root in a Binary Sort Tree is analogous to that of the pivot in the original version of Quicksort. For static lists, Binary Sort Tree is of no great value. However, as we will see in the next chapter, Binary Sort Tree is an outstanding sort when the list must be updated as well as sorted.

Exercise 6.14 In the above program, a procedure was used to calculate the median of three components. Could a function always be used instead ?

Hint: What if the component type of the array to be sorted were a string type?

Exercise 6.15 Determine the number of comparisons and the number of swaps in the above program if there are 1000 items, all of which have the same value.

	Sort effort	Order of sort effort	Worst case	Best case
Selection Sort	$0.5N^2 - 0.5N$	$O(N^2)$	$0.5N^2 - 0.5N$	$0.5N^2 - 0.5N$
Bubble Sort	$0.5N^2 - 0.5N \ln (N + 1) \cdots$	$O(N^2)$	$0.5N^2 - 0.5N$	$N - 1$
Insertion Sort	$0.25N^2 + 0.75N - \cdots$	$O(N^2)$	$0.5N^2 - 0.5N$	$N - 1$
Binary Sort Tree	$2N \ln N + 2 \ln N - \cdots$	$O(N \ln N)$	$0.5N^2 - 0.5N$	$N \log_2 (N + 1) + \log_2 (N + 1) + \cdots$
Merge Sort	$1.44N \ln N - 1.25N + \cdots$	$O(N \ln N)$	$1.44N \ln N$	$0.72N \ln N$
Quicksort	$1.7N \ln N - 3.7N + \cdots$	$O(N \ln N)$	$\dfrac{N^2 + 5N - 6}{2}$ (cutoff = 1)	$1.44N \ln N$

Figure 6.21 Comparison of several sort procedures.

Exercise 6.16 In Quicksorting a list of N elements in increasing order, no swaps occur. How many swaps occur in Quicksorting a list of N elements in decreasing order?

Exercise 6.17 Show how the partitioning method can be used to find the median of a list of numbers without completely sorting them.

Hint: At each stage, we partition only that subarray which includes the middle subscript(s) from the original array. For example, suppose we want the median of 9999 numbers stored in A[1..9999] and the first partition gives us a left subarray of A[1..3862] and right subarray of A[3863..9999]. Since the middle subscript, 5000, is in the right subarray, we can henceforth ignore the left subarray.

FILE SORTING

Because files must be accessed sequentially in Standard Pascal, sorting is a fairly common file operation. We now outline how this can be done efficiently. Suppose we want to sort a large file of random numbers. We assume that the maximum array size allowed is 10000, so we cannot simply read the file into an array, Quicksort the array, and then write the array out onto the file. Quicksorting will play a major role, but on pieces of the file, not the entire file.

We start by reading in the random number file, in blocks of 10000 numbers each. Each block is Quicksorted and stored, in an alternating fashion, on one of two temporary files: LEFT TOP and LEFT BOTTOM. See Fig. 6.22.

We then go through an alternating process which continues until all of the numbers are sorted and on a single file. The temporary files used in this process are LEFT TOP, LEFT BOTTOM, and RIGHT BOTTOM; RANDOM FILE itself plays the role of RIGHT TOP. At each stage, we merge a top and bottom pair of files, with the resulting double-sized blocks stored alternately on the other top and bottom pair. Figure 6.23 shows the first stage in this merge process.

If RIGHT BOTTOM is still empty after a left-to-right merge, then the sort is complete (and RANDOM FILE holds the sorted numbers). Otherwise a right-to-left merge is performed, after which we check to see if LEFT BOTTOM is still empty (in which case LEFT TOP is copied onto RANDOM FILE and the sort is complete).

A sorting method such as this is often used to provide a system sort utility or to implement COBOL's SORT verb. The sort effort is $O(N \ln N)$ since both Quicksort and Merge Sort have sort efforts that are $O(N \ln N)$.

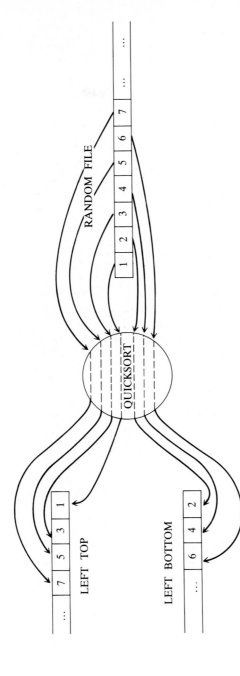

Figure 6.22 The first stage of the file sorting process —each numbered block, except the last, contains 10000 numbers. The last block may contain fewer than 10000 numbers.

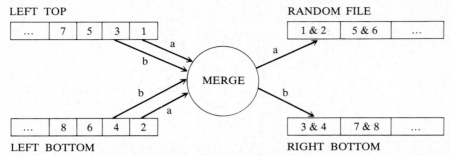

LEFT TOP   RANDOM FILE

LEFT BOTTOM   RIGHT BOTTOM

Figure 6.23 The first stage in merging. Each (numbered) block in LEFT TOP and LEFT BOTTOM is sorted and contains 10000 numbers. Each block in RANDOM FILE and RIGHT BOTTOM is sorted and contains 20000 numbers.

PROBLEMS

Problem 6.1 Comparing Binary Sort Tree, Merge Sort, and Quicksort

Design and write a program to solve the following problem: Determine the sort effort, in a given number of trials, to sort a given number of randomly generated zip codes by a Binary Sort Tree, by Merge Sort, and by Quicksort.

Clarification For each of the trials, generate the specified number of random zip codes and then sort them by the three methods. Print out the number of comparisons required by each method after each trial as well as the average (rounded to the nearest integer) for each method over all trials. In Quicksorts, use a cutoff of 12 for partitioning small arrays.

Sample Input

10 500

Sample Output

NUMBER OF COMPARISONS
TO SORT 500 RANDOM NUMBERS

TRIAL	BINARY SORT TREE	MERGE SORT	QUICKSORT
1	5140	3867	5172
2	4532	3870	5267
3	4340	3853	5288
4	4896	3856	5344
5	4755	3853	5352
6	4781	3862	5547
7	4506	3831	5325
8	4719	3860	5104
9	4625	3865	5308
10	4909	3860	5481

THE AVERAGE NUMBER OF COMPARISONS WAS AS FOLLOWS:
BINARY SORT TREE : 4720
MERGE SORT   : 3858
QUICKSORT   : 5309

Problem 6.2 Sorting a File of Random Numbers

Design and write a program to solve the following problem: Create and sort a file of random numbers.

Clarification Each random number will be a positive integer less than or equal to 131071 (see page 157). The input will consist of the seed and the number of random numbers to be generated. We assume, for specificity, that the maximum array size allowed is 1000 elements. The output will consist of the unsorted and sorted files.

Sample Input

5000   6500

Sample Output

THIS PROGRAM CREATES AND SORTS A FILE OF 6500 RANDOM INTEGERS, WITH EACH INTEGER HAVING A VALUE BETWEEN 1 AND 131071, INCLUSIVE.

THE SEED USED IS 5000.

WE ASSUME A MAXIMUM ARRAY SIZE OF 1000 LOCATIONS.

HERE ARE THE UNSORTED RANDOM NUMBERS:
 94460   127074 ...
   ⋮
 8517

(*new page*)

HERE ARE THE RANDOM NUMBERS IN INCREASING ORDER:
 17   20   22 ...
   ⋮
 130976

SEVEN

SEARCHING

In Chap. 6 we analyzed several sorting techniques with regard to their efficiency. In this chapter we present a parallel study of searching. The critical nature of these two operations can be seen from the fact that COBOL, the most widely used programming language, has both a SORT statement and a SEARCH statement, even though it lacks some other practical features (such as a CASE statement, dynamic variables, functions, and recursion).

MEASURES OF EFFICIENCY

Just as with sorting, searching a list poses the usual time-space-familiarity trade-offs. And again, once you have finished this chapter, familiarity should not be an important factor in your deliberations since you will have seen the most important searching techniques now being used. Similarly, space is seldom a key consideration in searching. Thus, the crucial criterion for judging a search technique's efficiency is how much time it takes to find an item (that is, component). We will not measure CPU time directly since this will vary from one computer to another. Instead, we will calculate each method's *average search length* (denoted by L): the average number of comparisons required to find the item we are searching for. The average is taken over the number of comparisons to find each item in the list. Specifically, assume that we have a list of N items

$$a_1, a_2, \ldots, a_N$$

and that we want to search through the list to find one of those items. Then

$$L = c_1 p_1 + c_2 p_2 + \cdots + c_N p_N$$

where, for each value of i between 1 and N,

c_i = the number of comparisons needed to find a_i

p_i = the probability that a_i is the item we are searching for

It often happens that each item in the list is equally likely to be accessed, that is,

$$p_1 = p_2 = \cdots = p_N$$

Since the sum of these probabilities is 1, each probability has a value of $1/N$, so we can write

$$L = \frac{c_1 + c_2 + \cdots + c_N}{N}$$

This situation occurs when information about previous searches is irrelevant or unknown. Sometimes, however, information from previous searches can suggest a rearrangement of the list to take advantage of the particular search method being used. For example, if some search technique always starts by considering the first item in the list, it may decrease the average search length if the item sought most often in the past were stored in the first position.

We make the following assumptions about the search methods we will investigate in this chapter:

1. Unless otherwise noted, we assume that each item in the list will be equally likely to be accessed.
2. Each item in the list will have a single *key field*, that is, the field by which the item is identified in the search. Each key value will be unique.
3. The search will conclude when either the item has been found whose key value matches the given key value, or it is discovered that no match exists.

SIMPLE SEARCH TECHNIQUES

The searches in this section will be conducted on the following list of (single-field) items:

546-3261
742-1950
742-8137
543-8080
742-3805
546-4611
749-1263
543-2007
742-1017
546-3565
749-2000
543-8181

Sequential Search This simplest search technique can be described as follows: Given a key value, first check the first item in the list to see if its key field contains a match of the given key value. If there is a match, the search concludes successfully; otherwise, check the second item for a match, then (if necessary) the third item, and so on.

The following procedure implements a sequential search on a list implemented as an array of records. MAXARRAYSIZE is a constant identifier and KEYTYPE can be any type for which " < " is defined.

```
TYPE   LISTSIZERANGE    = 1..MAXARRAYSIZE ;
       COMPONENTTYPE = RECORD
                          ⋮
                          KEYFIELD : KEYTYPE ;
                          ⋮
                       END ;
       LISTTYPE         = RECORD
                          A : ARRAY[LISTSIZERANGE] OF COMPONENTTYPE ;
                          N : LISTSIZERANGE
                          END ;

PROCEDURE   SEQUENTIALSEARCH(LIST              : LISTTYPE ;
                            KEYSOUGHT          : KEYTYPE ;
                            VAR     POSITION   : LISTSIZERANGE ;
                            VAR     MATCHFOUND : BOOLEAN) ;
```

(∗ Search LIST, that is, A[1..N] until we find a component   ∗)
(∗ whose KEYFIELD value matches the value of KEYSOUGHT. If ∗)
(∗ such a component is found, POSITION gets the subscript   ∗)
(∗ of that component and MATCHFOUND gets the value TRUE.   ∗)
(∗ Otherwise, MATCHFOUND gets the value FALSE.   ∗)

```
TYPE   POSINTEGER = 1..MAXINT ;

VAR    I : POSINTEGER ;

BEGIN
    (∗ Prepare for search. ∗)
    I                := 1 ;
    MATCHFOUND := FALSE ;

    (∗ Continue until match found or list searched unsuccessfully. ∗)
    WITH LIST DO
        WHILE (I <= N) AND (NOT MATCHFOUND) DO

            IF A[I].KEYFIELD = KEYSOUGHT THEN
                BEGIN (∗ Success! ∗)
                    POSITION     := I ;
                    MATCHFOUND := TRUE
                END
            ELSE
                I := I + 1
END ; (∗ of the procedure SEQUENTIALSEARCH. ∗)
```

For example, suppose the key value sought is 742-3805; then the search of the list on page 273 would require 5 comparisons. If each key value in the list is equally likely to be sought, then the average search length for a successful search would be

$$L = \frac{1 + 2 + 3 + \cdots + 12}{12}$$

$$= 6.5$$

In general, for a list with N items, where each is equally likely to be accessed, the average number of comparisons for a successful sequential search is given by

$$L = \frac{1 + 2 + \cdots + N}{N}$$

$$= \frac{N * (N + 1)}{2 * N}$$

$$= \frac{N + 1}{2}$$

That is, the average successful search requires looking at about half the list. For an unsuccessful search, the entire list must be accessed.

If we know how frequently each item was accessed in the past, then the calculation of average search length should take this into account (if we expect that the future will not be much different). For example, suppose we had the table of telephone numbers and previous accesses shown in Fig. 7.1.

For each telephone number, assume that the probability it will be sought is equal to its frequency divided by the sum of the frequencies. Thus

$$p_1 = \frac{50}{1300} = 0.038$$

$$p_2 = \frac{100}{1300} = 0.077$$

$$\vdots$$

$$p_{12} = \frac{100}{1300} = 0.077$$

TELEPHONE NUMBER	FREQUENCY
546-3261	50
742-1950	100
742-8137	70
543-8080	80
742-3805	150
546-4611	50
749-1263	80
543-2007	250
742-1017	120
546-3565	200
749-2000	50
543-8181	100

Figure 7.1 A list of telephone numbers and their access frequencies.

If we leave the list as it is, then for a successful search,

$$
\begin{aligned}
L &= c_1p_1 + c_2p_2 + \cdots + c_{12}p_{12} \\
&= (1)(0.038) + (2)(0.077) + (3)(0.054) + (4)(0.062) \\
&\quad + (5)(0.115) + (6)(0.038) + (7)(0.062) + (8)(0.192) \\
&\quad + (9)(0.092) + (10)(0.154) + (11)(0.038) + (12)(0.077) \\
&= 7.085
\end{aligned}
$$

You might now hastily conclude that knowledge of previous access frequencies *increases* the average search length from 6.5 to 7.085. Further reflection should convince you that such a suggestion is unsupported and, in fact, ludicrous! If the frequencies are as shown in Fig. 7.1, then the assumption of equiprobable access is apparently incorrect, so the calculated value of 6.5 for L is also incorrect. To put it another way, empirical observations do not yield higher search lengths, only more accurate search lengths.

Exercise 7.1 Modify the procedure SEQUENTIALSEARCH to search a linked-list instead of an array.

Ordered Sequential Search We can use the information about previous accesses to obtain somewhat faster sequential searches. To do this we must sort the list in order of decreasing frequencies, so that the most frequently accessed items will be at the top of the list. For example, if we sort the list in Fig. 7.1 by decreasing frequencies, the resulting table is shown in Fig. 7.2.

The average (successful) search length is then

$$
L = (1)\frac{250}{1300} + (2)\frac{200}{1300} + (3)\frac{150}{1300} + \cdots + (12)\frac{50}{1300}
$$

$$
= 4.738
$$

The trade-off for this improved search length is that the list had to be sorted by frequencies. A one-shot sort is not much of an expense, but static lists are the exception rather than the rule. As we will see in a later section, the problem of

TELEPHONE NUMBER	FREQUENCY
543-2007	250
546-3565	200
742-3805	150
742-1017	120
742-1950	100
543-8181	100
543-8080	80
749-1263	80
742-8137	70
546-3261	50
546-4611	50
749-2000	50

Figure 7.2 A list of telephone numbers, ordered by decreasing frequencies.

searching is often related to the problem of updating: Even if no *new* telephone numbers were to be added to the list in Fig. 7.2, the frequencies would be continually changing.

Binary Search This method also requires that the list be sorted, but here the sorting is by key field rather than frequency of access. Figure 7.3 shows the list of telephone numbers sorted into increasing order.

The binary search method works as follows: Suppose we seek the record whose key value is 742-1950. First, find the middle position† in the list, in this case, position 6. If the key field of the item in this position matches the given key value, we are done. Otherwise, determine if the middle item's key value (in this case, 546-4611) is less than or greater than the desired key (namely, 742-1950). Since it is less, we can ignore the items prior to position 6 and consider only the sublist in positions 7 to 12. The middle position is position 9. Since the ninth item's key, 742-3805, is greater than the key sought, 742-1950, we search the sublist in positions 7 through 8. Here the middle position is 7, and the key value there, 742-1017, is less than the key sought, so we search the trivial sublist in positions 8 through 8. Here a match is found.

In general, suppose we are searching the sublist from position FIRST to position LAST. If the key value at position MIDDLE is less than the key sought, we next search the sublist from position MIDDLE + 1 to position LAST. If, however, the key value at position MIDDLE is greater than the key sought, we next search the sublist from position FIRST to position MIDDLE − 1.

If there is no match of the key sought, we will keep searching smaller and smaller sublists, until eventually, we have an empty sublist to search. For example, if we were searching for 543-8457, the first, middle and last positions of the sublists searched would be as shown in Fig. 7.4.

If the key sought is smaller than any key value in the list, the final value of FIRST will be 1 and the final value of LAST will be 0. For a key sought that is greater than any key value in the list, the final value of FIRST will be one more than the size of the list; LAST's final value will be the list size.

† The list is, therefore, implemented contiguously, by an array.

543-2007
543-8080
543-8181
546-3261
546-3565
546-4611
742-1017
742-1950
742-3805
742-8137
749-1263
749-2000   **Figure 7.3** A list of telephone numbers in increasing order.

The following procedure implements a binary search on an array A[1..MAXARRAYSIZE] of records. MAXARRAYSIZE is a constant identifier and KEYTYPE can be any type for which " < " is defined. In comparing the middle record's key to the key sought, the result will be " < " or " > " more often than " = ". The nested IF statements were arranged to advantage of this fact (for the sake of efficiency).

```
TYPE   POSINTEGER      = 0..MAXINT ;
       SUBSCRIPTTYPE   = 1..MAXARRAYSIZE ;
       COMPONENTTYPE = RECORD
                          :
                          KEYFIELD : KEYTYPE ;
                          :
                       END ;
       ARRAYTYPE       = ARRAY[SUBSCRIPTTYPE] OF COMPONENTTYPE ;

PROCEDURE   BINARYSEARCH(A                   : ARRAYTYPE ;
                         FIRST, LAST         : POSINTEGER ;
                         KEYSOUGHT           : KEYTYPE ;
                         VAR POSITION        : SUBSCRIPTTYPE ;
                         VAR MATCHFOUND : BOOLEAN) ;
(* Conduct a binary search of A[FIRST..LAST] looking for a record whose key field matches  *)
(* KEYSOUGHT                                                                                 *)
(* Precondition: A[FIRST..LAST] in increasing order by key field.                           *)
(* Postcondition: If a record is found whose key field matches KEYSOUGHT, POSITION          *)
(* gets the subscript of the matching record and MATCHFOUND gets the value TRUE.            *)
(* Otherwise, MATCHFOUND gets the value FALSE                                                *)

VAR   MIDDLE : SUBSCRIPTTYPE ;

BEGIN

    MATCHFOUND := FALSE ;
    WHILE (FIRST <= LAST) AND (MATCHFOUND = FALSE) DO
        BEGIN

            MIDDLE := (FIRST + LAST) DIV 2 ;

            (* Compare the middle record's key to KEYSOUGHT. *)
            IF A[MIDDLE].KEYFIELD < KEYSOUGHT THEN
                FIRST := MIDDLE + 1
            ELSE
                IF A[MIDDLE].KEYFIELD > KEYSOUGHT THEN
                    LAST := MIDDLE - 1
                ELSE

                    (* Success! *)
                    BEGIN
                        POSITION     := MIDDLE ;
                        MATCHFOUND := TRUE
                    END

        END
END ;   (* of the procedure BINARYSEARCH. *)
```

FIRST	MIDDLE	LAST	RESULT
1	6	12	546-4611 > 543-8457
1	3	5	543-8181 < 543-8457
4	4	5	546-3261 > 543-8457
4		3	No match found

Figure 7.4 The steps in a binary search for 543-8457 in the list of Fig. 7.3.

In general, if each of N records is equally likely to have the desired key, then the average (successful) search length is, approximately, the number of times N must be divided by 2 to get a result of 1. That is, L is $O(\log_2 N)$—see Exercise 7.2. This search length is a considerable improvement over the sequential search length [which is $O(N)$] for large values of N, but the drawbacks are:

1. Information about previous access frequencies cannot be utilized since the keys themselves must be in order.
2. Since an array must be used, its maximum size must be specified in advance. This often wastes space.
3. In addition to the "cost" of the initial sort, updating the list requires substantial movement of records since an array is used.

Exercise 7.2 (This exercise requires familiarity with the principle of mathematical induction.) Show that the average (successful) search length for a binary search is $O(\log_2 N)$.

Hint: Assume, for convenience, that N is one less than a power of 2. Thus $N = 2^K - 1$ for some nonnegative integer K. Then one comparison is required for one record, the middle one. Two comparisons are required for 2 records, one a fourth of the way down the list and the other three fourths of the way down. Three comparisons are required for 4 records. Four comparisons are required for 8 records, and so on. Thus

$$L = \frac{1*1 + 2*2 + 3*4 + 4*8 + \cdots + K*2^{K-1}}{N}$$

$$= \sum_{i=1}^{K} \frac{i2^{i-1}}{N}$$

$$= \frac{K2^K - 2^K + 1}{N}$$

$$= \frac{[\log_2(N+1)](N+1) - (N+1) + 1}{N}$$

Note: We count as only one comparison the determination of whether a given key is less than, greater than, or equal to the key sought.

Exercise 7.3 For a fixed list of size 31, calculate, for a binary search:

1. The shortest (successful) search length
2. The longest (successful) search length
3. The average (successful) search length
4. The length of an unsuccessful search

BINARY SEARCH TREE

We noted above that a binary search requires an array implementation and is thus unwieldy for updating. A similar approach, the *binary search tree* (also known as the Binary Sort Tree, pages 212–213), provides $O(\log_2 N)$ search length and quick updating. To illustrate, we first sort the list on page 273 with a Binary Sort Tree, shown in Fig. 7.5.

To find the key with value 742-3805, only four keys need be examined: 546-3261, 742-1950, 742-8137 and 742-3805. For a perfectly balanced binary tree with N nodes, the average search length is the same as for the binary search of the previous section, namely $O(\log_2 N)$. If the original list were already in increasing (or decreasing) order, then the resulting tree would be a chain, with an average search length similar to that for a sequential search, namely, $O(N)$. For an arbitrary list, the average search length is still $O(\log_2 N)$; see Knuth, 1973, page 427, for details.

Exercise 7.4 Develop a procedure to search for a desired key in a binary search tree. The type KEYTYPE is any type for which " $<$ " is defined. Assume the following type definitions:

```
TYPE   POINTER = ^NODE ;
       NODE    = RECORD
                   :
                   KEYFIELD      : KEYTYPE ;
                   :
                   LEFT; RIGHT; POINTER
                 END ;
```

The procedure heading and initial comments are

```
PROCEDURE  BINARYSEARCHTREE(ROOT
                   : POINTER ;
       KEYSOUGHT          : KEYTYPE :
VAR    POSITION           : POINTER
VAR    MATCHFOUND : BOOLEAN) ;
```

(* Search the binary tree pointed to by ROOT for a node whose key field matches *)
(* KEYSOUGHT. If the node is found, POSITION points to it and MATCHFOUND gets *)
(* the value TRUE. Otherwise, MATCHFOUND gets the value FALSE.   *)

Hint: This procedure is analogous to the procedure BINARYSEARCH on page 278, with ROOT playing the role of MIDDLE.

For searching a static list, the binary search tree is no better than an array-based binary search. The average search lengths are both $O(\log_2 N)$. In fact, a binary search of an array is somewhat faster than a binary search tree since the array will always be "balanced." The space requirements are also similar: A binary search tree uses extra space for the pointers, but an array's maximum size must be specified in advance.

Updating a Binary Search Tree

The value of a binary search tree becomes evident when updating is attempted. Whereas an insertion or deletion in a sorted array forces about half of the elements to be moved, the same operation can be performed in a binary search tree by adjusting two pointers.

Insertion An insertion is handled easily because the new node becomes a leaf in the tree. For example, suppose we try to insert 546-9009 into the tree in Fig. 7.5. The insertion is effected as follows:

1. Since the tree is not empty, we compare 546-9009 with the root. Since 546-9009 > 546-3261, we try to insert 546-9009 in the root's right subtree.
2. Since that subtree is not empty, we compare 546-9009 with of that subtree's root. Since 546-9009 < 742-1950, we try to insert 546-9009 in that subtree's left subtree.
3. Since that subtree (the one with 546-4611 at its root) is not empty, we compare 546-9009 with that subtree's root. Since 546-9009 > 546-4611, we try to insert 546-9009 in that subtree's right subtree.
4. Since that subtree (the one with 742-1017 at its root) is not empty, we compare 546-9009 with that subtree's root. Since 546-9009 < 742-1017, we try to insert 546-9009 in that subtree's left subtree.
5. Since that subtree *is* empty, we insert 546-9009 as the root of that subtree.

The resulting tree is shown in Fig. 7.6.

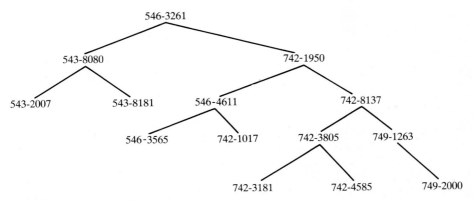

Figure 7.5 A binary sort (search) tree.

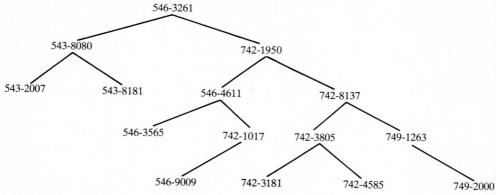

Figure 7.6 The binary search tree of Fig. 7.5 after 546-9009 is inserted.

If the phone number to be inserted matches the root of an already existing subtree, we have an attempt to insert an already existing phone number, so the insertion attempt fails.

Exercise 7.5 Develop a procedure to try to insert a node into a binary search tree. Assume the following type definitions, procedure heading and initial comments:

```
TYPE   STRING   = PACKED ARRAY[1..8] OF CHAR ;
       POINTER = ^NODE ;
       NODE     = RECORD
                     PHONENUMBER : STRING ;
                     LEFT, RIGHT     : POINTER
                  END ;
PROCEDURE   TRYTREEINSERTION(VAR   ROOT              : POINTER ;
                             CURRENTPHONENUMBER : STRING ;
                             VAR    SUCCESS          : BOOLEAN) ;
(* Try to insert CURRENTPHONENUMBER into the binary    *)
(* search tree pointed to by ROOT. If the insertion    *)
(* can be made, it is made and SUCCESS gets the value  *)
(* TRUE. If there is already a node in the tree whose  *)
(* phone number matches CURRENTPHONENUMBER, then the   *)
(* insertion is not made and SUCCESS gets the value    *)
(* FALSE.                                              *)
```

Deletion The degree of difficulty in deleting a node from a binary search tree depends on how many children the node has. For a node with no children, that is, for a leaf, we adjust its parent's corresponding pointer and then remove the leaf from the tree. Figure 7.7 shows what the binary search tree of Fig. 7.6 would look like after deleting 546-3565.

To delete a node with one child, adjust the node's parent's corresponding pointer to point to the child of the node to be deleted and then remove the node

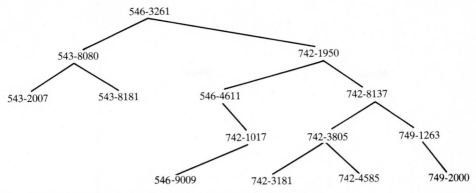

Figure 7.7 The binary search tree of Fig. 7.6 after the deletion of 546-3565.

from the tree. For example, to delete 546-4611 from the tree of Fig. 7.7, we would change the left pointer of the node with key 742-1950 so that the left pointer points to the node with key 742-1017. The resulting tree is shown in Fig. 7.8.

In "family tree" terminology, if a parent who has one child dies, the child is adopted by its grandparent.

In deleting a node that has two children, we must be careful to preserve the ordering of the tree. For any given phone number, each phone number in the left subtree must be less than the given phone number, and each phone number in the right subtree must be greater than the given phone number. To perform the deletion and still preserve this ordering, we replace the phone number to be deleted with the phone number of its immediate successor. The immediate successor of a node is the leftmost descendant of the node's right subtree.

For example, to delete 742-1950 from the tree in Fig. 7.8, we replace that phone number with the phone number of its immediate successor, namely 742-3181. The node which originally contained 742-3181 is then deleted. Figure 7.9 shows the resulting tree.

For a slightly more complicated example, suppose we want to delete 742-3181 from the tree in Fig. 7.9. This differs from the previous example only in that

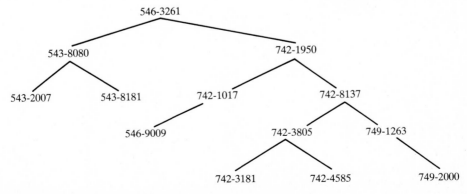

Figure 7.8 The binary search tree of Fig. 7.7 after deleting 546-4611.

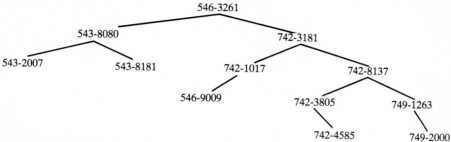

Figure 7.9 The binary search tree of Fig. 7.8 after deleting 742-1950.

the immediate successor, 742-3805, has a child of its own. We first replace 742-3181 with 742-3805. We then delete from the tree the node that originally contained 742-3805. This step is straightforward since we already know how to delete a node that has one child. Figure 7.10 shows the resulting tree.

As a final example of deletion, we delete 742-8137 from the binary search tree in Fig. 7.10. The only new feature here is that its immediate successor, 749-1263, is a *right* child rather than a left child. The result of the deletion is shown in Fig. 7.11.

The following procedures summarize the process of deletion from a binary search tree. We assume the type definitions from Exercise 7.5. Since each node in a tree is the root of some subtree, we consider only the case where the node to be deleted is a root. DELETEROOT can be called (recursively) by a procedure that deletes an arbitrary node from a binary search tree—see Exercise 7.7.

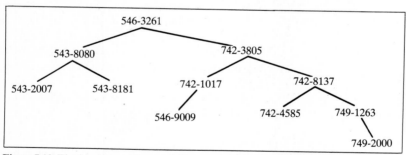

Figure 7.10 The binary search tree of Fig. 7.9 after deleting 742-3181.

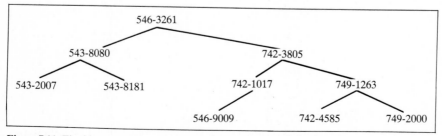

Figure 7.11 The binary search tree of Fig. 7.10 after deleting 742-8137.

```
PROCEDURE  FINDANDREPLACE(ROOT            : POINTER ;
                          VAR  SUCCESSOR : POINTER) ;

(* Find the ROOT's immediate SUCCESSOR, that        *)
(* is, the leftmost descendant in the root's right subtree.  *)
(* Replace the root's phone number with that of its successor *)
(* and then delete that successor from the tree.             *)


VAR     TEMPORARYPOINTER : POINTER ;

BEGIN
      IF SUCCESSOR^.LEFT = NIL THEN
          BEGIN (* We have found the root's immediate successor. *)
              ROOT^.PHONENUMBER := SUCCESSOR^.PHONENUMBER ;

              (* Delete SUCCESSOR^ from the tree. *)
              TEMPORARYPOINTER :=   SUCCESSOR ;
              SUCCESSOR            :=   SUCCESSOR^.RIGHT ;
              DISPOSE(TEMPORARYPOINTER)
          END
        ELSE
            FINDANDREPLACE(ROOT,SUCCESSOR^.LEFT)

END ;  (* of the procedure FINDANDREPLACE. *)

PROCEDURE  DELETEROOT(VAR  ROOT : POINTER) ;

(* Delete the root of a binary search tree. *)

VAR  TEMPORARYPOINTER : POINTER ;

BEGIN
    IF ROOT^.LEFT = NIL THEN

      BEGIN (* The root has no children or a right child only. *)
            TEMPORARYPOINTER := ROOT ;
            ROOT               := ROOT^.RIGHT ;
            DISPOSE(TEMPORARYPOINTER)
      END
    ELSE
      IF ROOT^.RIGHT = NIL THEN

        BEGIN (* The root has a left child only. *)
              TEMPORARYPOINTER := ROOT ;
              ROOT               := ROOT^.LEFT ;
              DISPOSE(TEMPORARYPOINTER)
        END
      ELSE

            (* The root has two children. Find the root's immediate  *)
            (* successor (the leftmost descendant of the root's right *)
            (* child). Replace the root's phone number with that of   *)
            (* its successor and then delete that successor from the tree. *)
            FINDANDREPLACE(ROOT,ROOT^.RIGHT)

END ;  (* of the procedure DELETEROOT. *)
```

Exercise 7.6 Make each of the following updates, one after the other, to the binary search tree of Fig. 7.10.

1. Insert 742-2222.
2. Insert 749-1568.
3. Delete 742-8137.

Exercise 7.7 Develop a procedure to try to delete, from the binary search tree pointed to by ROOT, the node whose phone number field matches CURRENTPHONENUMBER. Assume the following type definitions and procedure heading:

```
TYPE  STRING  = PACKED ARRAY[1..8] OF CHAR ;
      POINTER = ^NODE ;
      NODE    = RECORD
                    PHONENUMBER : STRING ;
                    LEFT, RIGHT  : POINTER
                END ;

PROCEDURE  TRYTREEDELETION(VAR     ROOT               : POINTER ;
                               CURRENTPHONENUMBER : STRING ;
                           VAR     SUCCESS            : BOOLEAN) ;
(* Try to delete, from the binary tree pointed to by      *)
(* ROOT, the node whose phone number field matches        *)
(* CURRENTPHONENUMBER. If there is such a node, it        *)
(* is deleted and SUCCESS gets the value TRUE.            *)
(* Otherwise, SUCCESS gets the value FALSE.               *)
```

Hint: TRYTREEDELETION should call DELETEROOT.

Balancing a Binary Search Tree

One potential problem with binary search trees is that they can become unbalanced through insertions and deletions. For example, if we start with an empty tree and make several insertions which happen to be in order, we get an unbalanced tree such as the one in Fig. 7.12.

Badly unbalanced trees can have average search lengths that are $O(N)$ instead of $O(\log_2 N)$. Fortunately, there are methods to restore balance to a binary

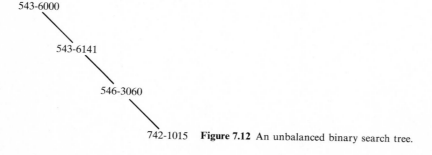

Figure 7.12 An unbalanced binary search tree.

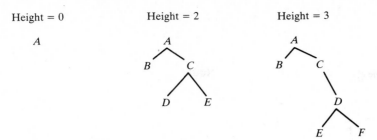

Figure 7.13 Several binary search trees and their heights.

search tree without destroying the ordering. One of these methods uses a type of binary search tree called an AVL tree, after its inventors G. M. Adel'son-Vel'skii and E. M. Landis (see Adel'son-Vel'skii, 1962).

Before we can define an AVL tree, we must define the "height" of a tree. The *height* of a nonempty tree is the number of branches from the root to its farthest descendant; the height of an empty tree is defined to be -1. Figure 7.13 shows the height of several binary search trees.

An *AVL tree* is a binary search tree which is empty or in which the heights of the left and right subtrees differ by at most 1, and in which the left and right subtrees are themselves AVL trees. Figure 7.14 shows several AVL trees, and Fig. 7.15 shows several binary search trees that are not AVL trees.

An AVL tree always has a certain degree of balance, but need not be perfectly balanced. To restore its balance after an insertion or deletion, we may have to restructure the tree. For example, if we start with the middle AVL tree in Fig. 7.14 and insert E as a left child of D, we get the non-AVL tree in the middle of Fig. 7.15. This can be rebalanced by "rotating" the tree to the left so that C becomes the root, as shown in Fig. 7.16.

Sometimes, a right rotation is required, as shown in Fig. 7.17.

For some trees that are almost AVL trees, a slightly more complex operation, called a "double rotation" is required. An example of a double rotation is shown in Fig. 7.18. Not all AVL trees become imbalanced after an insertion or deletion. In fact, an AVL tree will probably remain an AVL tree after a random insertion or leaf deletion.

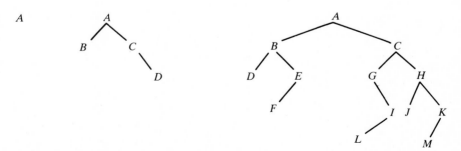

Figure 7.14 Three AVL trees.

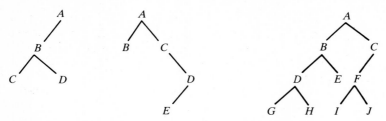

Figure 7.15 Three binary search trees that are not AVL trees.

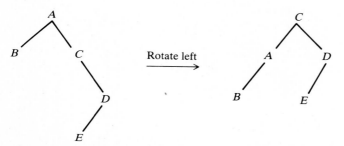

Figure 7.16 Restoring balance to a non-AVL tree. The tree on the right-hand side is an AVL tree.

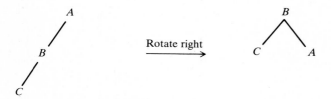

Figure 7.17 Using a right rotation to convert a non-AVL tree to an AVL tree.

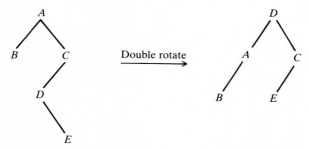

Figure 7.18 Using a double rotation to convert a non-AVL tree to an AVL tree.

A detailed discussion of AVL trees can be found in Kruse, 1984 as well as in Knuth, 1973. The principal advantage of AVL trees is that they restore their balance after each insertion or deletion, so searches do not become sequential. The tradeoff for this advantage is the extra work in restoring the balance.

Exercise 7.8 Create and maintain an AVL tree with the following insertions: 22, 85, 91, 17, 12, 36.

HASHING

Thus far our searches have been straightforward: sequential or based on sorted data. We now introduce a technique whose performance, in terms of search length, is much better than any of the other methods but does not require that the list be sorted. This is *the* search technique for large lists. We temporarily restrict our attention to the initial posting of the items. Later we will consider problems associated with updating.

Suppose we have a table with subscripts going from 0 to 999 and in that table we want to store a list of up to 1000 records. The key field will contain the social security number. To allow fast access, we can take the rightmost 3 digits of a social security number and store the entire record at the location whose subscript is that 3-digit number. For example, the record with a key value of 214-30-3261 (the hyphens are shown for readability only) would be stored at location 261. Similarly, the record with a key value of 033-51-8000 would be stored at location 0. You might already have noticed a potential pitfall with this scheme: Two distinct keys might have the same rightmost 3 digits, for example, 214-30-3261 and 814-02-9261. Such colliding keys are called *synonyms*. We will deal with collisions shortly. For now we simply acknowledge that the possibility of collisions always exists when the size of the key space, that is, the number of legal key values, is larger than the size of the address space, the number of locations available.

Hashing is the process of transforming a key into an address; the transformation involves some simple operation on the key. For an integer key, the operation is often

KEY MOD TABLESIZE

that is, the remainder when the key is divided by the size of the table. In the above example the table size is 1000, so the operation yields the rightmost three digits. Even when the key is not an integer, the MOD function can be used. For example, if each key were a five-letter name and the addresses ranged from 0 to 99, we could add up the ordinal values of the letters and take the remainder when that sum is divided by 100:

```
HASHTOTAL := 0 ;
FOR I := 1 TO 5 DO
    HASHTOTAL := HASHTOTAL + ORD(KEY[I]) ;

ADDRESS := HASHTOTAL MOD 100 ;
```

Thus, for the ASCII collating sequence, ADAMS would hash to 58 since (65 + 68 + 65 + 77 + 83) MOD 100 is 58.

The term "hashing" suggests that we scramble up the key in some way; in other words, that we "make hash" out of the key. No matter how successfully we hash the keys, collisions may still occur, so we must deal with them as part of our hashing algorithm.

Open Addressing

One way to resolve collisions is by *open addressing*: When a collision occurs, keep searching the table according to some strategy until an open address is found. The record is then stored at this address. To illustrate several open addressing schemes, consider the above problem of storing up to 1000 input records with social security numbers as keys. Suppose the list of keys is

214-30-3261

033-51-8000

214-19-9528

819-02-9261

033-30-8262

215-09-1766

214-17-0261

One simple hashing algorithm is this: Initialize the key field at each location in the table to 0. To post an input record with a given key, first calculate an address by taking the remainder when the given key is divided by 1000. If the address is already occupied, an offset of 1 is used; that is, we keep going through a loop until an open slot is found or we discover that all locations are occupied. In the loop, the new address is the remainder when the old address plus one is divided by 1000. If and when an unoccupied location is found, the input record is posted in that open slot. For the above list of keys, the first three records are posted at locations 261, 000, and 528, respectively, as shown in Figure 7.19. When we hash 819-02-9261, the resulting address is 261, which is already occupied. The next location, 262, is empty, so we post 819-02-9261 there. Since the next key, 033-30-8262 hashes to 262, an occupied spot, we must post it in the next empty location, namely 263. The key 215-09-1766 gets posted routinely at location 766, but the key 214-17-0261 finds its home at location 264, three positions away from its original hashed address. The resulting table is shown in Fig. 7.20.

A good hashing algorithm should minimize the occurrence of collisions, but it cannot eliminate them whenever the key space is larger than the address space. The above hashing algorithm appeared to cause clustering at location 261 only because the sample list was rigged for that purpose. The rightmost three digits of a company's list of social security numbers will probably be uniformly distributed between 0 and 999, so the above algorithm would actually avoid the

Subscript	Key	(Other fields)
0	033-51-8000	...
1	0	
.	.	
.	.	
.	.	
260	0	
261	214-30-3261	...
262	0	
.	.	
.	.	
.	.	
527	0	
528	214-19-9528	...
529	0	
.	.	
.	.	
.	.	
999	0	

Figure 7.19 A table to which three records have been posted (by hashing).

phenomenon known as *primary clustering*—the condition of having an excessive number of keys hashing to the same address.

However, the above hashing method does cause *secondary clustering*—the buildup of table entries along the path traced by synonyms from different collisions. For example, if we start with Fig. 7.20, a new key that hashes to 261, 262, 263, or 264 must travel to 265 to find an empty location.

Subscript	Key	(Other fields)
0	033-51-8000	
1	0	
.	.	
.	.	
.	.	
260	0	
261	214-30-3261	
262	819-02-9261	
263	033-30-8262	
264	214-17-0261	
265	0	
.	.	
.	.	
.	.	
527	0	
528	214-19-9528	
529	0	
.	.	
.	.	
.	.	
765	0	
766	215-09-1766	
767	0	
.	.	
.	.	
.	.	
999	0	

Figure 7.20 A table to which seven records have been posted (by hashing, with an offset of 1).

Any hashing method that entails secondary clustering is inefficient because it leads to sequential searches. As we will soon discover, a hashing algorithm that avoids primary and secondary clustering will, under most circumstances, have an average search length that is less than 2.0.

Could we have avoided secondary clustering if we had used an offset of 2? No, because the path for collisions at 261 would be 261, 263, 265, . . . ; the path for collisions at 263 would be 263, 265, . . . ; and so on. Clearly, any constant offset would still produce secondary clustering. In fact, some large constants would create an additional problem. For example, since 200 is a factor of 1000, an offset of 200 would imply that the path for synonyms would have a maximum length of 5 (such as 261, 461, 661, 861, 61). Thus if five synonyms had already been stored in the table, any additional synonyms would have no place to go!

Both of these difficulties can be overcome if we use the *quotient offset* method with a table size which is a prime number. A *prime number* is a positive integer, greater than one, which has no positive-integer factors other than 1 and itself. For example, if the table must accommodate up to 1000 records, we could choose a prime number slightly greater than 1000, such as 1009, as the table size. The subscripts would then range from 0 to 1008. For a given key, the original address would be the remainder when the key is divided by 1009. The offset would be the (integer) quotient of the key and 1009. If the original address is already occupied, we keep adding the offset to the address (MOD 1009) until we find an empty location. Since the quotient is independent of the remainder, two keys with the same remainder will (most likely) have different quotients and different offsets.

For example, suppose the first record to be posted had a key of 214-30-3261. Then the address calculated would be 214303261 MOD 1009, namely 742; the offset would be 214303261 DIV 1009, namely 212391. Since location 742 is empty (that is, has 0 in the key field), the record would be stored there. Now suppose that a later record had a key of 191-22-2386. Then the address calculated would be 191222386 MOD 1009, namely 742; the offset would be 191222386 DIV 1009, namely 189516. Since location 742 is already occupied, the next address tried is (742 + 189516) MOD 1009, namely 566. If, still further down in the list, we had a record with a key of 530-56-4221, the address calculated would be 530564221 MOD 1009, namely 742, but the offset would be 525831. So when it was discovered that location 742 was already occupied, the next address tried would be (742 + 525831) MOD 1009, namely 884, not 566. Thus secondary clustering is avoided since synonyms from different collisions (and even from the same collision) would not follow the same path. The resulting table is shown in Fig. 7.21.

Exercise 7.9 Use the "offset of 1" collision handler to hash the following keys to the table in Fig. 7.20:

802-57-8528

192-77-0562

Subscript	Key	(Other fields)
0	0	
.	.	
.	.	
.	.	
565	0	
566	191-22-2386	
567	0	
.	.	
.	.	
.	.	
741	0	
742	214-30-3261	
743	0	
.	.	
.	.	
.	.	
883	0	
884	530-56-4221	
885	0	
.	.	
.	.	
1008	0	

Figure 7.21 A table to which three synonyms have been posted by the quotient offset method.

Exercise 7.10 Use the quotient-offset collision handler to hash the following key to the table in Fig. 7.21:

214-73-2086

Hint: The quotient is 212816 and the remainder is 742.

Exercise 7.11 Why would it be inappropriate to use the first three digits of a social security number to get the table address?

Exercise 7.12 In the quotient offset method, what would happen if a collision occurred, but the quotient of the new record's key was a multiple of the table size? Show that this problem can be avoided if, whenever the calculated quotient is a multiple of the table size, we simply use 1 as an offset.

Exercise 7.13 (This exercise assumes familiarity with modular algebra.) Show that, if the change suggested in Exercise 7.12 is made, then, for each key, the set of offsets always covers the entire table. Specifically, show that the set of integers {(original address + $k *$ offset) MOD p, for $k = 0, 1, \ldots, p - 1$} has p elements.

Updating With Open Addressing

In the previous section we considered problems associated with the initial posting of hashed records when open addressing is used. Now we turn our attention to updating. We begin with a discussion of deletions since the method for handling deletions will affect how new records are inserted and how old records are accessed and changed.

Suppose we start with the table as given in Fig. 7.21. Note that 530-56-4221 originally hashed to 742. Since that address was occupied (by the record whose key is 214-30-3261), the offset was added to yield 884, and empty location. Now suppose we want to delete the record whose key is 214-30-3261. Since the initial hash address, 742, contains the desired key, we need look no further. But if we simply reset the key field to 0 at location 742, it would appear that no record had been posted there. This could lead to a problem if we later tried to insert a record with a key of 530-56-4221. Since that record had already been posted in Fig. 7.21, an error message should be generated to indicate that an attempt was being made to insert an already existing record. But since the initial hash address, 742, contained a zero entry, the insertion would erroneously be made at location 742.

To overcome this difficulty we include an additional field in each record. This field, known as the *deletion flag*, is initialized to FALSE and later set to TRUE if the record is deleted. This signals that before a record can be posted at that address, the offsets must be followed to make sure that the record had not been posted earlier at another address. Figure 7.22 shows what the table would look like after the initial three records have been posted and then the first one deleted.

Suppose we later tried to insert a record with a key of 124-56-7846. The initial hash address is again 742, but the insertion cannot be made yet because we do not know if the record has previously been posted. The quotient offset is 124567846 DIV 1009, namely 123456, so the new address is (742 + 123456) MOD 1009, namely 91. Since location 91 contains a zero entry in its key field, we infer that the record with key 124-56-7846 has not yet been posted. We could simply post it at location 91, but this would not utilize location 742, so we avoid wasting space by inserting the new record at location 742 (and resetting its deletion flag to FALSE). The resulting table is shown in Fig. 7.23.

Subscript	Key	Deletion flag	(Other fields)
0	0	FALSE	
.	.	.	
.	.	.	
.	.	.	
565	0	FALSE	
566	191-22-2386	FALSE	
567	0	FALSE	
.	.	.	
.	.	.	
741	0	FALSE	
742	214-30-3261	TRUE	
743	0	FALSE	
.	.	.	
.	.	.	
883	0	FALSE	
884	530-56-4221	FALSE	
885	0	FALSE	
.	.	.	
.	.	.	
1008	0	FALSE	

Figure 7.22 A table to which three synonyms have been posted and (then) the first one deleted.

Subscript	Key	Deletion flag	(Other fields)
0	0	FALSE	
.	.	.	
.	.	.	
.	.	.	
565	0	FALSE	
566	191-22-2386	FALSE	
567	0	FALSE	
.	.	.	
.	.	.	
741	0	FALSE	
742	124-56-3261	FALSE	
743	0	FALSE	
.	.	.	
.	.	.	
883	0	FALSE	
884	530-56-4221	FALSE	
885	0	FALSE	
.	.	.	
.	.	.	
1008	0	FALSE	

Figure 7.23 A table to which three insertions have been made, followed by a deletion and another insertion. All keys originally hashed to 742.

Exercise 7.14 Perform the following updates to the table in Fig. 7.23; the original addresses and the offsets are provided for your convenience.

1. Insert 214-19-0347; original address = 836; offset = 212279.
2. Insert 187-63-6494; original address = 836; offset = 185962.
3. Insert 334-85-4545; original address = 742; offset = 331867.
4. Delete 187-63-6494; original address = 836; offset = 185962.

Chaining

Open addressing, with a quotient offset, will resolve collisions. A simpler way to resolve collisions is to make each location the head of a linked list. In each linked list we will "chain" all the records whose keys hash to that address. For example, consider the above problem of storing up to 1000 records with social security numbers as keys. The hash function will be KEY MOD 1000. Initially, each location would contain a nil value. Figure 7.24 shows what we would have after posting records with the following keys:

214-30-3261

033-51-8000

214-19-9528

819-02-9261

033-30-8262

215-09-1766

214-17-0261

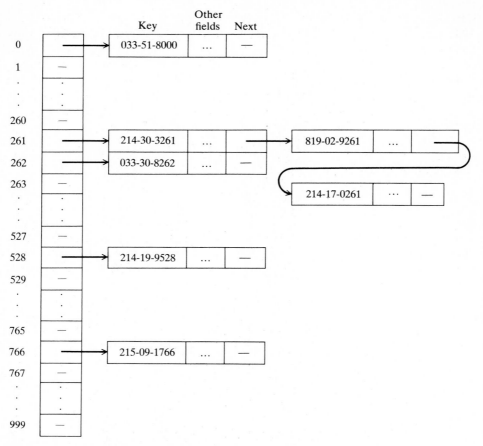

Figure 7.24 Posting seven records into a chained hash table.

There are several advantages to this method. First, collisions are easily (but sequentially!) handled. Also, secondary clustering has been avoided since each address has its own linked list (whether or not primary clustering is avoided depends on the hash function). A third advantage is that we may now store more than 1000 records. Also, deletions are no longer a problem—we simply use an algorithm for deleting (or trying to delete) from a linked list.

Which method uses more space, open addressing or chaining? The answer depends on the size of the records to be stored and the actual number of records stored. With open addressing, we must allocate enough space for the maximum number of records to be stored. Suppose, for example, that each record takes up twenty words of computer memory and the maximum number of records to be read in is 1000. Open addressing would require 20,000 words to be allocated; if only 500 records are actually stored, the wasted space will be 10,000 words. Chaining would initially allocate only 1000 words (assuming a pointer requires one word). If 500 records were read in, the words of memory used would be $1000 + 500 * 21 = 11{,}500$. In this case chaining would consume nearly 40 percent less space than open addressing. On the other hand, if the record size is small and the actual number of records read in is close to the maximum, open addressing can use as little as one-third of the space required for chaining.

Of paramount importance in analyzing a search technique is its average search length. We now calculate the average search length (for successful and unsuccessful searches) both for open addressing and for chaining.

The Average Search Length for Hashing

We claimed earlier that hashing was fast; we now show just how fast it is. We first calculate the average (successful) search length for hashing with open addressing. Note that the number of comparisons to access a hashed record is exactly the same as the number of comparisons needed to post the record originally. So let us assume that we have a table with P rows into which we will post N records. We further assume that the hashing algorithm is such that both primary and secondary clustering are avoided and that the offsets cover the whole table (see Exercise 7.13).

The number of comparisons to post the first record in the list is simply 1 or, to express it slightly differently, $(P + 1)/(P + 1)$. For the second record, only one comparison will be required unless the first and second keys are synonyms; this occurs only once in P times and requires 2 comparisons. Thus the number of comparisons to post the second record is

$$1 * \frac{P - 1}{P} + 2 * \frac{1}{P} \qquad \text{which is equal to} \qquad \frac{P + 1}{P}$$

For the third record, only one comparison is needed if the new key does not collide with either of the two preceding keys. Two comparisons must be made if the new key collided with one of the two preceding keys but the offset address did not collide with the other key. Finally, three comparisons are needed if the new key collided with one of the two preceding keys and the offset address collided with the other key. The number of comparisons to post the third record is thus

$$1 * \frac{P - 2}{P} + 2 * \frac{2}{P} * \frac{P - 2}{P - 1} + 3 * \frac{2}{P} * \frac{1}{P - 1} \qquad \text{which equals} \qquad \frac{P + 1}{P - 1}$$

In general, the number of comparisons needed to post (or access) the ith record is

$$\frac{P + 1}{P - i + 2}$$

This can be proved by mathematical induction: use double induction, on P and i.

Since, if there are N records posted, each one has a probability of $1/N$ of being accessed, the average search length L is calculated as

$$L = c_1 p_1 + c_2 p_2 + \cdots + c_N p_N$$

$$= \frac{1}{N}\left(\frac{P+1}{P+1} + \frac{P+1}{P} + \frac{P+1}{P-1} + \cdots + \frac{P+1}{P-N+2}\right)$$

L can be approximated as follows: let $l = N/(P+1)$; l is referred to as the *load factor*, roughly, the proportion of table entries that have been filled in. Then

$$L \approx \frac{1}{l}\ln\frac{1}{1-l} \qquad \text{(see Wirth, 1976, page 273)}$$

For an unsuccessful (open addressing) search, with N records posted, the average number of comparisons needed is simply the number of comparisons needed to post the $(N+1)$st record. Thus, for an unsuccessful search,

$$L = \frac{P+1}{P-(N+1)+2}$$

$$= \frac{P+1}{P-N+1}$$

$$= \frac{1}{(P-N+1)/(P+1)}$$

$$= \frac{1}{(P+1-N)/(P+1)}$$

$$= \frac{1}{1-N/(P+1)}$$

$$= \frac{1}{1-l}$$

If we use chaining instead of open addressing, the analysis is somewhat easier. Since we assume the N records are uniformly distributed over P lists, a successful search will examine a list in which there will be the record sought plus, on the average, an additional $(N-1)/P$ records. A successful, sequential search of a list requires (list size + 1)/2 comparisons—see page 275. Thus, for a successful search (with chaining),

$$L = \left(1 + \frac{N-1}{P} + 1\right)\Big/2$$

$$= 1 + \frac{1}{2}\left(\frac{N-1}{P}\right)$$

$$\approx 1 + \frac{1}{2}l$$

For an unsuccessful search (with chaining), we must search one entire list. Since each list contains, on the average, N/P records, the average search length for an unsuccessful search (with chaining) is given by

$$L = N/P$$
$$\approx l$$

This is slightly less than the average (successful) search length since an unsuccessful search of an empty list requires no comparisons between items.

Figure 7.25 summarizes these results. In each approximation, the value of L depends only on the load factor, not on the number of records posted!

To show you how startling these search lengths are, Fig. 7.26 approximates L for various load factors.

With chaining, the average search length is only one-and-a-half comparisons even if the load factor is 1.00! When this fact is coupled with the other advantages given on pages 296–297, we see that chaining is preferable to open addressing unless space is at a premium and all of the following conditions hold:

1. The information part of each record (that is, excluding the pointer field, if there is one) fits in one or two words of memory.
2. The actual number of records read in will be close to (but never greater than!) the specified maximum number.
3. Unsuccessful searches are rare.

The search lengths in Fig. 7.26 give credence to our earlier claim that hashing is *the* method of choice for searching large lists. The only exception occurs when the list must frequently be sorted. For example, suppose we want to read in a list

Open addressing	
Successful	$L \approx \dfrac{1}{l} \ln \left(\dfrac{1}{1-l} \right)$
Unsuccessful	$L = \dfrac{1}{1-l}$
Chaining	
Successful	$L \approx 1 + \frac{1}{2}l$
Unsuccessful	$L \approx l$

Figure 7.25 The relationship between the average search length L and the load factor l for hashing with open addressing and with chaining. The load factor is $N/(P + 1)$ where N is the number of records posted and P is the table size.

Load Factor	0.25	0.5	0.75	0.9	0.99
Open Addressing					
Successful	1.15	1.39	1.85	2.56	4.65
Unsuccessful	1.33	2.00	4.00	10.00	100.00
Chaining					
Successful	1.13	1.25	1.38	1.45	1.50
Unsuccessful	0.25	0.50	0.75	0.90	0.99

Figure 7.26 The approximate average search lengths for various load factors.

of names and, after each name is read in, print out the list (so far) in alphabetical order. In a case such as this, a binary search tree would be preferable to hashing.

In the next case study we hash a list of Pascal identifiers into a table. This is an important part in the construction of a symbol table, used by compilers, interpreters and assemblers to store information such as the location and data type of each identifier used in a program.

Exercise 7.15 With open addressing, an overflow occurs when N, the number of records in the list, exceeds P, the table size. What happens when N exceeds P if chaining is used?

CASE STUDY 7.1: HASHING IDENTIFIERS INTO A TABLE

Design and write a program to solve the following problem:

Problem

Hash a nonempty list of Pascal identifiers into a table. Calculate the actual average (successful) search length and compare this to the expected average (successful) search length.

Clarification Each line of input will contain one identifier. Only the first eight characters of an identifier will be hashed, but the entire identifier (30 characters) will be stored in the table, unless it is already there. If an attempt is made to store a duplicate identifier in the table, the identifier and an error message "Error: attempt to post a duplicate identifier" should be printed. Each entry in the table will also have a field which contains the actual number of comparisons needed to post the corresponding identifier. The table will have subscripts ranging from 0 to 250. The output of the table consists of each identifier (according to its position in the table) and the number of comparisons required to post that identifier into the table. The search lengths printed will be rounded to 3 decimal places.

Sample Input

```
HEAD
CURRENTPOINTER
CLASSTOTAL
UPDATERECORD
  :
RULE
NEXTTOKEN
```

Sample Output

IDENTIFIER	NUMBER OF COMPARISONS
CLASSTOTAL	0
PREVIOUSCHARACTER	0
NEXTTOKEN	1
UPDATERECORD	0
TOPOFSTACK	0
⋮	⋮

THERE ARE 101 IDENTIFIERS IN THE TABLE.

THE ACTUAL AVERAGE SEARCH LENGTH IS 1.198 COMPARISONS.

THE EXPECTED AVERAGE SEARCH LENGTH IS 1.199 COMPARISONS.

Solution Tree Whether we use open addressing or chaining, we must start with an empty table. After that, we read in and process all of the identifiers, print out the table, and calculate and print the average search lengths. Printing the table will be handled in a separate subtree. The initial version of the main tree is shown in Fig. 7.27.

Since the record size is not very small, chaining will be used (see page 299). Thus each record will consist of an identifier, the number of comparisons needed to post the identifier, and a pointer to the next record in the list.

To read and process all of the identifiers, we need to loop until we reach the end of file. Each time through the loop, we read in an identifier, calculate its hash address, and try to post it into the table. If the attempt fails because the identifier is already in the table, the identifier and the error message cited in the Clarification are printed.

The calculation of the actual and expected average search lengths will be made in a separate subtree, so the complete main tree is shown in Fig. 7.28.

The function subtree HASH will hash the current identifier to obtain an address in the table. We start by associating a number with the first eight characters (including, possibly, some trailing blanks) of the current identifier. We could simply add up the ordinal numbers associated with the characters and let the address be this sum MOD 251. To increase the likelihood that the addresses

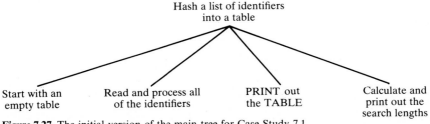

Figure 7.27 The initial version of the main tree for Case Study 7.1.

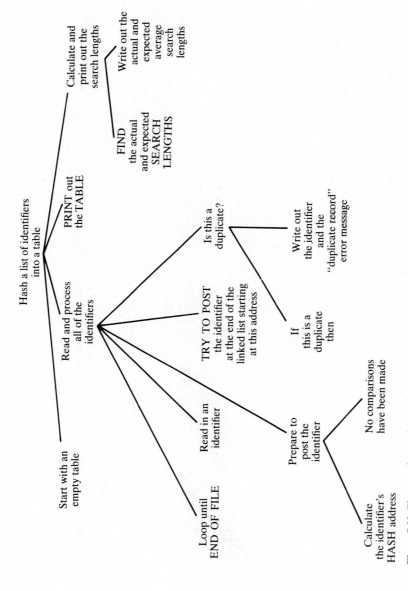

Hash a list of identifiers into a table

Start with an empty table

Read and process all of the identifiers

PRINT out the TABLE

Calculate and print out the search lengths

Write out the actual and expected average search lengths

FIND the actual and expected SEARCH LENGTHS

Loop until END OF FILE

Read in an identifier

TRY TO POST the identifier at the end of the linked list starting at this address

Is this a duplicate?

Write out the identifier and the "duplicate record" error message

If this is a duplicate then

Prepare to post the identifier

No comparisons have been made

Calculate the identifier's HASH address

Figure 7.28 The complete main tree for Case Study 7.1.

calculated will be scattered uniformly over the address space no matter what collating sequence is used, we multiply each partial total by 7 before adding the ordinal number of the next character.

The HASH subtree is shown in Fig. 7.29.

The subtree TRY TO POST will attempt to insert the current identifier at the end of the linked list that starts at the given hash address. There are several ways to attack this problem. A recursive approach, similar to the TRYTO-INSERT procedure on pages 64–65, is straightforward and so we adopt it here. If the list is empty, the posting is performed forthwith. Otherwise, we must compare the current identifier to the identifier at the head of the list. If there is a match, then we have found a duplicate; otherwise, we try to post the current identifier in the linked list pointed to by the head record's "next" field.

The TRY TO POST subtree is shown in Fig. 7.30.

One can argue that the overhead of recursive calls (see pages 256–257) makes the TRY TO POST subtree inefficient. There are several iterative alternatives, each with its own drawback. If we include a TAIL field with each linked list, an iterative subtree can easily be designed, but the initial size of the table will be doubled by the extra field at each table position. Another possibility is to start at the head of the list and then go through a loop in which we compare the identifier to be posted with each identifier in the list. We terminate the loop when we reach the end of the list or a duplicate is found. But, if the identifier is not on the list, we would have passed the last record in the list by the time we left the loop. This would make it somewhat more difficult to post the identifier at the end of the list.

Finally, the relative efficiency of the recursive and iterative approaches is not significant since, on the average, very few of the linked lists will have more than one record.

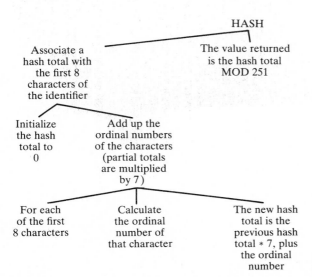

Figure 7.29 The subtree HASH.

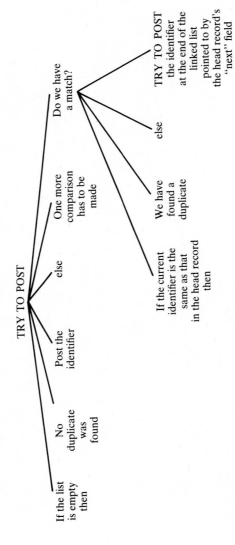

Figure 7.30 The subtree TRY TO POST.

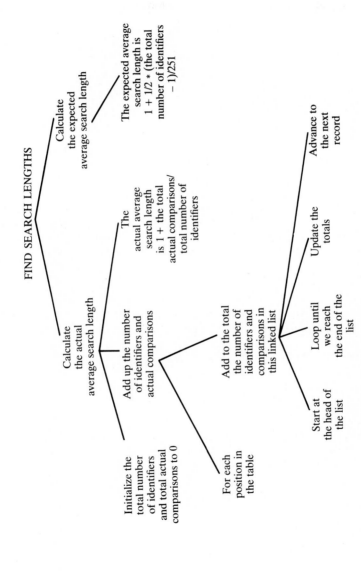

Figure 7.31 The subtree FIND SEARCH LENGTHS.

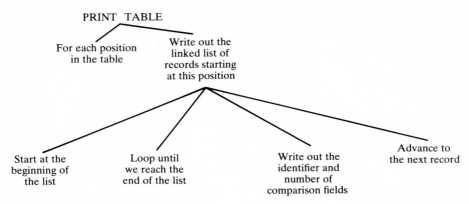

Figure 7.32 The subtree PRINT TABLE.

The FIND SEARCH LENGTHS subtree has two parts. To calculate the actual average search length, we initialize the total of actual comparisons and total number of identifiers to 0, then add up both totals in a loop. The search for any of the identifiers posted will be successful, so the number of comparisons for that search will be one plus the number of comparisons required to post the identifier originally. On the average, the number of comparisons to post an identifier is the total of actual comparisons divided by the total number of identifiers.

The calculation of the expected average search length follows the formula for a successful search on page 298. Since the total number of identifiers was determined while calculating the actual average search length, we need not recalculate that value.

The FIND SEARCH LENGTHS subtree is given in Fig. 7.31.

The PRINT TABLE subtree proceeds as follows: For each position in the table, we will write out the linked list (except for the pointer fields) starting at that position. The subtree is shown in Fig. 7.32.

Coding Each list in the table is implemented as a dynamic linked list. For the sake of information hiding, we initialize the table in a separate procedure. The hierarchy chart is shown in Fig. 7.33.

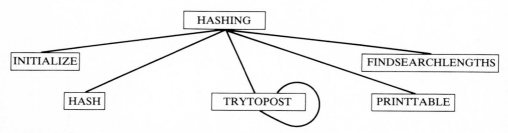

Figure 7.33 The hierarchy chart for the program HASHING.

```
PROGRAM  HASHING(INPUT, OUTPUT);

(******************************************************************)
(*                                                                *)
(*    PROGRAMMER: BILL COLLINS.                                   *)
(*                                                                *)
(*     This program will solve the following problem:            *)
(*   given a nonempty list of Pascal identifiers, post           *)
(*   them to a table by chaining. Only part of an                *)
(*   identifier is used in hashing the identifier.               *)
(*   After all the identifiers have been posted, each            *)
(*   one is printed, along with the number of                    *)
(*   comparisons needed to post that identifier.                 *)
(*   Finally, the actual and expected average search             *)
(*   lengths are printed.                                        *)
(*                                                                *)
(******************************************************************)

CONST TABLESIZE            = 251;
      LOWSUBSCRIPT         = 0;
      HIGHSUBSCRIPT        = 250;
      LENGTHOFIDENTIFIER   = 30;
      BLANK                = ' ';
      ERROROFDUPLICATION = 'ERROR: ATTEMPT TO POST DUPLICATE IDENTIFIER:';

TYPE  NONNEGINTEGER        = 0..MAXINT;
      STRING               = PACKED ARRAY[1..LENGTHOFIDENTIFIER] OF CHAR;
      SUBSCRIPTRANGE       = LOWSUBSCRIPT..HIGHSUBSCRIPT;
      POINTER              = ^ENTRY;
      ENTRY                = RECORD
                                IDENTIFIER            : STRING;
                                NUMBEROFCOMPARISONS : NONNEGINTEGER;
                                NEXT                  : POINTER
                             END;
      TABLETYPE            = ARRAY[SUBSCRIPTRANGE] OF POINTER;
      CHARCOUNTER          = 1..LENGTHOFIDENTIFIER;

VAR   IDENTIFIER                       : STRING;
      HASHADDRESS                      : SUBSCRIPTRANGE;
      TABLE                            : TABLETYPE;
      DUPLICATE                        : BOOLEAN;
      ACTUALAVERAGESEARCHLENGTH,
      EXPECTEDAVERAGESEARCHLENGTH : REAL;
      J                                : CHARCOUNTER;
      NUMBEROFCOMPARISONS              : NONNEGINTEGER;




PROCEDURE  INITIALIZE(VAR    TABLE : TABLETYPE);

(*  Make each list in the TABLE an empty list.   *)

VAR   I : SUBSCRIPTRANGE;

BEGIN

   FOR I := LOWSUBSCRIPT TO HIGHSUBSCRIPT DO
       TABLE[I] := NIL

END;  (*  of the procedure INITIALIZE.   *)
```

```
FUNCTION  HASH(IDENTIFIER : STRING) : SUBSCRIPTRANGE;

(*  Hash the IDENTIFIER to obtain a table address. To assure      *)
(*  that the identifiers will be scattered uniformly throughout    *)
(*  the table, partial hash totals will be multiplied by 7.        *)
(*  WARNING: Since the ORD function is used, the value calculated   *)
(*  depends on the collating sequence.                             *)

CONST INITIALSEGMENTLENGTH = 8;(* We will hash the first 8 characters.*)

      SCATTERFACTOR        = 7;(* To promote uniform distribution of *)
                               (* identifiers throughout the table.  *)

VAR   HASHTOTAL, ORDINALVALUE : NONNEGINTEGER;
      J                       : CHARCOUNTER;

BEGIN

   (*  Associate a hash total with an initial segment of the  *)
   (*  identifier.                                            *)
   HASHTOTAL := 0;
   FOR J := 1 TO INITIALSEGMENTLENGTH DO
      BEGIN
         ORDINALVALUE := ORD(IDENTIFIER[J]);
         HASHTOTAL    := HASHTOTAL * SCATTERFACTOR + ORDINALVALUE
      END;

   HASH := HASHTOTAL MOD TABLESIZE

END; (*  of the function HASH.  *)




PROCEDURE  TRYTOPOST(IDENTIFIER                 : STRING;
                     VAR    NUMBEROFCOMPARISONS : NONNEGINTEGER;
                     VAR    HEAD                : POINTER ;
                     VAR    DUPLICATE           : BOOLEAN);

(*  Try to post the IDENTIFIER, together with NUMBEROFCOMPARISONS, at  *)
(*  the end of the linked list pointed to by HEAD. If the given        *)
(*  identifier matches an identifier already in the list, no posting   *)
(*  takes place and DUPLICATE gets the value TRUE.  Otherwise,         *)
(*  DUPLICATE gets the value FALSE and the identifier is posted.       *)

BEGIN

   (*  Is the list empty?  *)
   IF HEAD = NIL THEN
      BEGIN
         DUPLICATE := FALSE;
         NEW(HEAD);
         HEAD^.IDENTIFIER         := IDENTIFIER;
         HEAD^.NUMBEROFCOMPARISONS := NUMBEROFCOMPARISONS;
      END
   ELSE
      BEGIN
         NUMBEROFCOMPARISONS := NUMBEROFCOMPARISONS + 1;

         (*  Have we found a duplicate of the given identifier?  *)
         IF IDENTIFIER = HEAD^.IDENTIFIER THEN
            DUPLICATE := TRUE
         ELSE
            TRYTOPOST(IDENTIFIER, NUMBEROFCOMPARISONS, HEAD^.NEXT,
                      DUPLICATE)

      END

END; (*  of the procedure TRYTOPOST.  *)
```

```
PROCEDURE  FINDSEARCHLENGTHS(TABLE                          :TABLETYPE;
                            VAR  ACTUALAVERAGESEARCHLENGTH,
                            EXPECTEDAVERAGESEARCHLENGTH      :REAL);

(*  Calculate the actual and expected average search  *)
(*  lengths, the latter from the formula on page 298. *)

VAR    TOTALNUMBEROFIDENTIFIERS,
       TOTALACTUALCOMPARISONS       : NONNEGINTEGER;
       I                            : SUBSCRIPTRANGE;
       CURRENTPOINTER               : POINTER;

BEGIN

   (*  Calculate the actual average search length.  *)
   TOTALNUMBEROFIDENTIFIERS := 0;
   TOTALACTUALCOMPARISONS   := 0;
   FOR I := LOWSUBSCRIPT TO HIGHSUBSCRIPT DO

      BEGIN

         (*  Add the number of identifiers and comparisons  *)
         (*  in this linked list.  *)
         CURRENTPOINTER := TABLE[I];
         WHILE CURRENTPOINTER <> NIL DO
            BEGIN
               TOTALACTUALCOMPARISONS     := TOTALACTUALCOMPARISONS +
                            CURRENTPOINTER^.NUMBEROFCOMPARISONS;
               TOTALNUMBEROFIDENTIFIERS := TOTALNUMBEROFIDENTIFIERS + 1;
               CURRENTPOINTER             := CURRENTPOINTER^.NEXT
            END
      END;

   ACTUALAVERAGESEARCHLENGTH := 1 +
            TOTALACTUALCOMPARISONS / TOTALNUMBEROFIDENTIFIERS;

   PAGE;
   WRITELN('THERE ARE ', TOTALNUMBEROFIDENTIFIERS:1,
           ' IDENTIFIERS IN THE TABLE.');
   WRITELN;

   (*  Calculate the expected average (successful) search length.  *)
   EXPECTEDAVERAGESEARCHLENGTH := 1 + (1/2) *
                            (TOTALNUMBEROFIDENTIFIERS - 1) / TABLESIZE
END; (*  of the procedure FINDSEARCHLENGTHS.  *)
```

```
PROCEDURE PRINTTABLE(TABLE : TABLETYPE);

(* Print out the TABLE. *)

VAR    I               : SUBSCRIPTRANGE;
       CURRENTPOINTER  : POINTER;

BEGIN

   (*  Print headings.  *)
   PAGE;
   WRITELN('IDENTIFIER': 20, 'NUMBER OF COMPARISONS': 51);
   WRITELN('-----------------------------':40,'---------------------':31);

   (*  Print out the table.  *)
   FOR I := LOWSUBSCRIPT TO HIGHSUBSCRIPT DO
      BEGIN

         (* Write out the linked list of entries starting *)
         (* at this position.                             *)
         CURRENTPOINTER := TABLE[I];
         WHILE CURRENTPOINTER <> NIL DO
            BEGIN
               WRITELN(CURRENTPOINTER^.IDENTIFIER:40,
                       CURRENTPOINTER^.NUMBEROFCOMPARISONS:21);
               CURRENTPOINTER := CURRENTPOINTER^.NEXT
            END
      END

END; (* of the procedure PRINTTABLE. *)
```

```
BEGIN   (*  the executable section of the main program.  *)

   PAGE;

   (*  Start with an empty table.  *)
   INITIALIZE(TABLE);

   (*  Read and process all of the identifiers.  *)
   REPEAT

      (*  Read in one identifier, character-by-character.  *)
      FOR J := 1 TO LENGTHOFIDENTIFIER DO
         IF NOT EOLN THEN
            READ (IDENTIFIER[J])
         ELSE
            IDENTIFIER[J] :=BLANK;
      READLN;

      (*  Prepare to post the identifier.  *)
      HASHADDRESS          := HASH(IDENTIFIER);
      NUMBEROFCOMPARISONS := 0;

      (*  Try to post the identifier.  *)
      TRYTOPOST(IDENTIFIER, NUMBEROFCOMPARISONS, TABLE[HASHADDRESS],
                DUPLICATE);

      (*  Is this a duplicate identifier?  *)
      IF DUPLICATE THEN
         WRITELN(ERROROFDUPLICATION, ' ',IDENTIFIER)

   UNTIL EOF;

   (*  Print out the table.  *)
   PRINTTABLE(TABLE);

   (*  Calculate the average search lengths.  *)
   FINDSEARCHLENGTHS(TABLE, ACTUALAVERAGESEARCHLENGTH,
                     EXPECTEDAVERAGESEARCHLENGTH);

   WRITELN('THE ACTUAL AVERAGE SEARCH LENGTH IS ',
           ACTUALAVERAGESEARCHLENGTH:6:3, ' COMPARISONS.');
   WRITELN;
   WRITELN('THE EXPECTED AVERAGE SEARCH LENGTH IS ',
           EXPECTEDAVERAGESEARCHLENGTH:6:3, ' COMPARISONS.');
   PAGE
END.
```

Program Testing

1. Testing the main program:

   Test 1a
   _____

   STACK3
   TOPOFSTACK
   RANDOMNUMBER2

2. Testing HASH :

   Test 2a   (a typical identifier, a short identifier, duplicate identifiers, and three
   _____   synonyms)

   ADDINGOPERATOR
   I
   TOPOFSTACK
   TOPOFSTACK
   FRANCHISE1
   FRANCHISE2
   FRANCHISE3

3. Testing TRYTOPOST (along with INITIALIZE and PRINTTABLE):

   Test 3a   (same as Test 2a)
   _____

   ADDINGOPERATOR
   I
   TOPOFSTACK
   TOPOFSTACK
   FRANCHISE1
   FRANCHISE2
   FRANCHISE3

4. Testing FINDSEARCHLENGTHS:

   Test 4a   (same as Test 2a)
   _____

   ADDINGOPERATOR
   I
   TOPOFSTACK
   TOPOFSTACK
   FRANCHISE1
   FRANCHISE2
   FRANCHISE3

   Test 4b   (A list of 101 identifiers)
   _____

   CLASSTOTAL
   PREVIOUSCHARACTER
   NEXTTOKEN
   UPDATERECORD
   TOPOFSTACK
   ⋮

Exercise 7.16 The problem statement for Case Study 7.1 specified that the list of identifiers was nonempty. Thus, a REPEAT statement was appropriate for the read-and-process loop. If we wanted to allow for an empty list, the REPEAT statement would have to be replaced by a WHILE statement. What other change would have to be made to the program?

RANDOM-ACCESS FILES (NONSTANDARD PASCAL)

Standard Pascal requires that each file be accessed sequentially, beginning with the first component in the file. In UCSD Pascal,† random-access files are also permitted. To access a component, we must first specify the position in the file where the component resides (or is to reside). This is done by means of the SEEK procedure, which has the file name and a nonnegative position number as parameters. For example,

SEEK(INVENTORY, ADDRESS)

sets the file position pointer for INVENTORY to the value of the variable ADDRESS. To retrieve the component at that position, a GET is used; to store a component in that position, use PUT.

The advantage of random-access files is that, no matter where you are in the file, you may access any component without first accessing all intervening ones. However, it is the programmer's responsibility to associate with each component in the file a position number. This can be done, for example, by hashing the component's key.

How are collisions handled? A variety of techniques are available (see Knuth, 1973, pages 534–538). One typical method is as follows: With each file position we associate a *bucket*: an area in which synonyms are stored. For example, if we choose a bucket size of 10, we may store up to 10 synonymous records in each bucket in the file. As shown in Fig. 7.34, the first 10 records whose keys hashed to 281 would be stored in that bucket. Later records whose keys hashed to 281

† Developed at the University of California at San Diego by Kenneth Bowles.

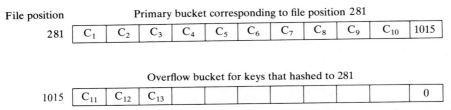

Figure 7.34 Hashing to a random-access file. Thirteen components have keys that hash to 281. The first ten records are stored in the bucket at file position 281. The remaining three are stored in an overflow bucket at file position 1015.

would be stored in an overflow bucket, for example at file position 1015. A zero value in a bucket's pointer field indicates that the bucket has not yet overflowed.

With the file organized in this fashion, each "component" corresponds to a bucket. Thus, each time the GET procedure is called, the contents of an entire bucket are brought into main memory. To extract the record sought from the ten just read in, a sequential (or other kind of) search would be performed.

PROBLEMS

Problem 7.1: A Realistic Scanner

Modify the program in Case Study 5.1 so that the procedure SCANNER hashes identifiers and reserved words into a symbol table.

Clarification Assume that the symbol table has subscripts ranging from 0 to 250. Only the names and their classifications (either identifier or reserved word) should be posted in the table. Numbers should be posted to a table of constants. At the conclusion of the program, both the symbol table and constants table should be printed out.

Sample Input
(See page 183)

Sample Output
(See pages 183–184)

SYMBOL TABLE

SUBSCRIPT	SYMBOL	CLASSIFICATION
28	CB	IDENTIFIER
41	BEGIN	RESERVED WORD
117	END	RESERVED WORD
182	B	IDENTIFIER

CONSTANTS TABLE

SUBSCRIPT	CONSTANT
72	2
178	10
231	5

Problem 7.2: Creating and Updating a Payroll File

(This problem deals with searching as applied to sequential files.) Design and write a program to solve the following problem: Create and update a *sequential* payroll file.

Clarification Each record in the payroll file will have a name field (30 characters, last name first) and a salary field (from $0 to $200,000). We assume that the input for the file-creation program is correct and in order by the name field.

Each update line will contain the type of update ('INSERT,' 'DELETE,' or 'CHANGE') in columns 1–6, the name in columns 10–39, and, for an insertion or change, the salary in columns 45–50. We assume that the input to the file updating program is in order by the name field. There may be more than one update per name. An exception report should be made of updates that contain any of the following errors:

1. MISSING UPDATE TYPE—If columns 1 through 6 are all blank.
2. MISSING NAME FIELD—If columns 10 through 39 are all blank.
3. MISSING SALARY FIELD—If columns 45 through 50 are all blank (and UPDATE TYPE is not 'DELETE').
4. ILLEGAL UPDATE TYPE—If the type of update contains nonblank characters but is neither 'INSERT,' 'DELETE,' nor 'CHANGE.'
5. SALARY OUT OF RANGE—If the salary is not in the $0–$200,000 range, the update is not made.
6. ATTEMPT TO ADD AN ALREADY EXISTING RECORD—If the update type is 'INSERT' but the record already exists in the payroll file.
7. ATTEMPT TO DELETE OR CHANGE A NONEXISTING RECORD—If the update type is 'DELETE' or 'CHANGE' but the record is not in the payroll file.

Sample Input (for the file-creation program)

```
ELZEY PENNY          28000
GREENE BEN           25000
SMITH JEFF           26000
```

Sample Input (for the file-update program)

```
INSERT    BANGOR JEAN        30500
CHANGE    BANGOR JEAN        31000
CHANGE    ELZEY PENNEY       29000
INSERT    GREENE BEN         25000
DELETE    GREENE BEN
INSERT    JAMES JESSE        30000
DELETE    JOHNSON LYNDON
INSRET    MILLER JOHN        31000
INSERT    PARKER DAVID       31000
CHANGE    PARKER DAVID       32000
DELETE    PARKER DAVID
DELETE    ROBERTS ROBIN
INSERT    ROBERTS ROBIN      31000
INSERT    ROBINSON JACK
CHANGE    SMITH JEFF         250000
INSERT    THOMPSON CURT      28000
```

The new version of the payroll file should be printed out after the exception report.

Sample Output (from the file-update program)

EXCEPTION REPORT

TYPE OF UPDATE	NAME	SALARY
INSERT	GREENE BEN	25000
ERROR—ATTEMPT TO ADD AN ALREADY EXISTING RECORD		
DELETE	JOHNSON LYNDON	
ERROR—ATTEMPT TO DELETE OR CHANGE A NONEXISTING RECORD		
INSRET	MILLER JOHN	31000
ERROR—ILLEGAL UPDATE TYPE		
DELETE	ROBERTS ROBIN	
ERROR—ATTEMPT TO DELETE OR CHANGE A NONEXISTING RECORD		
INSERT	ROBINSON JACK	
ERROR—MISSING SALARY FIELD		
CHANGE	SMITH JEFF	250000
ERROR—SALARY OUT OF RANGE		

(*new page*)

NEW PAYROLL FILE

NAME	SALARY
BANGOR JEAN	31000
ELZEY PENNY	29000
JAMES JESSE	30000
ROBERTS ROBIN	31000
SMITH JEFF	26000
THOMPSON CURT	28000

Problem 7.3: Class Roster, Revisited

Modify the design and program in Case Study 3.1 so that a binary search tree is used instead of a linked list.
Clarification See Case Study 3.1.
Sample Input See Case Study 3.1.
Sample Output See Case Study 3.1.

HEURISTIC SEARCHES

In the previous chapter, all of our searches were directed toward finding an item in a list. We now turn our attention to a more general and exciting kind of search: seeking a solution to a problem.

In developing a parser (Chap. 5), one of the options open to us was to use backtracking. That is, when presented with a choice of rules, we picked one of them at random and proceeded. If we later discovered that the parse could not succeed, we would go back to the point where the guess was made and make another guess. Because of the overhead involved in undoing bad guesses, backtracking is seldom used in parsing, especially since more efficient methods, such as recursive descent parsing, are available.

Although backtracking is an inefficient search technique, we must resort to it when no better method presents itself. This is similar to the situation we sometimes face when confronted by a problem: A trial-and-error approach is tedious and time-consuming, but it is preferable to failure. Human intelligence often enables us to shorten trial-and-error searches by using *heuristics*: rules of thumb, which are likely to succeed but not guaranteed to do so. For example, if you want to drive home from work in a minimum amount of time, you might decide, based on past experience, that the highway route is quicker on Monday through Thursday, but the back roads are a better choice on Friday because the highway gets congested then. Such hunches are invaluable aids to everyday life even though they sometimes fail.

Some other examples of heuristics are

1. If you are in a high tax bracket and are willing to dispose of some of your current investments, you should consider tax-sheltered investments.
2. In integrating a function, first try integration by parts.
3. In seeking the murderer, first consider the person with the best motive.

Computer scientists have employed heuristic search techniques in solving a wide variety of problems, such as chromosome matching, industrial scheduling, synthesizing organic compounds and robotics. The general field in which this research is conducted is *artificial intelligence*, which Marvin Minsky has defined as "the study of intelligence as computation." To put it another way, in artificial intelligence we make machines perform tasks that normally require human intelligence. In this section we will restrict our attention to the use of heuristic search methods in game-playing. The reason for this restriction is that the games can be represented simply and still provide situations complex enough to justify heuristic searches. It should be noted that much of the work on game-playing has contributed to progress in less frivolous areas. For a detailed treatment of what follows, the reader should consult Nilsson, 1971.

Since programs are written by humans, artificial intelligence is essentially a reflection on the intelligence of programmers, but the relationship between the programmer and program can be quite subtle. For example, one of the early efforts in artificial intelligence was a program called CHECKERS, written by A. L. Samuel (see Samuel, 1959). One interesting aspect of this program was that it played a better game of checkers than its author! This was not due merely to the computer's large memory, since an exhaustive, trial-and-error approach would take years to succeed even on the largest, fastest computer available today. The key to the program was its heuristic search method which incorporated learning from previous games.

The form we will use for representing problems is the *state-space representation*, which we now describe. A *state* is a value in some fixed data type. Thus a state may be a character string, a table, or even an entire network. We start with an *initial state* (or states) and try to obtain a *goal state* (or states). An *operator* transforms a state into another state. The *state-space* is the collection of all states that can be obtained from the initial state by applying some combination of operators; we include the initial state in the state-space. A *solution* to a problem is a path of operators that transforms an initial state into a goal state. We generally seek a solution that is *optimal*, that is, one for which no shorter path is a solution.

THE EIGHT-PUZZLE

For example, consider the eight-puzzle. We have eight numbered tiles in a three-by-three frame. A state is a configuration of the tiles in the frame, such as shown in Fig. 8.1.

The location of the blank is part of a configuration, so the state shown in Fig. 8.1 is different from the state shown in Fig. 8.2.

We can choose the state in Fig. 8.1 as an initial state. The goal state could be as shown in Fig. 8.3. An operator transforms one state into another by "moving" the blank space left, up, right, or down. Thus, there are four operators, some of which cannot be applied to a given state. For example, only three operators (left, up, right) can be applied to the initial state of Fig. 8.1. We can think of the state-

1	3	4
8	6	2
7		5

Figure 8.1 One state in the eight-puzzle.

1	3	4
8	6	2
7	5	

Figure 8.2 Another state in the eight-puzzle.

1	2	3
8		4
7	6	5

Figure 8.3 A possible goal state in the eight-puzzle.

space as a tree with the initial state as the root and operators as branches, with no states repeated. Figure 8.4 shows the state-space tree to a depth of 3; that is, the leaves result from the application of any sequence of three operators. The operators are always applied in the order left, up, right, and down. A solution is a path from the root to the goal state.

There are nine possible values for any single location in a state: a blank or a digit between 1 and 8. After we have selected a value for that location, there are eight possible values for any of the other eight locations. Continuing in this fashion, we see that the total number of states possible is $9 * 8 * 7 * 6 * 5 * 4 * 3 * 2 * 1$; that is, the number of possible states is 9 factorial. But from any given state, only half of the possible states can be obtained by applying the operators (see Gardner, 1959, pages 86–89). Thus, for a given initial state and a given goal state, there may not be a solution.

To determine if there is a solution path from a given initial state to a given goal state, we follow these steps:

1. In the initial state, move the blank to the same position it occupies in the goal state. Note: To move the blank from a corner position into the center requires two "moves."
2. Start with row 1, column 1 of the goal state and continue to row 1, column 2, and so on, finally, to row 3, column 3. For any position, if the goal state has a blank in that position, or if the tile in the goal state has the same value as the tile in the same position in the initial state, move on to the next position. Otherwise, the numbered tile, say *A*, in that position in the goal state is different from the numbered tile, say *B*, in that position in the initial state. Find where *A* is in the initial state and swap it with *B*. Thus, the initial and goal states will have *A* in the same position.
3. Count the number of swaps required in step 2 to transform the initial state into the goal state. If an even number of swaps was required, the goal state can be obtained from the initial state. In this case we say that the initial state and goal state have the same *parity*. If an odd number of swaps was required, no solution path is possible.

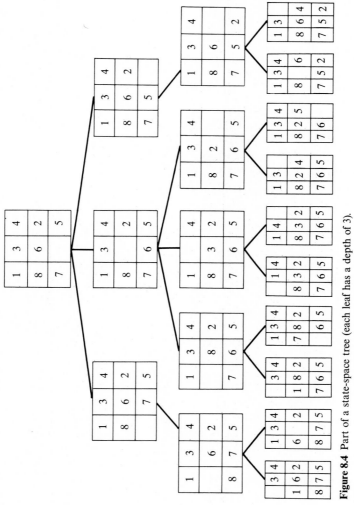

Figure 8.4 Part of a state-space tree (each leaf has a depth of 3).

Example 1

	Initial state			Goal state		

Initial state

1	3	4
8	6	2
7		5

Goal state

1	2	3
8		4
7	6	5

In the initial state, we move the blank up to get it in the middle position.

1	3	4
8		2
7	6	5

After swapping 2 and 3, and swapping 3 and 4, we get

1	2	3
8		4
7	6	5

Since an even number of swaps was required, the initial state and goal state have the same parity, so a solution can be found.

Example 2

Initial state

1	2	
8	3	4
7	6	5

Goal state

1	2	3
8		4
7	6	5

In the initial state, we move the blank left and then down to obtain

1	3	2
8		4
7	6	5

After only one swap (of 2 and 3), we obtain the goal state. Since an odd number of swaps was required, there is no solution possible.

Exercise 8.1 For which of the following pairs is a solution possible?

(*a*)   Initial state   Goal state

8	7	6
5	4	3
2	1	

1	2	3
4	5	6
7	8	

(*b*)   Initial state   Goal state

1	2	3
4	5	6
7	8	

1	2	3
8		4
7	6	5

(*c*)   Initial state   Goal state

2	1	6
4		8
7	5	3

1	2	3
8		4
7	6	5

Blind-Search Strategies

If you had no heuristic to guide you in finding a solution, you would have to rely on a *blind-search* method; that is, each time the method is used, the order in which the nodes have operators applied to them is the same. Two common blind-search methods are:

1. *Breadth-first Search.* Apply all possible operators to the root node (that is, the initial state), then to all the root's children (left-to-right), then to all the root's grandchildren (left-to-right), and so on. The search stops when the goal node is discovered.

   Figure 8.5 shows the ordering of nodes for a breadth-first search that starts with the initial state given in Fig. 8.1; the number next to each node is the order in which that node will be expanded.

2. *Depth-first Search.* It is convenient to explain a depth-first search in terms of a depth function. For any node n in the tree, we define a *depth function g* as follows:

   If n is the root node, then $g(n) = 0$. Otherwise, let m be the parent of n; then $g(n) = 1 + g(m)$. (Notice that this is a recursive definition.)

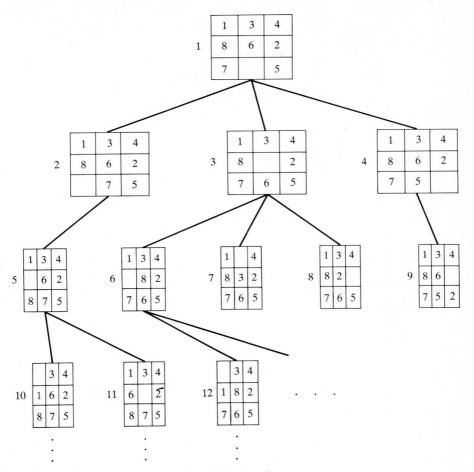

Figure 8.5 The ordering of nodes in a breadth-first search.

To put it another way, $g(n)$ is the number of operators that must be applied, starting at the root, to obtain n.

The deepest node in the partially developed tree is the one next selected for expansion. If several nodes have the same depth, the leftmost of those nodes is expanded. To prevent a long wild-goose chase down the left side of the tree, we start with a depth-bound of, say, 3. Thus, no node with a depth greater than 3 is expanded until all nodes with depths of 3 or less are expanded. If the goal state has not yet been reached, the depth-bound is increased to 6, and the search continues. Figure 8.6 shows the ordering of nodes for a depth-first search, with a depth-bound of 3, that starts with the initial state given in Fig. 8.1.

Incidentally, a depth-first search with no depth-bound is an NLR traversal (extended from a binary tree to an arbitrary tree).

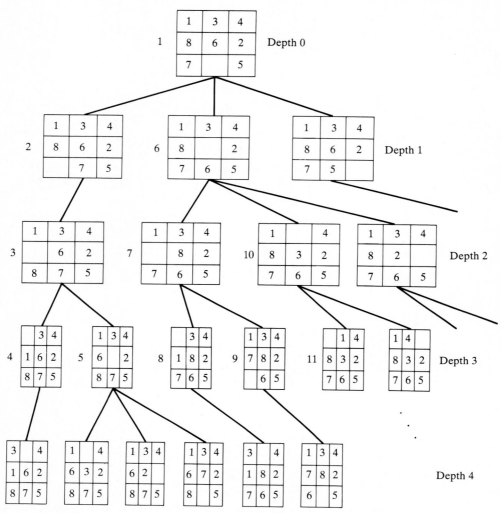

Figure 8.6 The ordering of nodes in a depth-first search, with a depth-bound of 3. The numbers next to the nodes indicate the order in which the nodes will be expanded.

Blind search methods are often not feasible because the state-space tree gets too large before the goal state is found.

Exercise 8.2 Complete the expansion of nodes, up to a depth-bound of 3, in Fig. 8.6.

Exercise 8.3 What is the relationship between a breadth-first search and a depth-first search with a depth-bound of 1?

Exercise 8.4 Both breadth-first and depth-first searches will always find a solution if one exists. Will both search methods always find an *optimal* (that is, shortest-path) solution if a solution exists?

Heuristic-Search Strategies

We now consider how a heuristic search strategy could be designed. Given a node in a search tree, we would like to evaluate how "promising" it is—that is, how likely that it will be on a (minimal) path to a goal node. One component of this evaluation is the depth of the node, as defined above.

In addition to calculating the value of the depth function g at a node, we need to estimate how far down from the node we will have to go to reach a goal node. The function that calculates this value is called a *heuristic function*. This function h will depend on the particular problem to be solved. For example, in the eight-puzzle, we might define, for any node n,

$h(n) = $ the number of misplaced (numbered) tiles in node n

Finally, we define the *evaluation function f* for any node n by

$$f(n) = g(n) + h(n)$$

For example, let n be the node

1	3	4
8		2
7	6	5

in the tree of Fig. 8.4. Then $g(n) = 1$, since n's parent is the root. Furthermore, tiles 2, 3, and 4 are not in the positions required for the goal node (tiles 1, 5, 6, 7, and 8 are correctly placed), so $h(n) = 3$. Thus $f(n) = 1 + 3 = 4$.

How do we select the next node to *expand*, that is, to apply the operators to and then evaluate the resulting nodes? From the list of unexpanded leaves, choose the leaf whose f value is lowest. If two or more unexpanded leaves are tied for lowest f value, we expand the one that was generated first. For example, Fig. 8.7 shows the search tree for the eight-puzzle with the initial state given in Fig. 8.1, the goal state from Fig. 8.3, and the heuristic function calculating the number of misplaced numbered tiles in a node. The f values for each node are circled and to the right of the node. Uncircled numbers to the upper left of nodes indicate the order in which nodes are expanded.

A search strategy based on an evaluation function will always find a solution if one exists, because g values are always higher as we go down the tree. Thus, if n is on a solution path, then n will be expanded before any node m which is "far down" in the tree, namely, any m such that $g(m) > g(n) + h(n)$. But, of course, a breadth-first search will also find a solution—in fact, an optimal one. What we need is a heuristic function that yields an optimal solution without expanding a lot of unnecessary nodes.

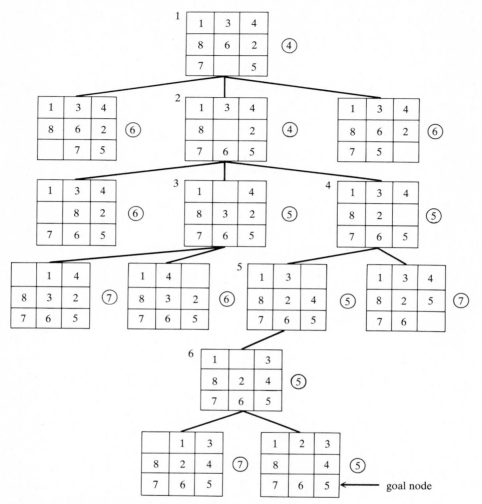

Figure 8.7 A heuristic search tree for the eight-puzzle.

For the heuristic function given on page 325, the application of one operator will, at best, correctly place one of the misplaced numbered tiles. Thus, for each node n, $h(n)$ is less than or equal to the actual number of nodes between n and a goal node. Under that circumstance, the resulting evaluation function is *guaranteed* to produce an optimal solution (see Nilsson, 1971, pages 59–61) if a solution exists.

If we are willing to forego the guarantee of minimal path, paradoxically we can sometimes devise a more accurate heuristic function. For example, the following heuristic function, suggested by Nilsson, usually generates solutions with fewer expansions than the heuristic function on page 325: For each node n, let

$$h(n) = P(n) + 3S(n)$$

$P(n)$ calculates the sum of the distances that each (numbered) tile in n is from where it belongs. $S(n)$ is also a sum: For each noncentral square, add 2 for a numbered tile not followed by its proper successor; finally, add 1 for a numbered piece in the center. For example, let n be the node

1	3	4
8	6	2
7		5

Then, moving clockwise from the top left square (and visiting the middle square last)

$$P(n) = 0 + 1 + 1 + 2 + 0 + 0 + 0 + 1 = 5$$
$$S(n) = 2 + 0 + 2 + 2 + 2 + 0 + 0 + 1 = 9$$

Thus

$$h(n) = 5 + 3 * 9 = 32.$$

Since this heuristic function does not provide a lower bound on the distance to a goal node, the evaluation function is not guaranteed to provide an optimal solution.

Exercise 8.5 Calculate the evaluation-function value of each node whose depth is $ <= 2$ in the partial state-space tree in Fig. 8.4. Use the evaluation function given on page 325.

Exercise 8.6 Solve the eight-puzzle with the heuristic function given on pages 326–327. Use the initial state given in Fig. 8.1.

Exercise 8.7 Solve the eight-puzzle with the heuristic function given on pages 326–327. Use the following initial state:

2	1	6
4		8
7	5	3

Note: This requires the expansion of 22 nodes. If you think that is a lot, try using the previous function (namely, $h(n) =$ the number of misplaced, numbered tiles in n) with this initial state—you will need a very large piece of paper!

In the next case study we implement a heuristic search method.

CASE STUDY 8.1: SOLVING THE EIGHT-PUZZLE

Design and write a program to solve the following problem:

Problem:

Implement a heuristic search technique for the eight-puzzle.

Clarification The eight-puzzle was described on pages 318–327. The first line of the input will consist of the initial state, row by row. The second line will contain the goal state, row by row; thus, the goal state need not be the same for every run of the program. The output will consist of a path from the initial state to the goal state. Use the heuristic function on page 325.

Sample Input

```
1348627 5
1238 4765
```

Sample Output

THE INITIAL STATE IS

```
134
862
7 5
```

THE GOAL STATE IS

```
123
8 4
765
```

(*new page*)
THE LOWEST EVALUATION-FUNCTION VALUE OF UNEXPANDED NODES IS 4, SO WE EXPAND

```
134
862
7 5
```

TO OBTAIN THE FOLLOWING NEW LEAVES:

```
134
862
 75
```

WITH AN EVALUATION-FUNCTION VALUE OF 6

```
134
8 2
765
```

WITH AN EVALUATION-FUNCTION VALUE OF 4

```
134
862
75
```

WITH AN EVALUATION-FUNCTION VALUE OF 6

(*new page*)
THE LOWEST EVALUATION-FUNCTION VALUE OF UNEXPANDED NODES
IS 4, SO WE EXPAND

```
134
8 2
765
```

TO OBTAIN THE FOLLOWING NEW LEAVES:

```
134
 82
765
```

WITH AN EVALUATION-FUNCTION VALUE OF 6

```
1 4
832
765
```

WITH AN EVALUATION-FUNCTION VALUE OF 5

```
134
82
765
```

WITH AN EVALUATION-FUNCTION VALUE OF 5

(*new page*)
THE LOWEST EVALUATION-FUNCTION VALUE OF UNEXPANDED NODES
IS 5, SO WE EXPAND

```
1 4
832
765
```

TO OBTAIN THE FOLLOWING NEW LEAVES:

```
 14
832
765
```

WITH AN EVALUATION-FUNCTION VALUE OF 7

```
14
832
765
```

WITH AN EVALUATION-FUNCTION VALUE OF 6

(new page)

THE LOWEST EVALUATION-FUNCTION VALUE OF UNEXPANDED NODES
IS 5, SO WE EXPAND

134
82
765

TO OBTAIN THE FOLLOWING NEW LEAVES:

13
824
765

WITH AN EVALUATION-FUNCTION VALUE OF 5

134
825
76

WITH AN EVALUATION-FUNCTION VALUE OF 7

(new page)

THE LOWEST EVALUATION-FUNCTION VALUE OF UNEXPANDED NODES
IS 5, SO WE EXPAND

13
824
765

TO OBTAIN THE FOLLOWING NEW LEAVES:

1 3
824
765

WITH AN EVALUATION-FUNCTION VALUE OF 5

(new page)

THE LOWEST EVALUATION-FUNCTION VALUE OF UNEXPANDED NODES
IS 5, SO WE EXPAND
1 3
824
765

TO OBTAIN THE FOLLOWING NEW LEAVES:

 13
824
765

WITH AN EVALUATION-FUNCTION VALUE OF 7

123
8 4
765

WITH AN EVALUATION-FUNCTION VALUE OF 5

(new page)
THE GOAL STATE HAS BEEN REACHED. THE SOLUTION PATH IS
      134
      862
      7 5
       *
       *
       *
       *
      134
      8 2
      765
       *
       *
       *
       *
      134
      82
      765
       *
       *
       *
       *
      13
      824
      765
       *
       *
       *
       *
      1 3
      824
      765
       *
       *
       *
       *
      123
      8 4
      765

Solution Tree The main tree should find and print out a solution, if one exists. We start by reading in the initial and goal states. A solution is possible if and only if they have the same parity (see Gardner, 1959, pages 86–89). Therefore, we next check to see if the initial and goal states have the same parity. If they do, we establish the preconditions for finding a solution, then find one and print it out. The preconditions are:

1. The root of the state-space tree is obtained from the initial state.
2. The root is the only leaf in the leaf-list, so far.
3. No solution has been found so far (unless the root is a solution).

If we started with the input given on page 328, then after the preconditions were established, the state-space tree-and-leaf list would be as shown in Fig. 8.8. So far, we know of only two fields in a node: the state and a pointer to the next leaf (with a bar to indicate a NIL or zero value). Other fields will be added as they are needed.†

The complete main Solution Tree is shown in Fig. 8.9.

The CHECK PARITY subtree will determine if the initial and goal states have the same parity, that is, if an even number of tile swaps of the initial state will transform it into the goal state.

Because only tile-swaps are counted, we must move the initial state's blank to the same position that the blank occupies in the goal state. At this point, no tile-swaps have been made. The transformation takes place in a loop that continues through each row and column in the goal state. Each time through the loop, we see if the initial state matches the goal state at this position. If not, we search through the remaining positions of the initial state to find the row and column where the tile does match. We then swap these tiles in the initial state and add 1 to the number of swaps.

The subtree is shown in Fig. 8.10.

The subtree MOVE THE BLANK will move the initial state's blank to the same position the blank occupies in the goal state. We first find the blank's position in both states. We then swap the blank with a succession of tiles until the blank is in the proper row, then repeat the process to arrive at the proper column.

The MOVE THE BLANK subtree, with some details omitted, is shown in Fig. 8.11.

The subtree FIND THE BLANK straightforwardly determines the row and column of the blank entry in the given state. See Fig. 8.12.

The subtree ADVANCE increments the column, unless it is already 3; in that case, the row is incremented and the column is reset to 1. (The reason for creating a subtree to solve such a simple problem is that the subtree is called several times in the course of designing the program.)

The ADVANCE subtree is shown in Fig. 8.13.

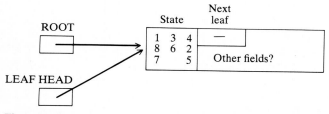

Figure 8.8 The state-space tree and leaf list at the beginning of the eight-puzzle, with the initial state given on page 328.

† The detailed structure of a node will be determined only after all the subtrees have been developed. That way, we will know what has to be included.

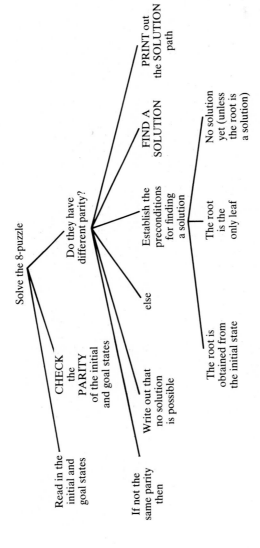

Figure 8.9 The main tree for the eight-puzzle.

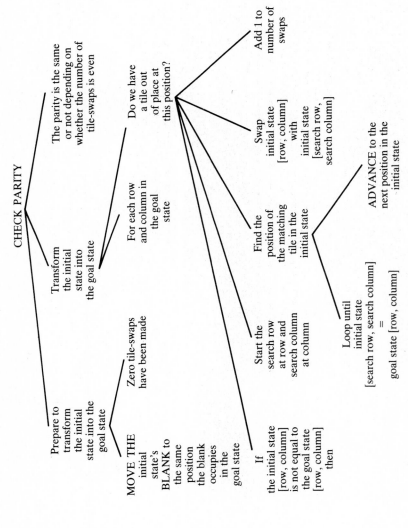

Figure 8.10 The CHECK PARITY subtree.

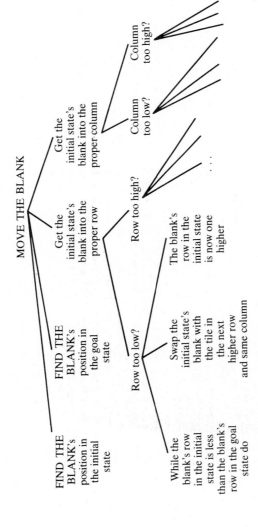

Figure 8.11 The subtree MOVE THE BLANK.

335

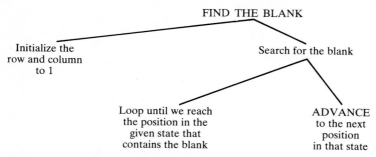

Figure 8.12 The subtree FIND THE BLANK.

The subtree FIND A SOLUTION loops until a solution is found. Each time through the loop, we find the leaf with the lowest evaluation-function value and then expand that leaf. After expanding that leaf, we must remove it from the leaf list.

The FIND A SOLUTION subtree is shown in Fig. 8.14.

The subtree FIND LOWEST VALUED LEAF will search through the leaf list to find the leaf with the lowest evaluation-function value. This subtree would be trivial if the leaf list were ordered by increasing evaluation-function values, but then each newly created leaf would have to be inserted into its proper position in the leaf list. The leaf list will be ordered as follows: Each time a new leaf is created, it will be tacked onto the end of the leaf list. It will be convenient for this if the leaf list has a tail as well as a head. To search through the list of leaves, we start at the head of the leaf list and we compare the evaluation-function value of each leaf to the lowest evaluation-function value seen so far. The evaluation-function value will be stored in each leaf when the leaf is created.

The subtree is shown in Fig. 8.15.

We next tackle the subtree EXPAND LOWEST VALUED LEAF. This sub-tree will apply each operator possible, and then check each state created to see if it is a duplicate or a goal state. We start by finding the position of the blank in the state of the lowest valued leaf. Then, for each operator, we apply the operator (if possible), thus creating a new state. We then search the tree to see if this new state is a duplicate. If not, we create a new leaf with the new state as its state and check to see if the new state matches the goal state. If there is a match, we must signify this new leaf as the goal leaf (to facilitate writing out the solution path).

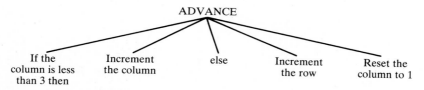

Figure 8.13 The ADVANCE subtree.

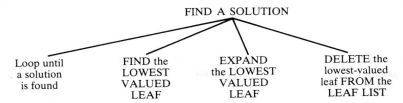

Figure 8.14 The subtree FIND A SOLUTION.

At this point in our design, the structure of each node is as shown in Fig. 8.16. The state-space tree and leaf list show how the situation might look right after the root was expanded and then deleted from the leaf list.

The subtree EXPAND LOWEST VALUED LEAF is shown in Fig. 8.17.

The subtree TRY TO APPLY OPERATOR will be given the leaf with the lowest evaluation-function value and will try to apply the given operator to that leaf. We say "try" because, for example, the blank can be moved to the left only if the column where the blank lies is greater than 1. Thus the row and column of the blank in the lowest leaf's state must also be provided to this subtree. The subtree will return an indication of whether or not the attempt was successful and, if so, also return the new state created. The specific attempt is different for each operator.

We show the details only for MOVE LEFT in the TRY TO APPLY OPERATOR subtree in Fig. 8.18.

The subtree SEARCH TREE FOR DUPLICATE will be called only if a new state was created in the TRY TO APPLY OPERATOR subtree. Thus, the SEARCH TREE FOR DUPLICATE subtree will be given the new state and the root of the state-space tree, and will return an indication of whether or not the new state duplicates the state of some node already in the tree. (Recall, from page 319, that a state-space tree has no duplicate states.)

Initially, no duplicate has been found. If the state-space tree is not empty, we check to see if the root's state matches the new state. If so, a duplicate has been

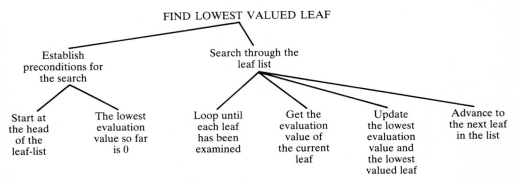

Figure 8.15 The subtree FIND LOWEST VALUED LEAF.

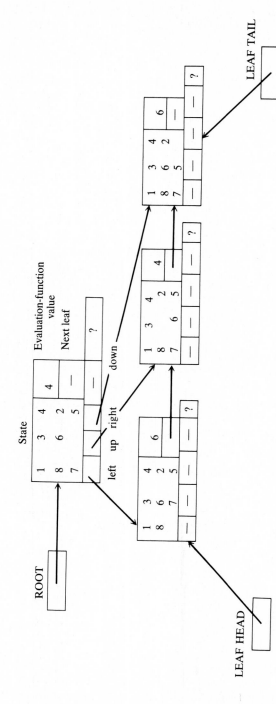

Figure 8.16 An illustration of what the state-space tree and leaf list might look like after the root was expanded and then deleted from the leaf list.

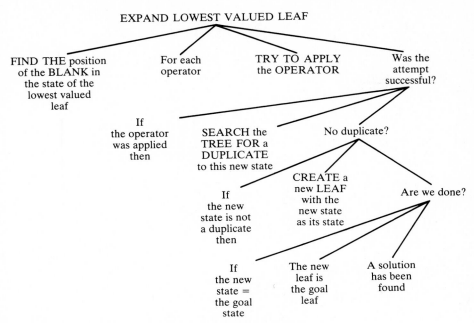

Figure 8.17 The subtree EXPAND LOWEST VALUED LEAF.

found. Otherwise, since each subtree of a state-space tree is itself a tree, we search the root's "left" subtree and, if necessary, the "up," "right," and "down" subtrees.

The SEARCH TREE FOR DUPLICATE subtree is shown in Fig. 8.19.

The subtree CREATE LEAF will create a new leaf from the state generated when an operator was applied to the lowest-valued leaf. After creating a new node and storing the new state in its state field, we calculate the node's heuristic

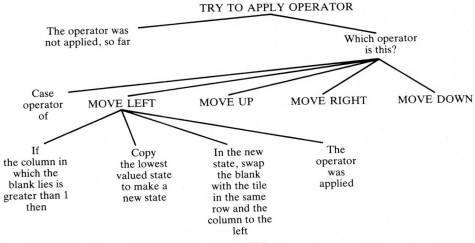

Figure 8.18 The subtree TRY TO APPLY OPERATOR.

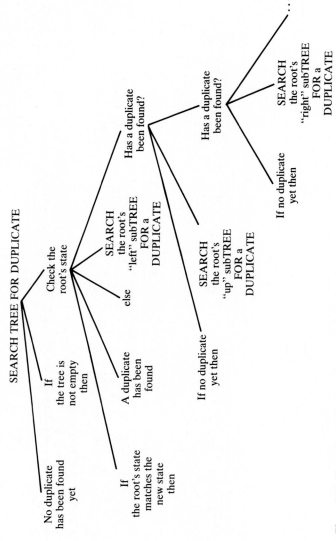

SEARCH TREE FOR DUPLICATE

No duplicate
has been found
yet

If
the tree is
not empty
then

Check the
root's state

If
the root's state
matches the
new state
then

A duplicate
has been
found

else

SEARCH
the root's
"left" subTREE
FOR a
DUPLICATE

Has a duplicate
been found?

If no duplicate
yet then

SEARCH
the root's
"up" subTREE
FOR a
DUPLICATE

Has a duplicate
been found?

If no duplicate
yet then

SEARCH
the root's
"right" subTREE
FOR a
DUPLICATE

...

Figure 8.19 The subtree SEARCH TREE FOR DUPLICATE.

value. To obtain the node's evaluation-function value, we need to add the heuristic-function and depth-function values. To facilitate this, we include a depth field in each node. The depth of a new leaf is one more than the depth of its parent, namely, the lowest valued leaf. Finally, we append this new node to the state-space tree and to the end of the leaf list.

The subtree is shown in Fig. 8.20.

To develop the subtree CALCULATE HEURISTIC VALUE, we will use the heuristic function given on page 325. This is straightforwardly implemented by a nested loop in which each nonblank entry in the current state is compared to the correponding entry in the goal state. (Thus, the goal state must be provided to this subtree, as well as to the calling subtree CREATE LEAF.)

The complete subtree is shown in Fig. 8.21.

The subtree DELETE FROM LEAF LIST will delete the lowest-valued leaf from the leaf list. If the lowest-valued leaf is not the head, then the next leaf field of the previous leaf should point to the next leaf after the lowest-valued leaf (the tail will be adjusted if that next leaf was the tail). If the lowest-valued leaf is the head of the leaf list, then the head (and, possibly, the tail) is adjusted to point to the next leaf after the lowest-valued leaf. We do not "dispose" of the leaf because it is still part of the state-space tree.

To facilitate accessing the previous leaf, we include a pointer field in each node to point to the node's previous leaf. Thus, the leaf list is a doubly linked list (see page 91).

The subtree is shown in Fig. 8.22.

The final subtree, PRINT SOLUTION, will be given the goal leaf. How can we access its ancestors? We simply include a "parent" field in each node. Since we want the path printed from the root downward, we call this subtree recursively.

The complete subtree is given in Fig. 8.23.

The complete structure of each node is given in Fig. 8.24.

Coding Some of the subprograms in the following program were not developed from subtrees. Two of these subprograms, READANDECHO and WRITE-STATE, deal with the details of input and output. Two others, OBTAINROOT and EQUALSTATES (discussed in the next paragraph) are concerned with implementation details.

To reflect the "natural" structure of a state, each one is implemented as a two-dimensional array. Since equality of two-dimensional arrays cannot be tested directly in Pascal, the boolean function EQUALSTATES is used in the procedures SEARCHTREEFORDUPLICATE and EXPANDLOWEST-VALUEDLEAF and in the main program. For example, in the subtree SEARCHTREEFORDUPLICATE we had

If the root's state matches the new state then . . .

In the procedure SEARCHTREEFORDUPLICATE, we have

IF EQUALSTATES(ROOT^.STATE, NEWSTATE) THEN...

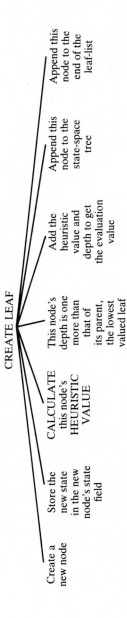

Figure 8.20 The subtree CREATE LEAF.

Create a
new node

Store the
new state
in the new
node's state
field

CALCULATE
this node's
HEURISTIC
VALUE

This node's
depth is one
more than
that of
its parent,
the lowest
valued leaf

Add the
heuristic
value and
depth to get
the evaluation
value

Append this
node to the
state-space
tree

Append this
node to the
end of the
leaf-list

CREATE LEAF

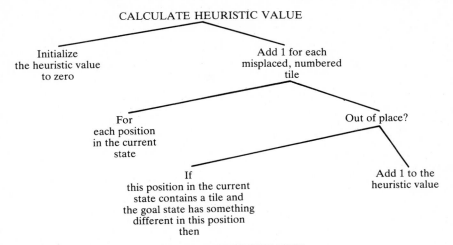

Figure 8.21 The subtree CALCULATE HEURISTIC VALUE.

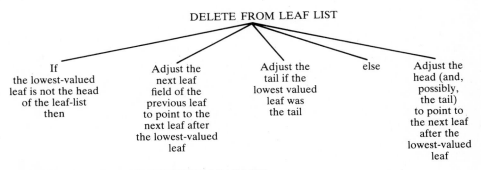

Figure 8.22 The subtree DELETE FROM LEAF LIST.

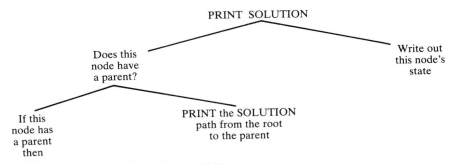

Figure 8.23 The subtree PRINT SOLUTION.

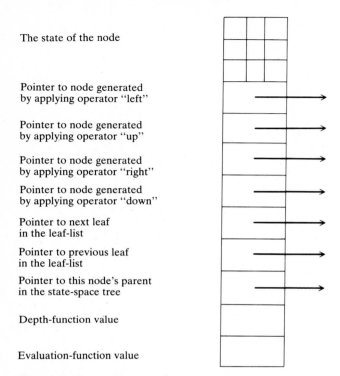

The state of the node

Pointer to node generated
by applying operator "left"

Pointer to node generated
by applying operator "up"

Pointer to node generated
by applying operator "right"

Pointer to node generated
by applying operator "down"

Pointer to next leaf
in the leaf-list

Pointer to previous leaf
in the leaf-list

Pointer to this node's parent
in the state-space tree

Depth-function value

Evaluation-function value

Figure 8.24 The structure of each node in the state-space tree.

The test for equality of the initial and goal states in the subtree CHECKPARITY is implemented by a test of their components in the procedure CHECKPARITY. This was done to avoid repetitious searching.

Finally, each state's two-dimensional array is "packed" to save space. Because a component of a packed array cannot be passed to a variable formal parameter, the procedure SWAP is slightly more cumbersome than if we had not used packed arrays.

The hierarchy chart is shown in Fig. 8.25.

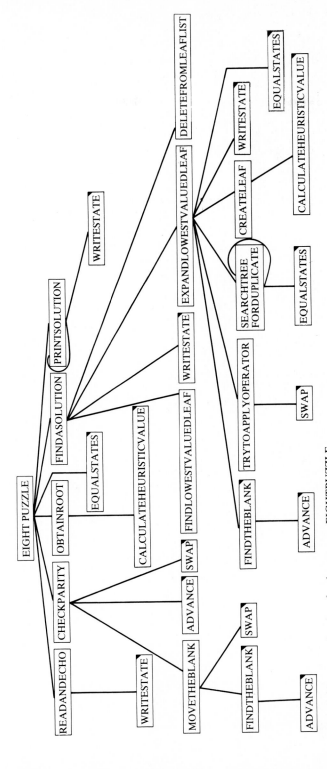

Figure 8.25 A hierarchy chart for the program EIGHTPUZZLE.

```pascal
PROGRAM   EIGHTPUZZLE(INPUT, OUTPUT);

(*********************************************************************)
(*                                                                 *)
(*   PROGRAMMER:  BILL COLLINS                                      *)
(*                                                                 *)
(*      This program will heuristically solve the eight puzzle.    *)
(*   Given an initial configuration of eight numbered tiles in     *)
(*   a three-by-three grid, the program will find a path to a      *)
(*   given goal configuration.  The path is obtained by applying   *)
(*   a succession of operators, where each operator moves the      *)
(*   blank space to the left, up, to the right or down in the      *)
(*   grid.  A solution path can be obtained only if the initial    *)
(*   and goal configurations have the same parity (see the         *)
(*   procedure CHECKPARITY).                                       *)
(*                                                                 *)
(*********************************************************************)

CONST SIDELENGTH    = 3;

TYPE  SIDETYPE      = 1..SIDELENGTH;
      NONNEGINTEGER = 0..MAXINT;
      BOARD         = PACKED ARRAY[SIDETYPE, SIDETYPE] OF CHAR;
      POINTER       = ^NODE;
      NODE          = RECORD
                          STATE                   : BOARD;
                          LEFT, UP, RIGHT, DOWN,
                          NEXTLEAF, PREVIOUSLEAF,
                          PARENT                  : POINTER;
                          DEPTH, EVALUATIONVALUE  : NONNEGINTEGER
                      END;
      TYPEOFOPERATOR = (MOVELEFT, MOVEUP, MOVERIGHT, MOVEDOWN);


VAR   INITIALSTATE, GOALSTATE    : BOARD;
      ROOT, LEAFHEAD, LEAFTAIL,
      GOALLEAF                   : POINTER;
      SAMEPARITY, SOLUTIONFOUND  : BOOLEAN;




PROCEDURE   WRITESTATE(CURRENTSTATE : BOARD);

(*  Write out the CURRENTSTATE, row-by-row.  *)

VAR   ROW, COLUMN : SIDETYPE;

BEGIN

   WRITELN;
   FOR ROW := 1 TO SIDELENGTH DO
      BEGIN
         FOR COLUMN := 1 TO SIDELENGTH DO
            WRITE(CURRENTSTATE[ROW, COLUMN]);
         WRITELN
      END;
   WRITELN

END; (*  of the procedure WRITESTATE.  *)
```

```
PROCEDURE  READANDECHO(VAR    STATE : BOARD);

(*  Read in and echo print the given STATE.  *)

CONST BLANK = ' ';

VAR   ROW, COLUMN : SIDETYPE;

BEGIN

   FOR ROW := 1 TO SIDELENGTH DO
      FOR COLUMN := 1 TO SIDELENGTH DO
         IF NOT EOLN THEN
            READ(STATE[ROW, COLUMN])
         ELSE (* If the blank is last and trailing blanks are ignored. *)
            STATE[ROW, COLUMN] := BLANK;
   READLN;

   WRITESTATE(STATE);
   WRITELN;
   WRITELN

END;  (* of the procedure READANDECHO.  *)




PROCEDURE  ADVANCE(VAR   ROW, COLUMN : SIDETYPE);

(*  Adjust ROW or COLUMN to advance to  *)
(*  the next position in the board.     *)

BEGIN

   IF COLUMN < SIDELENGTH THEN
      COLUMN := COLUMN + 1
   ELSE
      BEGIN
         ROW := ROW + 1;
         COLUMN := 1
      END

END;  (* of the procedure ADVANCE.  *)
```

```
PROCEDURE  FINDTHEBLANK(STATE              : BOARD;
                        VAR   ROW, COLUMN : SIDETYPE);

(*  In the given STATE, find the ROW and COLUMN  *)
(*  of the position where the blank lies.        *)

CONST BLANK = ' ';

BEGIN

   ROW     := 1;
   COLUMN  := 1;

   WHILE STATE[ROW, COLUMN] <> BLANK DO

      (*  Advance to the next position in the state.  *)
      ADVANCE(ROW, COLUMN)

END;  (*  of the procedure FINDTHEBLANK.  *)




PROCEDURE  SWAP(VAR     STATEA  : BOARD;
                ROWA, COLUMNA : SIDETYPE;
                VAR     STATEB  : BOARD;
                ROWB, COLUMNB : SIDETYPE);

(*  Swap the values of STATEA[ROWA, COLUMNA] and  *)
(*  STATEB[ROWB, COLUMNB].                         *)

VAR   TEMPORARY : CHAR;

BEGIN

   TEMPORARY    := STATEA[ROWA, COLUMNA];
   STATEA[ROWA, COLUMNA] := STATEB[ROWB, COLUMNB];
   STATEB[ROWB, COLUMNB] := TEMPORARY

END;  (*  of the procedure SWAP.  *)
```

```
PROCEDURE  MOVETHEBLANK(VAR    INITIALSTATE : BOARD;
                       GOALSTATE         : BOARD);

(*  In the INITIALSTATE, move the blank to the       *)
(*  same position that it occupies in the GOALSTATE.  *)

VAR   INITIALROW, (* the row containing the blank in the initial state. *)
      INITIALCOLUMN,
      GOALROW,
      GOALCOLUMN      : SIDETYPE;

BEGIN

   (*  Find the blank's position in the initial state.  *)
   FINDTHEBLANK(INITIALSTATE, INITIALROW, INITIALCOLUMN);

   (*  Find the blank's position in the goal state.  *)
   FINDTHEBLANK(GOALSTATE, GOALROW, GOALCOLUMN);

   (*  Move the initial state's blank into the proper row.  *)

      (*  Row too low?  *)
      WHILE INITIALROW < GOALROW DO
         BEGIN
            SWAP(INITIALSTATE, INITIALROW, INITIALCOLUMN,
                 INITIALSTATE, INITIALROW + 1, INITIALCOLUMN);
            INITIALROW := INITIALROW + 1
         END;

      (*  Row too high?  *)
      WHILE INITIALROW > GOALROW DO
         BEGIN
            SWAP(INITIALSTATE, INITIALROW, INITIALCOLUMN,
                 INITIALSTATE, INITIALROW - 1, INITIALCOLUMN);
            INITIALROW := INITIALROW - 1
         END;

   (*  Move the initial state's blank into the proper column.  *)

      (*  Column too low?  *)
      WHILE INITIALCOLUMN < GOALCOLUMN DO
         BEGIN
            SWAP(INITIALSTATE, INITIALROW, INITIALCOLUMN,
                 INITIALSTATE, INITIALROW, INITIALCOLUMN + 1);
            INITIALCOLUMN := INITIALCOLUMN + 1
         END;

      (*  Column too high?  *)
      WHILE INITIALCOLUMN > GOALCOLUMN DO
         BEGIN
            SWAP(INITIALSTATE, INITIALROW, INITIALCOLUMN,
                 INITIALSTATE, INITIALROW, INITIALCOLUMN - 1);
            INITIALCOLUMN := INITIALCOLUMN - 1
         END

END;  (*  of the procedure MOVETHEBLANK.  *)
```

```
PROCEDURE  CHECKPARITY(INITIALSTATE, GOALSTATE : BOARD;
                       VAR     SAMEPARITY          : BOOLEAN);

(*  Check to see if INITIALSTATE and GOALSTATE have the       *)
(*  same parity: If an even number of tile (that is, nonblank) *)
(*  swaps are required to transform the initial state into the *)
(*  final state, then SAMEPARITY gets the value TRUE. Otherwise *)
(*  SAMEPARITY gets the value FALSE.                           *)

VAR   NUMBEROFTILESWAPS        : NONNEGINTEGER;
      ROW, COLUMN,
      SEARCHROW, SEARCHCOLUMN : SIDETYPE;

BEGIN

   (*  Prepare to transform the initial state into the goal state. *)
   (*  Start by moving the blank in the initial state to the same  *)
   (*  position it occupies in the goal state.                     *)
   MOVETHEBLANK(INITIALSTATE, GOALSTATE);
   NUMBEROFTILESWAPS := 0;

   (*  Transform the initial state into the goal state.  *)
   FOR ROW := 1 TO SIDELENGTH DO
      FOR COLUMN := 1 TO SIDELENGTH DO

         (*  Do we have a tile out of place at this position?  *)
         IF INITIALSTATE[ROW, COLUMN] <> GOALSTATE[ROW, COLUMN] THEN
            BEGIN
               SEARCHROW    := ROW;
               SEARCHCOLUMN := COLUMN;
               REPEAT

                  (*  Advance to next position in initial state. *)
                  ADVANCE(SEARCHROW, SEARCHCOLUMN)

               UNTIL INITIALSTATE[SEARCHROW, SEARCHCOLUMN] =
                     GOALSTATE[ROW, COLUMN];

               SWAP(INITIALSTATE, ROW, COLUMN,
                    INITIALSTATE, SEARCHROW, SEARCHCOLUMN);

               NUMBEROFTILESWAPS := NUMBEROFTILESWAPS + 1

            END; (*  of the IF statement.  *)

   (*  The number of tile swaps is even if it leaves  *)
   (*   a zero remainder when divided by 2.           *)
   SAMEPARITY := NUMBEROFTILESWAPS MOD 2 = 0

END; (*  of the procedure CHECKPARITY.  *)
```

```
PROCEDURE  CALCULATEHEURISTICVALUE(CURRENTLEAF     : PCINTER;
                                   GOALSTATE       : BCARD;
                            VAR    HEURISTICVALUE  : NONNEGINTEGER);

(*  Calculate the HEURISTICVALUE of the CURRENTLEAF.  The      *)
(*  heuristic value of a node is the number of tiles in the    *)
(*  node that are in different positions from the GOALSTATE.   *)

CONST BLANK = ' ';

VAR   ROW, CCLUMN : SIDETYPE;

BEGIN

   HEURISTICVALUE := 0;

   (*  Add 1 for each numbered tile in the current leaf's     *)
   (*  state whose position is different in the goal state.   *)
   FOR ROW := 1 TO SIDELENGTH DO
      FOR COLUMN := 1 TO SIDELENGTH DO
         IF (CURRENTLEAF^.STATE[ROW, COLUMN] <> GOALSTATE[ROW, COLUMN])
               AND (GOALSTATE[ROW, COLUMN] <> BLANK) THEN
            HEURISTICVALUE := HEURISTICVALUE + 1

END;  (*  of the procedure CALCULATEHEURISTICVALUE.  *)




PROCEDURE  OBTAINROOT(VAR    ROOT                : POINTER;
                      INITIALSTATE, GCALSTATE : BOARD);

(*  Obtain the ROOT of the state-space tree from the INITIALSTATE.   *)
(*  To get the root's heuristic value field, we need to compare its  *)
(*  state to the GOALSTATE.                                          *)

VAR   HEURISTICVALUE : NONNEGINTEGER;

BEGIN

   NEW(ROOT);

   WITH ROOT^ DO
      BEGIN

         STATE          := INITIALSTATE;
         LEFT           := NIL;
         UP             := NIL;
         RIGHT          := NIL;
         DOWN           := NIL;
         NEXTLEAF       := NIL;
         PREVIOUSLEAF   := NIL;
         PARENT         := NIL;
         DEPTH          := 0;

         CALCULATEHEURISTICVALUE(ROOT, GOALSTATE, HEURISTICVALUE);

         EVALUATIONVALUE := DEPTH + HEURISTICVALUE

      END

END;  (*  of the procedure OBTAINROOT.  *)
```

```
PROCEDURE  FINDLOWESTVALUEDLEAF(VAR   LOWESTVALUEDLEAF : POINTER;
                                LEAFHEAD              : POINTER);

(*  Find the LOWESTVALUEDLEAF, that is, the leaf whose  *)
(*  evaluation-function value is lowest among all the   *)
(*  leaves in the leaf-list pointed to by LEAFHEAD.     *)

VAR   CURRENTLEAF : POINTER;

BEGIN

    (*  Establish preconditions for the search.  *)
    CURRENTLEAF      := LEAFHEAD;
    LOWESTVALUEDLEAF := CURRENTLEAF;

    (*  Search through the leaf-list.  *)
    WHILE CURRENTLEAF <> NIL DO
       BEGIN

          IF CURRENTLEAF^.EVALUATIONVALUE <
                LOWESTVALUEDLEAF^.EVALUATIONVALUE THEN
             LOWESTVALUEDLEAF := CURRENTLEAF;

          (*  Advance to the next leaf in the leaf-list.  *)
          CURRENTLEAF := CURRENTLEAF^.NEXTLEAF

       END

END;  (*  of the procedure FINDLOWESTVALUEDLEAF.  *)
```

```
PROCEDURE   TRYTOAPPLYOPERATOR(LOWESTVALUEDLEAF : POINTER;
                               OPERATOR         : TYPEOFOPERATOR;
                               ROWWITHBLANK,
                               COLUMNWITHBLANK  : SIDETYPE;
                               VAR   NEWSTATE   : BOARD;
                               VAR   THEOPERATORWASAPPLIED : BOOLEAN);

(*  Try to apply the given OPERATOR to the blank in the state      *)
(*  of the LOWESTVALUEDLEAF. We say "try" because, for example,    *)
(*  the blank can be moved to the right only if the blank is not   *)
(*  in the rightmost column. If the operator can be applied, then  *)
(*  a NEWSTATE will be created with the blank moved and            *)
(*  THEOPERATORWASAPPLIED will get the value TRUE. Otherwise,      *)
(*  THEOPERATORWASAPPLIED will get the value FALSE.                *)

BEGIN

   THEOPERATORWASAPPLIED := FALSE;

   CASE OPERATOR OF

      MOVELEFT  : IF COLUMNWITHBLANK > 1 THEN
                     BEGIN
                        NEWSTATE := LOWESTVALUEDLEAF^.STATE;
                        SWAP(NEWSTATE, ROWWITHBLANK, COLUMNWITHBLANK,
                             NEWSTATE, ROWWITHBLANK, COLUMNWITHBLANK - 1);
                        THEOPERATORWASAPPLIED :=TRUE
                     END;
      MOVEUP    : IF ROWWITHBLANK > 1 THEN
                     BEGIN
                        NEWSTATE := LOWESTVALUEDLEAF^.STATE;
                        SWAP(NEWSTATE, ROWWITHBLANK, COLUMNWITHBLANK,
                             NEWSTATE, ROWWITHBLANK - 1, COLUMNWITHBLANK);
                        THEOPERATORWASAPPLIED := TRUE
                     END;
      MOVERIGHT : IF COLUMNWITHBLANK < SIDELENGTH THEN
                     BEGIN
                        NEWSTATE := LOWESTVALUEDLEAF^.STATE;
                        SWAP(NEWSTATE, ROWWITHBLANK, COLUMNWITHBLANK,
                             NEWSTATE, ROWWITHBLANK, COLUMNWITHBLANK + 1);
                        THEOPERATORWASAPPLIED := TRUE
                     END;
      MOVEDOWN  : IF ROWWITHBLANK < SIDELENGTH THEN
                     BEGIN
                        NEWSTATE := LOWESTVALUEDLEAF^.STATE;
                        SWAP(NEWSTATE, ROWWITHBLANK, COLUMNWITHBLANK,
                             NEWSTATE, ROWWITHBLANK + 1, COLUMNWITHBLANK);
                        THEOPERATORWASAPPLIED := TRUE
                     END

   END  (*  of the CASE statement.  *)

END; (*  of the procedure TRYTOAPPLYOPERATOR.  *)
```

```
FUNCTION  EQUALSTATES(STATEA, STATEB : BOARD) : BOOLEAN;

(*  Return the value TRUE if STATEA and STATEB are the same state.  *)
(*  Otherwise, return the value FALSE.                              *)

VAR   ROW, COLUMN : SIDETYPE;

BEGIN

    EQUALSTATES := TRUE;

    FOR ROW := 1 TO SIDELENGTH DO
       FOR COLUMN := 1 TO SIDELENGTH DO
          IF STATEA[ROW, COLUMN] <> STATEB[ROW,COLUMN] THEN
             EQUALSTATES := FALSE

END;  (*  of the function EQUALSTATES.  *)




PROCEDURE  SEARCHTREEFORDUPLICATE(NEWSTATE          : BOARD;
                                  ROOT              : PCINTER;
                                  VAR    DUPLICATE  : BOOLEAN);

(*  Search the state-space tree pointed to by ROOT to see   *)
(*  if the NEWSTATE duplicates the state of some node in     *)
(*  the tree. If so, DUPLICATE gets the value TRUE;          *)
(*  otherwise, FALSE.                                        *)

BEGIN

    DUPLICATE := FALSE;

    IF ROOT <> NIL THEN
       IF EQUALSTATES(ROOT^.STATE, NEWSTATE) THEN
          DUPLICATE := TRUE
       ELSE

          (*  Check this root's subtrees.  *)
          BEGIN
             SEARCHTREEFORDUPLICATE(NEWSTATE, ROOT^.LEFT, DUPLICATE);
             IF NOT DUPLICATE THEN
                BEGIN
                   SEARCHTREEFORDUPLICATE(NEWSTATE, ROOT^.UP, DUPLICATE);
                   IF NOT DUPLICATE THEN
                      BEGIN
                         SEARCHTREEFORDUPLICATE(NEWSTATE, ROOT^.RIGHT,
                                                          DUPLICATE);
                         IF NOT DUPLICATE THEN
                            SEARCHTREEFORDUPLICATE(NEWSTATE, ROOT^.DOWN,
                                                             DUPLICATE)
                      END
                END
          END

END;  (*  of the procedure SEARCHTREEFORDUPLICATE.  *)
```

```
PROCEDURE  CREATELEAF(NEWSTATE                : BOARD;
                      LOWESTVALUEDLEAF         : POINTER;
                      OPERATOR                 : TYPEOFOPERATOR;
                      VAR   NEWLEAF, LEAFTAIL  : POINTER);

(*  Create a NEWLEAF with NEWSTATE as its state, and then insert    *)
(*  this leaf in the state-space tree with LOWESTVALUEDLEAF as       *)
(*  its parent.  We need to know which OPERATOR was applied to       *)
(*  obtain the new state so that NEWLEAF can be inserted in the      *)
(*  appropriate field in LOWESTVALUEDLEAF^. The new leaf is also     *)
(*  inserted at the end of the leaf-list whose last node is          *)
(*  pointed to by LEAFTAIL.                                          *)

VAR   HEURISTICVALUE : NONNEGINTEGER;

BEGIN

    NEW(NEWLEAF);
    NEWLEAF^.STATE := NEWSTATE;
    NEWLEAF^.LEFT  := NIL;
    NEWLEAF^.UP    := NIL;
    NEWLEAF^.RIGHT := NIL;
    NEWLEAF^.DOWN  := NIL;

    (*  Determine the depth and heuristic values of this leaf.  *)
    NEWLEAF^.DEPTH := LOWESTVALUEDLEAF^.DEPTH + 1;
    CALCULATEHEURISTICVALUE(NEWLEAF, GOALSTATE, HEURISTICVALUE);

    (*  Add the depth and heuristic values to get the evaluation value. *)
    NEWLEAF^.EVALUATIONVALUE := NEWLEAF^.DEPTH + HEURISTICVALUE;

    (*  Append this leaf to the state-space tree.  *)
    NEWLEAF^.PARENT := LOWESTVALUEDLEAF;
    CASE OPERATOR OF
        MOVELEFT  : LOWESTVALUEDLEAF^.LEFT  := NEWLEAF;
        MOVEUP    : LOWESTVALUEDLEAF^.UP    := NEWLEAF;
        MOVERIGHT : LOWESTVALUEDLEAF^.RIGHT := NEWLEAF;
        MOVEDOWN  : LOWESTVALUEDLEAF^.DOWN  := NEWLEAF
    END;

    (*  Append this leaf to the end of the leaf list.  *)
    LEAFTAIL^.NEXTLEAF      := NEWLEAF;
    NEWLEAF^.PREVIOUSLEAF := LEAFTAIL;
    NEWLEAF^.NEXTLEAF      := NIL;
    LEAFTAIL              := NEWLEAF

END;  (*  of the procedure CREATELEAF.  *)
```

```
PROCEDURE  EXPANDLOWESTVALUEDLEAF(LOWESTVALUEDLEAF, ROOT   : POINTER;
                                  GOALSTATE               : BOARD;
                                  VAR   LEAFTAIL, GOALLEAF : POINTER;
                                  VAR   SOLUTIONFOUND      : BOOLEAN);

(*  Expand the LOWESTVALUEDLEAF in the state-space tree pointed to   *)
(*  by ROOT. If a state generated does not duplicate any already     *)
(*  in the tree, a new node is created and appended to the state-     *)
(*  space tree and to the end of the leaf-list, whose last leaf       *)
(*  is pointed to by LEAFTAIL. If the new leaf's state matches        *)
(*  the GOALSTATE, then the new leaf is designated as the GOALLEAF    *)
(*  (to aid in printing the solution path) and SOLUTIONFOUND has      *)
(*  its value changed to TRUE; it had been initialized to FALSE       *)
(*  in the main program.                                             *)

VAR    ROWWITHBLANK, COLUMNWITHBLANK        : SIDETYPE;
       OPERATOR                             : TYPEOFOPERATOR;
       NEWSTATE                             : BOARD;
       THEOPERATORWASAPPLIED, DUPLICATE     : BOOLEAN;
       NEWLEAF                              : POINTER;

BEGIN

    FINDTHEBLANK(LOWESTVALUEDLEAF^.STATE, ROWWITHBLANK, COLUMNWITHBLANK);

    (*  Try to apply each operator.  *)
    FOR OPERATOR := MOVELEFT TO MOVEDOWN DO
        BEGIN

            TRYTOAPPLYOPERATOR(LOWESTVALUEDLEAF, OPERATOR,
                               ROWWITHBLANK, COLUMNWITHBLANK,
                               NEWSTATE, THEOPERATORWASAPPLIED);

            (*  Was the attempt successful?  *)
            IF THEOPERATORWASAPPLIED THEN
                BEGIN

                    (* Search the tree to see if the new state is a *)
                    (* duplicate.                                    *)
                    SEARCHTREEFORDUPLICATE(NEWSTATE, ROOT, DUPLICATE);

                    IF NOT DUPLICATE THEN
                        BEGIN

                            CREATELEAF(NEWSTATE, LOWESTVALUEDLEAF, OPERATOR,
                                       NEWLEAF, LEAFTAIL);

                            (*  Write out the new leaf's state.  *)
                            WRITESTATE(NEWSTATE);
                            WRITELN('WITH AN EVALUATION-FUNCTION VALUE OF ',
                                    NEWLEAF^.EVALUATIONVALUE:1);
                            WRITELN;
                            WRITELN;

                            (*  Are we done?  *)
                            IF EQUALSTATES(NEWSTATE, GOALSTATE) THEN
                                BEGIN
                                    GOALLEAF      := NEWLEAF;
                                    SOLUTIONFOUND := TRUE
                                END

                        END  (* of "IF NOT DUPLICATE ..." .  *)

                END  (* of "IF THEOPERATORWASAPPLIED ..." .  *)

        END  (*  of the FOR statement.  *)

END;  (*  of the procedure EXPANDLOWESTVALUEDLEAF.  *)
```

```
PROCEDURE   DELETEFROMLEAFLIST(LOWESTVALUEDLEAF          : POINTER;
                               VAR   LEAFHEAD, LEAFTAIL : POINTER);

(*  Delete the LOWESTVALUEDLEAF from the leaf-list. Special cases  *)
(*  occur if the lowest-valued leaf is the head or the tail. We    *)
(*  do not "dispose of" the deleted leaf because it is still a     *)
(*  node in the state-space tree.                                  *)

VAR   TEMPORARYLEAF : POINTER;

BEGIN

    IF LOWESTVALUEDLEAF <> LEAFHEAD THEN
        BEGIN

            (*  Delete the forward pointer to lowest-valued leaf.  *)
            TEMPORARYLEAF              := LOWESTVALUEDLEAF^.PREVIOUSLEAF;
            TEMPORARYLEAF^.NEXTLEAF := LOWESTVALUEDLEAF^.NEXTLEAF;

            (*  Have we deleted the tail?  *)
            IF LOWESTVALUEDLEAF = LEAFTAIL THEN
                LEAFTAIL := TEMPORARYLEAF
            ELSE
                BEGIN

                    (* Delete the backward pointer to lowest-valued leaf. *)
                    TEMPORARYLEAF                := LOWESTVALUEDLEAF^.NEXTLEAF;
                    TEMPORARYLEAF^.PREVIOUSLEAF := LOWESTVALUEDLEAF^.PREVIOUSLEAF

                END
        END
    ELSE
        BEGIN
            LEAFHEAD := LEAFHEAD^.NEXTLEAF;

            (*  Is the leaf-list now empty?  *)
            IF LEAFHEAD = NIL THEN
                LEAFTAIL := NIL
            ELSE

                (* Delete the backward pointer to lowest-valued leaf. *)
                LEAFHEAD^.PREVIOUSLEAF := NIL

        END

END;  (*  of the procedure DELETEFROMLEAFLIST.  *)
```

```
PROCEDURE   FINDASOLUTION(ROOT                                  : POINTER;
                          VAR   GOALLEAF, LEAFHEAD, LEAFTAIL : POINTER;
                          GOALSTATE                              : BOARD;
                          SOLUTIONFOUND                          : BOOLEAN);

(*  Find a solution to the 8-puzzle. A solution is a path from the  *)
(*  ROOT to some GOALLEAF, that is, a leaf that contains the         *)
(*  GOALSTATE. Adjust the leaf-list, pointed to by LEAFHEAD and      *)
(*  LEAFTAIL, as necessary. When a solution has been found,          *)
(*  SOLUTIONFOUND will have its value changed to TRUE (it was        *)
(*  initialized to FALSE in the main program).                       *)

VAR   LOWESTVALUEDLEAF : POINTER;

BEGIN

    WHILE NOT(SOLUTIONFOUND) DO
        BEGIN

            (*  Find the leaf with the lowest evaluation-function value.  *)
            FINDLOWESTVALUEDLEAF(LOWESTVALUEDLEAF, LEAFHEAD);

            PAGE;
            WRITELN('THE LOWEST EVALUATION-FUNCTION VALUE',
                    ' OF UNEXPANDED LEAVES');
            WRITELN('IS ', LOWESTVALUEDLEAF^.EVALUATIONVALUE:1,
                    ', SO WE EXPAND');
            WRITESTATE(LOWESTVALUEDLEAF^.STATE);
            WRITELN('TO OBTAIN THE FOLLOWING NEW LEAVES:');

            (*  Expand the lowest-valued leaf.  *)
            EXPANDLOWESTVALUEDLEAF(LOWESTVALUEDLEAF, ROOT, GOALSTATE,
                                   LEAFTAIL, GOALLEAF, SOLUTIONFOUND);

            (*  Delete that leaf from the leaf-list.  *)
            DELETEFROMLEAFLIST(LOWESTVALUEDLEAF, LEAFHEAD, LEAFTAIL)

        END

END;  (*  of the procedure FINDASOLUTION.  *)




PROCEDURE   PRINTSOLUTION(NODEPOINTER : POINTER);

(*  Print the solution path from the root to the  *)
(*  node pointed to by NODEPOINTER.               *)

BEGIN

    (*  Does this node have a parent?  *)
    IF NODEPOINTER^.PARENT <> NIL THEN
        BEGIN
            PRINTSOLUTION(NODEPOINTER^.PARENT);
            WRITELN('*':2);
            WRITELN('*':2);
            WRITELN('*':2);
            WRITELN('*':2)
        END;

    (*  Write out this node's state.  *)
    WRITESTATE(NODEPOINTER^.STATE)

END;  (*  of the procedure PRINTSOLUTION.  *)
```

```
BEGIN  (*  the executable section of the main program.  *)

    PAGE;
    WRITELN('THE INITIAL STATE IS');

    (*  Read in and echo print the initial state.  *)
    READANDECHO(INITIALSTATE);


    WRITELN('THE GOAL STATE IS');

    (*  Read in and echo print the goal state.  *)
    READANDECHO(GOALSTATE);

    CHECKPARITY(INITIALSTATE, GOALSTATE, SAMEPARITY);

    IF NOT(SAMEPARITY) THEN
        WRITELN('NO SOLUTION POSSIBLE: INITIAL AND GOAL STATES',
                ' HAVE DIFFERENT PARITY.')
    ELSE
        BEGIN

            (*  Establish the preconditions for finding a solution.  *)

                (*  Obtain the root from the initial state.  *)
                OBTAINROOT(ROOT, INITIALSTATE, GOALSTATE);

                (*  The root is the only leaf, so far.  *)
                LEAFHEAD := ROOT;
                LEAFTAIL := ROOT;

                (*  Are we done already?  *)
                IF EQUALSTATES(ROOT^.STATE, GOALSTATE) THEN
                    BEGIN
                        SOLUTIONFOUND := TRUE;
                        GOALLEAF      := ROOT
                    END
                ELSE
                    SOLUTIONFOUND := FALSE;

            (*  Find a solution.  *)
            FINDASOLUTION(ROOT, GOALLEAF, LEAFHEAD, LEAFTAIL,
                          GOALSTATE, SOLUTIONFOUND);

            (*  Print the solution path.  *)
            PAGE;
            WRITELN('THE GOAL STATE HAS BEEN REACHED. THE ',
                    'SOLUTION PATH IS');
            PRINTSOLUTION(GOALLEAF)

        END;

    PAGE
END.
```

Program Testing Because many of the subprograms are small, we will test several at a time.

1. Testing the main program, READANDECHO and WRITESTATE:

   Test 1a   (initial state = goal state)

   12345678β
   12345678β

   Test 1b   (the given Sample Input)

   1348627 5
   1238 4765

2. Testing CHECKPARITY and the procedures it calls:

   Test 2a   (no tile swaps needed to transform initial state into goal state)

   12345678β
   12345678β

   Test 2b   (one tile swap needed)

   1328 4765
   1238 4765

   Test 2c   (two tile swaps needed)

   1348627 5
   1238 4765

   Test 2d   (four tile swaps needed)

   2164 8753
   1238 4765

3. Testing OBTAINROOT, CALCULATEHEURISTICVALUE and EQUAL-STATES:

   Test 3a   (initial state = goal state)

   1238 4765
   1238 4765

   Test 3b   (initial state ≠ goal state)

   2164 8753
   1238 4765

4. Testing FINDASOLUTION and FINDLOWESTVALUEDLEAF:

   Test 4a   (the given Sample Input)

   1348627 5
   1238 4765

5. Testing EXPANDLOWESTVALUEDLEAF and TRYTOAPPLYOPERA-
   TOR:

   Test 5a   (the given Sample Input)
   _____

   1348627 5
   1238 4765

   Test 5b   (a hard puzzle)
   _____

   87654321♭
   12345678♭

6. Testing SEARCHTREEFORDUPLICATE and CREATELEAF:

   Test 6a   (the given Sample Input)
   _____

   1348627 5
   1238 4765

   Test 6b   (duplicates generated)
   _____

   87654321♭
   12345678♭

7. Testing DELETEFROMLEAFLIST:

   Test 7a   (the given Sample Input)
   _____

   1348627 5
   1238 4765

8. Testing PRINTSOLUTION:

   Test 8a   (the given Sample Input)
   _____

   1348627 5
   1238 4765

   Test 8c   (a hard puzzle)
   _____

   2164 8753
   1238 4765

Exercise 8.8 How difficult would it be to modify the program EIGHTPUZ-
ZLE to solve the 15-puzzle: 15 numbered tiles in a four-by-four grid? The 15-
puzzle was invented by Sam Loyd in 1878 (see Loyd, 1960). He offered a
huge prize to anyone who could solve the puzzle with an initial state of

$$
\begin{array}{cccc}
1 & 2 & 3 & 4 \\
5 & 6 & 7 & 8 \\
9 & 10 & 11 & 12 \\
13 & 15 & 14 &
\end{array}
$$

and a goal state of

$$
\begin{array}{cccc}
1 & 2 & 3 & 4 \\
5 & 6 & 7 & 8 \\
9 & 10 & 11 & 12 \\
13 & 14 & 15 &
\end{array}
$$

No one ever claimed the prize. Why?

Exercise 8.9 Discuss the tradeoffs with each of the following proposed changes to the program EIGHTPUZZLE:

1. Allow duplicate states in the state-space tree.
2. Order the leaf list in increasing order of evaluation-function values.
3. Use the heuristic function given on pages 326–327.

Exercise 8.10 In the program EIGHTPUZZLE, each state was implemented as a packed two-dimensional array of characters. Discuss the advantages and disadvantages of each of the following alternate implementations: a string; an unpacked, one-dimensional array of characters; a nine-digit integer (zero for the blank).

THE MINIMAX SEARCH STRATEGY

Let us now consider two-person, perfect information games, where the players alternate moves, each game results in a win, loss, or draw, and no chance is involved. Examples of such games are tic-tac-toe, checkers, chess, and go. The goal at each stage is to find the "best" move. Typically, we evaluate the possible future moves for several turns and then choose our move accordingly.

Tic-Tac-Toe

As a simple example, we will investigate a search strategy for tic-tac-toe. The first person to move will be PLUS, who will place an 'X' somewhere on the board, then MINUS will place an 'O', and so on. Whenever it is PLUS's turn, we will construct a tree of depth *two*. The root will be the current board configuration. The root's children will consist of all possible moves by PLUS; each of these nodes will have as children the possible moves that MINUS could then make.

We will evaluate each leaf from PLUS's perspective: a higher value suggests a better board for PLUS than a lower value does. We want an evaluation function that reflects PLUS's chances of winning. For example, for each leaf n, we can define f as follows:

If n is a winning position for PLUS, then

$$f(n) = 100$$

else, if n is a winning position for MINUS then

$$f(n) = -100$$

else

$f(n)$ = (the number of rows, columns, and diagonals that are still open for PLUS)
— (the number of rows, columns, and diagonals still open for MINUS)

For example, if n is

then $f(n) = 100$. If n is

then $f(n) = 3 - 3 = 0$.

Strictly speaking, this is a heuristic function. We refer to it as an "evaluation" function since the depth of each leaf is always 2.

Exercise 8.10 Evaluate each of the following board positions:

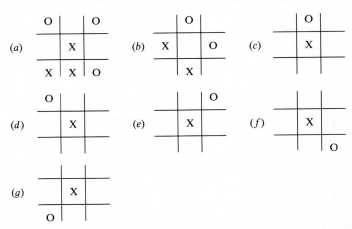

Notice that the last four positions in Exercise 8.10 are symmetrical, so it is sufficient to generate and evaluate only one such node. Early in the game, the tree is kept small by symmetries; later on it is kept small because there are few open spaces available.

How do we determine PLUS's best move in a given position? After all the leaves (to a depth of 2) have been evaluated, we proceed as follows: We assume that in each group of siblings, MINUS will choose the move that is worst for PLUS, that is, the move that has the lowest f value. For example, assume that MINUS has the following three choices (f values are encircled):

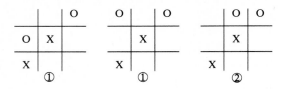

Since 1 is the minimum value among the siblings, MINUS will choose one of the moves with that value. We associate this minimum value with the parent node, namely

After associating the minimum value of its children with each node that is the parent of a leaf, we take the maximum of these values to determine PLUS's best move—on the theory that higher values represent better moves for PLUS. The term *minimax* is used to describe this strategy. For example, to determine PLUS's best move from the position

we generate the tree shown in Fig. 8.26.

Exercise 8.11 In Fig. 8.26, all 21 leaves were evaluated. Assuming that expansions and evaluations were performed from left to right, how many leaves could have remained unevaluated?

Hint: In the second set of siblings, the first leaf, namely

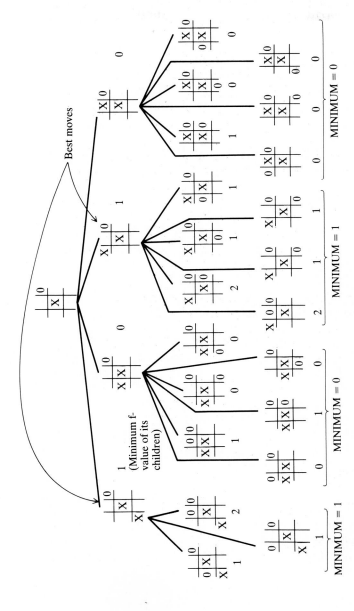

Figure 8.26 A minimax search tree for one position in Tic-Tac-Toe.

had an evaluation function value of 0. Thus, since MINUS will choose the minimum value among siblings, the highest possible value that could be associated with its parent's node is 0. Since that is smaller than the value already associated with the parent of the leftmost set of siblings (namely, 1), PLUS could not possibly choose the second node from the left, so the five siblings of

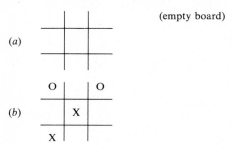

need not be generated nor evaluated.

Exercise 8.12 Use a minimax strategy to determine PLUS's best move in each of the following positions:

(empty board)

(a)

(b)

Exercise 8.13 Devise a new evalution function for tic-tac-toe.

Checkers

In Samuel's famous checker-playing program, the evaluation function was quite complex, involving such factors as piece advantage, number of kings and number of center squares controlled. The formula for calculating f at a leaf n was

$$f(n) = a * \text{piece advantage} + b * \text{number of kings} + c * \cdots$$

The weights $a, b, c \cdots$ assigned to these factors were learned by the program in two ways:

1. *From book games.* If the expert's choice differed from the minimax choice, the values of the weights were modified so that the program's choice would agree with the expert's choice in as many cases as possible.
2. *By consistency.* Note that the minimax value of a root is more accurate than its direct evaluation, so if there was a difference, the values of the weights were modified to make the direct value a little closer to the more accurate minimax value.

Interestingly enough, the values of the weights stabilized after only about 25 practice games!

PROBLEMS

Problem 8.1: Tic-Tac-Toe

Design and write a program to solve the following problem: Develop a heuristic strategy for playing tic-tac-toe.

Clarification The game will be played interactively. The program will generate moves for PLUS, and a mere human will specify moves for MINUS by entering the row and column in which the 'O' should be placed. An error message should be printed if the move is illegal, and then the human is asked to enter a legal move. Each game continues until a win, lose, or draw occurs, after which another game will be played if the human responds "YES" to the question "WOULD YOU LIKE TO PLAY ANOTHER GAME?" A response of "NO" terminates the program; any other response generates an error message and the question is repeated.

Sample Output, with Sample Input in boxes:

YOUR MOVE, HUMAN! ENTER THE ROW AND COLUMN, SEPARATED BY A SPACE, WHERE YOU WANT THE O TO BE PLACED.

| 1 3 |

YOUR MOVE, HUMAN! ENTER THE ROW AND COLUMN, SEPARATED BY A SPACE, WHERE YOU WANT THE O TO BE PLACED.

| 2 3 |

```
      | O
 ─────┼────
    X | O
 ─────┼────
  X   | X
```

YOUR MOVE, HUMAN! ENTER THE ROW AND COLUMN, SEPARATED
BY A SPACE, WHERE YOU WANT THE O TO BE PLACED.

3 3

NICE TRY, WET BRAIN! HOW ABOUT A LEGAL MOVE?

2 2

NICE TRY, WET BRAIN! HOW ABOUT A LEGAL MOVE?

1 1

```
O  |     | O
   |  X  | O
───┼─────┼───
 X |  X  | X
```

CARBON CHEMISTRY FAILS AGAIN! WOULD YOU LIKE
TO PLAY ANOTHER GAME? ANSWER YES OR NO.

NO

THANKS FOR GIVING MY CIRCUITS SOME EXERCISE. COME
BACK WHEN YOU HAVE EVOLVED INTO SOMETHING SMARTER!

THE SYNTAX OF PASCAL

The following list of grammatical rules differs from the format presented in Chap. 5 in that recursion is replaced by iteration. For example, consider a recursive definition such as the following ("#" represents the empty string):

⟨actual parameter list⟩ :: = (⟨actual parameter⟩ ⟨rest of actual parameter list⟩)

⟨rest of actual parameter list⟩ :: = # |, ⟨actual parameter⟩ ⟨rest of actual parameter list⟩

This can be simplified if we introduce the metalinguistic symbols { } to denote zero or more instances of whatever is inside those braces. Then we get

⟨actual parameter list⟩ ::= (⟨actual parameter⟩ {,⟨actual parameter⟩})

In deference to the terminology of Standard Pascal we use

"control variable"   instead of "loop counter,"
"identified variable" instead of "dynamic variable," and
"index"   instead of "subscript."

The Syntax of Pascal . . .

⟨actual parameter⟩ ::= ⟨expression⟩ | ⟨variable⟩ | ⟨procedure identifier⟩ |
                    ⟨function identifier⟩

⟨actual parameter list⟩ ::= (⟨actual parameter⟩ {,⟨actual parameter⟩})

⟨adding operator⟩ ::= + | − | OR

369

⟨apostrophe image⟩ ::= ″

⟨array type⟩ ::= ARRAY[⟨index type⟩ {,⟨index type⟩}] OF ⟨component type⟩

⟨array variable⟩ ::= ⟨variable⟩

⟨assignment statement⟩ ::= ⟨variable⟩ := ⟨expression⟩ |
                    ⟨function identifier⟩ := ⟨expression⟩

⟨base type⟩ ::= ⟨ordinal type⟩

⟨block⟩ ::= ⟨declarations section⟩ ⟨executable section⟩

⟨buffer variable⟩ ::= ⟨file variable⟩^

⟨case constant⟩ ::= ⟨constant⟩

⟨case constant list⟩ ::= ⟨case constant⟩ {,⟨case constant⟩}

⟨case index⟩ ::= ⟨expression⟩

⟨case list element⟩ ::= ⟨case constant list⟩ : ⟨statement⟩

⟨case statement⟩ ::= CASE ⟨case index⟩ OF ⟨case list element⟩
                {;⟨case list element⟩} END |
            CASE ⟨case index⟩ OF ⟨case list element⟩
            {;⟨case list element⟩} ; END

⟨character string⟩ ::= '⟨string element⟩ {⟨string element⟩}'

⟨component type⟩ ::= ⟨type denoter⟩

⟨component variable⟩ ::= ⟨indexed variable⟩ | ⟨field designator⟩

⟨compound statement⟩ ::= BEGIN ⟨statement sequence⟩ END

⟨condition⟩ ::= ⟨expression⟩

⟨conditional statement⟩ ::= ⟨if statement⟩ | ⟨case statement⟩

⟨constant⟩ ::= ⟨unsigned number⟩ | ⟨sign⟩⟨unsigned number⟩ |
          ⟨constant identifier⟩ | ⟨sign⟩⟨constant identifier⟩ |
          ⟨character string⟩

⟨constant definition⟩ ::= ⟨identifier⟩ = ⟨constant⟩

⟨constant definition part⟩ ::= ⟨empty⟩ | CONST ⟨constant definition⟩ ;
                    {⟨constant definition⟩;}

⟨constant identifier⟩ ::= ⟨identifier⟩

⟨control variable⟩ ::= ⟨entire variable⟩

⟨declarations section⟩ ::= ⟨label declaration part⟩
                  ⟨constant definition part⟩
                  ⟨type definition part⟩
                  ⟨variable declaration part⟩
                  ⟨procedure and function declaration part⟩

⟨digit⟩ ::= 0 | 1 | 2 | 3 | 4 | 5 | 6 | 7 | 8 | 9

⟨digit sequence⟩ ::= ⟨digit⟩ {⟨digit⟩}

⟨directive⟩ ::= ⟨letter⟩ {⟨letter⟩ | ⟨digit⟩}

⟨domain type⟩ ::= ⟨type identifier⟩

⟨empty⟩ ::=

⟨empty statement⟩ ::= ⟨empty⟩

⟨entire variable⟩ ::= ⟨variable identifier⟩

⟨enumerated type⟩ ::= (⟨identifier list⟩)

⟨executable section⟩ ::= ⟨compound statement⟩

⟨expression⟩ ::= ⟨simple expression⟩ |
     ⟨simple expression⟩⟨relational operator⟩
     ⟨simple expression⟩

⟨factor⟩ ::= ⟨variable⟩ | ⟨unsigned constant⟩ | ⟨function designator⟩ |
    ⟨set constructor⟩ | (⟨expression⟩) | NOT ⟨factor⟩

⟨field designator⟩ ::= ⟨record variable⟩.⟨field specifier⟩ |
      ⟨field designator identifier⟩

⟨field designator identifier⟩ ::= ⟨identifier⟩

⟨field identifier⟩ ::= ⟨identifier⟩

⟨field list⟩ ::= ⟨empty⟩ | ⟨fixed part⟩ | ⟨fixed part⟩; |
    ⟨fixed part⟩ ; ⟨variant part⟩ |
    ⟨fixed part⟩ ; ⟨variant part⟩ ; | ⟨variant part⟩ |
    ⟨variant part⟩ ;

⟨field specifier⟩ ::= ⟨field identifier⟩

⟨file type⟩ ::= FILE OF ⟨component type⟩

⟨file variable⟩ ::= ⟨variable⟩

⟨final value⟩ ::= ⟨expression⟩

⟨fixed part⟩ ::= ⟨record section⟩ { ;⟨record section⟩}

⟨for statement⟩ ::= FOR ⟨control variable⟩ := ⟨initial value⟩ TO
     ⟨final value⟩ DO ⟨statement⟩ |
     FOR ⟨control variable⟩ := ⟨initial value⟩ DOWNTO
     ⟨final value⟩ DO ⟨statement⟩

⟨formal parameter list⟩ ::= (⟨formal parameter section⟩
       { ;⟨formal parameter section⟩})

⟨formal parameter section⟩ ::= ⟨value parameter specification⟩ |
      ⟨variable parameter specification⟩ |
      ⟨procedural parameter specification⟩ |
      ⟨functional parameter specification⟩

⟨fractional digits⟩ ::= ⟨expression⟩

⟨functional block⟩ ::= ⟨block⟩

⟨function declaration⟩ ::= ⟨function heading⟩ ; ⟨directive⟩ |
     ⟨function identification⟩ ; ⟨function block⟩ |
     ⟨function heading⟩ ; ⟨function block⟩

⟨function designator⟩ ::= ⟨function identifier⟩ |
     ⟨function identifier⟩⟨actual parameter list⟩

⟨function heading⟩ ::= FUNCTION⟨function identifier⟩ : ⟨result type⟩ |
                            FUNCTION⟨function identifier⟩
                            ⟨formal parameter list⟩ : ⟨result type⟩

⟨function identification⟩ ::= FUNCTION⟨function identifier⟩

⟨function identifier⟩ ::= ⟨identifier⟩

⟨functional parameter specification⟩ ::= ⟨function heading⟩

⟨goto statement⟩ ::= GOTO⟨label⟩

⟨identified variable⟩ ::= ⟨pointer variable⟩^

⟨identifier⟩ ::= ⟨letter⟩ {⟨letter⟩ | ⟨digit⟩}

⟨identifier list⟩ ::= ⟨identifier⟩ {,⟨identifier⟩}

⟨if statement⟩ ::= IF⟨condition⟩THEN⟨statement⟩ |
                  IF⟨condition⟩THEN⟨statement⟩ELSE⟨statement⟩

⟨index expression⟩ ::= ⟨expression⟩

⟨index type⟩ ::= ⟨ordinal type⟩

⟨indexed variable⟩ ::= ⟨array variable⟩ [⟨index expression⟩
                     {,⟨index expression⟩}]

⟨initial value⟩ ::= ⟨expression⟩

⟨label⟩ ::= ⟨digit sequence⟩

⟨label declaration part⟩ ::= ⟨empty⟩ | LABEL⟨label⟩ {,⟨label⟩} ;

⟨letter⟩ ::= A | B | C | D | E | F | G | H | I | J | K | L | M | N | O|
         P | Q | R | S | T | U | V | W | X | Y | Z | a | b | c | d|
         e | f | g | h | i | j | k | l | m | n | o | p | q | r | s|
         t | u | v | w | x | y | z

⟨loop statement⟩ ::= ⟨repeat statement⟩ | ⟨while statement⟩ |
                  ⟨for statement⟩

⟨member designator⟩ ::= ⟨expression⟩ | ⟨expression⟩..⟨expression⟩

⟨multiplying operator⟩ ::= * | / | DIV | MOD | AND

⟨new ordinal type⟩ ::= ⟨enumerated type⟩ | ⟨subrange type⟩

⟨new pointer type⟩ ::= ^⟨domain type⟩

⟨new structured type⟩ ::= ⟨unpacked structured type⟩ |
                      PACKED ⟨unpacked structured type⟩

⟨new type⟩ ::= ⟨new ordinal type⟩ | ⟨new structured type⟩ |
            ⟨new pointer type⟩

⟨ordinal type⟩ ::= ⟨new ordinal type⟩ | ⟨ordinal type identifier⟩
⟨ordinal type identifier⟩ ::= ⟨identifier⟩

⟨pointer type⟩ ::= ⟨new pointer type⟩ | ⟨pointer type identifier⟩

⟨pointer type identifier⟩ ::= ⟨type identifier⟩

⟨pointer variable⟩ ::= ⟨variable⟩

⟨procedural parameter specification⟩ ::= ⟨procedure heading⟩

⟨procedure and function declaration part⟩ ::= {⟨procedure or function declaration⟩ ;}

⟨procedure block⟩ ::= ⟨block⟩

⟨procedure declaration⟩ ::= ⟨procedure heading⟩ ; ⟨directive⟩ |
      ⟨procedure identification⟩ ; ⟨procedure block⟩ |
      ⟨procedure heading⟩ ; ⟨procedure block⟩

⟨procedure heading⟩ ::= PROCEDURE ⟨procedure identifier⟩ |
      PROCEDURE ⟨procedure identifier⟩
        ⟨formal parameter list⟩

⟨procedure identification⟩ ::= PROCEDURE ⟨procedure identifier⟩

⟨procedure identifier⟩ ::= ⟨identifier⟩

⟨procedure or function declaration⟩ ::= ⟨procedure declaration⟩ |
      ⟨function declaration⟩

⟨procedure parameter list⟩ ::= ⟨actual parameter list⟩ |
      ⟨read parameter list⟩ |
      ⟨readln parameter list⟩ |
      ⟨write parameter list⟩ |
      ⟨writeln parameter list⟩

⟨procedure statement⟩ ::= ⟨procedure identifier⟩ |
      ⟨procedure identifier⟩ ⟨procedure parameter list⟩

⟨program⟩ ::= ⟨program heading⟩ ; ⟨program block⟩.

⟨program block⟩ ::= ⟨block⟩

⟨program heading⟩ ::= PROGRAM ⟨identifier⟩ |
      PROGRAM ⟨identifier⟩ (⟨program parameters⟩)

⟨program parameters⟩ ::= ⟨identifier list⟩

⟨read parameter list⟩ ::= (⟨variable⟩ {,⟨variable⟩}) |
      (⟨file variable⟩,⟨variable⟩ {,⟨variable⟩})

⟨readln parameter list⟩ ::= ⟨empty⟩ | (⟨variable⟩ {,⟨variable⟩}) |
      (⟨file variable⟩ {,⟨variable⟩})

⟨real type identifier⟩ ::= ⟨identifier⟩

⟨record section⟩ ::= ⟨identifier list⟩ : ⟨type denoter⟩

⟨record type⟩ ::= RECORD ⟨field list⟩ END

⟨record variable⟩ ::= ⟨variable⟩

⟨record variable list⟩ ::= ⟨record variable⟩ {,⟨record variable⟩}

⟨relational operator⟩ ::= IN | = | < > | < | > | < = | > =

⟨repeat statement⟩ ::= REPEAT ⟨statement sequence⟩ UNTIL ⟨condition⟩

⟨result type⟩ ::= ⟨scalar type identifier⟩ | ⟨pointer type identifier⟩

⟨scalar type identifier⟩ ::= ⟨ordinal type identifier⟩ |
      ⟨real type identifier⟩

⟨scale factor⟩ ::= ⟨signed integer⟩

⟨set constructor⟩ ::= [⟨empty⟩] |
           [⟨member designator⟩ {,⟨member designator⟩}]

⟨set type⟩ ::= SET OF ⟨base type⟩

⟨sign⟩ ::= + | −

⟨signed integer⟩ ::= ⟨unsigned integer⟩ | ⟨sign⟩⟨unsigned integer⟩

⟨signed number⟩ ::= ⟨signed integer⟩ | ⟨signed real⟩

⟨signed real⟩ ::= ⟨unsigned real⟩ | ⟨sign⟩⟨unsigned real⟩

⟨simple expression⟩ ::= ⟨term⟩ {⟨adding operator⟩⟨term⟩} |
           ⟨sign⟩⟨term⟩ {⟨adding operator⟩⟨term⟩}

⟨simple statement⟩ ::= ⟨empty statement⟩ | ⟨assignment statement⟩ |
           ⟨procedure statement⟩ | ⟨goto statement⟩

⟨special symbol⟩ ::= + | − | * | / | = | < | > | [|] | . | , | : | ; |
           (|) | ⟨⟩ | <= | >= | := | .. | ⟨word symbol⟩

⟨statement⟩ ::= ⟨simple statement⟩ | ⟨label⟩ : ⟨simple statement⟩ |
         ⟨structured statement⟩ | ⟨label⟩ : ⟨structured statement⟩

⟨statement sequence⟩ ::= statement⟩ { ; ⟨statement⟩}

⟨string character⟩ ::= ⟨one of a set of implementation-defined
          characters⟩

⟨string element⟩ ::= ⟨apostrophe image⟩ | ⟨string character⟩

⟨structured statement⟩ ::= ⟨compound statement⟩ | ⟨conditional statement⟩ |
           ⟨loop statement⟩ | ⟨with statement⟩

⟨structured type⟩ ::= ⟨new structured type⟩ | ⟨structured type identifier⟩

⟨structured type identifier⟩ ::= ⟨type identifier⟩

⟨subrange type⟩ ::= ⟨constant⟩..⟨constant⟩

⟨tag field⟩ ::= ⟨identifier⟩

⟨tag type⟩ ::= ⟨ordinal type identifier⟩

⟨term⟩ ::= ⟨factor⟩ {⟨multiplying operator⟩⟨factor⟩}

⟨total width⟩ ::= ⟨expression⟩

⟨type definition⟩ ::= ⟨identifier⟩ = ⟨type denoter⟩

⟨type definition part⟩ ::= ⟨empty⟩ |
           TYPE ⟨type definition⟩ ; {⟨type definition⟩ ; }

⟨type denoter⟩ ::= ⟨type identifier⟩ | ⟨new type⟩

⟨type identifier⟩ ::= ⟨identifier⟩

⟨unpacked structured type⟩ ::= ⟨array type⟩ | ⟨record type⟩ |
           ⟨set type⟩ | ⟨file type⟩

⟨unsigned constant⟩ ::= ⟨unsigned number⟩ | ⟨character string⟩ |
           ⟨constant identifier⟩ | NIL

⟨unsigned integer⟩ ::= ⟨digit sequence⟩

⟨unsigned number⟩ ::= ⟨unsigned integer⟩ | ⟨unsigned real⟩

⟨unsigned real⟩ ::= ⟨unsigned integer⟩.⟨digit sequence⟩ |
　　　　　　　　　⟨unsigned integer⟩.⟨digit sequence⟩E⟨scale factor⟩ |
　　　　　　　　　⟨unsigned integer⟩E⟨scale factor⟩

⟨value parameter specification⟩ ::= ⟨identifier list⟩ : ⟨type identifier⟩

⟨variable⟩ ::= ⟨entire variable⟩ | ⟨component variable⟩ |
　　　　　　　⟨identified variable⟩ | ⟨buffer variable⟩

⟨variable declaration⟩ ::= ⟨identifier list⟩ : ⟨type denoter⟩

⟨variable declaration part⟩ ::= ⟨empty⟩ |
　　　　　　　　　　　　VAR ⟨variable declaration⟩ ;
　　　　　　　　　　　　{⟨variable declaration⟩ ; }

⟨variable identifier⟩ ::= ⟨identifier⟩

⟨variable parameter specification⟩ ::= VAR ⟨identifier list⟩ :
　　　　　　　　　　　　　　　　⟨type identifier⟩

⟨variant⟩ ::= ⟨case constant list⟩ : (⟨field list⟩)

⟨variant part⟩ ::= CASE ⟨variant selector⟩ OF ⟨variant⟩ { ; ⟨variant⟩}

⟨variant selector⟩ ::= ⟨tag type⟩ | ⟨tag field⟩ : ⟨tag type⟩

⟨while statement⟩ ::= WHILE ⟨condition⟩ DO ⟨statement⟩

⟨with statement⟩ ::= WITH ⟨record variable list⟩ DO ⟨statement⟩

⟨word symbol⟩ ::= AND | ARRAY | BEGIN | CASE | CONST | DIV | DO | DOWNTO |
　　　　　　　ELSE | END | FILE | FOR | FUNCTION | GOTO | IF | IN |
　　　　　　　LABEL | MOD | NIL | NOT | OF | OR | PACKED | PROCEDURE |
　　　　　　　PROGRAM | RECORD | REPEAT | SET | THEN | TO | TYPE |
　　　　　　　UNTIL | VAR | WHILE | WITH

⟨write parameter⟩ ::= ⟨expression⟩ | ⟨expression⟩ : ⟨total width⟩ |
　　　　　　　　⟨expression⟩ : ⟨total width⟩ : ⟨fractional digits⟩

⟨write parameter list⟩ ::= (⟨write parameter⟩ {,⟨write parameter⟩}) |
　　　　　　　　　　(⟨file variable⟩, ⟨write parameter⟩ {,⟨write parameter⟩})

⟨writeln parameter list⟩ ::= ⟨empty⟩ |
　　　　　　　　　　　(⟨write parameter⟩ { ,⟨write parameter⟩}) |
　　　　　　　　　　　(⟨file variable⟩ {,⟨write parameter⟩})

STRING PROCESSING
(NONSTANDARD PASCAL)

String-manipulation functions are built in features of such languages as BASIC, COBOL, and FORTRAN. UCSD Pascal also provides these functions, but Standard Pascal does not. Can we simply define these general-purpose functions ourselves? Unfortunately, this is not straightforward because of Pascal's strong-typing facility: The type of each formal parameter must be prescribed when the program is written. Thus, we cannot write a function whose actual parameter for one call is a string of six characters and whose actual parameter for another call is a string of ten characters. We can get around this difficulty as follows: Let each string have the same fixed size—the maximum size needed. For each string, use a record with two fields: the string itself and its current length.

Since string manipulation in Standard Pascal cannot be easily handled in a general-purpose fashion, we summarize the string manipulation features of UCSD Pascal instead.

In UCSD Pascal, STRING is a predefined type. For example, we can write

VAR NAME: STRING[20];

NAME is thus declared to be (an identifier for) a string variable of up to 20 characters. The size of the variable can vary from 0 to 20 characters:

NAME := 'JOHN SMITH'

makes NAME have 10 characters, while

NAME := ''

gives NAME the value of the null string, that is, the string of length 0. A string variable can be declared to hold, at most, up to 255 characters:

VAR SENTENCE : STRING[255];

If the string's maximum length is not specified in square brackets, a string of up to 80 characters is assumed. Thus,

VAR MESSAGE : STRING;

is equivalent to

VAR MESSAGE : STRING[80];

In UCSD Pascal, there are six predeclared subprograms for string processing. The first two are procedures and the last four are functions.

1. INSERT(⟨string expression⟩, ⟨string variable⟩, ⟨starting position⟩). This procedure inserts ⟨string expression⟩ into ⟨string variable⟩, starting at position ⟨starting position⟩. For example, if MESSAGE has the value

   BET

   then INSERT ('UDG', MESSAGE, 2) will cause MESSAGE's value to become

   BUDGET

   An error occurs if the insertion increases the length of ⟨string variable⟩ beyond its maximum possible length.
2. DELETE(⟨string variable⟩, ⟨starting position⟩, ⟨length⟩). This procedure deletes ⟨length⟩ characters from ⟨string variable⟩, starting at position ⟨starting position⟩. For example, if MESSAGE has the value

   RESIST THE SILLY URGE TO CODE.

   then DELETE(MESSAGE, 12, 6) will cause MESSAGE's value to become

   RESIST THE URGE TO CODE.
3. LENGTH(⟨string expression⟩). The value returned is the number of characters in the current value of the string expression. For example, suppose we declare

   VAR   MESSAGE   : STRING ;
         MESSAGELENGTH : 0..80 ;

   Then the execution of

   MESSAGE := 'THE VIOLETS WILL BLOOM IN THE SPRING.';
   MESSAGELENGTH := LENGTH(MESSAGE)

   will give MESSAGELENGTH a value of 37. On input, an end-of-line marker serves to terminate an input string. Thus, if the Sample Input contains

   THE VIOLETS WILL BLOOM IN THE SPRING.

with an end-of-line marker immediately after the period, then the execution of

```
READLN(MESSAGE);
MESSAGELENGTH := LENGTH(MESSAGE);
```

will also give MESSAGELENGTH a value of 37.

4. POS(⟨string expression 1⟩, ⟨string expression 2⟩). The value returned is the starting position of the first occurrence of ⟨string expression 1⟩ in ⟨string expression 2⟩. For example, if we assign

MESSAGE := 'THE SNOW IS NOW ON THE GROUND.'

then POS('NOW', MESSAGE) is 6 since the first occurrence of 'NOW' in MESSAGE starts at position 6. Similarly, POS(' NOW', MESSAGE) is 12. Since 'OWN' does not occur in the value of MESSAGE, POS('OWN', MESSAGE) is 0.

5. COPY(⟨string expression⟩, ⟨starting position⟩, ⟨length⟩). The value returned is a copy of the part of ⟨string expression⟩ which starts at position ⟨starting position⟩ and whose length is ⟨length⟩. For example, if we assign

MESSAGE := 'BARE RUINED CHOIRS, WHERE LATE THE SWEET BIRDS SANG'

then COPY(MESSAGE, 8, 2) is 'IN'. Similarly, COPY(MESSAGE, 2, 3) is 'ARE'. Since LENGTH(MESSAGE) is 51, an error would occur if we called

COPY(MESSAGE, 40, 13)

or

COPY(MESSAGE, 13, 40)

6. CONCAT(⟨string expression⟩, ⟨string expression⟩ {, ⟨string expression⟩}). The value returned is the string expression obtained by concatenating (that is, joining together), in order, all of the string expressions given as arguments. For example, if we assign

MESSAGE := 'ABLE WAS I'

then CONCAT(MESSAGE, ' ERE I SAW ELBA.') is
'ABLE WAS I ERE I SAW ELBA.

Make sure that blanks are provided where needed. For example,

CONCAT(MESSAGE, 'ERE I SAW ELBA.') is

'ABLE WAS IERE I SAW ELBA.'

As an illustration of how these four functions can be used in concert, the following UCSD Pascal program converts a name such as

ULYSSES SIMPSON GRANT

to

GRANT, ULYSSES S.

```
PROGRAM  CONVERT(INPUT, OUTPUT);

(*****************************************************)
(*                                                   *)
(*    Programmer : Bill Collins.                     *)
(*                                                   *)
(*    This program, written in UCSD Pascal, will solve *)
(*    the following problem: Given a name in the form *)
(*       <first name> <middle name> <last name>      *)
(*    write it out in the form                       *)
(*       <last name>, <first name> <middle initial>. *)
(*                                                   *)
(*****************************************************)

CONST MAXLENGTH = 80;
      BLANK     = ' ';

TYPE  LETTER      = 'A'..'Z';
      STRINGLENGTH = 1..MAXLENGTH;

VAR   FULLNAME, FIRSTNAME, MIDDLELAST, LASTNAME,
      REVISEDNAME                               :STRING;
      MIDDLEINITIAL                             :LETTER;
      NAMELENGTH, FIRSTBLANKPOSITION,
      SECONDBLANKPOSITION                       :STRINGLENGTH;

BEGIN

   PAGE;
   READLN(FULLNAME);
   WRITELN('THE GIVEN NAME IS ', FULLNAME);

   NAMELENGTH := LENGTH(FULLNAME);

   (*  Find the first name.  *)
   FIRSTBLANKPOSITION := POS(FULLNAME, BLANK);
   FIRSTNAME := COPY(FULLNAME, 1, FIRSTBLANKPOSITION - 1);

   MIDDLEINITIAL := COPY(FULLNAME, FIRSTBLANKPOSITION + 1, 1);

   (*  Find the last name.  *)
   MIDDLELAST := COPY (FULLNAME, FIRSTBLANKPOSITION + 1,
               NAMELENGTH - FIRSTBLANKPOSITION);
   SECONDBLANKPOSITION := FIRSTBLANKPOSITION + POS(MIDDLELAST, BLANK);
   LASTNAME := COPY(FULLNAME, SECONDBLANKPOSITION + 1,
               NAMELENGTH - SECONDBLANKPOSITION);

   REVISEDNAME := CONCAT(LASTNAME, ',', BLANK, FIRSTNAME, BLANK,
                  MIDDLEINITIAL, '.');
   WRITELN('THE REVISED NAME IS ', REVISED NAME);

   PAGE
END.
```

The corresponding program in standard Pascal would be much longer since each string function would have to be simulated in a loop.

THREE

THE ASCII AND EBCDIC COLLATING SEQUENCES

1. ASCII (American Standard Code for Information Interchange)

Listed below are the internal values and corresponding characters. Characters with internal value below 32 or above 126 are unprintable control characters. They are included here for the sake of completeness. For a discussion of their significance, see Abd-Alla, 1976, pages 647–649.

Internal value	Control character representation	Meaning
00	NUL	Null
01	SOH	Start of heading
02	STX	Start of text
03	ETX	End of text
04	EOT	End of transmission
05	ENQ	Enquiry
06	ACK	Acknowledge
07	BEL	Bell
08	BS	Backspace
09	HT	Horizontal tabulation
10	LF	Line feed
11	VT	Vertical tabulation
12	FF	Form feed

Internal value	Control character representation	Meaning
13	CR	Carriage return
14	SO	Shift out
15	SI	Shift in
16	DLE	Data link escape
17	DC1	Device control 1
18	DC2	Device control 2
19	DC3	Device control 3
20	DC4	Device control 4
21	NAK	Negative acknowledge
22	SYN	Synchronize
23	ETB	End transmitted block
24	CAN	Cancel
25	EM	End of medium
26	SUB	Substitute
27	ESC	Escape
28	FS	File separator
29	GS	Group separator
30	RS	Record separator
31	US	Unit separator

32	:	blank	56	:	8	80	:	P	104	:	h
33	:	|	57	:	9	81	:	Q	105	:	i
34	:	"	58	:	:	82	:	R	106	:	j
35	:	#	59	:	;	83	:	S	107	:	k
36	:	$	60	:	<	84	:	T	108	:	l
37	:	%	61	:	=	85	:	U	109	:	m
38	:	&	62	:	>	86	:	V	110	:	n
39	:	'	63	:	?	87	:	W	111	:	o
40	:	(	64	:	@	88	:	X	112	:	p
41	:	)	65	:	A	89	:	Y	113	:	q
42	:	*	66	:	B	90	:	Z	114	:	r
43	:	+	67	:	C	91	:	[	115	:	s
44	:	,	68	:	D	92	:	/	116	:	t
45	:	—	69	:	E	93	:	]	117	:	u
46	:	.	70	:	F	94	:	^	118	:	v
47	:	/	71	:	G	95	:	_	119	:	w
48	:	0	72	:	H	96	:	`	120	:	x
49	:	1	73	:	I	97	:	a	121	:	y
50	:	2	74	:	J	98	:	b	122	:	z
51	:	3	75	:	K	99	:	c	123	:	{
52	:	4	76	:	L	100	:	d	124	:	|
53	:	5	77	:	M	101	:	e	125	:	}
54	:	6	78	:	N	102	:	f	126	:	~
55	:	7	79	:	O	103	:	g	127	DEL	Delete

2. EBCDIC (Extended Binary Coded Decimal Interchange Code)

64	:	blank	125	:	'	164	:	u	215	:	P
74	:	¢	126	:	=	165	:	v	216	:	Q
75	:	.	127	:	"	166	:	w	217	:	R
76	:	<	129	:	a	167	:	x	224	:	\
77	:	(	130	:	b	168	:	y	226	:	S
78	:	+	131	:	c	169	:	z	227	:	T
79	:	!	132	:	d	192	:	{	228	:	U
80	:	&	133	:	e	193	:	A	229	:	V
90	:	!	134	:	f	194	:	B	230	:	W
91	:	$	135	:	g	195	:	C	231	:	X
92	:	*	136	:	h	196	:	D	232	:	Y
93	:	)	137	:	i	197	:	E	233	:	Z
94	:	;	145	:	j	198	:	F	240	:	0
95	:	¬	146	:	k	199	:	G	241	:	1
96	:	−	147	:	l	200	:	H	242	:	2
97	:	/	148	:	m	201	:	I	243	:	3
107	:	,	149	:	n	208	:	}	244	:	4
108	:	%	150	:	o	209	:	J	245	:	5
109	:	_	151	:	p	210	:	K	246	:	6
110	:	>	152	:	q	211	:	L	247	:	7
111	:	?	153	:	r	212	:	M	248	:	8
122	:	:	161	:	~	213	:	N	249	:	9
123	:	#	162	:	s	214	:	O	250	:	|
124	:	@	163	:	t						

Only 94 of the 256 internal values are shown. The remaining 162 internal values are unused or else used for control characters or special graphics characters (see Abd-Alla, 1976, pages 92–93).

CODING CONVENTIONS USED IN THIS TEXT

1. Leave one blank line before and after all the LABEL declarations, one blank line before and after all the CONST definitions, one blank line before and after all the TYPE definitions, and one blank line before and after all the VAR declarations.
2. Leave one blank line before each comment (except in-line comments).
3. Line up the equal signs in CONST definitions. Also line up the equal signs in TYPE definitions, the colons in VAR declarations, and the " := " in consecutive assignment statements.
4. In each case study, use a type identifier for the type of each variable.
5. In each case study, each procedure declaration and function declaration will start at the top of a page or will not be split between two pages.
6. Indent three spaces after a line beginning with IF, ELSE, BEGIN, CASE, REPEAT, WITH, FOR or WHILE. Resume previous spacing before END, ELSE or UNTIL.
7. If an input or output statement will not fit on one line, continue it on the next line in the column after the first "(". For example,

   READLN(DISTANCE,FLIGHTNUMBER,DEPARTURETIME,
          ARRIVALTIME);

8. If an assignment statement will not fit on one line, continue it on the next line in the column after the " := ".
9. If a condition will not fit on one line, continue it on the next line and indent 6 more spaces than the word IF, WHILE or UNTIL.
10. Insert a blank space before and after each operator (such as :=, + or DIV).
11. Any two distinct identifiers will be unique through the first eight characters.
12. Global variables are permitted in subprograms only when this overcomes a defect in the Pascal language.

FIVE

COMPUTERS AND COMPUTER LANGUAGES

All computers, from the tiniest micros to the largest mainframes, have the same general organization, shown below.

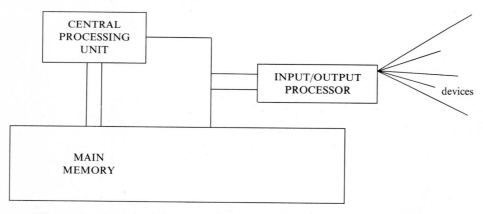

The central processing unit (CPU) controls the fetching, decoding and executing of machine-language instructions.† The instructions and operands are temporarily stored in the CPU in fixed locations called *registers*. The main memory

---

† The term *machine language* suggests that such instructions correspond to the actual wiring of the computer. This connotation was accurate for most computers until 1964, when IBM introduced the immensely popular 360 series of computers. The computers in this series were physically different from each other in terms of timing and other hardware features—but they all had the same machine language! This was because an intermediate level had been inserted between the machine-language level and the computer's wiring. This new level is referred to as "microprogramming": a technique for designing the decoding section of the CPU so that each machine-language instruction is executed as a sequence of elementary operations known as *microinstructions*. The concept of microprogramming was introduced by M. V. Wilkes in 1951. Virtually all computers since 1964 have been microprogrammed.

contains instructions and data stored in *cells*. An instruction in main memory must be fetched by the CPU before it can be decoded and executed. The input/output processor regulates communication with the outside world. Some larger computers have several input/output processors; each processor is then referred to as a *channel*.

The following is a machine-language instruction for an IBM 370 series computer:

0101100000110000110000000101010000

This tells the computer to load register 3 with the contents of the address formed by adding 80 to the number stored in register 12. When your computer language is machine language, the problem-solving process can be summarized as follows:

Problem statement in English

     | Analysis and design
     ↓

Algorithm

     | Coding
     ↓

Machine language program

     | Execution
     ↓

Solution

As you might imagine, the process of coding an algorithm in machine language is painstaking and error prone; attempting to debug a machine-language program is similar to trying to find a needle in a haystack.

Because of these difficulties, assembly language was invented. The assembly language version of the above instruction is

L 3,FIRST

The letter L indicates that a register is to be loaded with the contents of a memory address; 3 is the register to be loaded; FIRST is a name for the memory location 80 positions from the address stored in register 12. Since assembly language instructions are unintelligible to a computer, there must be a program to translate an assembly language program into the corresponding machine-language version. Such a translator program is called an *assembler*.† The

---

† Since only machine-language programs can be executed on a computer, the assembler itself must, ultimately, be a machine-language program. Initially, the assembler is written in assembly language. It could then be translated by hand into machine language. More likely, a *cross-assembler* would be used. A cross-assembler is a program written on computer *X* that inputs a program written in the assembly language for computer *Y* and outputs the machine-language version (in *Y*'s machine language) of the assembly language program.

corresponding problem-solving process is

Problem statement in English

     Analysis and design

Algorithm

     Coding

Assembly language program

     Assembly

Machine language program

     Execution

Solution

Assembly language programs are easier to understand and debug than their machine-language counterparts, but they are a long way from algorithms, partly because arithmetic and logical expressions cannot be straightforwardly represented in assembly language. For example, the fundamental instruction

Assign to AVERAGE the value of (FIRST + LAST)/2

would require several assembly language instructions.

From a programmer's point of view, a higher-level language such as COBOL (or Pascal or FORTRAN) is an enormous improvement over assembly language. But a COBOL compiler—a program that translates any COBOL program into machine language—is much more difficult to design and write than an assembler is: the COBOL programmer has less work, the computer has more. We then have the problem-solving process shown below:

Problem statement in English

     Analysis and design

Algorithm

     Coding

COBOL program

     Compilation

Machine language program

     Execution

Solution

Some programming languages, such as BASIC, APL, LISP, and SNOBOL, are not normally compiled; they are interpreted instead. For example, a BASIC interpreter is a program that investigates any BASIC program statement by statement; for each statement, the interpreter determines what the statement means (that is, interprets it) and then carries out the machine language instructions necessary to accomplish what the statement says. An interpreter produces answers, not a machine-language program! The corresponding problem solving process is

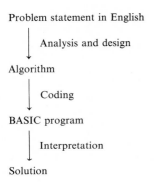

Problem statement in English

    Analysis and design

Algorithm

    Coding

BASIC program

    Interpretation

Solution

If you use a compiled language, a run-time error near the beginning of a program will not be detected until after the entire program has been translated into machine language, so a considerable amount of computer time may be wasted. With an interpreter, on the other hand, an early run-time error will be detected almost immediately. A similar situation exists for syntax errors (violations of the language's grammatical rules): with a compiler, no syntax error can be corrected until the entire compilation has been completed. Most interpreters, on the other hand, inform you immediately of your syntax errors and permit you to correct them before proceeding further. Thus interpreters tend to shorten the time needed to find errors in a program.

After a program has been debugged, a compiler is much more efficient than an interpreter, because once the compiler translates the debugged program into machine language, the compiler is no longer needed. The machine language program can be executed by itself. Since an interpreter does not produce a machine-language program, the interpreter must remain in main memory, along with the debugged program, to produce the solution to the original problem. Furthermore, an interpreter must classify each statement each time the statement is encountered—loops are especially time-consuming. Thus compilation is preferable for programs that will be run over and over again once they are debugged.

It would be convenient to have both an interpreter and a compiler for the same language. The interpreter would speed up the debugging and the compiler would produce the machine language version once the program had been debugged. The situation with Pascal is worth noting. On some systems a Pascal program is translated into a generalized type of machine language known as *p* code (for *pseudo code*). Since *p* code is machine independent, the translation from Pascal to *p* code is similar for all computers. The resulting *p* code can then be translated into machine language (or interpreted).

Exercise Suppose you could program in machine language and assembly language for your computer and you were equally proficient in Pascal and BASIC. If your computer already had a Pascal compiler, but not a BASIC interpreter, which language (Pascal, assembly language, machine language) would you prefer to write the interpreter in? Why?

BIBLIOGRAPHY

Abd-Alla, A. M., and A. C. Meltzer, *Principles of Digital Computer Design*, Prentice-Hall, Inc., Englewood Cliffs, New Jersey, 1976.

Adel'son-Vel'skii, G. M., and E. M. Landis, "An Algorithm for the Organization of Information," *Soviet Mathematics*, vol. 3, 1962, pp. 1259–1263.

Aho, A. V., J. E. Hopcroft, and J. D. Ullman, *Data Structures and Algorithms*, Addison-Wesley Publishing Company, Reading, Massachusetts, 1983.

Aho, A. V., and J. D. Ullman, *Principles of Compiler Design*, Addison-Wesley Publishing Company, Reading, Massachusetts, 1978.

American National Standard Pascal, The Institute of Electrical and Electronics Engineers, Inc., New York, New York, 1983.

Barrett, W. A., and J. D. Couch, *Compiler Construction: Theory and Practice*, Science Research Associates, Inc., 1979.

Bentley, J. L., "Writing Correct Programs," *Communications of the ACM*, December 1983, vol. 26, no. 12, pp. 1040–1045.

Bentley, J. L., "How to Sort," *Communications of the ACM*, April 1984, vol. 27, no. 4, pp. 287–291.

Calingaert, P., *Assemblers, Compilers and Program Translation*, Computer Science Press, Inc., Potomac, Maryland, 1979.

Cherry, G. W., *Pascal Programming Structures*, Reston Publishing Company, Inc., Reston, Virginia, 1980.

Collins, W. J., *An Introduction to Programming and Pascal*, Macmillan Publishing Company, New York, 1984.

Cooper, D., *Standard Pascal User Reference Manual*, W. W. Norton and Company, Inc., New York, 1983.

Gardner, M., *The Scientific American Book of Mathematical Puzzles and Diversions*, Simon and Schuster, 1959.

Gries, D., *Science of Programming*, Springer-Verlag, New York, 1981.

Griswold, R. E., J. F. Poage, and I. P. Polonsky, *The SNOBOL 4 Programming Language*, Prentice Hall, Inc., Englewood Cliffs, New Jersey, 1968.

Hoare, C. A. R., "Quicksort," *Computer Journal*, April 1962, vol. 5, no. 4, pp. 10–15.

Hogg, R. V., and E. A. Tanis, *Probability and Statistical Inference*, 2d edition, Macmillan Publishing Company, New York, 1983.

Hopcroft, J. E., and J. D. Ullman, *Formal Languages and Their Relation to Automata*, Addison-Wesley Publishing Company, Reading, Massachusetts, 1969.

Jackson, P. C., *Introduction to Artificial Intelligence*, Petrocelli Books, New York, 1974.

Jenson, and Cherrington, *The Business Management Laboratory Participants' Manual*, 2d edition, Richard B. Irwin, Inc., Homewood, Illinois, 1977.

Katzan, H., *Advanced Programming*, Van Nostrand Reinhold Company, New York, 1970.

Knuth, D. E., *The Art of Computer Programming*, Vol. 1: "Fundamental Algorithms," 2d ed., Addison-Wesley Publishing Company, Reading, Massachusetts, 1973. (1)

Knuth, D. E., *The Art of Computer Programming*, Vol. 2: "Seminumerical Algorithms," 2d ed., Addison-Wesley Publishing Company, Reading, Massachusetts, 1973. (2)

Knuth, D. E., *The Art of Computer Programming*, Vol. 3: "Sorting and Searching," Addison-Wesley Publishing Company, 1973. (3)

Korfhage, R. R., *Discrete Computational Structures*, Academic Press, New York, 1974.

Kruse, R. L., *Data Structures and Program Design*, Prentice-Hall, Inc., Englewood Cliffs, New Jersey, 1984.

Lewis, T. G., and M. Z. Smith, *Applying Data Structures*, 2d ed., Houghton Mifflin Company, Boston, 1982.

Loyd, S., *Mathematical Puzzles of Sam Loyd*, M. Gardner (ed.), Dover, New York, 1960.

Nilsson, N. J., *Problem-Solving Methods in Artificial Intelligence*, McGraw-Hill Book Company, New York, 1971.

Samuel, A., "Some Studies in Machine Learning Using the Game of Checkers," *IBM Journal of Research and Development*, vol. 3, no. 2, 1959, pp. 211–229.

Schneider, G. M., and S. C. Bruell, *Advanced Programming and Problem Solving with Pascal*, John Wiley and Sons, New York, 1981.

Sedgewick, R., "Quicksort," Ph.D. Thesis, *Stanford Computer Science Report*, STAN-CS-75-492, Stanford University, 1975.

Sedgewick, R., "The Analysis of Quicksort Programs," *Acta Informatica*, vol. 7, 1977, pp. 327–355.

Sedgewick, R., "Implementing Quicksort Programs," *Communications of the ACM*, October 1978, vol. 21, no. 10, pp. 847–857.

Shelly, G. B., and T. J. Cashman, *Advanced Structural COBOL: Program Design and File Processing*, Anaheim Publishing Company, Brea, California, 1978.

Singleton, R. C., "An efficient algorithm for sorting with minimal storage: Algorithm 347," *Communications of the ACM*, March 1969, vol. 12, no. 3, pp. 185–187.

Struble, G. W., *Assembler Language Programming: The IBM System/360 and 370*, 2d ed., Addison-Wesley Publishing Company, Reading, Massachusetts, 1975.

Tenenbaum, A. M., and M. J. Augenstein, *Data Structures Using Pascal*, Prentice-Hall, Inc., Englewood Cliffs, New Jersey, 1981.

Tremblay, J. P., and P. G. Sorenson, *An Introduction to Data Structures with Applications*, McGraw-Hill Book Company, New York, 1976.

Wiest, J. D., and F. K. Levy, *A Management Guide to PERT/CPM*, 2d ed., Prentice-Hall, Inc., Englewood Cliffs, New Jersey, 1977.

Wirth, N., *Algorithms + Data Structures = Programs*, Prentice-Hall, Inc., Englewood Cliffs, New Jersey, 1976.

INDEX